CAN DEMOCRACY TAKE ROOT IN POST-SOVIET RUSSIA?

Dilemmas of Democratization in Post-Communist Countries
Series Editors: Harry Eckstein, Frederic J. Fleron Jr.,
Erik P. Hoffmann, and William M. Reisinger

CAN DEMOCRACY TAKE ROOT IN POST-SOVIET RUSSIA?

Explorations in State–Society Relations

Harry Eckstein, Frederic J. Fleron Jr.,
Erik P. Hoffmann, and William M. Reisinger

with
Richard Ahl, Russell Bova, and Philip G. Roeder

ROWMAN & LITTLEFIELD PUBLISHERS, INC.
Lanham • Boulder • New York • Oxford

ROWMAN & LITTLEFIELD PUBLISHERS, INC.

Published in the United States of America
by Rowman & Littlefield Publishers, Inc.
4720 Boston Way, Lanham, Maryland 20706

12 Hid's Copse Road
Cumnor Hill, Oxford OX2 9JJ, England

British Library Cataloguing in Publication Information Available

Library of Congress Cataloging-in-Publication Data

Can democracy take root in post-Soviet Russia? : explorations in state–
society relations / Harry Eckstein . . . [et al.].
    p.   cm.
    Includes bibliographical references and index.
    ISBN 0-8476-8720-1 (alk. paper). — ISBN 0-8476-8721-X (pbk.: alk. paper)
    1. Political culture—Russia (Federation) 2. Democracy—Russia
(Federation) 3. Russia (Federation)—Politics and government—1991–
I. Eckstein, Harry. II. Series.
JN6699.A15C36 1998   97-41230
306.2'0947—dc21   CIP

ISBN 0-8476-8720-1 (cloth : alk. paper)
ISBN 0-8476-8721-X (pbk. : alk. paper)

Printed in the United States of America

♾ ™ The paper used in this publication meets the minimum requirements of
American National Standard for Information Sciences—Permanence of Paper
for Printed Library Materials, ANSI Z39.48–1984.

Contents

v

Foreword

It is an honor to write a foreword to the first volume of this multi-volume series, "Dilemmas of Democratization in Post-Communist Countries." The team writing and editing this series combines theoretical and technical sophistication and area depth with a patient recognition of the magnitude and complexity of the undertaking.

The authors have begun with a theory that avoids privileging particular explanatory perspectives, such as constitutional-legal engineering on one hand, or structural and cultural constraints on the other, or that relies exclusively or heavily on particular methods, such as survey research. Instead, the theory of congruence and balanced disparities proposed by Harry Eckstein early in the 1960s, as tested and elaborated since that time, is the explanatory framework of the present undertaking.

Eckstein's theory is both a general theory of political stability and, with its balanced disparities corollary, is a special theory of democratic stability. Congruence theory predicts political stability insofar as there obtains in a given country a substantial similarity in power relations in the political system and its various parts, and in the "adjacent" social agencies and organizations. This political stability is without regard to the form of its government. In other words, there is a general strain toward congruence in authority patterns. The special congruence theory of democratic stability proposes that "mixed" authority relations are more conducive to democratic stability than "pure" ones. Thus the stabilizing culture and structure of democracy is a mix of conflictual and consensual, obedient and participatory, passive and active components, and the like. The disparities help explain how authoritative decision making can be reconciled with popular participation.

If the theory is correct, one would predict from the political record of the tsarist and Soviet periods, and the contemporary patterns of the Russian Federation, a democratic minimalism with a variety of imperfections or distortions, or a collapse into authoritarianism. The authors' analyses add up to a prognosis of considerable doubt as to the effectiveness of the democratic transition in Russia or the prospects of consolidation. Elite culture in Russia is not responsive to constituents; mass culture does not accord legitimacy to Russian political institutions; a multi-party system with experience alternating in power as well as with independent bargaining interest groups has not emerged; a "neutral" civil service is nowhere near in place. Separation of powers and constitutionalism are "forms" and not "norms."

A process of democratization constrained by these authority patterns would be marked by instabilities in the interaction between the executive and the legislature and by executive gigantism alternating with stalemate. Efforts to deal with the two hundred odd frontier disputes among the ethnically varied members of the Russian Federation might take the form of failed federalist and consociational efforts à la Chechnya, rather than the "agreements to disagree" of the small democracies of Western Europe.

If, despite these gloomy and convincing forecasts of the honest and thorough scholarship of this volume, a recognizable democracy should survive in Russia (with turnovers of power, and relatively fair elections), how would this test affect the validity of congruence theory? In the concluding chapter Eckstein suggests that in such an event or series of events, and assuming an observable adaptation in changing political and social relations over a sustained period of time, the Russian case might prove to be a "crucial test case" confirming congruence theory. If, however, power patterns should go their separate courses, and remain incongruent, with Russian democracy surviving in at least a minimal sense, then congruence theory would be infirmed. And Russia, India-like, would float off into the future of political science, a vivid reminder of the ultimate inscrutability of human affairs. Whatever the outcome of these events and investigations, the Eckstein-Fleron-Hoffmann-Reisinger team has won the strongest claims among contemporary scholars to a "watching brief" of the historic Russian democratization drama. The authors have turned it into an "experiment" promising to yield significant knowledge, insofar as human ingenuity is capable of drawing lawful observations from the study of human affairs.

Gabriel A. Almond

Preface

This book is the first in a multi-volume series that examines the prospects for establishing viable democracies in former communist countries by focusing on the dynamics of state–society relations. Particular emphasis is given to the nature of authority patterns in state and society, the congruence between those authority patterns, the dynamics of political inclusion, and the balancing of governmental, economic, and social disparities. We approach these issues from the perspective that authority relations represent an important "linkage variable" that could provide a fresh view of democratization and democratic stability. Previous approaches have treated explanatory variables as either internal to government (e.g., structural and institutional arrangements) or external to government (e.g., level of economic development, political culture, intermediary associations, and social classes). The result has been a dichotomization of studies of democratization between state-centered (endogenous) approaches and society-centered (exogenous) approaches. Our focus on authority patterns in state and society, and their congruence, holds promise for transcending that dichotomy with a breakthrough in the understanding of democratic transitions and the prospects for viable democracy in Russia and other former communist and noncommunist regimes.

The volumes in this series explore ways in which theories of democracy and democratization can inform the study of postcommunist transitions, and how those theories must be refined, revised, or completely rethought in light of the experiences of former communist countries. As a result, the series should have wide appeal to students of comparative politics, democratic transitions, postcommunism, and the theory and practice of modern democracy.

Volume 1 constitutes a general examination of the dynamics of state–society relations with particular emphasis on Russia. We investigate the nature of authority patterns in state and society and the degree

ix

of congruence between those authority patterns, especially aspects of political inclusion such as the role of elites and the public in various phases of Russian democratization. The relationships among political attitudes, social institutions such as intermediary associations, and the architecture of governmental and economic institutions are analyzed. Finally, we assess the relative merits of state-centered and society-centered approaches to the study of democratic transitions, as well as the utility of survey research into public opinion and participation.

This volume demonstrates the viability of more detailed studies of authority patterns in the state–society relations of postcommunist polities to be presented in subsequent volumes. The project as a whole represents a major attempt to link postcommunist studies to the fields of comparative politics and political theory, especially theories of democratization and viable democracy, building democratic theory by empirical study of the building of democracy in postcommunist polities.

Efforts to understand the complicated process of establishing viable democracy in postcommunist countries must employ a wide variety of approaches from social science theory. The theoretical approach employed in this study is drawn from the theory of congruence in authority patterns formulated by Harry Eckstein several decades ago and refined in his three chapters in this volume. Our focus on the nature and degree of congruence of authority patterns in both state and social organizations seems to offer promising possibilities for new paths of inquiry.

This project grew out of my conversations concerning the nature of Eckstein's congruence theory and earlier efforts to test it with D. Munroe Eagles, my colleague at the State University of New York, Buffalo, who had studied with Eckstein at the University of California, Irvine. In an initial effort to apply the theory to the post-Soviet transition in Russia, I then wrote a background paper and convened a panel at the 1995 annual meeting of the American Political Science Association to explore the subject of "Cultural versus Structural Bases of Russian Democratic (In-)Stability: Eckstein's Congruence Theory Reconsidered." As this project gained momentum, I convened another panel, "Democratic Theories and Transitions from Communism: State-Centered versus Society-Centered Approaches," at the twenty-eighth national convention of the American Association for the Advancement of Slavic Studies in 1996. The discussions and papers from these two panels provided invaluable frameworks for developing this project and the chapters that follow.

Frequent communication among the authors in the past several years served to bring this project into sharper focus. We convened twice at the Center for Democracy at the University of California, Irvine, during which ideas were exchanged with members of the Center. The authors gratefully acknowledge the financial support of the Center in making these meetings possible.

Frederic J. Fleron Jr.

I
INTRODUCTION

1

Congruence Theory Explained

Harry Eckstein

The authors of the essays that constitute this book have made as its unifying thread a theory I first developed in the 1960s. This theory may be called "congruence theory." It has been elaborated several times, in numerous ways, since its first statement, but it has not changed in essentials.[1] I do not want to explain and justify the theory in all its ramifications here; for this, readers can consult the publications cited in the references. I do want to explain it sufficiently to clarify essentials.

The Core of Congruence Theory

Every theory has at its core certain fundamental hypotheses. These can be used as if they were axioms from which theorems (further hypotheses) may be deduced; the theory may then be tested directly through the axioms or indirectly through the theorems. A good deal of auxiliary theoretical matter is generally associated with the core hypotheses, usually to make them amenable to appropriate empirical inquiry. These auxiliary matters are subsidiary to the core postulates of a theory, but they are necessary for doing work with it and generally imply hypotheses themselves.[2]

Congruence theory has such an underlying core, with which a great deal of auxiliary material has become associated; the more important of these auxiliary ideas will be discussed later. The core consists of two hypotheses.

The first pertains to the viability and performance of political systems regardless of type. This says:

3

> Governments perform well to the extent that their authority patterns are congruent with the authority patterns of other units of society.

More specifically, high performance (above a threshold) requires high congruence, and, for all cases, performance increases monotonically as a function of congruence.

The second hypothesis pertains to the viability and performance of democratic governments. This says:

> Democratic governments perform well only if their authority patterns exhibit "balanced disparities"—that is, combinations of democratic and nondemocratic traits.

This hypothesis is not separate from the first but an extension of it. Congruence remains the fundamental condition of high performance by democratic governments, but the second hypothesis adds that the congruence condition will not be satisfied by democratic governments unless they exhibit such disparities.[3]

Hypotheses 1 and 2, then, are general and special versions of the same proposition. In this, hypothesis 2 differs from other hypotheses about the performance of democracies in an important way. Other hypotheses about the performance of democracies cover only democracies, not governments generally. This approach ignores the fact that democratic governments are governments, so that any general theory of governmental performance should hold in them as in other types. However, since democracies are a special type of government, special conditions of performance should also hold in them; but these should be consistent with, preferably derived from, the more general hypothesis. The fact that the congruence hypothesis connects a theory of democratic performance with a more general theory of governmental performance does not, of course, make it valid, but it does make it more "powerful" than competing hypotheses, if corroborated. This will especially be so if other well-grounded hypotheses about the performance of democracies can also be considered special instances of the general hypothesis. I will try to show later in this essay that they can.

Concepts

It is necessary now to clarify the concepts used in these core hypotheses. In this section, I will only deal with the concepts used in the general hypothesis; those used in the second will be discussed later.

Authority Patterns

General Nature of Authority Patterns

Patterns of authority are the structures and processes by which social units are directed or, put otherwise, their structures and processes of governance. *Authority relations* are the interactions that constitute the patterns.

We tend to think of "government" as pertaining only to the most inclusive level of society—the "State"—and to geographic subunits of the State. We extend study of the State to entities that directly affect it—political parties and pressure groups—but mainly in regard to how they do affect the State, not as social units that have systems of governance in their own right. Other units of society (e.g., families, schools, workplaces) we tend to ignore or treat superficially. We do relate general social conditions—like socioeconomic stratification, economic development, or literacy—to government, but not the particular units of society that do not comprise the State.

This tendency is unfortunate in that it leaves out of study most patterns of governance and most political relationships. Every social unit must be directed and managed in some way. Governance, in that broader sense, is found in political parties, workplaces and businesses, professional societies, trade unions, voluntary associations, community associations, friendly societies, hospitals, churches, sports teams and leagues, schools and universities, teams that produce films or plays, and, not least, families. What mainly distinguishes their governance from that of the State is scale, which may or may not be important. States also differ from other social units in complexity, but even rather small-scale entities, such as schools, have structures and processes of direction that are far from simple; and these, as Gurr and I (1975) have shown, vary on the same set of dimensions on which States vary. National government also is distinguished by its claim to sovereignty, or ultimate power, over all units of society; but even if this claim could be sustained, it does not mean that the State's authority patterns are constituted differently from others.

"Social units" are, so to speak, collective individuals, not just aggregates of individuals. They have their own identities, separate from the individual identities of members. Their members always, to some extent, define themselves in terms of the units—not only as, say, Americans, but also as Catholics, members of a university faculty, Republicans, and the like. The units persist despite turnover in their memberships, and they have goals of their own as well as their own functional differentiation of roles.

To function as entities, social units require governance. Governance is needed to define the unit's goals and means to attain them, to specify proper conduct in the unit, to "police" the members to ensure that propriety and directives are observed, to allocate roles and functions in the units, to coordinate these efficiently, and to relate the unit to others that affect it. The task of direction, in turn, always requires, to some extent, a certain inequality among members: hierarchical arrangements in which some direct, as superordinates, and others are directed, as subordinates. Something like universal and equal participation in governance may have been approached in some utopian communities, but just this fact may explain the characteristically short life spans of such communities.

Clearly, States and their governments are not the only structures of direction. Societies contain a multitude of social units, all having their own structures and processes of governance. If they did not, the units would be doomed to be chaotic and ultimately extinct.

Dimensions of Authority Patterns

We can argue this point further by showing that the elements of authority patterns are much the same in all social units, regardless of size or function.

Patterns of authority vary on many dimensions and subdimensions. Some of these refer to relations among superordinates and subordinates, others to relations among superordinates as decision makers and traits of the structures in which they operate. "Super-subrelations" obviously are at the core of authority, but authority patterns also vary in regard to relations among "elites" that occur in decision-making processes. These relations may in fact matter more in regard to efficacy than super-subrelations.

In a coauthored book, Gurr and I (1975) identified eleven general dimensions on which all authority patterns vary, and we divided these further into some forty subdimensions and elements. For comprehensive discussions of these, readers should consult the book, but summary discussions of a couple of the dimensions will illustrate the general nature of what we did. These discussions should help readers to see that authority patterns large and small, "public" or "private" (in the terminology used by Merriam [1944]), are much the same.

Directiveness. An important aspect of any authority pattern is what we call "directiveness," which denotes the extent to which activities in a social unit occur because of directives, not the free choice of members. This is plainly a continuum. At one pole it involves total regimentation of the unit's members; at the opposite pole is total permissiveness. These are abstractions to bound a directiveness scale, not conditions that might actually exist.

The degree of overall directiveness is the result of variations on several subdimensions that determine it in a "value-added" way. It involves, most basically, the extent to which directives exist that cover activities in a unit in the first place. This, however, never gives a complete description and measure of directiveness. Also important is the extent to which directives allow latitude to subs to choose particular actions under them. Latitude results mainly from the vagueness or generality of directives; for instance, the directive "Students should be neat in appearance" allows more choice than "Students must wear the school uniform." Also important is the extent to which activities are supervised; loose supervision or none obviously enlarges the extent to which personal choices of action may be pursued with impunity. For the same reason, directiveness also involves what might be called the unit's "sanction threshold": the severity of sanctions used in cases of noncompliance and the thresholds at which they are invoked. Lax sanctions, used only against extreme noncompliance, mitigate directiveness.

The most directive social authority pattern thus is one in which all the activities of subs are covered by highly detailed directives, close policing (supervision) is performed, and severe sanctions are used even against mild noncompliance.

To make this point concrete: A study by Schonfeld (1976) of authority in French schools found a level of directiveness in elementary schools that would certainly not even be approached in their American counterparts. Pupils' time is filled with study requirements defined by detailed national curricula, and these are further detailed by school administrators, senior teachers, and particular instructors. Not only is the work to be done prescribed in great detail, but so is the manner of doing it: the kind of pen to be used, the size of margins on pages, and so on. Proper comportment in class is also prescribed with petty precision. There is, in addition, continuous supervision to ensure compliance, and reports are made weekly in written evaluations of the pupil's work and conduct. Sanctions, however, are just "moderately severe" and not invoked against petty misconduct; however, one may suspect that the steady stream of reports leads to sanctions at home that may be more severe than those in schools.

This pattern changes when pupils enter higher grades, as detailed coverage decreases. However, says Schonfeld, explicit coverage is largely replaced by implicit coverage—that is, the internalization of directives by earlier conditioning. This changes the manner in which schools are directive, but not the extent to which they are. We may surmise that directiveness often occurs in this way—by internalization—rather than by explicit command.

High directiveness in the schools, however, does not mean high compliance; the French are not afflicted with what Germans call *Kadavergehorsamkeit*. Pupils frequently respond to high directiveness by rebellious behavior, especially by the *chahut*, an institution intended to cause teachers misery and embarrassment. Schonfeld speculates about the effects of this state of affairs on adult French orientations toward authority, on the plausible assumption that norms and practices of authority in childhood and youth will condition adult orientations.[4] Overall, he finds that childhood experiences provide bases for the alternation of authoritarian and liberal-revolutionary traditions that, so it was often argued, characterized French government and politics from Louis XVI to the Fifth Republic.

In my own work on the authority relations of poor people, such as people who live in the inner city or the lower working class in general, I have found even greater directiveness, including the frequent use of severe sanctions at low levels of noncompliance (1992a, chaps. 10 and 11). Moreover, authority in the social units of the poor seems to be similar regardless of the unit studied (e.g., families, schools, "street corner" societies) or the particular society and culture in which they exist. I have argued that this situation is the result of the very fact of poverty: the frustrations it induces and the adaptations required by having to manage with extreme scarcity. I have also argued that this helps to understand why a measure of "parochialism" (lack of involvement in politics)—most prevalent in lower socioeconomic groups— may be a constructive, perhaps even necessary, component of the "civic" culture that seems conducive to stable democracy.

Other general dimensions on which super-subrelations vary are participation, compliance, responsiveness, social distance, and comportment. I will not discuss any of these here, but it should be obvious that there can be more or less participation by subordinates in the direction of social units, more or less responsiveness to participation by superordinates, higher or lower general levels of compliance with directives, more or less distance in the general social positions of supers and subs, and more or less familiarity in their interactions.

Decision Rules. A critical aspect of superordinate behavior involves the rules that determine when decisions have in fact been taken, and taken properly, so as to be binding. Anyone familiar with the formal decision rules of national legislatures or constitutions, not to mention their informal norms, will realize that these rules vary greatly. So they do also in other social units.

In general, decision rules may be distinguished on a dimension defined by the number or proportion of participants in decision making required for a decision to be considered properly taken. At one extreme is "monocracy," in which the decision of a single individual prevails. (For instance, the traditional German family, the family of "Fatherland," was generally considered a model of monocracy.) At the other pole are consensual rules. These require the existence of a "sense of the meeting"—that is, the agreement of everyone, or nearly everyone, involved in deliberations about decisions, or at least their abstention from overt opposition. (Quaker meetings are an example.) Majority rule obviously is at midpoint between these poles, extraordinary majorities fall in the upper half of the dimension, and a variety of oligarchic rules fall in the lower ranges.

Decision rules are sometimes specified explicitly in constitutional documents, but more often they are implicit in the understandings of members of social units. Where the rules are formally explicit, operative decision rules often are different. The rules also are generally more complex than may seem to be the case on the basis of written rules pertaining to them.

As an example, consider the decision rules that seem to prevail in typical American academic departments, as I understand them.[5] Simple majority rule is always the formal rule in the departments; in the case of my university, it is specified again and again in voluminous written rules governing procedures. If we go by actual behavior, however, the operative rules are different and more complex. Gurr and I (1975) summarize them thus: (1) Simple majorities suffice in matters of routine departmental housekeeping. (2) On more consequential matters that do not involve personnel, majorities also prevail, but these must include members most affected by the decisions (e.g., course requirements, curricular innovations, or the frequency with which courses or seminars may be given); these are extraordinary majorities of a kind, or at least not "simple" majorities. (3) All decisions on faculty personnel—hiring, promotion, dismissal—are not regarded as properly taken unless agreed to by large extraordinary majorities, which must usually include a preponderance of the senior professors. (4) The more senior the faculty member, the closer decisions must approach unanimity.

Since, for the sake of departmental harmony, minor decisions usually are agreed to unanimously anyway, and since consequential ones are expected to approach unanimity, the overall rule seems to be consensus, or, perhaps better, quasi-consensus.[6] Pure consensus rules would probably not use voting at all; literal consensus emerges and is discovered, because the idea of consensus implies a unified collective will (a "corporate" will), whereas voting is done by separated individuals.[7]

A consensus process could not be effective unless certain conditions are observed.[8] Both an etiquette of consensual behavior and an operational code for achieving consensus apply where the consensus rule operates. No manual exists for these. They are learned by experience, as are all rules of etiquette and operational codes. The rule also has consequences that are probably the same for consensual decision rules regardless of social unit or general culture. Other decision rules, of course, have their own associated operational codes and consequences.

In these terms, a serious problem with radically "new" authority patterns will almost certainly be that no one quite knows what the operative rules are or, if they are known, how to operate them effectively.[9]

Forms, Norms, and Practices. Authority on these and other dimensions comes in three modes that should be distinguished. The discussion of decision rules exemplifies these.

One of the modes is the "forms" of authority—formal prescriptions pertinent to the dimensions, of the kind found in constitutions, charters, bylaws, or written compilations of conventions. A second is "norms" pertaining to the dimensions. These, as in the case of the academic decision rule just discussed, may differ substantially from the forms. The third is "practices"—that is, what is actually done, which may differ from both forms and norms of behavior.

Correspondence or the lack of it among forms, norms, and practices will probably have important consequences for the unit. One may surmise, for instance, that forms that do not correspond to norms will tend to be inoperative and that a disjunction of practices from norms will produce severe "dissonance," in the psychological sense (as, e.g., in France just before the revolution).[10] I have also tried to specify the special conditions under which forms will be taken particularly seriously, so that they will greatly determine behavior (1979b, 11–15).

Congruence

Ideally, congruence means isomorphism (sameness of form), as in geometry. In this sense it either exists or not, never as something more or less; figures either can or cannot be exactly superimposed. Congruence in this sense can only exist in geometric abstraction. The geometric conception, however, is derived from a more common, more inexact, and perfectly proper use of the term: congruence as a condition of broadly corresponding to something or being in agreement with it in essentials. The geometric use is an abstracted, idealized version of this more general meaning of the concept.[11]

It is manifestly unreasonable to expect all the multifarious units of societies to have identical authority patterns on all dimensions, or even to expect that all the patterns will greatly resemble one another. One plainly cannot hold this expectation in democracies, because some social functions simply cannot, for reasons of effectiveness, be performed in a highly democratic manner.[12] To determine whether congruence exists between "public" government and governance in "private" units, or in what degree, certain social units should be singled out as more, others as less, significant.

It is obvious that some social relationships impinge on government much less, or less directly, than others. Political parties, for instance, have a much closer bearing on government and politics than, say, sports teams. It should be obvious similarly that some units that do impinge on government do so only through intervening units, such as those that "aggregate" their interests. In the particular case of Great Britain, certain secondary schools—the public schools—have, in these senses, been more significant for government than other kinds of secondary schools (or perhaps any nonelite units), because of the large proportion of political and administrative leaders who were schooled and socialized in them.

Congruence, then, particularly requires resemblance among what I have called "adjacent" (or contiguous, or proximate) social units—units that impinge on government, or one another, directly and significantly. It is, of course, necessary to specify what these units are and, since they vary from case to case, to specify them in general terms that may have different "contents" in different instances.

I have stated two such general criteria for determining "adjacency" (1969, 296–97). One is that adjacency varies with extent of "boundary exchange" between social units—that is, the extent to which one unit serves as a special unit for recruitment into another, especially into its higher positions of superordination. In democracies, political parties always matter greatly in regard to this criterion. In particular democracies, other social units may matter as much—for instance, as stated, the British public schools, and especially a small number of them, the so-called "Clarendon Schools." In Norway, as another example, particularly close contiguity is apparent between local and national governance, in that national leaders (e.g., members of the Storting) typically serve long apprenticeships in local government, far more so than in other countries. In all cases, when evaluating congruence, one should thus start with the social units from which the political elite is predominantly drawn.

Second, social units are adjacent if one plays a significant role for socialization into another, for learning the norms and practices that pertain to the other unit's roles. What these are in regard to political socialization is, in all cases, a problem for research. One could, however, make plausible educated guesses about it. For instance, family life probably is less important for congruence in advanced societies than in others, because development is associated with the existence of numerous secondary or tertiary institutions that can attenuate primary socialization. This includes all of the organizations and institutions that have been called "civil society."

It follows that adjacency is greatest when a social unit serves as a source of both recruitment for another and socialization into it. Once more, the British public schools are a choice example. Other cases will not be so clear-cut, but we can, through research, find units that matter on both criteria. These, then, are, to use an awkward label, special "congruence-relevant" social units.

Although the more adjacent units count for more in regard to governmental performance, all units count for something, since all are contiguous with others. Families in advanced societies, for example, may not count for as much as in other societies, but socialization always begins in them and serves as a filter for later learning. The "primal" persists in the developed, but only as a note may persist in a chord (or, if the mixture is bad, a dissonance). Family socialization is followed, and may be attenuated, by socialization in elementary schools, the influence of which is attenuated, but never erased, by secondary schools, the influence of which, in turn, is mitigated by experiences in adult contexts. Despite all this attenuation, it is inconceivable that a democracy could be highly stable and effective if authority relations in families and/or schools are despotic.

From this discussion we can state two definitions of congruence:

1. Congruence exists if the authority patterns of all social units in a society are similar.

This definition is a slightly watered-down version of ideal congruence; but congruence even in this diluted form usually can only be approximated. The definition applicable to concrete cases is as follows:

2. Congruence exists if the authority patterns of a society exhibit a pattern of graduated resemblances.

This definition means that similarities are greater in more adjacent than in less adjacent units, but they exist to some extent in all, so that experiences in one social unit will in no case be sharply in conflict with those in other units with which it is connected. This will especially be the congruence condition in complex societies that have considerable functional differentiation, since traits of authority will to some extent be adapted to the effective performance of the different functions.

Performance

I discussed the meaning of governmental performance at length in a monograph on that subject (1971). In very brief summary: By "performance" I mean, of course, how well polities do what they are supposed to do; and this I consider to be a syndrome of conditions that are closely related to one another in that none is likely to exist in high degree without the others. These conditions are as follows:

1. Durability: the persistence of a polity over time
2. Civil order: the absence of collective resorts to violence, or other coercive actions, to achieve private or public objectives
3. Legitimacy: the extent to which a regime is considered by its members as worthy of support
4. Decisional efficacy (or output efficacy): the extent to which governments make and carry out policies in response to political demands and "challenges"

The monograph provides justifications for including each of these criteria in a general performance syndrome. It also describes extensive guidelines for empirical research into each of the criteria and for their measurement. This material should be useful aside from congruence theory for investigating any hypothesis about governmental performance.

The Bases of Congruence Theory

Congruence theory initially rested on four different bases, which can be sources of plausible hypotheses separately and which make hypotheses particularly plausible in conjunction.

Authority Relations as a "Linkage" (Relational) Variable

The process that led to congruence theory began with the compilation of an inventory of propositions about the conditions of stable democracy. I wanted to work on that subject and so wanted to know what others had said about it. One should, of course, always build upon existing ideas, to the extent that these exist and have merit.[13]

An extraordinarily large number of ideas turned up—several dozen.[14] These fell into two broad categories. Some invoked variables "endogenous" to government: traits of their internal structures and processes. As an example among many, it was argued that much of the secret of success of British parliamentary democracy has been the executive's unlimited power of dissolution over parliament. The reason for this was that the power supposedly started a chain of effects running from party discipline (to avoid the risks and costs of new elections), to cabinet stability, to decisional efficacy. Others invoked variables "exogenous" to government: traits of societies, or even larger environments, in which governments exist. Overall, there was scarcely an aspect of society that was not invoked as important for stable democracy by someone, from economic development, religion, and class structure, to climate, physical terrain, and geographic latitude.

Some of these hypotheses seemed well-founded, but none seemed fully convincing. Yet just about all conceivable exogenous and endogenous variables had been invoked. At the same time, it seemed hard to believe that the stability of governments should not have much to do with their internal structures or, conversely, that it had little to do with their social settings. The question then naturally arose whether there were any variables that were neither endogenous nor exogenous to government and perhaps ignored just because of that fact. The two broad categories, exogenous and endogenous factors, may seem to exhaust all the possibilities, but in fact a third possibility emerges: there might be variables both internal and external to government—in other words, traits shared by governments and their environments. From this idea, it was a small step to the general idea of authority, or governance, as something common to both governments and other social units.[15]

Using the concept of governance as a basis for theory about the performance of democracies had a particular advantage to recommend it. A problem with the then-existing hypotheses was that it was generally hard to see why their independent and dependent variables should be linked. The hypotheses specified empirical regularities, but they did not supply reasons to explain why the regularities should exist. For instance, level of per capita gross national product (GNP) and stability of democracy might be empirically associated, but the nature of the link between them is far from obvious or demonstrated.[16] This problem would not arise with variables that themselves describe how variables are linked or related—or, otherwise put, variables characteristic of the "field" between them, as in field psychology à la Lewin or in physics.

The idea of congruence suggested itself here as a condition that describes such a relationship, rather than disconnected traits of separate units.

The first basis of congruence theory thus was that it singled out a variable common to both governments and other social units (authority patterns) and also a variable that describes the "field" linking them (congruence).[17] This point in itself, however, only indicated that the theory might be on the right track. Additional bases for considering it plausible seemed necessary and were supplied.

The Empirical Basis

It is now generally supposed in political science that hypotheses should always be based on and supported by large bodies of data expressed in quantitative relationships. The data might preexist in numerical form (e.g., voter turnout, gross domestic product [GDP]), or they might be collected by systematic, large-n empirical researches, such as surveys. Hypotheses based on such data are generally called "grounded hypotheses." They identify regularities in phenomena and trust that these will reveal the underlying laws that explain them.

It is, of course, always desirable to have extensive empirical grounds for hypotheses. However, hypotheses may rest on other bases, including other empirical bases. The view that hypotheses apparently based on large aggregate data are somehow privileged over others—that is, that they are somehow validated by the researches themselves—is epistemologically naive. No matter where hypotheses come from, they must be corroborated by appropriate tests, preferably "strong" tests.[18] If so corroborated, their origins are irrelevant; appropriate tests equalize the status of hypotheses, however derived.

As originally stated, congruence theory did have an empirical basis, but this was not large-scale, original empirical research. Its empirical basis was wide and "deep" knowledge of two countries and their political systems that, it seemed, congruence theory had to fit to be plausible. These were Great Britain and Germany. Along with the United States, the former was generally used as the prototype of a stable, effective democracy,[19] whereas the Weimar Republic was generally used as an extreme case of the unstable, ineffective variety, which was surely correct. I knew both cases in depth since I had lived in these countries,[20] written extensively about their political systems, taught courses and seminars about them, done fieldwork (for two books) in Britain, and was schooled in the countries' histories and in sociological and social-psychological researches regarding them. Some of these researches, in both cases, were themselves extensive empirical researches, including survey researches.

It seemed to me then, as it still seems now, that this background was sufficient basis at least for an initial try at formulating a hypothesis that had a chance to stand up to tests; and it seemed to me then, as now, that the first requirement for testing an idea is to have one. Ideas may come from "intensive" (n = few) knowledge no less than from the extensive (n = many) variety.

Both countries supported the theory extremely well. I will not provide details of this work here, for reasons of space and because the supporting details can be read about in the original statement of the theory (Eckstein 1992b).

A more telling empirical basis was provided by a research project carried out in 1964–65, to help determine whether it might be worthwhile to invest more effort in the theory. I was aware from the start that the empirical researches called for by the theory would be unusually onerous—hard to carry out, expensive, and time-consuming. Not the least reason for this difficulty was the neglect by social scientists of researches into "private governance." Such researches had been repeatedly called for by political scientists (e.g., Merriam and Dahl), but nothing much had ever been done to respond to the calls. It was, of course, impossible to ignore entirely relations of authority in writings about social institutions, but the relations were rarely the focus of researches. Authority in social units other than government was then, and remains now, the terra incognita of social life, despite the fact that human lives are immersed in authority relations at all ages, in every sphere of existence. On the subject of authority patterns, then, nothing like accumulated research findings, let alone convenient data banks, existed. All the data requirements of the theory would have to be supplied nearly from scratch, and these were large and costly demands.

Before going on with the theory, then, it seemed desirable to do research that might establish its plausibility still more strongly—that is, that might indicate whether the theory's promised payoff might justify the onerous and costly researches for which it called.[21] For this purpose, I decided to do a field study of Norwegian government and social institutions. I had a special rationale for choosing Norway.

Norway is one of the oldest and most stable democracies, minimally on a par with the United States and Britain; but, beyond this, I knew almost nothing about it. Nor did others whose works might have informed me. Books and articles in English for learning anything about Norway were, to put it mildly, rare. This situation held true for other small European countries, but less was known about Norway than even some of these. A genuine predictive test was thus possible, and such tests are always the strongest that one can carry out, because they are risky—that is, likely to refute theory. The hallmark of strong corroboration of a hypothesis is that one has correctly deduced from it something previously unknown, by applying the hypothesis to known "initial conditions" (in this case, that Norwegian democracy was in fact very old and stable), in conformity with Hempel's (1965) analysis of "scientific explanation." The prediction, of course, was that great and manifest congruence between the governmental and other authority patterns would turn up. Not only was this matter unknown to me and other English-speaking researchers, but it was also unknown to Norwegian social scientists. Indeed, no research on the subject had ever been done, although many researches pertinent to it, but on other subjects, were available.

I will only outline some essential findings of the research in Norway here; for details and elaborations, readers should consult the book I wrote about Norwegian politics and society on the basis of the research (1966, chaps. 8 and 9).

1. An extraordinary degree of congruence turned up among all aspects of Norwegian life, from families to schools, workplaces, trade unions, trade associations, other associations, political parties, local governments, and national government. In all cases the themes manifested in authority relations were equality (low social distance), permissiveness, and participation. These, of course, turned up in different ways, in different degrees, in different social units, but they were major themes in all.

2. Particularly noteworthy was the fact that organizations and associations of all types were even more common than in the United States and Britain; they were ubiquitous and tended to have "dense" memberships.[22] They included not only large and familiar organizations, such as trade unions, but also small and exotic kinds (e.g., a Film Critics Society, which had all of twenty-eight members) and also a formal constitution. Almost without exception, in fact, organizations had written constitutions, and these were much alike, being modeled on the structure of local government, which means that they were highly democratic constitutions.

3. An extraordinary proportion of children and youths were active in such organizations and had occupied leadership positions in them.[23] Consequently, the experience of organizational authority, and authority in a particular form, is part of the early socialization process. The authority patterns experienced have all the trappings of democracy that are usually lacking in the experiences of young people: elections, service on collective decision-making bodies, coalition making, and so on.

4. Norway has political and social divisions that are normally associated with political instability. It is, in some ways, even a "plural society." However, it is extremely homogeneous in one respect: authority relations. The nature of such relations are in fact an essential aspect of Norwegian national identity.

Because of these and other findings, the research in Norway, which had been intended to be a "plausibility probe," might be considered to have amounted to much more—something like a strong test of congruence theory in a crucial case.

The Motivational Basis

One can show that associations between variables in the social sciences are genuine connections in another way. This is to demonstrate that the associations make sense (should exist) in light of well-established theories of human behavior. I thus tried to show, from the start, that congruence theory does make sense in this way. To illustrate this, I will discuss here just one such theory, that of "role strains."

Societies always have a division of labor, and in advanced societies functional differentiation is particularly complex. It is possible, therefore, to think of societies as complexes of "roles." It is also possible to think of individuals in this way. Doctor X, say, is a physician, a lecturer in a medical school, a businesswoman, a spouse, a mother, a member of the executive committee of her church, and a voter. This probably expresses the sum of her as a social (not individual) being. Throughout the day or week, she passes from one role to another. All of these roles are defined by complexes of norms, which may be similar or different. If the norms are contradictory, or inconsistent, Dr. X obviously might experience discomfort: "strain." A too familiar example is the sexual harassment of female subordinates by male superordinates; the roles of boss and employee and of being sexual partners are different and contradictory, but they can all too easily get mixed up.

Role strains can, of course, be "managed"—there are ways of reducing them. For instance, when a male doctor examines an undressed female patient, he is expected always to do so in the presence of another female. But all conflicting norms attached to roles can have more or less severe dysfunctional consequences, and all can reduce role performance.

The point is that congruence of authority relations means similar norms, thus less strain, as one passes from role to role in one's social existence. It should be evident that congruence also reduces the difficulties and costs of proper socialization into the variety of roles that

constitute individuals. A separate process of socialization for every social role might be imaginable, but even if it were possible, congruence
would reduce the burdens of socialization and, more important, increase the chances of its success by constant reinforcement.

Congruence Theory as Higher-Order Theory

Hypotheses can be supported not only by facts but also by other
hypotheses. Scientific progress in the more mature sciences often, in
fact, is made via higher-order, unifying theories that subsume separate
lower-order theories that are well corroborated themselves. The ability
to do this is in fact a particularly powerful way to progress from good
theory to better theory. The most powerful argument in favor of a
higher-order theory is the ability to show that it can account for everything that the separate hypotheses account for, and also more. One
way to do this is to show that the unifying theory explains both the
strengths and shortcomings of other hypotheses. Theories that can
pass muster as likely higher-order theories still require independent
testing, but evidence for subsumed lower-order theories also counts as
evidence for the higher-order hypothesis. This point is important because it means that evidence for a hypothesis may strengthen or
broaden the evidentiary basis of another that may seem different.

In my initial statement of congruence theory, I did in fact try to show
that it can serve as such a higher-order theory. This aspect of the theory
has been generally overlooked, but it was an especially important basis
for considering it plausible.

The inventory of hypotheses about stable democracy that led to the
original formulation of the theory suggested that three high-grade
(well-supported) hypotheses had considerable explanatory power, but
still not quite enough. One linked stable democracy to the influence of
religion; the second to level and rate of economic development; the
third (and, I thought, the most powerful) to the existence of "intermediate" organizations that operate in the space between individuals and
government—what is now called a strong "civil society." Both the
strengths and shortcomings of these hypotheses, I argued, could be
explained by congruence theory.

Here I will discuss only the civil society hypothesis. Many people
had argued this hypothesis over a long span of time—among others,
de Tocqueville, Ortega y Gasset, Mannheim, Lederer, Arendt, and especially Kornhauser (1959) and the great number of studies on which
he draws. It has always been well supported and is now particularly
strongly supported by Putnam (1993).

The connection between a vibrant group life in society and the con-

gruence variable should be rather straightforward to establish, just because the civil society hypothesis is such a strong hypothesis. Very
simply stated, it goes like this:

1. The primary institutions of society (family and kinship) and other
    institutions that almost everyone experiences (schools, work-
    places) can only be conducted democratically up to a point, for
    hard functional reasons. Parent-child relations or teacher-student
    relations can in some cases be more liberal, egalitarian, permis-
    sive, or participatory than in others, but they will be dysfunctional
    in all if they are liberal and permissive beyond a threshold. The
    dependency needs of children are always in conflict with permis-
    siveness, and the teacher-student relationship is, and must always
    be, asymmetrical to an extent. Workplaces generally are oriented
    toward some bottom line; therefore, they require considerable
    discipline, direction, and coordination. They can be more or less
    participatory, but never fully democratic. Thus, the most impor-
    tant institutions in which most lives are immersed will always be,
    to a greater or lesser extent, inconsistent with "pure" democracy.
2. A large number and variety of intermediary organizations can
    reduce the strains inherent in these facts and provide contexts for
    learning the more sophisticated patterns of democratic behavior.
    Along with local governments, they are, as de Tocqueville said,
    the "primary schools of democracy."
3. Intermediary groups are in fact logically necessary for "graduated
    resemblances" among the authority patterns of society to exist.

Hence the strong connection between a vital civil society and stable,
effective democracy.

But why is there not an even stronger connection? The reason provided by congruence theory is that organizations might themselves be
directed in authoritarian ways; in that case, these arguments are off.
Unless we assume, absurdly, that this is never the case, the association
between successful democracy and a strong civil society should be very
close but still imperfect—as seems to be the case.[24]

Putnam (1993) explains the association via the conception of "social
capital," which means, essentially, having learned how to function in
collective working relationships. I agree with him, except only for this
digression: the social capital for a "working democracy" cannot be developed if collective social life is itself inconsistent with democracy. Of
course, it remains to be shown that if a strong civil society and weak
democracy coexist, intermediary organizations will be found, in fact,

to be more schools for authoritarian than for democratic rule. Here is potential for a very strong predictive test of congruence theory.

The Balanced Disparities Hypothesis

On the basis of what has just been said, we can also explain why the balanced disparities hypothesis, stated at the start, should hold and how it is derived from general congruence theory, as applied to democracies.

If the social institutions that are the most widely experienced and consequential in people's lives are inherently inconsistent with pure democracy, it follows that high congruence is likely to exist only in democracies that, in some degree, combine democratic with other traits. The organizations that constitute civil, or intermediate, society may reduce the degree to which democratic elements must be balanced by others, but they can hardly eliminate the need for this altogether.

The position that mixed democracy, as it were, is the best-performing democracy has long been argued and is well supported in contemporary research. The most important corroboration comes from Almond and Verba (1963); they argue, and voluminously support with survey data, that the "civic culture" conducive to successful democracy is a compound of "participant" attitudes that pertain to political activism, with "subject" attitudes that pertain to subordination, with "parochial" attitudes that, in effect, detach people from politics. All the better for the performance of democracy if the parochials come mostly from social milieus in which authoritarian relations predominate—the milieus of lower socioeconomic groups—as, in fact, they generally do (Verba and Nie 1972, chap. 10).

Needless to say, not every mix of disparate elements is "balanced." Thus, we should be able to distinguish functional from dysfunctional mixes. This, however, is not possible in general terms, because it depends on the varying circumstances of societies—for instance, the extent to which institutions such as families have democratic traits, even if imperfectly; the extent to which economic stratification is great or small; and the extent to which intermediate organizations, democratically organized, exist. From the fact that a democracy has a mixed authority pattern, its success cannot be deduced. However, from the fact that a democracy is successful, one should be able to infer correctly that it is a mixed democracy.

A striking example of disparities in balance is again provided by Norway. As stated earlier, a high level of "democraticness" was predicted (correctly) to exist in Norway's social life. A second prediction was made at the same time: namely, that some element or elements of special authority would modify democraticness at the level of government, and perhaps in other organizations as well. This also turned out to be the case.

Liberal-democratic traits at the level of government were modified by a pervasive nondemocratic trait: deference to technical experts (including bureaucrats) on subjects of their expertise. The importance of such deference was augmented by a tendency to regard many realms, including rather unlikely ones, as areas of technical expertise, hence substantially out of the realm of normal democratic politics. This deferential element, I argued, supplied much of the energy and decisional efficacy of Norwegian government. It also seemed to "balance" without great dissonance the highly egalitarian principles of Norwegian authority, since it located special authority in abstract knowledge and skill, not directly in persons. This tendency to defer to assumed expertise in fact turned up in other realms of social life as well. Thus, Norway displayed congruence, as it should have, in almost an ideal way for the functioning of democracy: high similarity of authority patterns, the general existence also of balanced disparities and of similarly balanced disparities in authority patterns, and a particular mix of democratic and nondemocratic traits that was bound to limit perceptions of dissonance.

Nondemocratic aspects of democratic governments not only may enhance congruence but are required to energize government, to provide leadership, to allow a degree of autonomous action (which is often necessary for effective government), in addition to reasons of symbolism and ceremony: to provide figures above mundane politics and figures that somehow "embody" the idea of the political system. Constitutional monarchies, for example, are not anomalies in democracies but strongly associated with their success. In Britain, also, the prime minister and cabinet enjoy a great deal of autonomy; they govern. They are "constitutionally" subject to parliamentary controls, but these, in practice, are more fictional than real, though they are fictions that have useful effects.

Change toward Congruence

What happens to authority patterns if they are incongruent and if, in consequence, performance problems arise? In what ways can congruence be established or enhanced?

A frequent misinterpretation of congruence theory has been that congruence can only be enhanced by adapting government to conform to social authority patterns. This opinion would preclude the effective and creative construction of governmental structures—successful "constitutional design" or "engineering." It is thought that the theory implies that either social authority is mimicked on the governmental level or else government is condemned to low performance.

If this were really so, one might be disappointed, but the theory's plausibility would not be impugned; nothing says that only happy theories are valid. However, it is not so. The allegation comes from a misreading of the original statement of congruence theory and from overlooking a subsequent companion essay (Eckstein 1969). The latter work explicitly explores the question of how social units, including governments, may respond to the existence of incongruence and its effects. This is an important part of congruence theory, which should at least be summarized here.[25]

The core hypothesis concerning how authority patterns change if seriously incongruent is as follows:

Incongruent authority patterns tend to change toward increased congruence.

One could call any such a process toward greater congruence "adaptive" change. The hypothesis implies that congruence should be considered the "normal" state—not necessarily the most frequent state (which depends on what research turns up) but the state toward which sociopolitical systems always tend.[26]

On what is this hypothesis based? One reason for it is that the bearing of incongruence on performance might be "sensed" even if not consciously understood. Revolutionaries who try to transform society, for example, have always seemed to sense that transformation must proceed on all fronts of society to succeed on any—thus their attempts to reconstruct not only government or the economy but family life, education, workplaces, and so on.

Another, more tangible reason for the hypothesis exists. Incongruence in authority patterns must induce a degree of "cognitive dissonance," similar to what we called strain, and such dissonance is always discomfiting and may be seriously damaging. It must be uncomfortable to live with norms in one context of one's life that are contradicted in another but binding in both. It must also be uncomfortable, and certainly confusing, not to be able to transfer practices learned, at cost to the learner, from one context to another. One can therefore posit a general tendency to try to make perceptions and beliefs about authority consistent. There is much experimental evidence to the effect that reducing dissonance of any kind is in fact a general tendency in human behavior (Festinger 1957).

It is true that two inconsistent beliefs can often be squared by a third that reconciles them. A simple example (from the real world): You believe that businessmen only do things that are good for the bottom line. You learn that the CEO of a large firm has installed an ambitious program of workers' participation in management and that he says that he has done this "to save his soul" (Witte 1980). You could make these perceptions consistent by changing your whole conception of managerial behavior, but that approach would entail changing many, probably deep, beliefs. The more "efficient" solution is to conclude that the CEO has not been candid but has in fact installed the scheme for self-interested ends, like to glean more commitment and production by workers or to undermine a trade union.

It is not as easy to manage the dissonance that results from norms and practices in one kind of social unit being contradicted by those of others; there are no simple "third-sentence" solutions in that case. One might perhaps reduce dissonance in such a case by attributing the differences simply to different functional requirements, but this strategy calls for much sophistication and will certainly not get rid of the inconsistency. The best way to reduce dissonance in this case clearly is to reduce incongruity itself.

This is not to say, of course, that adaptation must succeed. Institutions may resist adaptive changes for a variety of reasons, and people often do wrong things for right reasons. Wherever there is adaptation there is also the possibility of maladaptation. Consequently, the hypothesis posits only a tendency.

Incongruence in authority patterns, in light of earlier arguments, might be reduced in one or both of two ways: by changes in the patterns that increase their similarity or, because of the notion of graduated resemblances, by the creation of intermediary units that increase the distance between incongruent units. But what changes to conform to what?

Logically, congruence might be increased by changes in either the governmental pattern or that of social authority patterns. One has no logical reason to suppose that it must always be the governmental pattern that is adapted. Consequently, the direction of change should be stated in a more general manner. I do this by a second hypothesis that is "auxiliary" to the first:

> Adaptation toward increased congruence occurs toward conformity with authority in the less labile social units—those most resistant to change.

This hypothesis may be considered a version of the apparently universal tendency of any motion to take the path of least resistance.

It is not true, though widely believed, that governments are always artificial and other aspects of society somehow "natural," so that government, but not society, can be adaptively engineered. This view is very dubious: governments can certainly be less labile than other social units. What, then, makes social units more or less labile?

We may posit, first, that lability varies with strength of institutionalization: the more deeply norms of behavior pertinent to certain social units are internalized, the less labile are the units. Given the well-supported hypothesis that early socialization generally goes deeper than later socialization—that it acts as a "filter" for the later processes—we can infer that childhood patterns (family, school) generally tend to dominate adult patterns of all kinds. Hence, perhaps, arose the Confucian belief (and Montesquieu's) that the well-constructed kingdom must be like a well-constructed family.

However, it is certainly possible that norms pertaining to government and politics could dominate other norms. If internalized early and deeply, and held intensely, such norms may certainly induce a tendency to change others. In all advanced democratic societies, in fact, a strong tendency now exists to democratize "everyday life"—to make it more permissive, participatory, and inclusive—so that it will be more consistent with deeply held political values. How far this process can go is still open to question, particularly since the imperative to adapt toward congruence will often clash with the imperative to adapt institutions to functions, but that the process goes on is certain.

Lability will also vary with the capacity to control and resist. Here modern governments have a great advantage over other social units because of their monopoly on legitimate coercion—the ability to impose violent sanctions and other severe deprivations—and, less obviously, because of the technical and administrative capacities they command, alongside overwhelming resources of wealth and numbers. It might, in fact, be hypothesized that, as societies advance, the realm of government constantly becomes stronger (less labile) vis-à-vis other social realms, so that the tendency toward congruence increasingly involves the adaptation of social to governmental patterns.[27]

Adaptation toward congruence thus may occur in both directions and is likely to involve the adaptation of social authority patterns to the governmental pattern at least in certain specifiable conditions. This point implies further that "constitutional engineering" is possible but also unlikely to succeed if not extended in some degree to other social units, especially those adjacent to government.

Congruence Theory and Democratization

Since this book deals with democratization, it is appropriate to make some remarks about the bearing congruence theory might have on that process.

Needless to say, congruence theory says nothing directly about democratization. It is certainly not a theory of democratization of the currently dominant genre, transition theory.[28] This sort of theory, as I understand it, is concerned with the problem of how a new democracy might be safeguarded against early demise—political infant mortality, so to speak. This problem is obviously important; for there can be no long run without a short run. The leading idea about it is pact theory, or the practice of garantismo. This theory says that new democracies can only be safeguarded if existing elites perceive a critical need to institute them (through shortcomings in the old regime, exacerbated by "crisis") and if, by a series of understandings akin to treaties, the old elites (economic, military, bureaucratic, religious) are guaranteed that their special interests will not be seriously harmed by the change to democracy.

This theory makes sense as far as it goes. Existing elites always command powerful resources for resisting and undermining major changes. But, for two reasons, it does not go far enough. First, regimes can fail for reasons other than the opposition of old elite groups. Regimes may fail to persist simply because of their inefficacy; if they are seriously ineffective, then of course all interests will be adversely affected and pacts are beside the point. Also, much historical evidence indicates that opposition by old elites tends to become serious mainly when normal government is weak, especially if, as in the case of Weimar Germany or prefascist Italy, it is paralyzed in the face of situations that call urgently for action. Second, it is not reasonable, by logic and evidence, to hold that a transition to a new order is accomplished when the order has made it through a few years, through infancy. If that were so, then almost all failed democracies had made successful transitions.

How long is a transition, anyway? I have heard it said that the transition to democracy is over when democratic institutions have been put in place. Clearly, this perspective trivializes the idea of transition. A more extensive period must be involved; but how much more extensive?

I will argue (chap. 10) that this point depends on the extent to which conditions under which democracies may flourish are already in place when democratization starts, which seems truistic. Even if we lack exact knowledge about this, however, we can make a stab at specifying a minimal time period for accomplishing transition by calculating, as Gurr (1974) has, the statistical chances of longer-term survival if a regime has lasted a specified period of time. In general, this seems to be something approaching a generation. In less time just about anything still seems equally likely, from early demise to eternal life. This also makes intuitive sense in light of conspicuous cases. For instance, the Bonn Federal Republic was not generally regarded as entrenched until the late sixties or early seventies. The Fifth French Republic was regarded, for a similar period, as DeGaulle's personal regime (which, so it was assumed, would vanish with him) rather than as an entrenched impersonal order.

It seems clear, then, that a good deal of governmental efficacy is required for successful passage through a transitional period. It is just as clear that foundations for enduring democracy must be laid during this period or at least begun to be laid. It is sometimes argued (e.g., Di Palma 1990) that the only such foundation needed is a constitutional order, but this view flies in the face of all historical evidence. A proper social environment for democracy is also required. This is elementary logic, if the fact of democratization does not insulate, or separate, the polity from society; if anything, democracy, being an "open" system, has the opposite effect. In any case, societies do not come neatly divided into hermetically sealed compartments, corresponding to the subjects of academic departments. On these grounds, it is inconceivable that, aside from pacts, only the constitutional order should affect governments in transition.

Thus, the prudential maxims of pact theory must be supplemented, even during initial transition, by prudential maxims based on general theories of democratic performance. Here, of course, enters congruence theory (or other theories about governmental performance). What sort of prudential counsels for transition might it imply? I will outline a couple.

No doubt a constitutional order of some sort is needed almost immediately after an authoritarian regime disintegrates, and this order requires constitutional design. A sizable new literature on constitutional design has recently come into being. This literature, however, is flawed by treating the design of governmental institutions as if it occurred in a social vacuum. Are presidential systems, it is asked, superior to parliamentary regimes, or vice versa? Should there be strong or weak emergency powers, or none? What is a good electoral system? The answer to all such questions should be "it depends"—it depends on traits of the society for which governmental constitutions are designed.

Engineering of any kind always requires originality and imagination, mostly in finding ways to accomplish goals in contextual givens.

For the civil engineer—or anyone—an abstract question like "What is a good bridge to build?" would be absurd. Obviously, it depends; you would not want to imitate, say, the Golden Gate Bridge, which is certainly good, if you wanted to bridge the Charles River. What you engineer depends on what you want to bridge, the loads the bridge is expected to bear; the materials you have to work with, and numerous other factors, not excluding aesthetics. So it is also with constitutional contrivances.

We need research and thought about the appropriateness of new institutions to varying social conditions; this will be difficult research requiring knowledge of institutions, social conditions, and how the latter affect the former. It will certainly require the collaboration of theorists (who have general hypotheses) with country and area specialists (who can contribute deep contextual information). Unfortunately, our theories say next to nothing about fitting engineered political institutions to given conditions, simply because of the fact that the issue, remarkably, is not raised.[29]

Congruence theory implies that new institutions must be designed at least in a way that does not dramatically violate the congruence condition—in other words, that adapts, in some degree, to the preestablished order. If it is advisable to pacify old elites by guaranteed concessions, then it is also advisable to come to terms with the fact that there are old ways of doing things—old patterns of socialization, old organizational behavior patterns, and so on. New regimes, like it or not, must compromise with old regimes, of both persons and of institutions.

If congruence theory has merit, then two things follow for the practice of democratization. One is that the crucial consideration in fitting new structures to old is the nature of preexisting authority patterns, particularly those "close" to the realm of government. The other is that laying long-run foundations for democracy means to democratize, as much as possible, social life in general. Since this approach is hardly possible on a comprehensive scale, it requires fostering intermediary institutions (of the right kind) that link and mediate between government and aspects of social life resistant to democratic traits.

In some cases, this may permit democratization in early stages only in a petty sense. A saving grace here is that constitutional orders may be treated as provisional, while foundations for more permanent orders are developed. Another saving grace is that the constitutional order, if "short and vague," might adapt itself, little by little, without overrational design, to fit social conditions, in something like an evolutionary manner. In that case, history might do what is hard or impossible to contrive. The more long-lived democracies in history developed in that manner anyway.[30]

Empirical Demands of the Theory

Congruence theory has come in for its share of objections, some of which need to be taken seriously in developing the theory and basing work on it. Here I will only go into the objection most commonly made and most consequential for the theory's future. This is that the demands the theory makes on empirical inquiry are too great ever to be satisfied. The researches called for by the theory, so it is alleged, are so taxing as to be paralyzing, so that the theory is doomed always to have a flimsy empirical basis. This point, if true, would of course be a fatal flaw.

I agree with some of this criticism: the theory does impose heavy tasks in regard to all facets of empirical research. Indeed a genuinely convincing empirical "test" of it, consisting of hard data, is probably at this point impossible. Consider that authority patterns exist in all social units and that there are many kinds of social units, even in relatively simple societies, and that the patterns vary on many dimensions and subdimensions, each of which poses considerable difficulties of its own in regard to conceptualization, appropriate research methods, and measurement. Not least, determining degrees of congruence among many units as a summary of their variations on the various dimensions of authority is an intimidating task.

These tasks can be lightened by focusing on special "congruence-relevant" social units, as discussed earlier. As Gurr and I (1975, 208–21) suggested, the task can be lightened further by positing that certain dimensions of authority will also be particularly congruence relevant and confining research to these.[31] Both of these modes of lightening the empirical load contain hypotheses of their own, but, as stated at the start, it is normal and necessary to posit untested auxiliary hypotheses in relating theory to empirical research. But even if these ways of narrowing the researches called for by the theory make sense, it remains empirically onerous.

The problem is compounded by the extraordinary paucity of research, especially systematic research, into the subject of private governance. As I said earlier, it is almost impossible to write about social units without touching on their authority relations, but statements about them are scattered in a myriad of books and articles, very few of which deal thoroughly and directly with the subject. The researcher thus is faced with the need to start practically at the bare beginning in

regard to empirical information, concepts, methods, and measure-
ments.

I speak here from experience. Shortly after publishing the original
statement of the theory, I began a large project of empirical study inspired by it. Fourteen graduate students, plus a codirector and research
assistant, participated in this work over several years. The students
were to do (and did) fieldwork on authority patterns in a large number
of societies. The directors supplied the field-workers with most of the
voluminous materials later published in Eckstein and Gurr (1975).
These materials were worked out initially over a period of a year and
refined later. They included careful conceptualization of all the dimensions and subdimensions, detailed discussion of appropriate sources
and techniques for inquiry into them (including questionnaire items
for surveys), and specified modes of expressing research results in
numbers.[32] The participants in the project thus went into the field
armed with an almost unprecedented amount of conceptual and operational material to inform their work.

The project certainly produced results (summarized in Eckstein and
Gurr 1975, x–xi) but far fewer and flimsier results than expected. The
studies certainly did not provide a basis for an extensive comparative
evaluation of congruence theory. Why? No doubt for more than one
reason. But the most important reason, I now think, was precisely the
fact that so much conceptual and operational material was provided
to the field-workers, in an attempt to make the researches readily comparable and cumulative and the results exact. Although the participants themselves wanted guidelines as comprehensive as possible for
their researches, overall these must have had a paralyzing effect on
them when confronted with the actual tasks of research.

More would surely have been done if less had been expected. This
point especially applies to demands for rigor and exactitude. These are
crucial scientific values in the abstract, but there is such a thing as
premature, thus dysfunctional, empirical rigor in practice. Particularly
in the early stages of research, the important thing is that studies report
some findings (almost any) pertinent to a large subject, so that cumula-
tion can begin and exactitude can gradually be increased. Genuine science cannot be rushed or produced by following guidelines. The
participants in the project would probably have accomplished more if
advised to do more impressionistic work, if that was necessary to get
work done in the first place.

I would now even advance this as a general methodological precept,
so that useful work might be done on important new subjects, and so
there would be less choosing of research subjects just for their condu-
civeness to exactitude, not their significance—a regrettable trend in

contemporary political science. Exactitude increases in the course of normal scientific development, as one of several aspects of scientific progress, but it is never absolute, and, most important, it is not the only, or even the dominant, scientific value.

The efforts that went into the guidelines to research have surely not been wasted, because their published results are available to guide anyone who might want to do research on authority patterns. There exists a framework, the result of much labor, that can inform researches into the subject. But this framework, at this stage, is to be treated cautiously. It should be used only as an aid to research, not as an extensive program for research.

The definitive rejoinder to the objection that the theory makes daunting empirical demands is, however, very simple: difficulty is not a reason for not trying, only a reason for trying harder. The only issue is whether a theory promises enough to be worth making the efforts for which it calls.

Readers should bear these points in mind as they read the subsequent chapters in this book. Not having deep and systematic researches into Russian authority patterns on which to draw, the discussions here, inevitably, are preliminary and tentative, but they do make a substantial start. I hope that these discussions will encourage others to widen and deepen knowledge of authority in Russia and elsewhere and of its consequences for the processes of democratization now under way.

Notes

1. The restatements and elaborations of the theory include Eckstein (1966, 1969, and 1992b) and Eckstein and Gurr (1975).

2. Consider one of the most widely used research techniques, survey research, as an example. Survey researchers know that some respondents answer dishonestly or express "nonattitudes." Nevertheless, they posit that the overall results of surveys researches are trustworthy. This is a hypothesis. The fact that we cannot test all matters auxiliary to hypotheses, and auxiliary to the auxiliary hypotheses, is one reason that scientific theories are never definitively established.

3. We can probably leave the word *democracy* undefined, without serious consequences. Most people probably would agree on whether most regimes are democratic. However, things are not so simple when we talk about democratic aspects of authority patterns, as we often will here. For this purpose, Dahl's (1971) conception of "polyarchy" is particularly useful. Polyarchy, à la Dahl, has two broad facets: "public contestation" (institutionalized competition) for positions of leadership and inclusive rights for citizens to participate

in leadership and contestation for it. Dahl further argues that a certain "liberal" order is required to make contestation and inclusive participation meaningful. This includes the right to vote and run for offices, freedom of expression, freedom to form organizations, and the existence of alternative sources of information. We might add to this list the possibility of directly participating in decision making, as a kind of inclusion that goes beyond voting. All of these traits are dimensional; each exists in greater or lesser degree in particular cases. On this basis, one can speak of organizations and institutions as having democratic traits in certain respects and degrees. For instance, families will not have voting for office, but they may have free expression, openness instead of secretiveness, and participation by children in family decision making. These criteria for degree of "democraticness," so to speak, will be especially important for grasping the notions of congruence and balanced disparities discussed later in this chapter.

4. For full discussion of Schonfeld's findings, consult Schonfeld (1976).

5. I have discussed this subject at length in Eckstein and Gurr (1975, 126–32).

6. Shortly after I wrote these lines, my department deliberated on a mid-level professorial appointment. A majority of nine to four was in favor of making the appointment. The matter was dropped.

7. The rule set discussed here is far from universal. As stated, it is, by my experience, typical. However, I have the impression that the idea of a university department as a "corporation," not just an aggregate of individuals, has weakened (though not yet disappeared) during the course of my academic life. In the United States, the decision rules have become more congruent with the individualistic biases and practices of the larger society.

8. These are discussed in Eckstein and Gurr (1975).

9. Other general dimensions of authority patterns include the structural conformation of the patterns (e.g., their simplicity or complexity in various senses), recruitment to superordinated positions, and bases of legitimacy.

10. This is discussed further in the next section.

11. Congruence also sometimes denotes being in harmony with something or being fit or suitable for a condition (e.g., the reception of divine grace). Almond and Verba (1963) seem to me to use the concept in the latter sense, despite reference to my use.

12. This point is discussed more fully later, in the section that gives the basis for the balanced disparities hypothesis.

13. Inventories of findings and hypotheses are not compiled enough in the social sciences. This is one reason for their lamented lack of cumulativeness. Inventories have yielded important results before. The most fruitful was an inventory of existing knowledge about political behavior conducted in the fifties in Columbia University's Bureau of Applied Social Research. This opus led to several truly seminal works: Lipset on the social bases of politics, Hyman on political socialization, and Kornhauser on mass society. It is high time to repeat that inventory.

14. Most of the propositions were pretty low-grade—vague interpretations

of a case, or notions without discernible basis. Several hypotheses, however, were substantial and seemed important to take into account as a basis for possibly still better theory. This was done in the development of congruence theory, as discussed in the section on congruence as a "higher-order variable."

15. Reading Merriam (1944) at this time no doubt suggested this point.

16. Lipset (1960) does supply post hoc explanations of the empirical association. In the original statement of congruence theory, I showed that these explanations could be subsumed under congruence theory.

17. Other variables might satisfy this criterion, but I have not been able to think of any.

18. For the nature of "strong tests," see Watkins (1984, 294–97).

19. For example, Great Britain was so used by Almond and Verba (1963)—a work written and published at about the same time as congruence theory.

20. This basis of hypotheses has been reviled as merely "anecdotal" and also dignified by a technical methodological expression: "participant observation."

21. I have called researches so conducted "plausibility probes" (Eckstein 1979a), suggesting that such probes should be far more commonly used in the field than they are.

22. Density here refers to the proportion of eligibles who actually are members.

23. A survey of 11,000 nineteen-year-olds, conducted in 1952, found that 22 percent had served as officers of organizations (Eckstein 1966, 104).

24. This point applies most obviously to societies in which typical organizations, or those "close" to government, are governed in authoritarian ways. But even if organizations are not generally authoritarian, some—including some close to government—may be. Readers should not have difficulty thinking of American cases in point.

25. For elaboration, see Eckstein (1969, 315–22).

26. Such change can, of course, be the result of human contrivance, in which case it may well lessen congruence.

27. I argued a more general version of this point in Eckstein (1992b).

28. Some leading examples of the genre are Linz and Stepan (1996a); O'Donnell, Schmitter, and Whitehead (1986); and Di Palma (1990).

29. An honorable exception to this is Lijphart's (1977) counsels on constitutional orders appropriate for "plural societies."

30. In 1969 I made an important addition to congruence theory that I called "consonance theory." I will not describe this theory here because it is complicated and because it was always treated as subsidiary to congruence theory as a hypothesis about successful government.

31. The dimensions we singled out for this purpose were recruitment, directiveness, and participation (in that order of importance).

32. The students themselves contributed a great deal to these guides to fieldwork. They were devised in many hours of discussions with them.

2

Congruence Theory Applied: Democratization in Russia

Frederic J. Fleron Jr.

Beginning in the period 1989–91, the so-called third wave of democratization has come to include many of the former communist countries stretching from the Pacific Rim in the East to the Elbe River in the West. Of the twenty-seven former communist regimes in the region, about one-third can be classified as democracies, one-third as semi-democracies, and one-third as authoritarian regimes. Recent debates (particularly in the pages of the *Slavic Review*) have raised questions concerning the unique characteristics of these countries and, therefore, the appropriateness of considering their political transitions from the perspective of the experiences of countries in South America, southern Europe, and East Asia toward democratic transition and consolidation. The resolution of these questions is obviously an empirical matter that cannot be settled in advance of research efforts aimed at establishing the similarities and differences of the democratization process across regions.

One of the more arresting questions concerning Russia in the post-Soviet era is the prospect for a viable, effective, and stable democratic political order. This is a multifaceted question that requires consideration of a wide range of factors: institutional arrangements, the personalities of leaders, historical influences, cultural traditions and conditions, and both domestic and international political, economic, and social conditions. A constitution has been promulgated, legislative bodies have been established, and elections have been held, but are these enough to ensure a viable, effective, and enduring democratic political order? The domestic economy is in shambles and violent crime is rampant, especially in major Russian cities. The president of the country, Boris Yeltsin, is known for his authoritarian behavior. All of these factors raise serious doubts about the ability of democracy to develop and survive (assuming it has arrived), let alone become stable.

Yet even in the absence of such factors, the prospects for stable democracy appear dim in a country with a tradition of deep-grained conservatism and even authoritarianism, an absence of strong and consistent democratic traditions, and a "legacy of cynicism and lawlessness," plus a political culture defined by such attributes as "a feeling of powerlessness in relation to political authorities"; "a fear of disorder and chaos"; an emphasis on order, stability, and predictability; "a reluctance to engage in autonomous political activity"; an obsession with secrecy, the "absence of a secular and bargaining political culture"; a tradition of "loyalty to a person rather than to political, and particularly legal, institutions"; a "suspicious attitude toward representative democracy"; an "indifference to the rule of law"; and a "lack of political tolerance." These are some of the defining characteristics of Russian/Soviet political culture found in the works of leading scholars. They are no doubt quite familiar to students of Russian history and politics; indeed, they have become part of our "folkways" about "Russian political folkways" (Keenan 1986). Whereas students of Western democratic systems have viewed strong intermediary associations as necessary, but not sufficient, conditions for the maintenance of a democratic political order, scholars studying Russia and the USSR have found a "lack of autonomous sub-group activity," the "concentration of power in the political organism as distinct from the social organism," and "the subordination of other groups—be they boyars or managers and/or intellectuals—to the state."[1] All of these factors require analysis, but where do we start?

This chapter is an initial application of congruence theory to assess the possibilities for viable, effective, and stable democracy in post-Soviet Russia. After revisiting the central hypotheses of the theory, we will consider balanced disparities in congruence among authority patterns. Next we explore the nature of authority patterns in intermediary associations and the role of authoritarian elements in Russia's transition. Since congruence theory does not require absolute congruence of authority patterns in the state and all societal units, we will consider the issues of relative congruence and the adjacency of organizations and institutions to the state-society nexus. Comparisons of Russia and France will suggest the significance of primary societal units—the family, schools, and the workplace—for an assessment of congruence in authority patterns between state and society. We then examine authority patterns as a linkage variable that may enable us to overcome the intellectual divide between state-centered and society-centered approaches to the study of Soviet and post-Soviet politics. Finally, we will suggest specific possibilities for testing congruence theory through analysis of authority patterns in post-Soviet Russia. The discussions in this chapter are structured to provide a guide to analyses in the chapters that follow.

Congruence in Authority Patterns and Balanced Disparities

The major proposition in Eckstein's congruence theory of democratic stability is stated as follows:

1. A government will tend to be stable if its authority pattern is congruent with the other authority patterns of the society of which it is a part. (Eckstein 1992b, 188)

After explicating the key concepts, Eckstein restates this major proposition as follows:

2. Government will be stable (1) if social authority patterns are identical with the governmental pattern, or (2) if they constitute a graduated pattern in a proper segmentation of society, or (3) if a high degree of resemblance exists in patterns adjacent to government and one finds throughout the more distant segments a marked departure from functionally appropriate patterns for the sake of imitating the governmental pattern or extensive imitation of the governmental pattern in ritual practices. (Eckstein 1992b, 191)

Eckstein goes on to add:

3. By the same token, governments will be unstable (and the authority patterns of a society incongruent) if the governmental authority pattern is isolated (that is, substantially different) from those of other social segments, or if a very abrupt change in authority pattern occurs in any adjacent segments of society, or if several different authority patterns exist in social strata furnishing a large proportion of the political elite (in the sense of active political participants). (Eckstein 1992b, 191–92)

Eckstein's theory has two parts: (1) the question of congruence "in the relations between governmental and nongovernmental authority patterns" and (2) in democratic systems the existence of "balanced disparities in the governmental pattern" such that "the governmental authority pattern contains a balance of disparate elements, of which democracy is an important part (but only a part)" (Eckstein 1992b, 207). The importance of balanced disparities recognizes, as Thompson, Ellis, and Wildavsky (1990, 215–216) have put it, "that competing ways of life exist within a single country"; that is, countries are constituted of competing political cultures, not a single political culture. With regard to Russia, for example, Petro (1995, 2) has gone so far as to argue that the existence of a democratic counterculture throughout much of Russian history explains the rapid emergence of democratic values following the collapse of communism.

> The historical persistence of an alternative political culture is the key to understanding the survival of democratic ideals after 1917. . . . Hence, the emergence of pluralism in the late 1980s was not a *new* ideal for Russian political culture, but the first *public* manifestation of an ideal centuries old.

Although a minority view among students of Russian history, this idea of competing political cultures is quite consistent with the unexpected finding of Almond and Verba (1963) that "stable democracies have mixed participant-subject-parochial cultures" (Eckstein 1980, 10, n. 11).

Regarding the first element of Eckstein's theory, it is still an open question whether there is in contemporary Russia a congruence "in the relations between governmental and nongovernmental authority patterns." The question simply has not yet been examined but is a promising area for exploration. As for the second aspect of the theory, the elements of authoritarianism in Yeltsin's government and constitution may prove to be a blessing in disguise. While some purists find these authoritarian elements alarming, Eckstein (1992b, 215) suggests that the greatest problem for democratic stability occurs in societies in which (1) democracy is very pure and (2) "associational life is poorly articulated." This disparity appears to be especially important in countries where strong elements of authoritarianism appear in the traditional culture—that is, countries such as Russia (Reisinger et al. 1994, 183).

At first glance, contemporary Russia would seem to be a classic case of the "blending of disparities" that Eckstein (1992b, 218) suggests is characteristic of more stable democracies: a "mixture of modern and premodern patterns." But on closer examination, there may be important similarities between Russia and Weimar Germany. In a passage particularly appropriate to post-Soviet Russia, Eckstein (1992b, 218) warns:

> Worst of all, the sudden creation of an advanced democracy will abruptly liberate men politically, while the exigencies of rapid industrialization

will subject them, in the short run, to unprecedented disciplines and compulsions. In this way, rapid industrialization not only unsettles the social order in general, but tends to create particularly great strains between government and other aspects of social life.

No claim is being made here that an "advanced democracy" has been created in Russia. But if one substitutes marketization for industrialization, the same warnings apply to contemporary Russia: rapid marketization appears to be unsettling the social order and creating "great strains between government and other aspects of social life." Indeed, the Russian case may prove to be an important test for Eckstein's propositions concerning congruence and balanced disparities, for it represents a new type of case: one in which industrialization had largely taken place but before both democratization and marketization.

The most advanced industrial countries are those in which industrial development occurred gradually. Here is an important lesson for Russia, since it was in those countries that "industrialization was associated with the relatively slow growth of populistic democracy and the gradual adaptation, never complete displacement, of preindustrial patterns" (Eckstein 1992b, 219). In this respect, the rapid industrialization of Russia in two waves (the 1890s and the 1930s) may have had a lasting and negative impact on the ability of Russia to develop that pattern of "balanced disparities" Eckstein views as so critical to democratic stability. Both periods of industrialization were characterized by the dominant role of the state, which, no doubt, accounted for the paucity of intermediary associations with their ability to balance the disparities between old and new created by the industrialization process.

Intermediary Associations and Authoritarian Elements in Russia's Transition

In Eckstein's (1992b, 221) view, a "vigorous associational life" has two positive consequences for democracy: (1) it "permits authority patterns to be congruent," and (2) it "leads also to one of the balanced disparities that democracy seems to require—a balance between governmental authority and dependence, 'democracy' and 'authoritarianism.'" Consideration of these questions from Eckstein's theory appears to be prior questions to the now fashionable debate over the relative merits of presidential and parliamentary government in Russia. Nevertheless, they have yet to receive any attention.

It is the purpose of this book to inquire into the relevance of authority patterns and the balance between authoritarian and democratic elements for democratic stability in contemporary Russia. All of this has important implications for democratic consolidation in Russia. If the analysis works, it would tend to support those who see some authoritarian elements as necessary to the democratic transition in opposition to those who want too much democracy too soon. A contrary view has recently been set forth. Przeworski and others (1996, 39–55) "dispel the myth . . . that 1) dictatorships are better at generating economic development in poor countries, and that 2) once countries have developed, their dictatorial regimes will give way to democracy." Since "transitions to democracy are random with regard to the level of development," it stands to reason that "to strengthen democracy, we should strengthen democracy, not support dictatorships." But how do we strengthen democracy, and what is the importance of balanced disparities in that process?

It appears that many of the old social structures (or transmission belts) of communist Russia have been eliminated and not yet replaced by new ones.[2] Steven Fish (1995b, 94) has pointed to the "syndrome of ineffectiveness" that retarded the development of intermediary associations in post-Soviet Russia. As we explore this dimension of congruence in authority patterns, it will be useful to consider Robert Putnam's (1993) work on social trust and social capital. (Erik P. Hoffmann analyzes the relevance of this line of inquiry in chapter 4.) Contrary to Putnam's view in *Making Democracy Work*, Anatoly M. Khazanov (1995, 50) argues that "effective democratic society needs not interpersonal trust based on strong ties of reciprocity and mutuality, but a specific form of generalized trust rooted in modern individualist norms."

A potential problem with the authoritarian transition in Russia has been addressed by Steven Fish in his exploration of the state corporatist alternative to civil society. In his view (1994, 40), "the state-led organization of societal interests" would undermine the ability of Russian society to create truly intermediary associations. The result would be the perpetuation of a feeble civil society. Regarding both points, it might be useful to explore the parallels between Weimar Germany and Yeltsin's Russia (Starovoitova 1995, 138–45).

Eckstein (1992b, 197) argues that British government has been stable because "British life . . . illustrates the congruence of social authority patterns in all its aspects and degrees." The Weimar Republic, on the other hand, was "one of the least stable of all modern governments" because "[d]emocracy, in interwar Germany, was, for all practical purposes, isolated at the level of parliamentary government, but at that level it was organized in an almost absurdly pure and exaggerated manner." In other words, the Weimar Republic was "a government violently contradictory to all nongovernmental aspects of life" (Eckstein 1992b, 199).

This should be a warning to some Westerners who worry too much about strong authoritarian elements in either Russian government or society that appear to compromise democracy. They may be attempting to foist off too much democracy too fast onto a society that is striking for its lack of democratic traditions (as that term is usually understood in the West). In post-Soviet Russia, as well as in Weimar Germany, too pure a democratic government may be "a government violently contradictory to all nongovernmental aspects of life" (Eckstein 1992b, 199).

What is the meaning of Eckstein's (1992b, 209) assertion that "democratic governments require a healthy element of authoritarianism"? On the one hand, stable democracy requires the following elements:

1. "congruence of authority patterns between government and segments of social life that resist democratization"
2. "balances of contradictory behavior patterns, in such a way that the balances do not lead to undue strain and intolerable anomie"
3. "a certain similarity among authority patterns, but not to the extent that basic human needs are thwarted" (Eckstein 1992b, 223)

On the other hand, Eckstein (1992b, 224) sees semiauthoritarian government as "the most stable of all possible governments, owing precisely to its impurity and easy congruence with primary group patterns." Semiauthoritarian government is that in which "strong, preferably ascriptive, authority is mitigated by adherence to impersonal rules, paternalistic benevolence, institutionalized channels of representation, and a vigorous corporate life" (Eckstein 1992b, 224). Not all of these attributes are present in contemporary Russia, which has a tradition of both strong and ascriptive authority. Despite Galina Starovoitova's (1995, 133) hopeful assertion that "[r]ational ways *can* be applied to this country, too," Russia currently lacks the adherence to impersonal rules, institutionalized channels of representation, and vigorous corporate life that are essential to mitigating such authority. Furthermore, Eckstein (1992b, 210) sees authoritarianism as that form of government that has "a high capacity to control social relations toward desired ends." Authoritarian or not, the present Russian government does not appear to have that capacity.

Fish (1994, 31) argues that the many groups that emerged during the Gorbachev era developed "significant mobilization and expressive capacities," but few of them "managed to assume genuine intermediary functions." He also affirms that "the interests, issues, and divisions around which political and social organization normally develop are now far more weakly present and much less differentiated in Russia than in most other countries" (Fish 1994, 33).

> The total ban on free association for political, economic, or social ends—the essential defining feature of totalitarianism—meant that the intermediary realm between state and society was driven out of existence. In sociopolitical terms, Soviet Russia consisted on the one hand of a state that monopolized all associational life, and on the other of an ultraprivate realm of networks of individuals bound together by ties of kinship, ethnicity, personal friendship, or informal economic exchange. With the state fractured and disintegrating and the ban on autonomous associations only a memory, the enormous breach between the state and the individual has become a powerful vacuum. (Fish 1994, 33)

Yet there are promising signs for the creation of an increasing number of intermediary associations: producers' associations, professional associations, and so forth. Indeed, Fish (1994, 37) feels that "while autonomous organizations are still weak, they are now far better endowed than they were during the Gorbachev period." He also suggests, "Elections and electoral reform represent a second aspect of political change that has prompted the growth of intermediary groups." The December 1993 parliamentary elections, for example, brought forth "more highly structured and more clearly differentiated parties." Those elections also "induced major figures . . . to launch their own parties and work hard at building them up" (Fish 1994, 38). Intermediary associations are important linkages between state and society in many political systems, but they are not the only institutions that perform this linkage function. Political parties and legislatures are also important because of their adjacency to the boundaries of state and society. Hence, the character of their authority relations has special relevance to any consideration of the congruence of authority patterns in state and society.

Relative Congruence and Adjacency

Eckstein's hypothesis that governments tend to be stable and effective if "their authority patterns are congruent with the authority patterns of other units of society" (Eckstein in chap. 1; see also 1969, 294–8; 1992b, 188) does not require absolute congruence: a high "degree of resemblance among all social units." Rather, it requires only relative congruence: "the resemblance of a limited number of dyads, regardless of what is the case for the others." This is based on the assumption "that some social relationships affect government much less than others" (Eckstein 1969, 294). As a result, Eckstein holds that "congruence theory might work well enough if the concept of congruence were taken in a relative sense: the resemblance of the government authority pattern to specified other patterns in a society, but not to all" (Eckstein 1969, 295). But this leaves us with the question of which social units are most important in assessing congruence.

Authority patterns perform an important linkage function between state and society. As Eckstein points out, however, it is not to be expected that all social units are of equal importance in this regard. Social units of greatest importance in this linkage function are those most adjacent to government. The degree of adjacency of a social unit is determined by four criteria:

1. "the frequency of *direct boundary-exchange* among social units, i.e., the extent to which one serves as a special unit of recruitment for another"
2. "the significance of a social unit for *socialization* into another, or for learning the norms and practices entailed in its roles"
3. "the frequency and importance of *cross-boundary interaction* between members of different social units"
4. "the strength of *de facto role segregation* between social units, i.e., the extent to which actors can shift from roles in one into those in others without experiencing sharp contradictions" (Eckstein 1969, 296–7).

From the bottom-up perspective, political parties are particularly important "congruence-relevant" social units because of their high degree of adjacency to government. After all, a primary function of parties is boundary exchange between government and other social units. In addition, political parties are "congruence relevant" in that they play a key socialization role.

In established democracies, political parties are "special recruitment units for the chief governmental decision-making positions, and governmental leaders generally serve simultaneously as party leaders as well" (Eckstein 1969, 269). This function of parties may be problematic in the case of democratizing countries, at least in the early stages of democratization. In many democratizing countries, political parties are a recent creation, and their leaders have been socialized in other social structures that have their own authority patterns. Hence, the importance of political parties as adjacent structures may be weaker in the transition phase, stronger in the consolidation phase of democratization, and strongest after a democratic political system has been up and running for a long time.

But this all depends on at least two factors: (1) whether political parties are new creations or have existed for some time and, if the latter, (2) whether the predemocratic authoritarian social milieu placed its stamp on the authority pattern within the party. For example, before October 1917 the Bolsheviks operated underground in a conspiratorial context, and the authority patterns in the party reflected this fact. Once in power, this conspiratorial view of the world continued, and the Bolsheviks attributed to their political enemies their own conspiratorial motives before they achieved state power. Indeed, the Bolshevik experience in this regard is a striking example of the importance of adjacency.

In light of these considerations, it will be important to follow the nature of authority patterns that develop in Russia's political parties. Not only will those authority patterns influence the relationships between leaders and rank-and-file party members, but they will undoubtedly help to define the relationship of parties to both the government and other social units.

To illustrate the significance of this approach, compare the nature of authority patterns in the Communist Party of the Soviet Union (CPSU) to those in the "movement organizations" Fish (1995b, 81) examines: organizations that "spoke for and acted on behalf of previously unmobilized constituencies and sought to advance goals and preferences that previously enjoyed no organized expression in the political arena." In the CPSU, authority relations between superordinates and subordinates, as well as those among supers, were governed by democratic centralism, the Resolution on Party Unity, and what Roeder (1993) calls "the constitution of Bolshevism" founded on the principle of "bureaucratic reciprocal accountability" and "a conscious plan to eliminate the accountability of those exercising the polity's policymaking power to the larger populace." In sharp contrast, authority relations in the "movement organizations" and proto-parties of the late 1980s and early 1990s were prone to "hyper-democracy" that reduced the social distance between superordinates and subordinates and contributed to "difficulty of collective identity formation within groups" and other "dysfunctional traits and behaviors" that Fish (1995b, 94, 96) has called a "syndrome of ineffectiveness." This rendered them unable to organize and structure themselves internally to perform the "normal" functions of political parties—constituency representation, the election of candidates to government office, the structuring of preferences about issues and candidates during elections, the organization of policy and voting blocs in the legislative branch, and other functions associated with their role as intermediaries between state and society—

thereby greatly reducing their significance as congruence-relevant social units.

From the top-down perspective, legislatures are probably the most
congruence-relevant governmental institutions. Of all government institutions, they are the most adjacent to society, since one of their primary functions is to represent constituent interests, and ultimately
they are responsible to the electorate through the vote. As Colton
(1995, 67, 77) has reported, however, Russian legislators have had only
a "fitful and lackadaisical interaction with constituents," and "[r]epre-
sentation was indisputably a low priority."

Nevertheless, focus on authority patterns in two of the most congruence-relevant institutions—parties and legislatures, and perhaps also
intermediary associations—could tell us much about the nature of
state-society relations in contemporary Russian politics. Eckstein
(chap. 1) and Bova (chap. 7) discuss the importance of less adjacent
primary societal units—the family, the schools, and the workplace—
and comparisons of Russia and France in the next section explore the
significance of these primary societal units for an assessment of congruence in authority patterns between state and society.

Comparisons of Russia and France

Empirical research on authority patterns in France suggests theoretically significant avenues of inquiry into Russian authority patterns and
also some important similarities between the two countries. As with
Eckstein's work on congruence theory, much of what Schonfeld (1976)
and Stanley Hoffmann (1974) describe about authority patterns in
France strikes a chord of resemblance to Russia, at least during the
Soviet period. Schonfeld (1976, 7) sought "to create an understanding
of how the French *behave* toward authority," and his research consisted
of "empirical case studies conducted in two distinct types of social
units—an agency of general, mass socialization (secondary schools)
and an agency of elite training and recruitment (the École Nationale
d'Administration)." Among his more interesting findings are that responses to teachers "are not internally derived but rather are imposed
or are perceived of as being imposed upon oneself by others," models
of behavior are transmitted "by outside authorities," and avoidance of
uncertainty is coupled with constraint. Indeed, constraint is the "price
paid" for "avoidance of the anxiety which stems from inhabiting an
uncertain universe" (Schonfeld 1976, 21).

Similar attachments to order, stability, and predictability are widely
held to be central elements of Russian/Soviet political culture.[3] What

happens to the "avoidance of anxiety" resulting from certainty when the norms and institutions of the Soviet ancien régime (authority patterns, social safety net, etc.) are destroyed and not replaced by alternative norms and institutions that are viewed as legitimate by large segments of the population? Recent survey research (explored by Fleron and Ahl in chap. 11) has discovered what is purported to be widespread acceptance of democratic norms, yet other research (Pammett and DeBardeleben 1996; Fleron 1996b) suggests that there is considerable and growing skepticism concerning democratic practices (including elections). Still others (Starovoitova 1995) have identified what they term an "ideological vacuum" in post-Soviet Russia. In addition, evidence indicates that at least some of the political institutions of Russia are not representative of the larger society (Starovoitova 1995). The result is that so far, at least, Russia resembles the former USSR in that social pluralism is not matched by political pluralism (Fleron 1969).

Another similarity relates to Schonfeld's (1976, 65) observation that "French children seem to develop a legitimacy notion based on forcefulness and fail to learn how to set self-limitations on their own behavior." This is reminiscent of the consequences of swaddling infants in Russia as described by Gorer and Rickman (1962) in which limitations on behavior are viewed as *external* constraints. A similar view of authority in the traditional Russian character structure was described by Mead (1955, 26): "control was seen as imposed from without." Yet both of these early interpretations run counter to evidence on Soviet education suggesting that "self-discipline is internalized obedience— fulfilling the wishes of adults not as commands from without but as internally motivated desires" (Bronfenbrenner 1970, 10).

One of the most striking similarities between the two countries relates to an issue area that has long perplexed students of political culture: the apparent divergence between attitudes and behavior. In France, Schonfeld (1976, 59) found considerable "conflict between the expressed norms and the actual behavior of (French) students," which he characterized as a "dualistic normative structure" and "dual and segregated guides to action" (1976, 64). Stanley Hoffmann (1974, 69) discovered a related phenomenon in which the French system of authority patterns "results for the individual in a kind of double bookkeeping: he complies with the rules (explicit and assumed) of the social units he lives and works in, as long as they are not arbitrary; yet his private beliefs remain unaffected by, and often are quite contrary to his public behavior."

A similar phenomenon has been observed in Russia—what a number of scholars have labeled the *dual persona*. Both personae are real, argues White (1979, 111), because "both *personae* in fact share elements of both spuriousness and authenticity." This dualism appears to be the result of "the institutionalized hypocrisy which the Soviet system continues to demand of its citizens if they are to live a normal family and occupational existence within its boundaries, and the ambivalence and 'linguistic dualism' which these pressures impose upon them" (White 1979, 111). And it must be added that this dualism had its origins not in Sovietism but rather in tsarist Russia, as much of nineteenth-century Russian literature testifies. To be sure, it was both intensified and reinforced in the Soviet period. During the Brezhnev era, writes Colton (1988, 154), it was manifested in "a seeping increase in 'double morality' (*dvoinaya moral*) and 'divided consciousness' (*razdvoyennoye soznaniye*), in which individuals pay lip service to approved values while scoffing at them in action." Tucker (1987, 184) found evidence of the bifurcated personality in the era of glasnost taking the form of "cross-thinking (rather like having a cross-eyed mind), in which one part of the head pronounces correct words while another part guides actions quite incompatible with those words." The dual persona found in both French and Soviet/Russian authority patterns is but an extreme form of what Eckstein (1992a, 275) (following Northrop) has called an "epistemic gap" "between objective behavior and subjective dispositions." Bridging this epistemic gap has proved to be a task every bit as formidable as attempting to overcome the Cartesian dualism or the Kantian antinomies.

The duality between "a 'false' subjectivity oriented toward public consumption and a 'real' one in the smaller community" (Sakwa 1995, 953) has important consequences for the formation of individual subjectivity crucial to the development of a stable democratic political order in post-Soviet Russia. In particular, argues Richard Sakwa (1995, 952), it affects the manner in which individual citizens will or will not interiorize patterns of authority, in contrast to the Soviet period, which was "characterized by the exteriorization of authority patterns." The importance of subjectivity to the convergence or divergence of congruence of authority patterns among societal units is demonstrated by Sakwa's (1995, 946) observation that "if patterns of politics are dissonant not only with technological and other socio-cultural developments (the old modernization argument), but above all with the forms of subjectivity, then society seeks to 'reject' or 'modify' those politics to pursue life-styles more congruent with intrinsic patterns."

The phenomenon of the dual persona poses difficult questions for the issues of continuity and change in Russian political culture. There appear to be several possible explanations of the public support for democratic norms in post-Soviet Russia reported in much contemporary survey research.[4] The first explanation is that the rapid social trauma of the collapse of communism led to an equally rapid reorientation in political culture. Yet Eckstein (1992a, 275) suggests that such an explanation is "precluded by culturalist assumptions," since cultural change is a slow and long-term process. Therefore, it is not likely that a democratic political culture could develop in the short period of a few years.

A second explanation might be that the public persona of the Soviet period conformed to official ideology, whereas the private persona supported democratic norms. Now that the official ideology is no longer official, it appears that public and private personae are now congruent in such a way that there is continuity with the old private persona but discontinuity with the old public persona. But we currently lack evidence to support such an interpretation. What is the justification for the assumption that, after more than a century of dual personality under both tsarism and Sovietism, Russians now suddenly have a unified persona that publicly supports private orientations in favor of democratic norms? If "orientational inertia" (Eckstein 1992a, 275) exists with regard to the structure of belief systems as well as the content of belief systems, then such a rapid transformation would appear highly unlikely. Indeed, Eckstein's (1992a, 275) approach to a culturalist theory of political change suggests that "changes in political culture that occur in response to social discontinuity should initially exhibit considerable formlessness." In other words, anomie and political extremism, not rapid developments of new cultural orientations such as democracy, are the expected outcomes of extreme social, political, and/or economic discontinuity (Eckstein 1992a, 274–275). This point may help to explain the significant decline in support for democratic norms in Russia since 1991 and the strong support for Zyuganov's Liberal Democratic Party in the 1993 parliamentary elections, the Communists in the 1995 parliamentary elections, and the Communist candidate Zyuganov in the 1996 presidential election.

A resulting methodological problem is suggested by what Eckstein (1992a, 267) calls the "postulate of oriented action" in which "actors do not respond directly to 'situations' but respond to them through mediating 'orientations.' " This view suggests that the Russian subjects surveyed about democratic norms may have been responding to the "situation" of the interview and not to real-life situations involving democratic practices. Orientational inertia would lead us to believe that the dual persona still exists. As a result, Russians surveyed expressed public opinions supportive of democracy, but they may have held quite different private opinions. Hence, evidence purporting to find values supportive of democracy based on survey research of opinions may be no evidence at all, for it taps only the public persona and in no way speaks to the private persona. Given the history of the dual persona in Russian culture, those who argue otherwise are obliged to produce evidence that is more stringent than that which taps only the public persona.

A third possible explanation for the nature of Russian support of democratic norms points to the connection between what Russians say and what they actually believe. As Ahl and I note in chapter 11 (in the section on "Social Context and the Nature of Democracy"), public opinion surveys conducted before 1992 found high support for democratic norms, while those conducted after 1992 found positive but declining support. This decline could be interpreted as a consequence of the ephemeral nature of support for democracy (Fleron 1996b). But at least some survey researchers (Hahn and Reisinger in Fleron, Hahn, and Reisinger 1997) are confident that Russians' verbal support for democratic norms reflects genuine commitment to those norms. To the extent they are correct, therefore, it appears that the more modest support for democratic norms noted in recent surveys is nevertheless accompanied by a strong commitment to democracy. This is an important point, for it signifies a greater congruence between attitudes and beliefs than we have heretofore recognized, and it increases the likelihood of greater congruence between attitudes and behavior supportive of democracy (Erik P. Hoffmann, personal communication).

Yet another dimension of the similarity between French and Soviet/Russian authority patterns can be found in what Stanley Hoffmann (1974, 70) identifies as the characteristic of *homeorhesis*, which he defines as "a refusal to retrogress or a resentment at failing to progress during a process of change that improves the lot of others; it is the rejection of absolute or relative *declassement*. It is based on the fear of insecurity." Hoffmann (1974, 70) feels that this term applies to the French polity "where there is a pervasive dislike for change that disturbs the existing hierarchy of ranks and statuses and the existing leveling within each stratum, a willingness instead to tolerate either the *status quo* or, if it is untenable and provokes excessive strains, change that affects the whole society yet preserves the delicate harmony of hierarchy and equalitarianism." This view seems similar to the culture of envy and negative equalitarianism that many observers of Russian culture have noted (see, inter alia, Brown 1989; Breslauer 1991; White 1979; Smith 1989).

Finally, there may be similarities between the two countries in terms of crisis leadership. Following Michel Crozier's lead, Stanley Hoffmann (1974, 71) observes that "the French style of authority produces an alternation of routine and crisis." This remark sounds very much like the Soviet campaign mentality that produced such phenomena as the collectivization of agriculture, the five-year plans, and the Virgin Lands Program.

None of this is to suggest that there are no differences in the nature of the authority patterns in France and Soviet/Russia. Indeed, a number of important differences are apparent. First, in France "there is very little attempted control over the ideas which pupils should express" (Hoffmann 1974, 25). This was certainly *not* the case in the USSR, where concerted institutionalized efforts were made to control thinking from cradle to grave. Schonfeld reports that, in sharp contrast to the USSR, "an integral part of the (French) system is an overt attempt not to restrict or influence the ideological options open to the individual" (Hoffmann 1974, 25).

Second, in France there is an "absence of face-to-face relations" (Hoffmann 1974, 25), whereas in the Soviet Union great importance was attached to face-to-face relations and interpersonal trust. As Crozier (1964, 229) observes, "Only because, at the middle and lower levels, people trust each other and are ready to enter into all the necessary deals and semi-legal or illegal arrangements can the most glaring discrepancies between the announced objectives and the means provided to achieve them be glossed over and the orders of the sacrosanct 'Plan' respected." Hence the presence of such "informal adjustment mechanisms" as *blat'* and the *tolkachi* in the USSR. At the present time, however, there is conflicting evidence concerning interpersonal trust in post-Soviet Russia.[5]

Third, in France "impersonal rules" (Hoffmann 1974, 71) have central importance, whereas in Soviet authority patterns strong elements of particularism are noted (Hough 1969). Indeed, it was this "rampant particularism" (Jerry Hough's term) that led Jowitt (1983) and Walder (1986) to characterize Leninist systems as neotraditional, thus suggesting that they lie beyond the scope of Max Weber's classical categories. In this vein, Crozier (1964, 229) characterizes the Soviet regime "as an attempt to integrate primary groups more and more within the sphere of influence of the central power and within the domain of rationality and efficiency." Very revealing of the similarities and differences between the two countries would be a comparison of the Crozier-Hoffmann discussion of "the fragility of 'routine authority' " (Hoffmann 1974, 74–75) in France with Yanov's (1977) description of "the boss" and the nomenklatura telephone in the Soviet Union. Also useful here might be a comparison of Crozier's (1964, 229) discussion of how Soviet bureaucracy "escapes the French type of bureaucratic vicious circle" and Hough's (1972) reply.

Authority Patterns as a Linkage Variable between State-Centered and Society-Centered Approaches

In discussions leading to the preparation of this volume, Eckstein wondered whether Russia is a case that provides a basis for arguing that authority patterns should be included in political analysis. While the following chapters support an affirmative answer, a direct case needs to be made at the outset for the relevance of authority patterns in comprehending the Russian transition. In developing that case, I take as a point of departure the controversy between state- and society-centered approaches to the study of Soviet/Russian politics.

The "bringing the state back in" movement of the mid- to late 1980s was the result of a perception among some scholars that society-centered approaches (especially pluralism, structural-functionalism, and neo-Marxism) prominent in earlier decades had not given sufficient attention to the importance of states as relatively independent actors and instead tended to treat them as mere referees of competing social interests. In reaction to this perceived privileging of society over the state, state-centered explanations staged a comeback in the ensuing decade as it became "fashionable to treat states as actors and as society-shaping institutional structures" (Skocpol 1985, 6). In this view, the state is "much more than a mere arena in which social groups make demands and engage in political struggles or compromises" (Skocpol 1985, 8). Indeed, states have considerable autonomy: "as organizations claiming control over territories and people [they] may formulate and pursue goals that are not simply reflective of the demands and interests of social groups, classes, or society" (Skocpol 1985, 9). Accordingly, the state is viewed as "an *actor* whose independent efforts may need to be taken more seriously than heretofore in accounting for policy making and social change" (Skocpol 1985, 21). Skocpol (1985, 21) has suggested that the even greater importance of the state is its impact on society:

> In this perspective, states matter not simply because of the goal-oriented activities of state officials. They matter because their organizational configurations, along with their overall patterns of activity, affect political culture, encourage some kinds of group formation and collective political actions (but not others), and make possible the raising of certain political issues (but not others).

All of this suggests to Skocpol (1985, 21) the likely emergence of a "new theoretical understanding of states in relation to social structures."

The new institutionalists have expanded this critique of modern political science beyond the charge of reductionism to argue that it is also contextual, utilitarian, functionalist, and instrumentalist. Not only the state but all political institutions are denied the status of independent actors. In other words, according to March and Olsen (1984, 735), society-centered approaches have tended to see "politics as subordinate to exogenous factors": they viewed "the causal links between society and polity as running from the former to the latter, rather than the other way around."

Dissenting from this view, Gabriel Almond (1990a, 189) holds that so-called society-centered approaches are not society centered at all, for they are not "societally reductionist, according no autonomy to state structures and politics and hence fundamentally lacking in explanatory power." Rather than privileging society, he argues (1990a, 192), "They grew out of a realism that recognized the processual character of politics, and examined institutions . . . in terms of what they actually did." After an extensive search of the mainstream literature in political science, Almond concludes that the statist critique of societal reductionism does not hold for either pluralism or structural functionalism, although it is essentially correct regarding neo-Marxism. Not only is the critique of mainstream literature flawed, but "[i]ts assertion that a statist approach is both different from prevailing views in mainstream political science research and a distinctly improved approach to political explanation also fails to convince" (Almond 1990a, 215).

Despite these problems, the statist approach was a hallmark of traditional Soviet studies as reflected in the works of Merle Fainsod, Robert C. Tucker, and Adam Ulam, and it continues to have its advocates and practitioners. In his book *Red Sunset*, Roeder (1993) takes an extreme and avowedly state-centered (endogenous) institutionalist approach that he juxtaposes to the society-centered subjectivist approaches that some scholars have employed "to explain the causal mechanisms" of change in the USSR. Roeder's conceptualization suggests a 2×2 table (figure 2.1), but then his analysis addresses only two of the four cells. All society-centered approaches are seen as subjectivist (and conversely all subjectivist approaches are viewed as society centered) and all state-centered approaches as objectivist. What Roeder's analysis ignores are the other two possibilities: state-centered subjectivist and society-centered objectivist approaches. Are not elite approaches both subjectivist and state centered? And are not modernization theories and demographic analyses both objectivist and society centered?

In further developing Roeder's (1993) conceptualization, Reisinger (chap. 9, figure 9.1) identifies a number of studies of elite political culture, ideology, or interests that exemplify what might be termed state-

FIGURE 2.1
Subjectivist versus Objectivist and State-Centered versus Society-Centered
Explanations: Roeder's (1993) Analysis

	State-Centered	Society-Centered

Subjectivist		*Subjectivists*
		Culture: Stephen F. Cohen
		Ideology: Friedrich and Brzezinski
		Political psychology: Carl Linden
		Values: Gail W. Lapidus
		Morals: Daniel Chirot
		Learning: George W. Breslauer
		(Roeder 1993, 14-15)
		
		Society-Centered
		Pluralism: Isaac Deutscher
		Urbanization &
		professionalization:
		    Moshe Lewin
		    Geoffrey Hosking
		Generations: Robert V. Daniels
		Generations: Timothy J. Colton
		(Roeder 1993, 17)

Objectivist	Roeder (1993, 14)	

centered subjectivist approaches. In addition, he views applications of modernization theory as examples of a society-centered objectivist approach. Reisinger's analysis provides us with a much deeper understanding of the full range of approaches: state-centered subjectivist, state-centered objectivist, society-centered subjectivist, and society-centered objectivist.

Unlike transitions in the South that were accomplished primarily through elite pacts, transitions in the East have tended to be through a combination of elite pacts and mass participation (Bunce 1995a, 90). In chapter 11, Ahl and I discuss what difference this makes in terms of the continuing importance of mass publics, especially for the consolidation of democracy in Russia.

Whereas traditional Sovietology focused on elites and adopted a view from the top down similar to state-centered approaches, the revisionist historians of Russia took the view from the bottom up.[6] One problem of our attempts to understand perestroika was that we tended to rely too much on the Moscow intellectuals—a view from the top. Lest we repeat that error, Fish (1996, 105–7) has recently presented evidence that counters a number of pessimistic myths about the Russian masses that have been propagated by "the Moscow intelligentsia and Western observers." He concludes that Russian voters are much more "engaged and sophisticated" than the view from the top suggests.

The opening of the former Soviet Union to empirical field research has enabled us to gather information and data that give us a better view both from the top down and the bottom up. Roeder's (chap. 8) and Reisinger's (chap. 9) analyses provide us with some important insights into the connection between these two perspectives.

Reisinger (chap. 9) nicely fills in the two missing cells of Roeder's (1993) implicit 2×2 table in chapter 2 of *Red Sunset*. More important, he provides us with analysis that suggests how we can bridge the gap among these four different perspectives. Quite significant is his admonition to bring society back into the thick of things, for otherwise the utility of neoinstitutional approaches cannot be properly assessed. Reisinger stresses, however, that bringing society back in does not mean that our analyses of "social change should be entirely society-centered.' "

Roeder (chap. 8) focuses on *process* in a way that views the design of institutions as the outcome of bargaining among political elites. In his view, "The outcome of this bargaining depends on the balance of power among them and this is principally created by the preexisting political institutions within which they operate." As a result, the elite bargaining process over constitutional design in the fifteen successor states of the former Soviet Union was "constrained by the preexisting Soviet institutional structure of each union republic." Roeder discounts the importance of mass publics and societal constraints on elites because the "forced departicipation" of the Soviet era resulted in an "atomized public sphere" that presumably was incapable of placing societal constraints on elites.

On the other hand, as Kullberg and Zimmerman (1996, 31) have suggested, the "real constraints on the politically possible" emanate from mass publics who are empowered by the process of democratization. Their data indicate that elites and mass publics have "divergent" or "discordant" interests. Since, as they affirm, there is also a "weakness of post-communist 'linkage mechanisms'—i.e. social organization, political parties, and legislatures," mass publics can pursue their own interests in few ways. This results in a greater absence of societal constraints on elites than one generally finds in democracies based on market economies. In the relative absence of such societal constraints, it appears that the primary factors constraining elite behavior are the structural political factors identified by Roeder. Those structural political factors relating to the balance of power among elites probably always affect elite behavior, but they take on a more exclusive role in the relative absence of linkage mechanisms with society. In light of this, it is probably the case that structural political factors were not privileged so much by Roeder, but rather they received primacy of place in his analysis because of a weak civil society. That is, the privileging was in the phenomenon, not the observer.

These considerations may provide us with important insights into the particular characteristics of postcommunist transitions that transcend the dichotomy between state-oriented endogenous variables and society-oriented exogenous variables. Namely, where society is weak and less able to exert constraints on elites, structural-state factors will have a correspondingly greater impact on elite calculations and behavior in the manner suggested by Roeder's elite-oriented structural analysis. In this respect, Roeder (chap. 8) and Reisinger (chap. 9) may be describing two sides of the same coin rather than providing contradictory perspectives.

Eckstein came upon the idea of authority patterns as a "linkage variable" that could provide a fresh way to view democratic stability and performance. Previous approaches have treated explanatory variables as either endogenous or exogenous. Endogenous theories focused on factors internal to government, including structural and institutional arrangements (Skocpol 1985; 1994, 3–20, 301–37). Exogenous theories emphasize factors external to government, for example, level of economic development (Lipset 1959), political culture (Almond and Verba 1963; Inglehart 1988, 1990), intermediary associations (Kornhauser 1959; Putnam 1993), and social classes (Rueschemeyer, Stephens, and Stephens 1992). The result has been a dichotomization of studies of democratization between state-centered approaches that emphasize the importance of endogenous variables and society-centered approaches that tend to privilege exogenous variables. In Eckstein's (1992a, 180) view, authority patterns are found both in governments and other social units; hence, they are "a factor both endogenous and exogenous, and also neither: a possible 'linkage variable' that might connect governments and their contexts, and through which brute contextual factors could work effects upon governments (and vice versa)." As a linkage variable, authority patterns transcend the dichotomy between state-centered and society-centered approaches. By requiring us to examine both norms and practices, authority patterns perform an additional linkage function: they also transcend the subjectivist-objectivist dichotomy (figure 2.2). And unlike competing theories of government performance and durability, congruence theory privileges neither the state nor society. Eckstein (1969, 318) explicitly rejects the assumption "that 'social' structures are always somehow natural givens and 'political' ones always artificial contrivances."

Hence, Eckstein's congruence theory of democratic stability has several advantages in our efforts to assess the prospects for democracy in Russia. First, as a theory of the middle range, it should be amenable to

FIGURE 2.2
Subjectivist versus Objectivist and State-Centered versus Society-Centered Explanations: Fleron's Analysis (based on Roeder 1993)

	State-Centered	*Transcend State-Centered vs. Society-Centered Distinction*	*Society-Centered*
Subjectivist	Elite approaches		*Subjectivists* Culture: Stephen F. Cohen Ideology: Friedrich and Brzezinski Political psychology: Carl Linden Values: Gail W. Lapidus Morals: Daniel Chirot Learning: George W. Breslauer (Roeder 1993, 14-15) *Society-Centered* Pluralism: Isaac Deutscher Urbanization & professionalization: 　Moshe Lewin 　Geoffrey Hosking Generations: Robert V. Daniels Generations: Timothy J. Colton (Roeder 1993, 17)
Transcend Subjectivist vs. Objectivist Distinction		With the concept of "authority patterns" as a linkage variable, Eckstein's congruence theory transcends both dichotomies.	Sergeyev and Biryukov (1993, ix) attempt to overcome the divide between subjectivists and objectivists.
Objectivist	Roeder (1993, 14) Fish (1995)		Modernization theories Demographic analysis

empirical testing. Second, it may help to "bridge the gap between top-down and bottom-up theories of democratization" that Reisinger (1993, 276) has argued should be a goal of future research. Third, analysis of congruence in authority patterns is an important aspect of "elite-mass linkages" that are undergoing such dramatic and rapid transformation in the post-Soviet era. Fourth, as Reisinger observes in chapter 5, "congruence theory asks us to consider aspects of Russian life that remain little studied." Most important of these aspects are the nature of authority patterns in both state and society and the requirements for congruence and balanced disparities of these authority patterns for viable, stable, and effective democratic government. It is precisely these aspects of Russian life that will be examined in the case studies in volume 2 of this series.

Early in the Brezhnev era, Meyer (1967) argued that the Soviet political system was a system designed to withstand change. He concluded that "the Soviet system has shown little talent for smooth self-regulation," and, as a result, was unable to restructure itself in response to substructural changes. As Evans (1990, 29) put it more recently, it had been unable "to institutionalize the dynamic of constant adaptation," a point forcefully argued by Roeder (1993). In this respect, the Soviet system was far from Karl Deutsch's conception of a well-functioning political system as a "self-regulating automatic machine" (Meyer 1967). The Novosibirsk Report (generally considered the founding charter of perestroika) argued that one of the greatest problems of the Soviet system was that the political system had placed artificial constraints on the ability of the productive relations of Soviet society to keep up with changes in the productive forces (economic, scientific, and technical developments). As a result, Soviet society (and its citizens) had experienced a retarded development. For a system based on neotraditionalism and welfare-state authoritarianism, that outcome was not a problem. For a system undergoing perestroika, it proved to be a fatal flaw.

Although the political system of post-Soviet Russia has changed in some very basic and dramatic ways, many social, political, and economic problems remain and new ones are being created. One of the most important things to have changed is that the political system is now in the vanguard. No longer retarding superstructural change, the political system now requires it. To develop further, however, the nascent democratic political system in Russia requires certain social mechanisms that the retarded development of Russian society simply cannot provide at the present time. These include various aspects of civil society and civic culture.

Eckstein (chap. 10) contends that the dilemmas of democratization relate to the pace, scope, and sequence of change. He further suggests that these dilemmas of democratization have no real solution. To the extent this is so, it may be quixotic to keep looking for solutions. Thus, our task as scholars is not so much to find solutions as to further the understanding of the process of democratization and its attendant dilemmas. Such understanding may at least contribute to an avoidance of solutions that could lead to either of the two extremes of degeneration: chaos or a return to authoritarianism. In addition, it could help reduce some other negative consequences along the way. Hence, analyses of what seems to work and what does not can provide critical information. This is the import of Eckstein's (chap. 10) proposal for "a comprehensive, explicit, detailed, and scheduled agenda for proceeding from partial to full democratization." It is also the import of his argument for "proceeding in a manner that may suffice to buy time early on without overloading the process and then continuing sequentially, in some reasoned manner, over a good deal of time, so that changes can be 'digested' and so that they can prepare the way for further changes." One of the issues joined in this book concerns the utility of various approaches to further that understanding. The chapters in Part III examine the merits of state- and society-centered approaches, suggesting that these two perspectives need not be mutually exclusive.

Testing Congruence Theory: Authority Patterns in Post-Soviet Russia

In his assessment of congruence theory, Reisinger (chap. 5) writes that it would be a "daunting task" to "gather from scratch sufficient information to credibly assess the theory's propositions." He posits as a more appropriate goal the effort "to broadcast as widely as possible within the field the advantages of bearing congruence theory in mind so that the work of many different scholars becomes more likely over time to produce a body of knowledge that permits an assessment of the congruence of different authority patterns in Russia." But what is this likely to yield in the absence of explicit attempts to test propositions from the theory? This chapter concludes by assessing several promising avenues for testing propositions from congruence theory in the context of contemporary Russian politics.

One suggestion is to build on the research of Sergeyev and Biryukov (1993) in *Russia's Road to Democracy: Parliament, Communism and Traditional Culture*. This work is an effort to consider the "interdependence of political institutions and political culture" in light of "the rise and fall of a particular social institution"—the USSR Congress of People's Deputies. The authors state that their approach was "also based on a study of the evolution of political ideas that influenced the fate of Russia, for any attempt to introduce representative institutions into its political life was bound to run against the suspicious attitude toward representative democracy embedded in the national political culture" (Sergeyev and Biryukov 1993, ix).

Sergeyev and Biryukov found that basic elements of traditional Russian culture were reflected in the debates of deputies elected to the Congress of Peoples Deputies in 1989. Paramount among these was the idea of *sobornost*—the idea of communion or "some mystic union of humanity" that was "opposed to the individualism believed to be a characteristic feature of Western (unorthodox) culture: *sobornost*, by contrast, was exemplified by the collectivist totality of the Russian Orthodox *mir*, or self-governed village commune" (Sergeyev and Biryukov 1993, 34). If *sobornost* is alive and well at this level of elite behavior (in this case, parliamentary debate), then congruence theory suggests that we might look for signs of *sobornost* at the level of mass opinions and behavior in various societal units, particularly in rural Russia, and also in other aspects of elite verbal and nonverbal behavior. Yet most opinion surveys to date have looked for signs of mass values supportive of democracy and democratic values rather than signs of the durability of traditional Russian cultural values. Hoffmann explores the significance of *sobornost* in contemporary Russian politics further in chapter 4.

Yet *sobornost* is only one element of traditional Russian culture to which we must be sensitive. There are many others, as indicated at the beginning of this chapter. Following the research of Willerton (1992) and others on the salience of particularistic norms in Soviet elite politics, such as personal ties and patron-client relations, Reisinger writes in chapter 5 that "congruence theory suggests that Russia must develop a form of democracy that allows personalistic ties to continue and yet does not undermine genuine democracy." This statement suggests that Russians must construct political institutions that are congruent with the authority patterns characteristic of their society, a topic Bova explores in chapter 7. Yet a question remains whether such institutions would be democratic in nature. And we are immediately confronted with a question that is currently at the forefront of research in comparative politics: What is the relationship between democratic institutions, on the one hand, and behavior and values, on the other? In other words, which way does the causal arrow point: from institutions to values and behavior, or vice versa? In light of our earlier discussion, we would also want to ascertain which side of the dual persona is presumably affected by institutions: the public or the private.

Recent survey research on Russian opinions of democracy has found considerable support for democratic values. It is even suggested that these values are both strong and stable and therefore unlikely to be abandoned because of major disruptions in society brought on by economic chaos (Duch 1995). Nevertheless, such judgments are based on evidence that may be ephemeral in nature (see chap. 11). If so, then a quite different conclusion may result from the analysis of demonstrably more enduring authority structures and relationships when viewed in comparative perspective (Eckstein 1992b, 188–201).

For this reason, it might be useful to view the congruence between authority patterns in government and society in light of Wuthnow's (1989, 3) identification of the problem of articulation between cultural artifacts and their social environment:

> Great works of art and literature, philosophy and social criticism, like great sermons, always relate in an enigmatic fashion to their social environment. They draw resources, insights, and inspiration from that environment: they reflect it, speak to it, and make themselves relevant to it. And yet they also remain autonomous enough from their social environment to acquire a broader, even universal and timeless appeal. This is the problem of articulation: if cultural products do not articulate closely enough with their social settings, they are likely to be regarded by the potential audiences of which these settings are composed as irrelevant, unrealistic, artificial, and overly abstract, or worse, their producers will be unlikely to receive the support necessary to carry out their work; but if cultural products articulate too closely with the specific social environment in which they are produced, they are likely to be thought of as esoteric, parochial, time bound, and fail to attract a wider and more lasting audience. The process of articulation is thus characterized by a delicate balance between the products of culture and the social environment in which they are produced.

Wuthnow adds that "[t]he problem of articulation is particularly enigmatic in the case of discourse that specifically challenges the status quo." And that is precisely what the reforms of the Gorbachev and post-Soviet era are attempting to do. Unlike the reformers of the Protestant Reformation described by Wuthnow, the political and economic reformers of Russia in the past decade have not succeeded in winning the support of large segments of their society, although the Russians, like the Lutherans, had engaged in the process now fashionably known as collective learning (Breslauer 1990; Breslauer and Tetlock 1991). Whereas for Wuthnow (1989, 4) "[t]he Reformation spoke to the needs and longings of men and women living in sixteenth-century towns and villages," it appears that the Russian reformers are not speaking to the needs of Russian townspeople and villagers.

Wuthnow's (1989, 5) analysis of the Protestant Reformation, the Enlightenment, and the rise of Marxist socialism "is a study of the ways in which social conditions in each period made cultural innovation possible." By contrast, social and economic conditions in contemporary Russia may make cultural innovation difficult. At present, it is too early to tell the degree of fit or articulation between the mode of discourse characterizing the reformist ideology and its social context.[7]

In terms of late Soviet and post-Soviet Russia, a major question seems to be whose program articulates best with the social environment? The answer has changed rather dramatically in the last five years. In 1991, Yeltsin. In late 1993, Zhirinovsky. In late 1995, the Communist Party. In 1996, Yeltsin again, but with substantial support for the Communist Zyuganov. Since 1991, it appears that the democratic and market reformers have not been able to articulate well with the post-Soviet environment in Russia, except the intellectuals (Hockstader 1996, 23). Why is this the case?

Political culture change in Western democratic, capitalist countries was a response to economic changes. In those countries, democracy was the result of the struggle for political power of a class that had already won economic power: the bourgeoisie. Hence, democratization in the West was a more incremental process that unfolded on the heels of the Industrial Revolution and, in some measure, was coterminous with it. In Russia, on the other hand, artificial constraints in the form of a monopoly of political power by the CPSU, with all its attendant manifestations of totalitarian controls, prevented such an incremental development even as the country underwent its own industrial revolution. Current conditions in Russia, including simultaneous efforts at marketization and democratization, may result in what both Putnam (1993, chap. 5) and Wuthnow (1989, 530) have described as a "relatively abrupt period of cultural upheaval."[8] "Rather than envisioning the Reformation, the Enlightenment, and socialism as instances of long-term, unilineal, or deterministic tendencies associated with the general growth of modernization or capitalism," Wuthnow (1989, 535) "made an effort to suggest specific historical conjunctures that made cultural innovation possible." Such an approach, he argues, "runs against the grain of the dominant ways in which cultural change has been conceived in the theoretical literature,"[9] in both the cultural adaptation theories of Émile Durkheim, Talcott Parsons, Niklas Luhman, Robert Bellah, and Jurgan Habermas and the class legitimation theories of Karl Marx and Max Weber.

A very different approach is taken by Petro (1995, 1), who blames the failure to predict the collapse of the communist system in Russia on the conventional wisdom about Russian political culture held by Western analysts.

> Despite their political and methodological differences, nearly all students of Russian and Soviet politics agreed that Russian political culture could safely be characterized as more centralist, more interventionist, and more collectivist than its North American or European counterparts.
> Perestroika, however, laid bare the inadequacy of this received wisdom. The astonishing upsurge in civic activism after 1987 (more than sixty thousand independent associations involving nearly fifteen million people emerged) was clearly inconsistent with the image of a politically passive population.

Against this "received wisdom," Petro (1995, 2) argues, "The historical persistence of an alternative political culture is the key to understanding the survival of democratic ideals after 1917." And that alternative political culture is characterized as more democratic than the official ideology of Russian communism. Furthermore, he affirms (1995, 2) that without such an understanding it is impossible to comprehend how and why "alternative political values emerged so quickly" after the collapse of communism.

> "The rapid collapse of the Soviet regime and the sudden emergence of a civic culture supportive of democratic values suggest that a fundamentally different approach is required to understand political culture in totalitarian countries. If one accepts that basic values cannot be formed overnight, one must allow for the possibility that alternative values were somehow preserved in Russia despite the constraints imposed by the regime." (Petro 1995, 20)

The thrust of the book is to demonstrate that a democratic political culture has a long tradition in Russia.

In sharp contrast to a big-bang interpretation (such as Putnam's) that describes a "relatively abrupt period of cultural upheaval" (Wuthnow 1989, 530), Petro (1995, 21) advocates a more incremental interpretation: "Of special significance to understanding cultures are the patterns reflected in action over time, rather than those observed at any given moment." In his view, a major shortcoming of the mainstream approach to Russian political culture is that it did "not allow for the simultaneous existence of two competing political cultures with a single nationality," and it did not "look far beyond the public expression of political views to ascertain deep-seated political values" (Petro 1995,

3). But exactly how does one get at such "deep-seated political values"? That is a question that has confounded many analysts. Petro's (1995, 4–5) proposed solution is that "political culture must move beyond its behavioral origins and embrace the more pluralistic analytical approaches used in history and anthropology." Only in this way can the manifestations of political values be comprehended, for they are "not likely to be revealed to itinerant Western pollsters." They can, however, "be gleaned through intense study of the interaction of deeply rooted symbols" (Petro 1995, 8).

Among these "deeply rooted symbols" are to be found reflections of authority patterns (Anderson, Chervyakov, and Parshin 1995). And here we see a high degree of continuity between tsarist and Soviet Russia as revealed in the following observation by Daniels (1988, 130):

> The prospects for a reform that would consummate the moderate revolutionary revival in Russia are further limited by historical circumstances. Thanks to Stalin's postrevolutionary assimilation of the Russian past into the Soviet present, the system still embodies the long Russian tradition of centralized, bureaucratic, and despotic government, endowed by its exclusive official faith with what Gorbachev himself has condemned as an "infallibility complex."

A question of great concern to students of Russian politics is the degree of continuity between Soviet and post-Soviet Russia in terms of institutions, values, and behavior. As we proceed to examine that question, Millar and Wolchik (1994, 1–2) have suggested that we must distinguish between the legacies of communism and its aftermath. They differentiate these terms as follows:

> Technically, the term "aftermath" refers to the condition of a field after the harvest. For grain, for example, it would consist of stubble, chaff, weeds, and gleanings; conceptually, these leftovers are usually thought of as transient and possible negative features. Thus, in Russia, the poor quality of medical care, for example, may be regarded as part of the social aftermath of Soviet communism. A legacy, on the other hand, is usually conceived of as an enduring intergenerational transfer from the past to the present.

Millar and Wolchik (1994, 1, 4) identify two distinct types of legacies: (1) "legacies that flow from the tacit social contract between the population and the state" and (2) "legacies that represent values, attitudes, and behavior that the state attempted to either instill or extirpate in the subject population." Aftermath, on the other hand, is described as "the unintended consequences of communist rule" that are usually "transient" and "negative." This distinction can have a profound impact on the ability of democracy to survive in post-Soviet Russia.

In an effort to explain differences in degree of effective government in four Russian oblasts, Kathryn Stoner-Weiss (1997, 23) found (contrary to Putnam's study of Italy) that "social context did not yet appear to matter much." In the Russian case, what does seem to matter is "the residue of former economic institutions which affected relationships between key economic and political actors in new political institutions." Is this "residue of former economic institutions" one of the legacies of communism or part of its aftermath (in the terms of Millar and Wolchik)? If a legacy, then the Millar-Wolchik list needs to be augmented to include legacies that flow from old institutions (and not only economic institutions). If part of the aftermath of communism, then their definition of "aftermath" needs revision, for "the residue of former economic institutions" may be neither transient nor negative. As Stoner-Weiss (1997, 54–55) puts it, "new institutions, and political and economic actors that operate within them, do not start with a tabula rasa. Behaviors emanating from institutional context and history influence the way actors respond to the incentives that new political institutions provide."

Such considerations resonate with Reisinger's observations (chap. 5) concerning the importance of knowledge about authority patterns in the assessment of elite behavior and the performance of transplanted democratic institutions. Indeed, he emphasizes that to "apply congruence theory to a given country, one must know something about long-term historical developments and how those influenced the rise of certain authority patterns throughout the society." However, he cautions, we must be careful not to assume that those historical factors continue to have an impact in the absence of confirming evidence.

Some important recent evidence suggests that certain pre-Soviet peasant authority patterns continued throughout the Soviet period and perhaps were even reinforced. Research by Fitzpatrick (1994) documents the forms of "everyday resistance" and "subaltern strategies" employed by the peasants to survive collectivization, including methods by which the peasants could cope with authority. And Viola (1996, 7) found that the "[f]undamental structures and institutions of peasant community persisted, demonstrating the durability and adaptability of the peasantry as a culture." Not only were the peasants successful in retaining traditional values in the rural setting, but evidence suggests that those values survived in the urban setting. As a result of the great urban migration of Russian peasants in the 1930s "village networks" (*zemliachestvo*) developed that perpetuated village values in the new urban setting. Contacts established among peasants from the same village resulted in "clusters of fellow villagers . . . living in the same neighborhood and working in the same factory or at the same construction site" (Hoffman 1994). The results included the undercutting of managerial authority in the workplace and undermining Soviet efforts to form new identities and the New Soviet Man. In some cases, Erik Hoffman (1994) reports, these village networks "allowed immigrants to preserve a form of peasant culture in the city"; "in other cases, new cultural forms were adopted, but imbued with traditional meanings." Hence, I would agree with Reisinger that "[e]vidence of authority patterns toward the end of the Soviet period is likely to prove most helpful, because of its temporal proximity, for assessing contemporary Russian authority patterns," but we must be sensitive to the significance of historical patterns and traditions *if* it can be demonstrated that they were either continued or reinforced. For this reason, it is important that any collective efforts to test congruence theory in the context of postcommunist polities include both anthropologists and historians, as well as political scientists and sociologists.

Continuity of traditional authority patterns down to the present is but one possible interpretation of current developments in Russia. A quite different picture has been presented by some Russian observers who argue that Russia has not yet experienced its "bourgeois democratic revolution," and therefore "a decisive break with the communist totalitarian past has not yet occurred." One author even suggests that what has transpired in Russia since 1991 is "not a revolution, not a transformation of basic structures but, rather, a decomposition of the political, economic and cultural structure of Soviet society" (quoted in Aron 1995, 306). This decomposition is purported to be a result of the fact that the present political regime in Russia "is not democratic but 'embarrassed authoritarian' "; it is a regime "merely hiding behind external attributes of democracy" (Aron 1995, 306). If this interpretation is correct, it signifies a violation of one of Eckstein's (1992b, 184) two conditions for genuine democracy: that "democratic structures must not be mere facades for actual government by nondemocratic structures."

A closely related problem is that a new relationship between polity and society is being forged in Russia. As Erik Hoffmann points out in chapter 4, a great transformation is taking place in terms of who is important and why. At the core of this transformation is a shift from a purely ascriptive system in which nomenklatura connections meant everything to one in which money talks. This new system is a modern clan system that is much less ascriptive than the nomenklatura system it is replacing, he suggests, but one that does not conform to standard Weberian notions of achievement norms. These clans are based on money, but the acquisition of this money has been largely based on the ability to rip off the old system. As a result, a whole new system of social stratification is emerging. A major question for congruence theory is the extent to which this will change traditional authority patterns. Those who have benefited from this wholesale theft of state property want stability, especially property rights to protect their new acquisitions. Hence, democratic forms are being used to legitimize and preserve former theft. As a result, Hoffmann (chap. 4) concludes, "The transformation of democratic *forms* into democratic *norms*—especially the constitutional, civil, criminal, electoral, and tax laws—is crucially important for democracy to take root throughout Russia."

Whether unfolding events in Russia can be interpreted as continuity with traditional authority patterns, a decisive break with communist traditions, or a decomposition of structures from the Soviet past is unclear at present. A focus on authority patterns could be an important link in our efforts to understand these processes, for as Eckstein (1992b, 180) has observed, authority patterns represent a " 'linkage variable' that might connect governments and their contexts."

The following chapters suggest that to test propositions from congruence theory in postcommunist polities, several conceptual, theoretical, and methodological issues must be clarified. First, what are the basic propositions of congruence theory, and how must they be clarified to guide empirical research? These issues are addressed by Eckstein in chapter 1 and Reisinger in chapter 5.

Second, what are the dynamics of state-society relations in post-Soviet Russia and how can congruence theory contribute to our understanding of those dynamics? Hoffmann examines these issues in chapters 3 and 4.

Third, a critical factor is how to measure some of the key variables in congruence theory that address questions of authority patterns. Reisinger (chaps. 5 and 6) provides a preliminary analysis of this issue.

Fourth, what is the methodological status of congruence theory and authority patterns as a linkage variable, especially in relationship to state- and society-centered approaches that have dominated research in the past? The present chapter, along with chapters 7 through 9 in Part III, address this question.

Fifth, the matter of appropriate empirical referents looms large. Congruence theory was originally formulated to assess stability in democratic governments. In that context, the question of "balanced disparities" was relatively easy to assess. Postcommunist countries have not yet experienced democratic consolidation, and it is still unclear whether congruence theory can tell us much about democratizing countries. Balanced disparities are hard to maintain under revolutionary circumstances such as one finds in postcommunist countries. Among other factors, distribution of the costs of marketization in Russia has been very uneven, which has resulted in increasing social friction. Hoffmann (chap. 4) and Eckstein (chap. 10) analyze these factors.

Sixth, what is the nature of the postcommunist transition in Russia, and what can the experiences of other transitions tell us about the postcommunist experiences, particularly in the realm of state-society relations? These questions are addressed by Eckstein in chapter 10 and by Ahl and me in chapter 11.

Finally, a number of important issues await further detailed analysis. One result of weak national government in Russia is that the national government is not exercising enough political influence throughout the whole system. Hence, congruence in authority patterns may exist in parts of the system but not throughout the whole system. This matter signals the importance of examining authority patterns at the level not only of national government but of regional and local government as well. It signals also the necessity of identifying and comparing the nature of authority patterns in particular social and governmental units, especially in the most adjacent and "congruence-relevant" units. These and related issues will be addressed more fully, and with a much wider range of case studies and empirical evidence, in subsequent volumes of this series.

Notes

Earlier versions of this essay were presented at the 1995 Annual Meeting of the American Political Science Association, Chicago, August 31-September 3, 1995, and at the Center for the Study of Democracy, University of California at Irvine, February 19, 1996. I wish to thank Erik P. Hoffmann for comments and suggestions on earlier drafts of this chapter.

1. The characteristics cited come from the following works: Cohen (1985), White (1979), Brown (1989), Breslauer (1991), Tucker (1987), Feshbach and Friendly (1992), Joyce (1984), Naylor (1988), Smith (1989), Melville (1993), Remnick (1993), Brzezinski (1976), Sakwa (1989), Sakwa (1990), and Sergeyev and Biryukov (1993).

2. An exception appears to be the trade unions: "The CPSU is gone; the Soviet Union, with its ministries, state committees, and Supreme Soviet, is gone. But the structures of old, 'official' trade unionism remain" (Connor 1994, 338).

3. See Brown (1989), Cohen (1985), Breslauer (1991), White (1979), Sakwa (1989), and Sakwa (1990).

4. Hahn (1993b); Gibson, Duch, and Tedin (1992); Miller, Reisinger, and

Hesli (1993); and Reisinger, Miller, Hesli, and Maher (1994). For analysis and critique of this and related survey literature, see Fleron (1996b).

5. See, for examples, Melville (1993), Wyman (1994), and Reisinger, Miller, and Hesli (1995).

6. See, for examples, Suny (1994); Koenker, Rosenberg, and Suny (1989); Fitzpatrick, Rabinowitch, and Stites (1991); and Rosenberg and Siegelbaum (1993).

7. To paraphrase Wuthnow (1989, 10). Wuthnow (1989, 16) defines "ideology" in this context as "an identifiable constellation of discourse that in fact stands in some degree of articulation with its social context."

8. Putnam's interpretation is described as a big-bang explanation in Laitin (1995, 172).

9. However, on the rapid remaking of German political culture in the post-World War II period, see Baun (1995).

3

The Dynamics of State–Society
Relations in Post-Soviet Russia

Erik P. Hoffmann

This chapter seeks to elucidate perennial questions about states and societies in order to understand the fitful democratization of state–society relations in early post-Soviet Russia. Basic questions include the following: Should one focus on the state–society nexus or take a state-centric or society-centric perspective? Should one employ a dichotomous "state-versus-society" or a disaggregated "state-in-society" approach? Should one emphasize zero-sum conflict or multiple-sum cooperation? Are "congruent authority patterns" in state and social institutions and "balanced disparities" throughout the polity and society essential for successful democratization and viable democracy? How can one study state–society relations when it is not at all clear that certain political institutions (e.g., regional and local governments) and economic institutions (e.g., banking and media conglomerates) are part of the state or society? How do coalitions of state and social institutions compete and collaborate with other "clans" for oligarchic power and democratic authority? Can a noncivil society, noncivil economy, and noncivic culture be transformed into a civil society, civil economy, and civic culture without governmental protection of minority interests, state-enforced property rights, and considerable elite and mass commitment to the rule of law? Is the surest path to constitutional democracy via constitutional authoritarianism or nonconstitutional democracy? Are prosperous domestic and foreign markets strengthened by a slow and regulated denationalization of a state-controlled economy or by rapid and unregulated privatization? How can one explain state–society interaction when the external borders and administrative subdivisions of the state are in dispute at home and abroad? And how do interstate and intersocietal relations influence intrastate and intra-societal relations?[1]

To try to answer such questions we will briefly discuss some perti-nent Western theories about the dynamics of state–society relations. We will then analyze contemporary Russian experience and historical legacies in light of these theories.

Western Theories of State–Society Relations: Domestic and International Dimensions

Definitions of "state" and "society" are myriad. A "state," according to *The Concise Oxford Dictionary of Politics* (McClean, 1996, 461–62, 472–76), is "[a] distinct set of political institutions whose specific concern is with the organization of domination, in the name of the common inter-est, within a delimited territory"; and "[t]he English word 'society' can be stretched or narrowed to cover almost any form of association of persons possessing any degree of common interests, values, or goals." The World Bank's (1997, 20, italics in original) definitions are more succinct and interrelated: "*State*, in its wider sense, refers to a set of institutions that possess the means of legitimate coercion, exercised over a defined territory and its population, referred to as society. The state monopolizes rulemaking within its territory through the medium of government."

Most international affairs specialists equate *a* state with an entire nation or country. But many comparativists equate *the* state with the government (which includes only state institutions and personnel) or the polity (which includes both political and civil society), and they do not presume that the state encompasses or dominates the society. Some analysts dichotomize the state and its society and discount external influences on their interaction. And others emphasize that state institu-tions are embedded in their own societies and the international com-munity, with countless opportunities for mutual benefit or harm in both interdependent arenas.

I do not wish to endorse any definition of "state" or "society," be-cause this chapter's primary purpose is to encourage thoughtful recon-ceptualization of these key analytical terms and creative theorizing about their relationships under conditions of enormous flux, such as in post-Soviet Russia. But I use "state" and "society" mostly in refer-ence to particular "state institutions" (e.g., cabinets, courts, and ar-mies) and "social institutions" (e.g., banks, schools, and churches), not state functions or activities and social forces or strata. I limit the con-cept of "institution" to organized structures, excluding policies (e.g., fiscal and environmental policies) and policymaking procedures (e.g., formal constitutions and informal sanctions). Also, de jure state institutions (e.g., strong local governments and weak national legislatures) can be de facto social institutions, and de jure social institutions (e.g., multinational corporations and business communities) can be de facto state institutions. One's categorization depends on the concentration of state power and authority in its central institutions and on the extent of state power and authority in society as a whole.

Effective and legitimate social institutions (e.g., political parties, interest groups, business firms, and television networks) are often "adjacent" to or "intermixed" with state institutions because of the juxtaposition or overlapping of their primary interests and activities. But state and social institutions are rarely monolithic or impermeable and do not permanently abut or predictably orbit one another. Rather, institutions are multifunctional and multilayered organisms (like the human brain) that can have beneficial, neutral, or detrimental effects on one another and their environments (like an ecosystem). One must underscore the dynamism and complexity of institutional relationships. Although core functions of an institution (e.g., authority patterns) are less likely to be altered near its periphery than deep within it, any intermixing segments of two institutions can have a powerful impact on the entire institutions and their surroundings.

Social institutions are sometimes part of the state, surrounding or suffusing state agencies and combining or alternating private and public sector roles. Politically influential social institutions are always part of "political society," which is a prominent segment of "civil society" in a stable democracy. "Political institutions" can originate in either the state or society, and their power depends on their linkages or proximity to the center of state power and/or a power base in society. Closely adjacent state and social institutions influence one another's structures and policies, and their interests may coincide and their personnel interchange for private, parochial, and public ends. In constitutional democracies these quasi-state or quasi-social institutions do not absorb or supplant one another and have distinguishable boundaries regulated by law. And "societal units," such as workplace, family, and voluntary membership organizations, are free to choose their own agendas and authority patterns.

In an authoritative recent survey of the field of comparative politics, Mair (1996, 320–23) concludes that researchers are preoccupied with the *effects* of political institutions rather than their *determinants*. When comparativists have devoted attention to the causes or antecedents of democratization, they have underscored the importance of state rather than social institutions and have marginalized socioeconomic, demo-

graphic, and ecological conditions such as industrialization, urbanization, and educational, pollution, and health-care levels. Also,
comparativists often describe rather than explain how a state functions; presume that the state's structures are stable and strong; forget
that socioeconomic associations can perform traditional state functions
and that subnational political institutions can play traditional socioeconomic roles; do not monitor the transformations in state–society relations; and ignore the origins and impacts of these transformations,
which include creating new bonds and tightening old ones, widening
gaps in interests and ideologies, and heightening indifference to constituent needs and wants by coalitions of state and social organizations. Bluntly put, the state has been brought back into comparative
political studies with a vengeance (or is behaving like a bull in a china
shop, at the very least).

Surprisingly, recent developments in the field of international relations have taken a very different tack and provide much better guidance for post-Sovietologists. "Whereas the discipline of IR remains
unquestionably state-centric in its choice of *explananda*, that is not true
so far as its *explanantes* are concerned," observes Goldmann (1996, 407,
italics in original). In other words, the state is still the chief dependent
variable in the study of international relations, but it is one of many
independent variables, including "intra-state and non-state factors" as
well as their transnational and intersocietal interactions. The relative
importance of these independent variables, especially the appropriate
emphasis on the central government, multinational corporations, and
social movements, is the subject of spirited academic dispute but-
tressed by mounting empirical evidence.

I submit, however, that the comparative politics and international
literatures are insufficiently connected to one another to the detriment
of both. For instance, it would seem axiomatic that a state's relations
with its own society (e.g., legitimacy, stability, and efficacy) greatly
influence a state's relations with other states (e.g., diplomatic, economic, and military power). And it is quite likely that a state's behavior
in the international arena will be similar to its behavior in the domestic
arena. Hence, it may prove fruitful to apply some traditional approaches from the study of interstate relations to the study of state–
society relations, with emphasis on their reciprocal influences and
possible systemic interaction.

A case in point is the study of Soviet foreign policy and three Western schools of thought about the motivations and perceptions of top
Soviet leaders: (1) communist expansionism, (2) realpolitik expansionism, and (3) realpolitik self-defense (Herrmann 1985). The first orientation emphasizes the relentlessly aggressive but sometimes cautious

pursuit of ideologically determined goals by an "inherently weak" state. The second orientation emphasizes the opportunistic adaptation of short-term tactics but not of long-term aggressive strategy by a "profoundly insecure and defensive" state. The third orientation emphasizes the pragmatic adaptation of short-term tactics and long-term strategy by a "profoundly conservative state," whose leadership is striving to enhance its own power and national security at minimal risk and cost. And all of these orientations presume that the primary goal of Soviet foreign policy was to preserve the party-state's illegitimate dominance over its own long-suffering society.

Cyberneticists will immediately see that the first approach underscores the *lack* of feedback mechanisms; the second underscores goal-*seeking* feedback; and the third underscores goal-*changing* as well as goal-seeking feedback. Moreover, Sovietologists will quickly recognize that the first approach is *essentialist* (the essence or core elements of the Soviet polity and society as well as its foreign and domestic policies are unchanging); the second is *mechanistic* (core elements adapt tactically but not strategically to unexpected events, and policies are automatically pursued until they meet counterforce and are "contained"); and the third is *learning* (core elements change at historical turning points, and both ends and means are periodically adjusted to opportunities and problems in the fluid domestic and international environments).

These three orientations not only emphasize the domestic sources of foreign policy but have their counterparts in the study of state-society relations. Communist expansionism, realpolitik expansionism, and realpolitik self-defense are all characterizations of a state's goals and capabilities vis-à-vis its own society. Also, there will probably be intense competition among such different orientations, especially in polities undergoing rapid reforms or revolutionary changes. This competition will surely take place within and among governmental bureaucracies and perhaps in the mind of the same leader. Furthermore, traditional questions about the international policies of a political leader and institution should also be asked about their domestic policies. Are the leader and an institution trying to expand the power of the state over society, and are they motivated by ideological and/or nonideological beliefs? Do a politician and bureau alter their priorities in specific time periods, geographical regions, or issue areas? And, under both Nikita Khrushchev and Mikhail Gorbachev, were not the uncoordinated mixes of domestic and foreign policies largely the *residue* of fierce competition among rival oligarchs and their bureaucratic clients?

Like interactions between two states, interactions between a state and its society can range across the following spectra: congruent to dissonant, viable to ineffectual, radical to reactionary, ideological to pragmatic, expansionist to reclusive, institutionalized to amorphous, unreactive to interactive, undifferentiated to differentiated, extractive to symbiotic, domineering to responsive, confrontational to collaborative, high to low risk and cost, and many more. Some of these examples may not be spectra at all but parts of complicated multidimensional grids and multicausal linkages. And researchers must pay close attention to political actors' distinctive assessments of their choices and environments at home and abroad. For instance, I included above "expansionist to reclusive" rather than "expansionist to defensive," because Lenin, Stalin, and many post-Stalin conservatives believed that "a good offense is the best defense."

The distinction between state and society should not be overdrawn. The state is part of a society or the society is part of a state (depending on one's definitions), and state and society share the same territory (even if some ethnic groups have a sizable number of brethren abroad). Joel Migdal rejects the state–society dichotomy altogether, conceptualizing the state as one of many institutions in a highly competitive "mélange of social organizations" (Migdal 1991, 50–52; see also Migdal et al. 1994, 1–33, 293–326). One can presume that the state institutions are usually predominant in an industrialized society and a mixed economy, but wide variations can be expected among developing polities of different types and sizes and within polities in different geographical and issue areas. State–society and interstate relations are hardly immutable, even in the short run, and all must be documented by longitudinal and differentiated empirical evidence. Evaluating the seminal political science research of the 1980s and early 1990s, Rogowski (1993, 439–41) rejects "sweeping assessments of state capacity" and disputes the proposition that "state elites were in significant degree autonomous from society." He praises authors who found that differences in governmental capabilities do not explain policy variations (among and within polities), and he tentatively concludes that the state "is at best an intervening variable, which itself responds (or fails to respond) to social pressures and needs."

Political, economic, and social problems and opportunities are increasingly emanating from the international environment because of the growing permeability of national borders. Arguably, the structures of various states are becoming less dissimilar and less decisive for policy outcomes because of the mounting influence of world markets, modern computer and telecommunications technology, and interstate, transnational, and intersocietal interactions. Like it or not, the governmental and business elites seeking economic growth and productivity must adapt to the financial, legal, managerial, and accounting criteria and standards of the Bretton Woods institutions, the huge multinational firms, and the potentially behemoth regional trading blocs. Furthermore, most nations' mutuality of interests on global issues, as well as the urgency of ecological, demographic, health, food, energy, and nuclear proliferation dilemmas, gives greater meaning to the concept of "global community" and less weight to the "sovereign state." According to Cerny (1997, 286, 314; see also Cerny 1990), "globalization is a multilayered phenomenon that incorporates the state and sustains many of its ostensible functions, while at the same time altering its very essence and undermining its constitutional foundations. . . . The state today is, therefore, a potentially unstable mix of civil association and enterprise association—of constitutional state, pressure group, and firm—with state actors, no longer so 'autonomous,' feeling their way uneasily in an unfamiliar world."

These interconnected domestic and international developments raise serious questions for the student of state–society relations. Obviously a state and society have to be "disaggregated," and obviously political and social institutions interact with one another as well as with the political and social institutions of other countries. But what are the boundaries or junctures of major governmental and nongovernmental institutions, such as national or regional executive agencies and multinational corporations and banks? When do symbiosis, collaboration, and durable coalitions obliterate the distinct identities (de facto, if not de jure) of state and social institutions? To what extent can a multinational corporation not based on the territory of a state really function as part of that state? Do strong regional and local governments function as state institutions in the international system, and do weak national legislatures and judiciaries function as social institutions in their own political system?

Responses to such questions are crucial, because they will decisively influence one's conceptualization of the reciprocal relations or feedback loops between state and societal organizations. For example, Harry Eckstein's theories of viable democracy and successful democratization rest heavily on the distinction between state and society, but he stresses the importance of interelite and elite-mass linkages. Eckstein argues that governmental performance depends on congruent authority patterns and balanced disparities among adjacent state and social institutions. Comparing the authority patterns of various governmental bodies with those of political parties, lobbying groups, business firms, trade unions, and professional associations is especially important in understanding the recruitment and socialization of different types of political leaders. Where, for example, do national politicians acquire the attitudes toward authority and the interpersonal skills needed to compete or cooperate with their most powerful constituents? Work in subnational governments and private organizations is a common source, but early experiences in educational and religious institutions as well as in family and ethnic networks can have a lifelong impact.[2]

Stages in democratic institution-building are accompanied by stages of market-building and culture shift.[3] The precise nature of these stages and their sequencing is the subject of much dispute, with Gorbachev initiating political reforms before economic reforms, Jiang Zemin doing the opposite, and Boris Yeltsin trying to manage a hybrid authoritarian/democratic polity and a transitional centralized/market economy. But academics and policy analysts are giving increasing weight to the role of the state, with the best research focusing on state–society relations. For example, Linz and Stepan (1996a, 7–19 ff.) view democracy as an "interacting system" comprised of five mutually dependent "arenas"—the state apparatus, the rule of law, political society, economic society, and civil society.[4]

Also, the World Bank (1997, 27) has enumerated "minimal," "intermediate," and "activist functions" of the modern state that "address market failure" and "improve equity" and that may identify state priorities in successive phases of democratization and marketization. The minimal functions are defense, law and order, property rights, macroeconomic management, public health, antipoverty programs, and disaster relief. The intermediate functions are basic education, environmental protection, utility regulation, antitrust policy, insurance (health, life, pensions), financial regulation, consumer protection, redistributive pensions, family allowances, and unemployment insurance. And the activist functions are fostering markets, private enterprise initiatives, and asset redistribution.

All of these functions are being performed very weakly by the current Russian state. True, some regional and local governments are functioning adequately in a few spheres (e.g., basic education). But national state institutions are barely fulfilling *any* of the World Bank's "minimal functions," with the possible recent exception of macroeconomic management (e.g., financial stabilization). Especially serious are the deficiencies in law and order, property rights, public health, and environmental protection which, together with insufficient tax collection, undermine the fulfillment of all of the other functions, as well as the very survival of the Russian people.

A state's capability to formulate and implement economic policies profoundly affects every citizen and social unit as well as its domestic and international environments. The success of economic policy outcomes is a major source (often *the* major source) of a state's authority and stability, including its national security, which is increasingly defined in socioeconomic as well as military-diplomatic terms. In post-Soviet Russia sources of legitimacy include free elections and free speech, but the state's viability depends heavily on performance factors such as economic prosperity, social services, physical safety, and international accomplishments. Although viable constitutionalism has begun to take root, it can grow only if the Russian state does a much better job of distributing the diminishing public goods and regulating the burgeoning private sector.

To understand postcommunist transformations, it is essential to focus on the distinctive origins of these states and societies and their interrelationships (Migdal 1997a, 14). Because of the remarkably peaceful and telescoped revolutions of 1989 and 1991, a tabula rasa was not created in any of the countries of Eastern Europe, the Baltic states, and the Commonwealth of Independent States. Soviet political and social legacies were especially fresh and powerful in the Russian Federation and other CIS countries. Very portentous were the consequences of economic exploitation and institutional centralization and of cultural chauvinism and ideological orthodoxy in the "metropole" and internal and external "colonies" of Soviet Russia (and of tsarist Russia, to a much lesser extent). For example, Russia suddenly faced a national identity crisis as well as an influx of Russian migrants from neighboring countries.

Thus, the unexpected nature and speed of the USSR's demise were key dependent variables in laying the bases of the postcommunist order, not the revolutionary ideals and institutions or military conquests and charisma of the Russian Federation's founding fathers. Arguably, the weak and conflicting ideals and institutions of Russia's regime-building coalition, to say nothing of their incompatible ambitions and interests, were more influential still. But the disintegration of the Soviet state and society had a major impact on the composition and balance of power among the new elites and on the formation of the post-Soviet state and society and the post-Cold War world.

Transforming State–Society Relations in Post-Soviet Russia

I will save for another occasion a full discussion of Russia's international relations and will focus in the rest of this chapter on Russia's state–society nexus. To do so, the distinctive features of Russian concepts and institutions must be noted immediately.

The first article of the present constitution proclaims Russia to be "a democratic federative law-governed state (*gosudarstvo*) with a republican form of governing (*pravlenie*)." And the preamble enumerates many reasons for adopting the constitution, including "preserving the historically established state unity." But fundamental questions about the state's responsibilities to society and the public's restraints on governmental powers are vaguely addressed or ignored. The general population's rights to monitor and control its appointed executives and to be represented and served by its elected officials are not underscored. Language to this effect was included in draft versions of the constitution and deleted from the final version. Also, the constitution endorses general principles but does not usually obligate or enable particular institutions to safeguard or implement these principles. Why and how, for example, is "[t]he President . . . the guarantor . . . of human and civil rights and freedoms" and "the State [the guarantor of] the equality of rights and freedoms," including the "freedom of thought and speech" and "[t]he freedom of the mass media"?[5]

The Russian state is a territorially delineated legal entity, but national state (*gosudarstvennye*) institutions are not limited to those of the "Government" (*Pravitelstvo*). The executive branch now includes the Administration of the President (*Administratsiia Prezidenta*) as well as the governmental ministries. The legislative branch's upper chamber, the Federation Council, consists of 178 elected "senators" (a prestigious informal term) who represent the legislative and executive bodies of each of the Russian Federation's 89 "constituent entities"; and the lower chamber, the State Duma, consists of 450 elected deputies (the official term) who represent political parties and 225 single-member districts nationwide. The judicial branch consists of the Constitutional Court, Supreme Court, and Supreme Arbitration Court. And the president is an eighth "institution" dominating or overseeing all the others. He is the "head of state," and it is his constitutional duty to "ensure the coordinated functioning and interaction of the bodies of state power," which substantially undermines the principles of federalism and separation of powers. Also, "executive power" is to be exercised by the "Government of the Russian Federation," which signifies that the president has much broader unchecked and unbalanced powers, such as the right "to form and head the Security Council" and "to form the Administration of the President."[6]

In contrast, the USSR Constitution included sham federalism but no separation of powers or checks and balances. The actual Soviet state incorporated (literally and figuratively) the hierarchies of the ministries and state committees and of the national and subnational soviets or councils. The Communist Party was "[t]he leading and guiding force of Soviet society and the nucleus of its political system, of all state organizations and public organizations," under the Constitution (Article 6) (see Sharlet 1978). CPSU officials were beholden to Party Rules that did not include subordination to the Constitution. And, for ideological purposes only, the CPSU was deemed a "social" or "public" (*obshchestvennaia*) organization, thereby lumping it together with the *Komsomol*, trade unions, and lesser mass organizations.

The Russian concept of "society" (*obshchestvo*) now rivals its Western counterparts for elasticity and vagueness. But it is not just a residual category. It connotes an organization, group, or stratum that is "nonstate." This has cognitive and emotive significance for most Russians because of the present gulf between elites and masses and the Soviet legacy of state domination over society. The official Soviet concept was a little more precise. Society was divided into the worker and peasant "classes" and the intelligentsia "stratum." And many social organizations were called "societies," as they are in post-Soviet Russia.

The dissonance between Soviet ideology and reality is another matter entirely. In fact, the dominant institution of the Soviet state was not a state organization, and the dominant class was not a class. Hence, the importance of the Western term "party-state" (except under Stalin) and of the Soviet term *nomenklatura* (which connotes both a privileged class and a patronage list). Whereas Soviet intellectuals distinguished between the government, intelligentsia, and people (*narod*), party-state officials distinguished chiefly between the nomenklatura and *narod*. And citizens of all kinds distinguished sharply between their *pravitelstvo* and *obshchestvo*, as they continue to do in today's Russia.

The post-Stalinist party-state was an integrated but increasingly ossified political system, and when a few fundamental components and bonds weakened or relaxed, other brittle elements and "transmission belts" broke rapidly. The postcommunist changes in Russia's state and society were made possible by the Soviet polity's functional breakdown, which ended the CPSU's domination of the national and subnational state agencies and of the territories forcibly incorporated into the tsarist and Soviet empires. Or, to use Sakwa's (1996, 117) striking simile, "Interwoven like a double helix, the collapse of the Communist Party to a degree also entailed the collapse of the state."

Yet most Soviet institutions, especially their interpersonal networks and cultures, did not dissolve. Gorbachev (mostly unintentionally) and Yeltsin (mostly intentionally) disconnected the linkages among core elements of the Soviet political system, leaving intact large pieces of the former institutional colosi and freeing their members to adapt to and thereby to help shape the revolutionary new circumstances. Republic leaders were given taxation powers, and other nomenklatura officials were given financial inducements that spurred them to radicalize Gorbachev's reforms for parochial and personal benefit. Also, the disagreements among top Soviet leaders accelerated a revolution of rising economic and ethnic aspirations. And the steady crumbling of centralized economic planning and management, as well as the oscillating relaxation of political and social controls over the non-Russian nationality groups, made possible the emergence of new economic strata and national identities at home and in the "near abroad."

Key interrelated features of the postcommunist Russian experience are the 50 percent or so decline in economic growth and productivity, caused by the severing of the connections in the Soviet command economy, and the sudden ambiguities in national identity in the Russian Federation, caused by the breakup of the Soviet Union. New economic and political institutions that bring a higher standard of living to most segments of the population and a greater legitimacy to the ideal of democracy are obvious priorities in the early phases of democratization, and the paucity of such institutions has been a very serious shortcoming in the immediate post-Soviet period. Although the distinction between an ethnic Russian (*russkii*) and a citizen of Russia (*rossianin*) is potentially destabilizing, the assertiveness of ethnic minorities has been considerably tempered by economic circumstances, from the prosperity of Tatarstan to the poverty of Tuva. But the war in Chechnya was horrific, and the other multinational and international disputes over the internal subdivisions and external boundaries of the country are troublesome. And Great Russians' angst over the contemporary soul (*dusha*) and fate (*sudba*) of Russia is significant. The formation of a Russian national consciousness is a necessary condition, but by no means sufficient, for the emergence of a Russian civic culture.

The creation of a national identity in the Russian Federation is probably important for short-term democratization as well as long-term democratic consolidation. State-building is much more than institution-building when a new state's raison d'être is unclear to the dominant nationality group in a multinational citizenry. And the development of a state is especially difficult if its sovereignty is rejected by a militant national minority, its external and internal borders are challenged by regional ethnic and economic interests, its twenty-five million Russian diaspora is the subject of chauvinistic partisanship in the legislature, and its tsarist and Soviet legacies are debated by all nationalities, perhaps especially among Great Russians themselves.

Since Gorbachev's liberalization many ethnic Russians have felt the need for *gosudarstvennost* (statehood). A legitimate and effective polity and a prosperous and peaceful citizenry, with emphasis on governmental influence abroad and social entitlements at home, seem to be the only common denominators in this widely held desire. Abundant pride in Russia's cultural achievements has been accompanied by greater acceptance of cultural heterogeneity, especially now that over four-fifths of all *rossiane* are *russkie*. And considerable distress over Russia's reduced status in world affairs has been manifested in more international accommodation, necessitated by a dramatic decline in nonnuclear military forces.

But ambiguities and tensions abound in the concept of *gosudarstven-nost*. Ethnocentrism and multiculturalism have long been competing components. Now Russians' hopes for constructive governmental action are often directed toward subnational governments rather than the national government. Because central executive and legislative institutions simply have not "delivered," today's citizens have greatly reduced expectations of government and greatly increased self-reliance. Indeed, Russians have little trust in new or old state and social institutions; only the Orthodox Church was trusted by 50 percent of the population in 1994, according to an authoritative study. Trust in the next-highest-ranked institutions (the army, 40 percent; peasants' organizations, 26 percent; the mass media, 23 percent) has probably dropped considerably since 1994. And political parties and market enterprises as well as workers' and patriotic associations are particularly distrusted (White et al. 1997, 50–54).

It is easy for most Russian politicians to view the state as no longer "Soviet" and for some citizens to criticize social groups whose authority patterns have retained their bossy or obedient Soviet mentality. But it is not so easy to disgorge such authoritarian elements of Soviet political culture as *nachalstvo* (self-important authorities, usually arbitrary commanders) and *sovok* (literally "dustpan," but colloquially an "ignorant, narrowminded, doctrinaire [Soviet-type] person") (Shlyakhov and Adler 1995, 185). Indeed, it is difficult for state and social institutions to prioritize the core values of a post-Soviet culture (e.g., to replace ideological intolerance, nomenklatura privileges, and male chauvinism with the rule of law, distributive justice, and gender equality). And, because economic competition is fierce and legal restraints are few, it is most difficult to transform enlightened elite values into mass norms and enlightened mass norms into elite values.

True, Russia's cultural revolution has been launched by selected governmental policies and considerable citizen activism and has been advanced by education, persuasion, sanctions, and trial-and-error. New values, attitudes, and beliefs have produced and been shaped by personal accomplishments, frustrations, and hardships. But a viable relationship between state and social institutions has not been established. For example, a consensus on decisionmaking rules and incentives and a balance of interests and ideologies simply does not exist.

The Soviet system's congruence (authoritarian elites and complaisant followers) has been shattered, but a democratic system's congruence (responsive leaders and assertive masses) has barely begun to take root.[7] The instability of the current transitional period is considerable and could lead toward steady-state (pun intended) equilibrium of either kind.

Gosudarstvennost is a sociopsychological phenomenon—collective and individual characterizations of Russia's physical and spiritual essence and assessments of its accomplishments and potentials—and it is not to be confused with the political institutions of the state or the officials of the current government. But *gosudarstvennost* includes expectations about the appropriate role of one's government and the degree to which it is meeting these expectations. As Sakwa (1996, 37, 336, 369; see also Breslauer and Dale 1997) perceptively observes,

> The development of gosudarstvennost took a distinctive form in the post-communist Russia. The regime system of government was entwined with the emerging state and to a degree became a substitute for the state itself. . . .
> If the regime substituted for the state, a complex elite system substituted for the development of civil society. The typical political expressions of civil society, like parties, parliament and the rule of law, were subverted by intra-elite negotiations based on personal ties and informal bargaining processes. . . .
> The system was relatively stable as long as the various elite interests were balanced, but the very gulf between the regime and society threatened the emergence of a new anti-elite insurgency.

Yet state–society relations are hard to describe, let alone explain, when a highly centralized one-party system suddenly fragments, many of its national and regional leaders place parochial and personal interests above the survival of the polity, most of its nationalized industrial enterprises are privatized, and its ethnic and nonethnic administrative units are given tax collecting authority by the country's top politician. State and social institutions become tangled as their functions and roles intermix. State and society are considerably blurred when government ministers sell off large chunks of valuable state property at bargain prices to their favorite businessmen or bankers, who compete murderously (literally and figuratively) with other coalitions of political officials and private entrepreneurs. State and society overlap further when all of these major coalitions buy or control the major banks and mass media, with prominent businessmen shuttling in and out of government service or seeking election as legislators to gain immunity from anticipated criminal prosecution. And state and society become indistinguishable—even Kafkaesque—when most government bureaucrats don two hats, public and private, and most public agencies double as privatized cooperatives. For just one small example, which the author has personally experienced, a district housing bureau in Moscow is open for government business only one day a week and for private business four days a week, and is staffed by the very same personnel in the very same office for the very same work. Only the prices and the speed of work vary!

The uncertainties of state–society relations are unsettling for most Russians, and the analytical and empirical implications of these new realities are challenging for all researchers. Our conclusions depend heavily on our conceptualization of the components of Russia's state and society, to say nothing of their capabilities and limitations in specific policy spheres. But how does one determine whether specific clusters of institutions, distinctive types of institutions, and individual institutions are part of the state or part of the society? For example, how does one categorize the weak legislatures and courts at all levels? Are most regional and local executive bodies, political parties, business firms, mass media, and segments of the Russian Orthodox Church part of the current Russian state or society? All of these questions are complicated enormously by the speed of change in Russia's polity and society and by political socialization (e.g., nationalist awakening) and social modernization (e.g., demographic trends). But these are very basic questions that must be provisionally answered and continuously reassessed by detailed empirical investigations. Fortunately, the classification of professional and voluntary associations, non-Russian ethnic and non-Orthodox religious groups, and environmental, women's rights, and other special interest lobbies seems clearer.

It is not easy to describe state and social institutions' authority patterns (balanced or unbalanced) and to identify the causes and consequences of these patterns (homogeneous or differentiated), as well as their evolutionary or revolutionary changes. But then the real work begins—analyzing the congruence or dissonance between the authority patterns of specific state and social institutions. It may prove fruitful to study the relationships between *exogenous* authority patterns (between state and social institutions) and *endogenous* authority patterns (within state and social institutions). And one cannot presume the insignificance of weakly organized or unorganized social forces or of economic strata with amorphous or latent authority patterns.

Identifying Russia's most powerful political and social organizations is not difficult, but the nature of their interaction is often shrouded in secrecy. Although degrees and kinds of adjacency and intermixing can be hypothesized, they must be documented by empirical evidence and periodically redocumented. Given the highly personalistic nature of postcommunist politics and business, as well as the much greater importance of "know-who" than "know-how," a particular institution's power and property and even its classification as a state or social institution can shift abruptly.

Closely adjacent political-administrative and socioeconomic institutions sometimes coalesce. The former may mobilize the latter to help win bureaucratic struggles, and the nongovernmental body may then begin to perform governmental functions. To be sure, close collaboration between state agencies and social associations does not make them identical. But a symbiotic relationship can easily lead to the overlapping of institutional jurisdictions and incentive structures, especially if policymaking practices and economic policies, as well as the lack of judicial and ethical restraints, make it difficult to define, let alone impose sanctions on, illegal or deviant behavior. Keenly sensitive to the cultural context of crime and corruption, Sergeyev (1998) questions the very meaning of illegality and deviance in a society where legal and moral moorings have been jarred loose and are in flux. These problems are endemic to all democratizing polities and marketizing economies, but they are perhaps most acute in a democratizing postcommunist polity and a marketizing postcommand economy with a weakly enforced new criminal and civil code and a weakly embedded elite and mass legal culture, as well as both emerging and reemerging religious and ethnic identities.

Consider, especially in the light of our discussion of congruence and adjacency, the following insightful observations of Huskey (1996a, 369):

> What makes the ministries such potent actors in Russian politics? Put simply, the synergism of bureaucratic and sectoral interests. The interests of the ministries are often identical with the interests of broad sectors of the Russian economy and society. Thus, the ministries not only govern Russia, they represent it—or at least its most powerful interests. . . . Whereas in democratic countries political parties are the primary mediating institutions between the state and society, ministries perform that function in Russia. The sources of ministerial legitimacy, therefore, are not limited to the formal rules of state. As extensions of powerful social and economic interests, the ministries have been able to flaunt Western conceptions of collective responsibility, which would impose discipline on a fractious Russian executive.

Although Huskey is analyzing state–society relations in the postcommunist period, much of his characterization also applies to the post-Stalin era. And the Soviet political-administrative mentality, the nomenklatura's "golden parachute" from the Gorbachev to Yeltsin years, and the post-Soviet choices to build weak legislatures and political parties have powerfully influenced the structures and functions of the current Russian state. Many old institutions, practices, and leaders not only survived the putsch of August 1991 and the breakup of the USSR in December 1991 but weathered the constitutional crisis and presidential consolidation from October to December 1993, adapting well, even thriving, thereafter.

The fact that so many political-administrative and socioeconomic networks have changed so little after the collapse of the USSR confirms the fragmenting rather than dissolving of the Soviet state and highlights the corporate rather than participatory character of the current Russian polity. The CPSU terminated its control over the national and republic ministries and the soviets and production enterprises, but few bureaucratic and sectoral or regional and local coalitions disintegrated. Indeed, many patron-client networks became stronger by using their freedom from central directives to overcome new obstacles and to seize new opportunities. The tumultuous executive-legislative struggle from 1991 to 1993 enhanced the autonomy of traditional managerial and production fiefdoms, and the subsequent deep divisions among national institutions continue to give these fiefdoms considerable leeway in Moscow and the provinces.

Many bureaucratic and social interests are being articulated, but only the former are being systematically aggregated in the national executive and legislative branches of the Russian government. Bureaucratic pluralism may foster but does not ensure social pluralism.[8] Only the broadening of interest representation in various regions and localities gives promise of democratization. Optimally the Russian state and society will democratize "from above" and "from below," with synergistic effects accelerating the process, but a modicum of democratic thinking and behavior from any source constitutes progress.[9]

The Russian Federation has neither a strong constitutional authoritarian state nor a strong constitutional democratic state, which makes it not only very difficult to regulate the lobbies and cartels entrenched throughout the country but also virtually impossible to formulate and implement a national economic policy in the national interest. Even with a highly professional and diversified council of economic advisors, it would be an insurmountable hurdle for the courts to enforce the new Civil Code (Russia's so-called economic constitution) and to oversee all high-stakes programs, especially the privatization of the Soviet state's most valuable industrial assets and properties and the export licensing of oil and natural gas.

Some of Russia's state institutions (or segments thereof) are quite powerful and well funded, and others are not (in whole or in part). But the relationships among these institutions are fragile and fluid and are governed by few checks and balances in theory or practice. Although the constitution and enabling legislation have established a rough division of powers, the interaction of national institutions with one another, with the eighty-nine constituent entities of the Russian Federation, and with the rapidly growing private sector is predominantly informal, interpersonal, secretive, unregulated, and asymmetrical. The many rigged auctions of state property, the shifting alliances among officials of the two highest executive and two highest legislative bodies, and the thirty or so bilateral treaties negotiated between Yeltsin and republic and province leaders are notable examples.

Russia still lacks a stable, meritocratic, efficient, nonpartisan, and law-governed civil service with Weberian-type managerial skills and technocratic traditions. Top-level businessmen have quickly rotated in and out of top-level government offices, including the national security council and the state information agency. Also, there are insufficient incentives to recruit and retain professional administrators and to stipulate and enforce the rules under which they interact with political and social institutions. All bureaucrats face enormous temptations to use their offices for personal gain at the expense of their sectoral and regional rivals and the general public. Talented and well-connected technocrats can now easily quit for lucrative jobs in the private sector, and some take part-time business consultancies *during* their public service.

Moreover, Russian ministers have sharply divergent interests and motivations as well as dual sources of power and authority—the formal "metapolicies" (policies on how to make policy) of a nascent constitutional democracy and the informal metapolicies of well-established networks from the Soviet era. The unofficial metapolicies (e.g., personal loyalties and "insider" deals) invariably conflict with the official metapolicies (e.g., administrative regulations and transparent information), and the former have frequently prevailed and will continue to prevail until the chief executive recognizes the importance of establishing a genuine rule of law and a permanent civil service. To date, he has relied mainly on the presidential administration, not on the governmental ministries, let alone the legislative and judicial institutions at the national and subnational levels. The president may well feel accountable to the electorate, as he interprets its needs and wants, and to the law, as he promulgates it through decrees, but he surely does not feel restrained by checks and balances on his power. Huskey (1996b, 465, 467) rightly concludes that "the most effective set of checks and balances in Russia is the tension between sectoral elites rather than between state institutions," and that "the greatest peril facing Russia is not authoritarianism but warlordism, whether regional or departmental."

The Politics and Economics of Cronyism

"Warlordism" is a concept that reminds us of the weakness of national state institutions as well as the viciousness of the competition among subnational quasi-states. But it does not do justice to crucial Russian realities—namely, the state's reliance on banking/media conglomerates to fund basic state functions, the corruption of state officials by these conglomerates, the ability of conglomerates to subvert the rule of law, and the power of conglomerates over state policies (domestic and foreign) and the policy process (including elections and appointments). The root of this disaster or bonanza (depending on one's point of view) is well-known: the Soviet state's property is being privatized prior to the codification or enforcement of laws guaranteeing the transparency of these disbursements and the rights of property owners. To protect one's business and personal property, however acquired, one must rely on private security forces and extralegal means, especially cronyism and bribery and more than occasionally extortion and violence. Furthermore, the state's inability to collect taxes, pay wages, and administer entitlements has made it highly dependent on the wealthiest private institutions, which are eager to buy valuable state assets cheaply and can put hard cash immediately into the state coffers and into the pockets of state bureaucrats. As Raitsin (1997a, 13) concludes,

> [T]he line between the state and private sector has been significantly eroded with the formation of a new financial oligarchy comprised of Russia's largest banks. These banking concerns include Oneximbank, Most Bank, Capital Savings Bank, Menatep, Alfa Bank, Imperial and Inkombank. Information channels, such as newspapers and television stations, have already been divided up among these banks, which also control many key state posts.

The "Big Seven" banks are parts of "financial-industrial groups" (FIGs), some of which include military manufacturing enterprises. These huge conglomerates are proliferating. In July 1997 there were 62 registered FIGs that included over 1,000 industrial institutions (e.g., metallurgical factories) and over 90 financial institutions (e.g., commercial banks), and dozens of new FIGs were forming (Sirotin 1997, 30–31; see also Johnson 1997). The growth of domestic and transnational FIGs virtually ensures greater competition and conflict among and within them. It also creates the possibility of stronger countervailing forces and legal restraints on the largest and most aggressive FIGs, which now enjoy enormous powers over fiscal and monetary policies, especially when they collude. Prime Minister Viktor Chernomyrdin (quoted in Raitsin 1997b, 44) has promised better legal regulation of FIGs and more transparency in their financial transactions, but it is problematical that his office or any combination of presidential and governmental agencies has the will and ability to do so.

An Association of Financial-Industrial Groups was established in January 1996 and is headed by Oleg Soskovets, ex-prime minister and ex-presidential campaign director. Soskovets bemoans the slow progress in his association's "working relationship with the executive and legislative branches," especially the government's "clearly . . . insufficient" support of the new domestic FIGs and its virtual failure to fulfill "promised guarantees," such as purchases of state property and awards of government contracts. However, the development of FIGs and their professional association has major ramifications for state–society relations in Russia and its international economic relations. Soskovets and others are keenly aware that FIGs can become powerful independent institutions profiting from their ties with selected government and commercial institutions at home and abroad. Almost all domestic FIGS have been created by their members, not by government diktat, and at most 25 percent of a FIG's holdings consists of state property (e.g., railroads) (Sirotin 1997, 31). Transnational FIGS have been "founded not by command from above, but from below, as an expression of cooperative and regional interests," and "sprang up precisely on the basis of bilateral and multilateral intergovernmental agreements." Soskovets (quoted in Sourzhansky 1997, 28–29) adds:

> FIGs are ready to establish a partnership between large private capital interests and the government. Each side is taking upon itself distinct, sufficiently stiff obligations: the FIGs are implementing federal and regional programs, and the government is making a commitment to provide the necessary customs, tax and insurance conditions and relevant guarantees.

In short, FIGs have the potential to become Western-type domestic and multinational corporations. Whether this potential can be fulfilled is a key variable that will influence state-society relations in Russia for the foreseeable future.

True, some Russian FIGs have aroused considerable interest in the European Union and from foreign investors. These exchanges have already begun to move Russian legal, managerial, and accounting practices in the direction of their Western counterparts. But it will be quite difficult for Russia to establish independent government and business organizations that interact under the rule of law. When Anatolii Chubais, first deputy prime minister and twice chief architect of privatization policy, was asked in August 1997 how he would cope with "the very powerful criminal, financial and industrial groups who simply have little or no respect for the government," he responded:

> I will never, never accept the view that the government or the Ministry of Finance is just another group. The government is not a player in the game. It will always be making the rules of the game. This is the reason for my fundamental disagreement with some of the leaders of the powerful Russian banking elite. I will never compromise on this principle. . . . *I think that now the rule of government is probably priority number one in all of Russian political life. . . .*
> The major problem today is the rule of law. The government has to convince or, if necessary, force all participants in the economy to play by the rules. I will work within the government as long as I am able to make clear the difference between the government making the rules and private interest groups abiding by such rules within the country. (Chubais quoted in Kim 1997, 35, italics added)

Regardless of political intent, this is an authoritative and lucid acknowledgment of the weakness of Russia's national government.

Chubais expresses a strong desire to consolidate the dominant role of the state as rule maker and rule enforcer and to create legal constraints on the most powerful and adjacent social institutions. While these goals are laudable, the processes of achieving them have just begun at the national level and have progressed farther in only a few localities, including the communist-dominated city of Ulyanovsk, which has had "the highest standard of living for the majority of its residents since the start of reforms in 1991," according to American economist Robert McIntyre. "Rather than being 'anti-market,' (the Ulyanovsk policymakers) take seriously the institutional requirements for the successful functioning of markets. Because criminalization couldn't develop and entrench itself, markets are better able to function now" (quoted in Helmer 1997, 41). In contrast, the national government and the vast majority of subnational governments lack the political will, administrative skills, and tax incentives to combat corruption, enforce laws, and spur economic and social progress.

One cannot agree with Chubais (quoted in Kim 1997, 34) that "The [privatization] system has proven itself" and that "the government is strong enough to introduce new rules to make the system clear and transparent and, more importantly, to force all participants to follow these rules." Crony capitalism and "crony reformism" (to use *The*

Economist's apt phrase; "Russia's Reforms . . ." 1997, 24) will continue to retard economic growth and constitutional democracy until the top oligarchs in the private sector and their collaborators in the public sector choose otherwise. The president has the power to issue decrees but not to impose controls. And self-restraint or self-regulation on the part of the major business/government clans seems quite unlikely to develop in the near future for at least four reasons.

First, Chubais himself made a deal with the leaders of the Big Seven FIGs to finance Yeltsin's presidential bid of 1996 and to use their media affiliates, especially national television, to ensure a grossly biased campaign. The quid pro quo was to give these FIGs preferential treatment in the sale or auctioning of the best state property or simply to let the top oligarchs divide up the spoils as they saw fit. Chubais's subsequent rhetoric about honest government notwithstanding, his wealthy benefactors were incensed that he welshed on a huge debt and viewed themselves as "king-makers" who had been double-crossed. True, drafting and obeying campaign finance laws are especially difficult in the earliest stages of democratization. But Russia's first free presidential election may not have considerably strengthened the prospects for constitutionalism.

Second, Chubais was seriously threatened and weakened for trying to change the rules of the game between government and business and for creating obstacles to mega-FIG influence over marketization and privatization. One can only imagine the nature of these direct and indirect threats, but they surely included the murder of his friend and associate, Mikhail Manevich, head of privatization in St. Petersburg. Also, Chubais and four colleagues greatly damaged their own credibility and that of the entire national government by accepting $90,000 each in royalties from a publishing company owned by a FIG that had recently profited lucratively from government favoritism in an allegedly competitive auction. The discovery of these royalties was made by a FIG's private investigators and disseminated by a FIG's mass media, not by a court of law.

Third, the Russian state's extractive, regulatory, and distributive capacities are woefully inadequate to maintain the legal boundaries between big business and government and to resist the former's thoroughgoing manipulation or cooptation of the latter. The low salaries of government officials, the constant temptations to take bribes for issuing licenses and documents, and the national and subnational bureaucracies' lack of capitalist managerial skills and modern information technology will delay the formation of a professional civil service for a long time. Politically and bureaucratically effective administrators like Chubais are few and far between. Also, the president has negoti-

ated different tax laws with different republic and regional governments. Most important, a vicious cycle has been set in motion: the
national government cannot collect enough taxes to pay its public servants, so it sells off its best revenue-producing properties to pay current debts. These properties, of course, cannot bring the state
continuous revenues in the future, and the newly empowered private
firms can evade taxes with greater impunity.

Fourth, the presidential campaign did serious damage to the integrity and independence of the mass media and journalistic profession.
Every major television channel and national newspaper is now an instrument of one or another government/business clan. After every
major auction of state property, for example, the winners praise the
results through their media and the losers condemn the results
through theirs. In short, the establishment of a "fourth estate" has been
delayed indefinitely, which bodes ill for the democratization of all
state-society relations, especially the protection of property and minority rights and the assurance of fair and free elections. It would be hard
to cite reasons why the presidential campaign and voting in the year
2000 will be more democratic than their 1996 counterparts.

In a September 1997 address to the Federation Council, President
Yeltsin affirmed the need "to establish . . . clear rules of economic behavior" that apply equally to business enterprises of all sizes and governmental institutions at all levels. To reach this ideal, he called for
greater national and subnational state supervision of the private sector:
"We are resolutely moving from a policy of 'noninterference' to a policy of preemptive regulation of economic processes and oversight of
vitally important branches of the economy and the effectiveness of
budget spending" (Yeltsin 1997, 3). Two journalists (Koshkaryova and
Narzikulov 1997, 5) vividly describe the probable motivations behind
this policy adjustment:

> It seems that the genie of market freedom that Yeltsin let loose six years
> ago is becoming more and more frightening to the President. This year
> [1997] has shown that big Russian capital has become stronger than the
> state and is trying to impose its own rules of play on it. The President has
> come to the conclusion—albeit belatedly—that a strong economy means
> not only a market but a strong state as well.

Can "the genie of market freedom" be put back in the bottle? Can a
Western-type mixed economy be built? Not without breaking the illicit
relationships between Russian business and government elites. And
not without much stronger property, land, labor, and tax laws as well
as a much stronger civil service and independent judiciary. The presi-

dent himself has acknowledged that recent anticorruption initiatives are meeting "stiff opposition" *within* the state apparatus, "primarily from those for whom a market without rules is advantageous" (Yeltsin 1997, 3). And an unregulated and manipulable market is even more beneficial to the largest FIGs.

Hence, Yeltsin and his closest aides have begun to talk more openly about the need for new policymaking rules but have made no concerted efforts to end the national government's dependency on powerful business/media conglomerates, let alone fundamental changes in state–society relations. The only thing keeping the most powerful clans from replacing the state is their intense and sometimes violent competition with one another. As a result of this competition, the state is being infiltrated, manipulated, and enervated. The state's prime assets are being parceled out to the best-connected bidder, and the state's top officials are concentrating on nonstate or personal interests. As Migranyan (1997, 1–2) puts it,

> [V]arious clans, both inside and outside the structures of power, are creating their own financial/media empires that are independent of the state's control, establishing close connections with key figures in the government and on the President's staff and using them in an effort to snatch even richer pieces of property during the upcoming redistribution of remaining state property. . . . At present, the President sees his basic political task as restoring a certain balance of forces so that he can once again become an arbiter between warring groups.

And, as Shevtsova (1997, 4) affirms,

> What we in Russia call the "oligarchy" . . . is made up of influence groups, lobbies and clans. Our state is much closer to a bureaucratic-authoritarian state whose distinguishing feature is that no one force—neither the bureaucracy nor influence groups—can monopolize power. It is important that in this state the leader be stronger than the corporate groups, because then he can appeal to the apparatus, to the regional bosses and, finally, to the people. That is the powerful guarantee against purely oligarchic rule.

From these similar premises Migranyan and Shevtsova draw very different conclusions—the former overly pessimistic and the latter overly optimistic. Migranyan (1997, 3) sees the next presidential election as a contest between one candidate willing to preside over "the dissolution of the Russian Federation as a state" and the other seeking to restore viable government by "creating authoritarian rule and a corporate state." Shevtsova (1997, 4) contends that the "heyday" of the powerful clans ended in early 1997 because of excessive bickering and insufficient subnational support, and declares that "the logic of strengthening the regime itself [now] requires clearer rules of play and restrictions on excessive appetites."

Predicting the future of state–society relations in Russia is hazardous, but it seems safe to say that they will develop along some nonlinear course between the Migranyan and Shevtsova scenarios. The chief imponderables are the initiatives of the Russian leaders who are emerging in the public and private sectors as well as the behavior of the Russian citizens who are deeply pessimistic and dissatisfied with current socioeconomic conditions. The vast majority of public officials are putting their private interests over the collective interests of their organizations and are jeopardizing the survival of the current government and even the Russian state. And many average citizens are nostalgic for the Leonid Brezhnev period, which suggests that material, physical, and psychological security are valued more highly than free elections, free markets, and free speech. Some public opinion polls highlight generational, demographic, and geographical differences, with younger and urban citizens voicing more support than older and rural citizens for governmental and economic reforms, especially those at the regional and local levels (e.g., Fleron et al. 1997, 15 and passim). However, a recent sociological survey (Gorshkov 1997a, 4–5) concludes:

> Evidently, political forms of defending their vital interests are not especially popular among Russian citizens. . . . The experience of recent years has convinced the majority of the country's population . . . that there are no effective ways of influencing the authorities in Russia (almost 60% of those surveyed believe this). . . .
>
> What kind of social base is there for the current Russian reforms and their further development? It's good, of course, when the authorities can rely on the support of young people in the 18–20 age group, and it's good that such social groups as entrepreneurs and students properly appreciate the reform policy. But isn't that too little for Russia as a whole? For the sake of whom and what has there been so much agony during the reforms, and when will they begin to meet the interests of the majority of Russian citizens? Unless they answer these questions, today's reformers, without even realizing it, may end up driving (if only figuratively) all of Russia into the world of yesterday.

This analysis suggests that socioeconomic pressures for political counterreforms are building, but another Russian sociological study (Byzov et al. 1997, 14), based on similar findings at the exact same time, comes to a very different conclusion:

Psychologists observed long ago that the more helpless society feels and the more profoundly people sense that they are incapable of doing anything to improve their lives, the stronger will be their urge to counter-balance this cold, hostile world by creating an imaginary parallel world where powerful emotions surge and noble heroes triumph. In a country where the majority of citizens—about 62% according to the September [1997] figures—report that they are barely managing to survive day to day, the dominant mood of the masses is not so much a desire to change the world as a willingness to resign oneself to the inevitability of what is happening.

Under Yeltsin many Russians are experiencing a revolution of *declining* expectations, which may have unpredictably powerful effects because it abruptly reversed the revolution of *rising* expectations launched by Gorbachev.

My best guess—on the basis of social science theory and information about Russia—is that this second interpretation of state-society relations is closer to the mark and that antidemocratic counterreforms are not imminent. It was de Tocqueville (1955), after all, who posited that social revolutions are most likely to be sparked by state leaders who initiate liberal reforms and activist citizens who see an opportunity for major change, not when elite structures appear stable or personal circumstances look hopeless to the downtrodden masses. And it was the public's response to the reforms of Alexander II and Gorbachev (Lenin, too, arguably) that proved de Tocqueville correct in the Russian context.

True, elite structures are not stable and personal circumstances are not hopeless in present-day Russia. Many Russians who grew up in the Gorbachev and Yeltsin years seem to feel indifference, not anger, toward their ineffectual governmental institutions. Although citizens lack political efficacy, they enjoy personal opportunity. Entrepreneurs of various ages and backgrounds are prospering from minimal government intervention in their lives and are thankful for their freedom from the state. But apathy and alienation abound, particularly in rural provinces and "rust-belt" cities. The most impoverished and disoriented individuals have their scapegoats and feel futility and frustration because their life's work has been devalued or their life's plans have been derailed. Some people are suffering acutely from financial pressures and loss of status. They have been immobilized by unexpected developments, have ignored new opportunities, and may feel some guilt about their inaction or inadequacies. Small wonder that alcohol consumption has risen considerably beyond its alarming level prior to Gorbachev and is threatening to become a demographic catastrophe, especially for men. Women have coped better with the strains and up-heavals of perestroika and postperestroika. However, both sexes have become much less interested in politics since the heyday of glasnost and especially since the president's shelling of the parliament in 1993. Robert C. Tucker's (1971, esp. chap. 6; 1987) "dual Russia" has survived the transition from the Soviet era. And the deepening or narrowing of this multifaceted gap between the governors and the governed, especially between their respective ideologies and interests, will have a profound impact on state–society relations in the early post-Soviet period.

Conclusion

This chapter has sought to refocus scholarly attention on the interaction between Russia's state and society. These dynamic linkages are probably the most important variables shaping core elements of the nascent Russian polity and influencing governmental performance in domestic and foreign arenas. A sharper focus on state–society relations not only will help post-Sovietologists to understand the realities of contemporary Russian politics but can help comparativists to build theories of successful democratization.

There are, of course, various paradigms in comparative politics research—for example, rationalist, structural, culturalist, and historical institutional (e.g., Lichbach and Zuckerman 1997). A leading specialist (Migdal 1997b, 231) on state–society relations favors an amalgam that emphasizes the latter two approaches, and he reaches conclusions that are remarkably relevant to postcommunist studies:

> States have been unable to transform societies sufficiently so as to solve the paradox of being simultaneously apart from society and a part of society. More than that, the engagement of the state with society, which has created sites of struggle and differences in society, subverting the state's efforts at uniformity, has also transformed the state. The mutual transformation of state and society has led to contending coalitions that have both cut across and blurred the lines between them. It is within these dynamic institutional arrangements that we must now approach the study of the state—an organization divided and limited in the sorts of obedience it can demand. We must abandon approaches that isolate the state as a unit of analysis. To do that, we must develop the means to forge the efforts of the historical institutionalists and culturalists, who until now have worked mostly in splendid isolation from one another.

Especially pertinent to an understanding of post-Soviet Russia are Migdal's (1997b, 208–9, 224, 230) emphases on the "limited state," the "engagement" of state institutions with social groups, "the authority deriving from collective consciousness" (national identity), and the need to shift our "analytic focus from the state as a freestanding organization to a process-oriented view of the state-in-society."

There are also various approaches to the study and practice of democratization—for example, societal modernization, comparative history, intraelite interaction, and institutional design (e.g., Reisinger 1997). All have their merits and liabilities depending on one's theoretical paradigm and methodological preferences as well as one's pragmatic priorities and material resources. But all of these orientations must address state-society relations, albeit in distinctive ways and with different emphases. For example, a democratic government's responsiveness and representativeness can strengthen both its state and society. Also, a strong civil and political society can *empower* a state by *constraining* it. The state's policies and policymaking procedures become more legitimate and effective because of its law-regulated and limited powers. And state officials will find it is much easier to stimulate and regulate a highly productive and growing private sector through fiscal and monetary policies than to create and sustain a technologically innovative and efficient public sector through centralized planning and management.

Particularly important may be the complex and fluid configurations of authority patterns between state and social institutions and their domestic and international environments. To be sure, Russia's most adjacent state and social institutions are not clearly distinguishable and their relationships are not stable, which makes its more difficult to study state–society relations. But if one's purpose is to explain governmental performance in a nascent democracy, it is quite useful to compare the authority patterns of various powerful institutions and to monitor the changes in these patterns and relationships. And it would be shortsighted to analyze interelite bargaining without examining elite efforts to mobilize mass support. Interelite conflict can easily disrupt congruent authority patterns between political and social institutions and create or deepen fissures among social classes or strata.

Moreover, a salient feature of state–society relations may be the public's distrust of or apathy toward both state *and* social institutions. In present-day Russia, for instance, many average people seem to believe that social institutions cannot effectively represent their needs and wants and that state institutions are unresponsive to group and mass interests. To date, most elected deputies (especially at the national level) have not given much weight to their role as representatives or spent much time with their constituents. Some segments of the population appreciate the greatly reduced governmental interventionism after the oppressive Soviet controls. But the current Russian state's actions and inaction have intruded powerfully into most citizens' daily lives—first in the form of rampant inflation, decontrolled prices, and product and service shortages and now in the form of still high prices, low unpaid wages, reduced social services, corrupt bureaucrats, heightened crime, dangerous pollution, poor health care, and a host of other socioeconomic ills.

Furthermore, the drafting of a democratic constitution cannot ensure the launching of a constitutional democracy. The former depends on the political acumen and technical skills of activist elites, but the latter depends on the legitimacy of a constitution's promulgation and the fairness of its metapolicies in the eyes of most citizens. Key variables explaining the development and consolidation of viable constitutionalism are the equitable distribution and judicious uses of authority—perhaps especially the balance of power among coalitions of state, class-based, and transnational institutions.[10]

I agree with two comparativists (Bratton and van de Walle 1997, 276, italics in original) who contend that "a major weakness of the prodigious institutional literature on the state—and the slim institutional literature on civil society—is that it tends to leave politics out." But I disagree with their conclusion that "a *politico*-institutional approach brings politics back in." Although such an approach may be entirely appropriate for analyzing the neopatrimonial polities and preindustrial economies of Africa and moderately appropriate for the most authoritarian "postcolonial" countries of the Commonwealth of Independent States, it is merely a first step toward understanding the politics of state-building and society-building in Russia, the Baltic nations, and much of Eastern Europe.

Students of postcommunism need to bring society back in. They can do so by focusing on emerging social institutions and movements and their symbiotic or strained relationships with state institutions and individual bureaucrats. Privatization by its very nature enlarges the society at the expense of the state, and public assets cannot be privatized without the collaboration of state officials. The legality or venality of these transactions depends entirely on the new political rules of the game, which can be democratized and stabilized only through codification and enforcement by legitimate state institutions. These formal and informal metapolicies can accumulate legitimacy through procedural rights (especially free elections) or substantive accomplishments (especially economic prosperity). But a high voter turnout and a high standard of living cannot by themselves instill a democratic legal culture; workplace democracy and grassroots activism may be even more important. And a consensus about new policymaking procedures cannot be built without elite *and* mass support or acquiescence. Effective public policies probably cannot be formulated and surely cannot be implemented without the legally regulated participation of political parties, professional associations, business firms, trade unions, environmental activists, independent mass media, financial-industrial groups, and administrative agencies representing social and economic interests.

Post-Sovietologists must continue to accumulate knowledge about the impact of cracked and splintered bureaucratic monoliths, the adaptation of ethnic and socioeconomic networks, and the obstacles toward establishing (or resistance toward even trying to establish) law-governed states and markets as well as political and civil societies. But to accomplish these goals we must underscore the abrupt severing of linkages between the former party and state and between the party-state and social institutions. And, because of the unsettled transformations and mounting tensions in the state-society relations of many postcommunist countries, we must continuously reassess the causes and consequences of these linkage variables. In a word, our primary focus should be on continuity and change in the nexus between state and society.

The briefest possible answers to the questions with which we began this chapter are as follows: Yes, the reciprocal relations of state and social institutions, including their international and transnational relations, are key linkages that must be studied as dependent and independent variables to advance understanding of the theory and practice of democratization, perhaps especially in postcommunist protodemocracies such as Russia. Analysts have to disaggregate state and social institutions and strata and highlight the stiff competition or symbiotic collaboration between state and social institutions at the national and subnational levels. Zero-sum and multiple-sum approaches are both useful, but the latter may be more fruitful in present-day Russia because of the persistence of weak national state institutions and their penetration by powerful social institutions, and because of the stable and unstable alliances and networks between state and social institutions at all levels.

Also, there is a clear need for further study of congruent authority patterns and balanced disparities in democratizing and democratized countries. But it is not clear that these linkages are possible or desirable in every phase of state-formation and society-formation, and that the origins and effects of key linkages can be empirically verified with a considerable degree of confidence. Because it is hard to classify and categorize the state and social institutions of a transitional polity and because their structures and functions are fluid, it is quite difficult to

discern the fit between institutional authority patterns and the equilibrium among disparate political bodies. During democratization there
may be *dysfunctionally congruent* relationships among the oligarchic coalitions of state and social institutions or at least among their corrupt
officials. And there may be *functional imbalances* (e.g., judicious executive or legislative leadership) that propel a state from authoritarian to
democratic stability. Because congruent authority patterns can be either democratic or authoritarian, the balancing of disparate institutional interests and of mixed political cultures is critical to the
establishment and consolidation of a viable democratic polity.

Furthermore, the rule of law is absolutely crucial for democratic
state-building and society-building. A balance of power can be temporarily achieved among political-administrative and financial-industrial
conglomerates and even among criminal communities, but a law-governed state and society has much greater potential for long-term stability and viability. Legislative acts codify the formal rules and shape the
informal rules of policy making—that is, they establish policies on how
to make policy—and independent courts ensure compliance with these
metapolicies. Also, the rule of law is essential for market-building at
home and abroad. And, for most or all countries, the best path toward
viable democracy and successful marketization is via constitutional
guarantees of civil liberties and property rights, prior to or simultaneous with the enfranchisement of the entire population and the emergence of a multiparty system. The vital first step is to establish a
democratic legal culture among the elites and masses and to elect legislators, appoint judges, and train civil servants who are honest, skillful,
and farsighted.

But Russia has not taken many of these paths, in part because of its
tsarist and Soviet statist traditions, the calculations and mistakes of
recent top leaders, and the needs and wants of newly poor and rich
citizens. Also, the sudden shift from a collectivist mentality to an individualist mentality has been jarring for numerous Russians. And the
development of a distinctive Russian national consciousness and *gosudarstvennost* is very important for the future of state–society relations
as well as interstate and intersocietal relations, especially with the
countries of the former Soviet Union and Soviet bloc.

Thus, post-Sovietologists face a significant challenge in trying to understand the shifting realities and potentials of the state–society nexus
in the Russian Federation and of the international activities and aspirations of its many state and social institutions. A distinguished Russian
cultural historian, Likhachev (1990, 16–17), once said that Russians live
only in the past and the future. But the immediate present is crucial
for Russia, because the current priorities of its politicians and citizens

and their collective and individual actions will have powerful long-term effects. This is not only their personal fate—it is the *sudba* of the entire country. Like a growing fetus in the womb, which is predominantly formed in the earliest stages of its development, the foundations of the postcommunist Russian state and society are being formed *now*. The collective dilemma of present-day Russia and of many of its individual citizens is illuminated in Dostoevsky's (1991, 634–35 and passim) *The Brothers Karamazov*. Noble and base aspects of Ivan Karamazov's personality are in sharp conflict, and the former urge him to testify in court that his brother, Dmitri, is innocent of murdering their father. But Ivan's apparition or "devil" reappears just before Dmitri's trial, and Ivan is deeply distressed that he feels helpless when it is of the utmost importance to speak and act "boldly and resolutely."[11] When Ivan needs to have all of his physical and mental facilities functioning at their very best, his struggle with himself and others intensifies and he can barely muster enough strength and sanity to survive. The outcome of Ivan's prolonged and anguished quest for self-knowledge and self-fulfillment is never revealed. But Dostoevsky provides many indications that his protagonist's ordeal will eventually reintegrate his personality and regenerate his life.

Notes

I am grateful to Nadia Kavrus-Hoffmann for her thoughtful critique of this chapter and especially for elucidating the political and social connotations of key Russian concepts. Also, I wish to thank Frederic J. Fleron Jr., Robert Sharlet, and William M. Reisinger for their very helpful comments on this chapter.

1. For many additional questions, concepts, and theories applicable to state–society relations in contemporary Russia, see the other essays in the present volume.

2. See especially Eckstein's three chapters in the present volume.

3. For elaboration of these themes, see my other two chapters in this volume.

4. For analysis of this book and other major books on state–society relations, see my other two chapters in this volume.

5. Compare the Russian and English versions of the 1993 constitution in *Konstitutsiia Rossiiskoi Federatsii: The Constitution of the Russian Federation* (Moscow: Iuridicheskaya Literatura, 1994), 5–6, 13, 17, 43, 83–84, 91, 94–95, 120.

6. *Konstitutsiia Rossiiskoi Federatsii: The Constitution of the Russian Federation*, 43, 45–46, 61, 120, 123, 138.

7. See Eckstein's three chapters in this volume; Putnam 1993, 104 ff.

8. On the importance of "bureaucratic pluralism" and "centralized pluralism" in the Soviet political and economic systems respectively, see Hammer 1990, 172 and passim; Nove 1987.

9. On Soviet liberalization and post-Soviet democratization in regional and local governments, see Hahn 1996a and Stoner-Weiss 1997.

10. For three different approaches to these interrelated themes, see Rueschemeyer, Stephens, and Stephens 1992, especially chaps. 1 and 7, Baaklini and Desfosses 1997, and Ahdieh 1997.

11. For analysis of the impact of Ivan Karamazov's ideas on the development of his personality and of the painful but *positive* role played by his "devil," see Hoffmann 1992.

II
THEORY AND METHOD

4

Democratic Theories and Authority Patterns in Contemporary Russian Politics

Erik P. Hoffmann

Theories of democracy and democratization may help to explain contemporary developments in Russia as well as in the other countries of the former Soviet Union and former Soviet bloc. But data from former communist countries are essential to verify, refine, or reject existing democratic theories. Western theories probably have much more to *gain* from than *contribute* to our understanding of postcommunist politics in Eurasia and Eastern Europe. The distinctive political and economic legacies of these societies, to say nothing of the demographic and ethnic divisions within societies, are providing abundant new data on transitions from authoritarianism and totalitarianism. We are witnessing transitions to anarchy, sultanism, protodemocracy, and democracy. Such transitions provide unprecedented opportunities to test theories about the origins and stabilization of democratic institutions and cultures. Also, we may need to reconceptualize core elements of disintegrating empires, democratic consolidation, and viable constitutionalism (Hoffmann 1993, 1994, 1997; Fleron and Hoffmann 1993; Fleron 1993; Walker 1993).

I am not suggesting that the Soviet Union and post-Soviet Russia are "unique" and therefore their structures and processes are impervious to insights from other contexts. Rather, I am underscoring the need to focus on the distinctive features—indeed, the unprecedented combination of features—in the transitional politics of the former Soviet Union and Soviet-bloc countries. I am also highlighting the importance of continuity as well as change in withdrawals from authoritarianism and totalitarianism. Some core elements of the disintegrating polities have persisted in the emerging polities. And new political and economic institutions are performing traditional functions in certain countries, provinces, or localities.

The demise of the USSR and the Berlin Wall notwithstanding, there are many political, economic, military, environmental, territorial, ethnic, and geostrategic links between communist and postcommunist systems. The networking of nomenklatura elites, the institutionalized clientelism of production executives and their workers, nuclear and conventional weapons conversion, decaying Chernobyl-type nuclear reactors, over two hundred border disputes within the Russian Federation, about twenty-five million Russians living in the "near abroad," and Baltic and East-Central European pressures for NATO expansion are examples of each of these linkages, respectively. Hence, political scientists would be wise to view theories of Third World "modernization" and Third Wave "democratization" as signposts rather than hitching posts in the study of postcommunist politics.

This essay will use democratic theories to interpret developments in post-Soviet Russia and will use Russian experience to assess democratic theories, in particular the "congruence" theory of Harry Eckstein and others. I will discuss, in turn, general theoretical issues; specific propositions, hypotheses, and approaches; the theory and practice of authoritarian withdrawal (1991 to 1993); the theory and practice of emerging democracy (1994 to the present); and the prospects for democratic consolidation.

General Theoretical Issues

Political analysts have developed at least two very different theories of democracy and democratization. The first stresses elite-mass consensus, political inclusion, civil liberties, socioeconomic equality, citizen activism, and responsive national, regional, and local government bodies; and the second stresses interelite competition, procedural rules, mandates of elected representatives, interest group politics, an effective civil service bureaucracy, and public acquiescence to national policies. The former can be traced from Aristotle, Rousseau, and de Tocqueville to Seymour Lipset, Harry Eckstein, and Robert Putnam, with empirical support from institutional and cultural data. The latter can be traced from Plato, Burke, and Weber to Joseph Schumpeter, Robert Dahl, and Samuel Huntington, with evidence from studies favoring both presidential and parliamentary forms of government.[1] As Reisinger (1993, 275–6, italics added) notes, some analysts emphasize the need for "high levels of interpersonal *trust* in the society and popular *trust* in government and *a close match* between governmental policies and public values." Others stress the importance of political leaders' choices and institutional design at critical phases of democratization, and "they focus on the interaction of such elites as party, military, and union leaders, charismatic politicians, representatives of the business sectors, . . . and politicians representing regional and ethnic interests." Whereas the first approach focuses on the cultural as well as the socioeconomic preconditions of democracy, the second approach contends that "democratic institutions and norms can emerge and receive support as a by-product of intra-elite power struggle, without a 'democratic' populace being in place."

Is it necessary to choose between elite-mass and interelite (or intra-elite) theories of democracy and democratization? Should "grassroots" and "trickle-down" approaches be compartmentalized?

Common sense tells us that "bottom-up" and "top-down" theories are *complementary* and that these theories should be *integrated* to the extent warranted by diverse kinds of empirical data. Common sense also tells us these theoretical approaches reinforce one another, probably simultaneously and almost surely sequentially, and that both approaches are necessary to avoid unidimensional, partial, or misleading explanations. And common sense tells us that theoretical and methodological pluralism are especially important in the infancy of postcommunist political systems and of the post-cold war international system, because theories of democratization and multipolarism have not incorporated newly available data about elite collaboration and public opinion in the diverse countries of the Commonwealth of Independent States.

But common sense is not common. Western students of democratization have insufficiently examined the synergies between interelite and elite-mass behavior as well as the linkages between bottom-up and top-down theories of democratization. And analysts have not focused on the interaction of state and society or the interaction of both state and society with their international environment. An impressive exception is the historically grounded and cross-national research of Rueschemeyer, Stephens, and Stephens. They (1992, 5, italics in original) focus on "the balance of power among different *classes and class coalitions,*" "the *state apparatus* and its interrelations with civil society," and "the impact of *transnational power relations* on both the balance of class power and on state–society relations." And they conclude that the working class played a decisive role in the democratization of most South American, Central American, Caribbean, and northern and southern European countries. "It was neither capitalists nor capitalism as such but rather the contradictions of capitalism that advanced the cause of political equality. Capitalism contributed to democracy primarily because it changed the balance of class power in favor of the subordinate interests" (Rueschemeyer et al., 1992, 302 ff.).

Other notable studies are grounded on the distinction between political rights (freedom *to* participate in governmental policymaking) and civil liberties (freedom *from* governmental intervention).[2] Open elections and independent mass media are well-known examples of these "positive" and "negative" freedoms, respectively. Fair campaigning, however, is an often overlooked component of a viable or would-be democracy. Political candidates' access to television and radio, as well as to governmental and nongovernmental campaign funds, are key political rights, and manipulation of the voters through governmental domination of the mass media, as well as through promised disbursements of governmental largesse (i.e., "pork"), are infringements of civil liberties. Whether such rights and liberties are feasible and desirable in the initial stages of authoritarian and totalitarian withdrawals is a moot point among democratic theorists and activists.

In a comprehensive book, Linz and Stepan (1996a) contend that a modern consolidated democracy consists of "five major inter-relating arenas": civil, political, and economic society as well as the rule of law and a state apparatus. Viewing democracy as "an interacting system" in which no arena "can function properly without some support from one, or often all, of the other arenas," Linz and Stepan (1996a, 8–9, 13, 15ff., italics in original) underscore the importance of elite-mass linkages in every phase of democratization.

> For modern democratic theory, especially for questions about how to consolidate democracy, it is important to stress not only the *distinctiveness* of civil society and political society, but also their *complementarity*. . . . A robust civil society, with the capacity to generate political alternatives and to monitor government and state can help transitions get started, help resist reversals, help push transitions to their completion, help consolidate, and help deepen democracy. At all stages of the democratization process, therefore, a lively and independent civil society is invaluable.

Also skillfully integrating bottom-up and top-down approaches, Eckstein's theory of viable democracy focuses on the reciprocal influences between governmental and nongovernmental authority patterns. He views elite-mass bonds as core elements of an inclusive polity capable of adapting its goals and methods to changing domestic and international environments. The centerpiece of this school of thought is "congruence" theory—Eckstein's idea that *"a government will tend to be stable if its authority pattern is congruent with the other authority patterns of the society of which it is a part "* (Eckstein 1992b, 188, italics in original)[3] and Putnam's (1993, 101) idea that governmental performance is enhanced if "[a]uthority relations in the political sphere closely mirror authority relations in the wider social setting." Putnam (1993, 104 ff., italics in original) affirms:

> Elite and mass attitudes are in fact two sides of a single coin, bound together in a mutually reinforcing *equilibrium.* . . . [T]hese distinctive elite-mass linkages have evolved over a very long time. Under these circumstances, it would be surprising if elite and mass attitudes were not *congruent.* A situation of authoritarian elites and assertive masses cannot be a *stable equilibrium,* and a pattern of obeisant leaders and complaisant followers is hardly more permanent.

Hence, according to congruence theorists, the combination of authoritarian elites and docile masses is most conducive to hierarchical or nondemocratic forms of stability. And the combination of responsive leaders and assertive masses is most conducive to horizontal or democratic forms of stability.

Eckstein and Putnam include behavioral as well as attitudinal components in their conceptualization of authority patterns (e.g., Eckstein examines national governments and primary social organizations, such as schools and churches, and Putnam investigates subnational political elites and socioeconomic networks, including civic associations and recreational clubs). Most important, the two authors *compare* elite and mass authority patterns, looking for similarities and differences that help explain governmental performance. The researchers then link individual authority variables and their configurative relationships to tangible and perceived dimensions of performance (e.g., political legitimacy, public satisfaction with socioeconomic programs, decision-making effectiveness, bureaucratic responsiveness to citizen requests, and efficient use of scarce financial resources). Putnam (1993, 105) finds that in Italy "[t]he effectiveness of regional government is closely tied to the degree to which authority and social interchange in the life of the region is organized horizontally or hierarchically. Equality is an essential feature of the civic community." Eckstein (1992b), on the basis of field research in Western Europe and the United States, rejects Lipset's contention that power can be centralized *within* the civilian political and social institutions of a democratic polity. And both Eckstein and Putnam discover a strong correlation between successful governmental policies and democratic authority patterns throughout society.

Significantly, Eckstein (1992b, 207–9) emphasizes that stable democracy requires "a balance of disparate elements," including "a healthy element of authoritarianism." A "pure" or homogenous society is neither possible nor desirable, because both the methods of pursuing it and the end product will be authoritarian or totalitarian. Most human conflicts and differences (e.g., political, economic, social, cultural, ethnic, religious, ideological, geographical) cannot be eliminated, and democratic institutions and politicians do not try to do so. Instead, democracies fragment power and create incentives for power sharing, thereby managing, mitigating, and "grounding" conflicts and frustrating the aggressive ambitions of individuals, groups, and majorities. James Madison and other American founding fathers had a keen understanding of the darker side of the individual psyche and had no illusions about the perfectibility of human nature. Even with the untapped riches and beckoning opportunities of the American continent, they highlighted the inevitability of scarce material resources and the importance of nonmaterial values (e.g., power, status, security). By contrast, Karl Marx looked forward to a harmonious, prosperous, and classless utopian "communist" society, and many of his followers used highly repressive means in the alleged pursuit of this conflict-free ideal.

Following counterintuitive observers from Aristotle and Aquinas to Gabriel Almond, Sidney Verba, and Eckstein, contemporary social theorists affirm that "a balance of political cultures" is essential to "sociocultural viability" and that competing political interests and "ways of life" must coexist or be balanced in a stable democracy. Thompson, Ellis, and Wildavsky (1990, 96–97) conclude:

> A nation in which [the five and only five] ways of life are nicely balanced (or, at least, "never entirely excluded") is less prone to being surprised and will have a wider repertoire to draw from in responding to novel situations. It will still blunder, of course, but it will blunder less than its more monolithic competitors. The more ways of seeing that are included, the less there is that will go unseen. Those regimes that have largely excluded a particular cultural bias lose the wisdom attached to that bias, and thus inevitably pile up trouble for themselves. If this reasoning is valid, it implies that those political systems that promote a diversity of ways of life are likely to do better than those that repress the requisite variety. Governments need not let a thousand flowers bloom, but they may do well not to nip any of the five cultural biases in the bud.

The key component of a stable democracy is the institutional and attitudinal response to diversity and conflict. Diverse political forces must tolerate and compromise with one another—preferably respect and cooperate with each other—and thereby preserve the basic institutions and traditions that restrain or reduce conflict. Even governmental gridlock will probably protect political rights and civil liberties, although it will surely reduce governmental effectiveness in responding to problems and opportunities and in producing outputs and outcomes beneficial to the majority of the population. The major exception to this generalization is a federal system, or phase in its evolution, during which stalemate among branches of the national government enables regional governments to repress the rights and liberties of segments of their populations.

Eckstein's theory of "congruence" and "balanced disparities" helps to explain the stability and performance of established democracies—the kinds of polities that emerge after "democratic consolidation," variously defined. Also important is Eckstein's concept of "adjacency," which underscores the socialization and recruitment functions of subnational governments, political parties, interest groups, business corporations, trade unions, and other institutions that interact directly with national governmental bodies. For instance, if local politicians acquire democratic skills and are frequently elected to national offices, then the viability of a democracy is enhanced. Conversely, if military leaders often become chief executives and national legislators, then a democracy's viability is undermined. Eckstein (1992b, 224) observes that stable democracy (as well as stable totalitarianism) is rare indeed, and he contends (invoking Weber) that "semiauthoritarian government . . . is bound to be the most stable of all possible governments, owing precisely to its impurity and easy congruence with primary group patterns." Whether he would apply this argument to a proto-democratic polity and a weak state emerging from totalitarianism under revolutionary socioeconomic conditions, as we are witnessing in contemporary Russia, is a moot point.

Although primarily a theorist of stable democracy rather than of unstable democratization, Eckstein exhorts political scientists to explain systemic "dynamics, change, [and] adaptation" toward undetermined goals. He underscores the difficulty of managing conflict in consolidated democratic orders: "While degrees of stability, or rates of change, may vary, no form of government can be inherently stable—if only because no form of government can escape the dilemma of managing strains by increasing the probability of others" (Eckstein 1980, 32; see also 1992b, 224; and chap. 10 in this volume). Moreover, Eckstein emphasizes the close connections between elites and masses, structure and process, and authority patterns and governmental performance. His key dependent variable—stability—is just one dimension of performance. And his focus on political-administrative and socioeconomic outcomes is essential to an understanding of the obstacles and challenges to democratization as well as the tensions and trade-offs in a viable democracy. Explicitly and implicitly, Eckstein is constantly bridging the gap between grassroots and trickle-down theories about nascent and established democracies.

But the mere presence of various "disparities" or "ways of life" does not ensure that they will foster political stability or governmental performance, and it is exceedingly difficult to balance competing political interests without creating policy-making gridlock, permanent advantages for certain groups, or a reversion to authoritarianism. Especially in the transition from a totalitarian polity and a command economy, might it not be more fruitful and less difficult to institutionalize conflict resolution mechanisms between old and new *elites* than to try to build *congruent* authority patterns throughout the society? Might not elite consensus on new decision-making rules counterbalance discordant organizations and movements, whose no-holds-barred rivalries could prove fatal to the democratization of a recently authoritarian or totalitarian polity? Might not the breadth and depth of mass commitment to representative institutions depend heavily on socioeconomic achievements and prospects, which can be realized only through coalition building among political, economic, military, and ethnic leaders? And might congruence among authority patterns and consonance within them, which are essential to the stability of a responsive and effective democratic polity, not be feasible or desirable in the early stages of many successful democratic transitions (e.g., if many citizens still favor state socialism or great-power chauvinism and elect predominantly Communist or military leaders at the national, regional, and local levels)?

All such questions underscore the need to distinguish between theories of stable democracy and theories of democratization and to investigate creatively the interconnections between the two. Equilibrium theories focus on the congruence of political-administrative and socioeconomic variables after democratic consolidation. Disequilibrium theories focus on the preconditions of and transition to democracy, especially elite consensus on new policy-making practices and property redistribution. Both theories stress the procedural elements of democracy and conflict management, and both try to explain the enhancement of political legitimacy and effectiveness.

Democratization can be viewed as the shift from a noncivil society, noncivil economy, and noncivic culture to a civil society, civil economy, and civic culture. The most probable sequence is fivefold: (1) a stable and monolithic totalitarian (or corporatist authoritarian) polity and a predominantly centralized economy, (2) an unstable and predominantly authoritarian polity and an emerging mixed economy, (3) an unstable and hybrid authoritarian/democratic polity and a transitional centralized/market economy, (4) an unstable and predominantly democratic polity and a consolidating mixed economy, and (5) a stable and multi-institutional democratic polity and a predominantly market economy. Inevitably, there will be backward lurches and zig-zags in this sequence of shifts. But the institutionalization and legitimation of a democratic policy process and a prosperous market economy are most likely to be accompanied by a narrowing gap between state and society and their increasing interdependence. Fewer interelite pacts and more elite-mass bonds (e.g., congruence between elite and mass authority patterns and interests, à la Eckstein and Putnam; responsiveness and accountability between the governors and the governed, à la Linz and Stepan) may be causes or consequences of democratization and marketization.[4]

A peaceful and speedy transition is desirable but not necessary or sufficient for democratic consolidation and successful markets. Sometimes bloodshed or policy failures can bring intemperate leaders to their senses or wiser leaders to the fore. Also, "velvet" revolutions can leave authoritarian political and economic elites with much of their power intact. And the new governmental and nongovernmental institutions of a civil society and economy must start functioning before the wide and deep inculcation of a civic culture. But a democratic state cannot emerge without the democratic and entrepreneurial aspirations of a determined minority of elites and, at the very least, the acquiescence of the masses. Civic institutions and traditions cannot be imposed from above or below; they are the fruits of initiatives and responses from both the elites and masses. And they can be rooted only in the congruence of interests and the balancing of disparities among all citizens—that is, majority rule with minority rights and free election of accountable representatives with constitutional restraints on the governors as well as the governed.

In the first phase of democratization, however, the most crucial endeavors are institution building and institution dismantling, while adapting old institutions to new conditions whenever possible. The very survival of a democratic experiment may hinge on the motivations, skills, and decisions of the new leaders, who are seeking to accumulate power and authority through charisma, elections, policy successes, and/or institutional support. Also significant is the interaction between political elites and counterelites, who may or may not accept the concept of "loyal opposition" or even agree on the territorial boundaries of the country. And absolutely critical are law-based policies on how to make policy (i.e., *metapolicies* that establish, sustain, and broaden and deepen democratic governance). Metapolicy making includes constitutional bargaining, which can be a highly contentious and prolonged process. But regime-founding elites must establish inclusive and transparent rules of political decision making for a democratic transition to proceed. Elites can disagree on substantive policies and decisions, not on the lawful procedures for allocating values and resources and constraining power and ambition.

For democratization to develop and stabilize, "congruence" between elite and mass authority patterns may or may not be necessary in all or most stages. This is an important theoretical issue that has not received its due and a thorny empirical question that has not been resolved. But one can more confidently affirm, on both theoretical and empirical grounds, that "balanced disparities" must be quickly and firmly established among elites and their institutions and cultures, and eventually among mass institutions and cultures. A fuller understanding of the distinctive disparities between the elites and masses, and especially of the symbioses, synergies, and feedback loops between these two sets of disparities, awaits the maturation of congruence theories of democratization and democracy. For now, one can only emphasize that progress in the initial phase of democratization may depend heavily on the democratic instincts of leaders who have the power to be autocratic or oligarchic. Progress may also result from the positive side effects of political stalemate, such as the need to compromise with one's adversaries, to mobilize broader elite and mass support for one's powers and policies, and to accept certain decision-making procedures or rules of competition, in the belief that they may further one's personal ambitions or group's interests in the foreseeable future.

Majority rule without minority rights can undermine or reverse democratization, and authoritarian governance can subvert or swallow up democratic ideals. Finding the balance or sequence that nurtures democratization is a challenge that can be met only by widely respected and transformational leaders with an intimate knowledge of the domestic and international context or with extraordinary luck, intuition, persuasiveness, charisma, or spiritual insight. Although visionary goals may guide and energize the democratic reformer or revolutionary, pragmatic thinking is urgently needed to move from undesired toward desired conditions and to assess the costs and risks of alternative priorities and methods at successive stages of democratization.

Specific Propositions, Hypotheses, and Approaches

How can democratic theories enhance, and be enhanced by, our growing knowledge of post-Soviet Russia? Five propositions can be proffered:

1. The ongoing debate about elitist and populist theories of democracy must focus on the state-society nexus in various stages of democratization, with particular emphasis on the constraints and obstacles bequeathed by authoritarianism or totalitarianism and generated by the initial phase of political and economic adjustment.
2. Theories of democratization must pay much greater attention to the interaction of political and economic variables, especially to the distinctive legacies of centrally planned and managed economies, the sequencing of political and economic reforms, and the international security and transnational market environments.
3. Theoretical and methodological pluralism is essential to develop the middle-range social science theories, especially the combinations of domestic and international theories about institution building and incentive structures, that can help explain democratic transitions in the post-cold war era.
4. Interdisciplinary and cross-national research is essential to understand postcommunist polities, economies, and societies as well as postcommunist countries' evolving ties to one another, their geostrategic regions, and major world powers.
5. Analysts must understand diverse and changing *Russian* theories and conceptions of democracy and democratization and compare them with their Western, Third World, East European, and other postcommunist counterparts.

For a start, Eckstein's ideas about congruence and balanced disparities can enrich the argumentation, conceptualization, and data gathering of Russian and non-Russian theorists. He identifies some important institutional and cultural variables, which enable one to hypothesize about the origins and effects of democratization as well as of stable democracy. Eckstein sensitizes us to the reciprocal influences between the emerging organizations of the state and society, especially the imbalances, tensions, and "contradictions" at various stages of their development. Also, Eckstein's concept of governmental performance is quite useful under conditions of rapid and multifaceted change in national, regional and local politics. Furthermore, given the continuing cohesiveness of socioeconomic networks in Russian factories and farms, as well as the increasing numbers of enterprise directors and *kolkhoz-sovkhoz* chairmen elected to regional parliaments, Eckstein's emphasis on elite-mass linkages seems well placed. Finally, his attention to mass political culture and authority patterns is a helpful corrective to the overly elitist theories of democracy and democratization, such as Joseph Schumpeter's and Phillipe Schmitter's, and to the insuf-

ficiently cultural and attitudinal "new institutionalism," such as Philip
Roeder's and M. Steven Fish's.

Eckstein's general theories and Robert C. Tucker's insights about political culture and leadership in Russia might be fruitfully integrated.
More than three decades ago, Tucker (1971, 122 ff.) wrote: "The image
of dual Russia is not simply a conception of the state and people as
two different Russias ["official" and "popular"]. It also comprises an
evaluative attitude, or rather a range of attitudes." Many scholars have
underscored the stability or symbiosis of these authoritarian ties between the Russian elites and masses. Tucker, however, highlights the
discordant side of this relationship and the mounting pressures for an
"unbinding" of the state's control of society. Instead of being a complaisant or acquiescent citizen, Tucker's *muzhik* views "autocratic state
power as an *alien* power in the Russian land"; his *kolkhoznik* resists
becoming a "cog" in Stalin's social engineering; and his bureaucratic
elites do not uniformly embrace "dual Russia." Reformers who sought
to reduce the gulf between state and society included tsar Alexander
II as well as the nobles, army officers, intelligentsia, clergy, urban bourgeoisie, workers, peasants, minorities, and women who made increasingly assertive petitions for policy and systemic changes, especially in
the 1760s, 1860s, and 1905–1906. Nikolai Bukharin, Nikita Khrushchev,
and Mikhail Gorbachev were Communist Party liberalizers, and Andrei Sakharov, Aleksandr Solzhenitsyn, and Roy Medvedev were diverse dissidents from the Soviet era.

In significant ways, Tucker's "dual Russia" is alive and well in post-
Soviet Russia. Because of the remarkably rapid and peaceful demise of
the USSR, "much of the statist Soviet system and its political culture
survived into the 1990s" (Tucker 1995, 9). Also, as early as November
1992, Liliya Shevtsova (quoted in Colton and Tucker 1995, 64) be-
moaned the "crisis of the democratic movement and deepening despair and fatigue on the part of the masses." Explaining the widening
gulf between the Russian political leadership and populace, she affirmed:

> Our political institutions are oriented only toward themselves and con-
> centrate on their own survival. This conclusion is eloquently confirmed
> by what goes on in the Russian parliament. . . . [It] long ago lost ties with
> society and turned itself into something self-sufficient. The presidential
> camp has also been incapable of sustaining constant communication with
> society. And so it has not created a mass base for its political course. It
> has not managed to find even a narrower foothold for itself in the form
> of a steady dialogue, with appropriate mutual obligations taken on by
> the participants, with so much as a few of our political groupings.[5]

For an important example, in 1994 Yeltsin launched a vicious civil war in Chechnya at the urging of a few personal advisers and with the unanimous backing of his Security Council, which included the two leaders of parliament's chambers. He probably did not consult with any other parliamentarians and did not discuss his decision in public for over a month. In fact, Yeltsin tightened government controls over the mass media, which had quickly reported the genocidal realities in Chechnya to the disapproving citizenry. And he allowed his personal security forces or chief of staff to insulate him from dissenting voices and constructive critics.

Moreover, the ultranational Communists and neofascists were not alone in characterizing Yeltsin's government as a "foreign" and "occupying regime." Prime Minister's Viktor Chernomyrdin's new party was called "Russia Is *Our* Home," but average citizens immediately dubbed it "Russia Is *Their* Home"—a bitter joke that expressed a deep feeling of alienation. Even Yeltsin, in his 1995 "State of the Federation" speech, frankly acknowledged that "[t]he overcoming of totalitarian oppression has not diminished the alienation of society from authority" (*Daily Report*, February 16, 1995, 8). Perhaps referring to the tsarist, Soviet, and post-Soviet periods, Chernomyrdin subsequently opined, "People in Russia have never liked authority. Not only have they not liked it, they have feared it. And with reason. In public they swore to love it, while in their soul and in the kitchen they reviled it" (*Daily Report*, September 13, 1995, 19).

Political alienation did not abate with the advent of a new constitution in 1993 and a presidential election in 1996. Indeed, mass cynicism about national politics rose steadily after the August 1991 putsch. By the mid-1990s, one could no longer plausibly contend that every Russian was a political theorist and a political scientist, or that every *apparatchik* and *babushka* was thinking about the functions of government and his or her role in it. Although Yeltsin won post-Soviet Russia's first presidential election, few citizens felt that he was *their* president. Voters chose Yeltsin over Gennady Zyuganov as the lesser of two evils, were more afraid of the Communists' return to power, or did not want further destabilizing changes. Contempt for most national politicians, especially their love of power, money, and perquisites, was widespread among the voters, to say nothing of the nonvoters.

Public disillusionment with national politicians increased in October 1996 when Yeltsin angrily fired Security Council head Aleksandr Lebed, the popular ex-general and ex-presidential candidate, amid a barrage of venomous charges about power grabs in the Kremlin, incipient mutinies in the armed forces, and treasonous peace accords and war profiteering in Chechnya. Top government, business, and media leaders across the political spectrum quickly voiced their support for Yeltsin's sacking of the overtly ambitious Lebed. But the gulf between the elites and masses perceptibly increased. Many Russian citizens— especially the 15 percent of the electorate that voted for Lebed— viewed him as an honest and incorruptible populist, who was cynically co-opted to help elect an unpopular president and was victimized by collusion among government-business clans to perpetuate their power and wealth. Public cynicism about the democratic process, especially the widespread corruption and unaccountability at all levels of government as well as the transparent Kremlin infighting and manipulation of election campaigns on television, was reflected in broader and deeper mass political apathy and atomization. "Democratic forms" had been rendered meaningless by "totalitarian counterweights" in the Soviet period, as John Hazard long ago observed, and many Russians were finding depressing evidence of authoritarian counterweights to democratic forms in post-Soviet Russia.

Dualism is not limited to conflicts within and among political, economic, and social strata; democratic and authoritarian impulses can compete within the head and heart of an individual Russian. For instance, Chernomyrdin stated in an interview that politicians should be respected, not feared, and that citizens should think for themselves, not rely on iron-fisted leaders. "We must awaken the sense of our own worth, in order to realize at last that we must count on ourselves above all." But a minute or so later he added, "Heaven forbid that anyone consults with his wife. I do not let people like that come anywhere near me. I never repeat my invitation. When I was still working as a [factory] director I realized for the rest of my life what kind of people these were—those who invariably consult with their wives on such occasions" (*Daily Report*, September 13, 1995, 18–19).

Tucker's emphasis on the *instability* of "dual Russia" and on the socioeconomic pressures for political change is especially important in the postcommunist context. So is Eckstein's concern about insufficient congruence and imbalanced disparities, and perhaps even Marx's analysis of intensifying "contradictions" between state and society and within society. Consider the following assessment of mid-1995 Russia by a team of Russian academicians that was deeply concerned about the exacerbation of political, economic, social, and ethnic conflicts and the dissipation of social capital. The Conflict Research Center of the Russian Political Science Association and Russian Academy of Sciences concludes:

> The current socio-political situation in Russia may be characterized as latent conflict. . . .

The outward semblance of stability is by no means a consequence of effective management—it is the result, on the one hand, of the micro-adaptation of a large part of the population to current conditions; and, on the other hand, of the weakness of the public and political institutions that have been called upon to defend the interests of the population. This adaptation is occurring not thanks to, but rather in spite of, the authorities' efforts, i.e., it is of a semi-official, unofficial, or generally criminal nature, which is associated in all instances with estrangement from or distrust of state and other institutions, whose sources of legitimacy are almost exhausted. . . .

There is the "specter" of a new political and economic redistribution, which is almost always associated in our country with social upheavals, "stalking" across Russia. (*Daily Report Supplement*, September 21, 1995, 30)

According to these Russian scholars, the most portentous "contradictions" and "conflict potential" emanate from the ambiguous roles of important state organs, especially the national legislature and armed forces; of key nonstate organs, especially the mass media and trade unions; and of fast-growing social strata, especially the "underclasses" and entrepreneurs. In 1995 over 50 percent of the electorate held "centrist" views, which were weakly articulated and aggregated by the 250 or so political parties with or without deputies in legislative bodies. Also, the approximately thirty-three thousand "public associations" were "extraordinarily poorly included in the general political processes." And a "negative consensus" was emerging between state and society. Citizens did not strenuously object to government policies or policy-making practices, but they resisted government intrusions into their private lives, especially into their financial and ethnoreligious activities. The Russian analysts concluded that this "negative consensus" was unlikely to foster democratization or even protodemocratic consolidation. On the contrary, they feared that the "atomization" of individuals, the "economic nationalism" of republics, and the "regional self-consciousness" of provinces were likely to hasten authoritarian consolidation, surely in some localities and possibly on the national level (*Daily Report Supplement*, September 21, 1995, 31–32 ff.).

Using considerable public opinion data, Kullberg and Zimmerman (1996, 9, 32) document the "ideological discord" and "interest divide" between Russia's national elites and masses.

In short, the post-Soviet Russian experience, trends in other former socialist states, and a growing body of empirical evidence support the proposition that in the absence of a well-developed market economy, economic reform, while in the interests of elite democratizers, may be starkly at odds with the interests of broad segments of their publics. Moreover, the trends suggest that this discordance may persist for relatively long periods of time. The presence of a substantial elite/mass interest divide violates a central assumption of transitions theory, and therefore undermines its contention that mass disaffection from democracy is typically both temporary and harmless. . . .

In Russia and other states of the former Soviet Union the psychological, ideological, and organizational disconnectedness of elites from mass may bring about the failure of democratic regimes.

According to Kullberg and Zimmerman, the Russian national elites and general public have vastly divergent ideologies (value and belief systems), interests (needs and wants), and opportunities (economic and social), all of which are seriously jeopardizing democratization. Their argument is strengthened by a number of mutually reinforcing factors: the dramatically widening gap in living standards between Russia's nouveaux riches and nouveaux pauvres; the strong elite support for market democracy and the widespread mass support for socialist democracy; the huge impact of money on Russian electoral politics and access to the mass media; the weakness of associational groups in representing interests and political parties in aggregating them; the extensive corruption in most governmental and nongovernmental institutions; and the ambiguities of constitutional and civil statutes as well as the fragility of law enforcement and judicial administration. Hence, de facto and de jure economic and political power are being consolidated by a narrow strata of old and new elites. For example, middle-aged nomenklatura officials and factory managers, as well as young entrepreneurs and technocrats, have solidified the personal connections and amassed the money to win elected or appointed positions in the executive, legislative, and judicial branches at all levels of government. And reputed mafia leaders have sought and occasionally won parliamentary seats to avoid criminal prosecution.

In early 1995, presidential aspirant and economist Grigory Yavlinsky declared:

We are at a crossroads today. We can still try to turn in the direction in which people will become independent. Or we may, with greater ease, go the way we are going on the basis of an oligarchy among the authority of money, business, and monopoly groups. In this sense we have not changed the old system at all: it was a supermonopoly, and this is the way it has stayed. In the past, decisions were made by 15 Politburo members; now they are made, for instance, by 10 monopoly groups which are not difficult to enumerate. (*Daily Report*, March 8, 1995, 20)

To understand the complexities and ramifications of these choices and developments, *it is necessary to construct a theory of interelite (hori-*

zontal) congruence as well as a theory of elite-mass (vertical) congruence and to try to link the two. Ideally, one could identify feasible and desirable stages of democratization and the relative significance of different types of congruence at different stages. A decisive "takeoff" from a stable or unstable protodemocracy is essential, but both trajectories to democracy have their pitfalls. A stable protodemocracy can easily perpetuate itself by supporting state socialism or an "uncivil" economy, and an unstable protodemocracy can easily vote into office reactionary legislators or oligarchic rulers. Hence, balanced disparities among the elites, balanced disparities among the masses, and legally regulated competition among elite-mass coalitions may be crucial at every stage of successful democratization, as well as to stable democracy.

A gradual shift from interelite to elite mass congruence also seems essential to democratic transitions, but there would surely be exceptions and reversals whose origins and impact would have to be explained. Both major schools of democratic theory—interelite consensus building and elite-mass consensus building—can help clarify the product and the process of democratization. And greater understanding of insufficient congruence and imbalanced disparities in protodemocracies may broaden and deepen our understanding of viable democracies.

For example, Tucker's "image of dual Russia" helps to explain both the tsarist and Soviet legacies, including the current gap between elite and mass perspectives, pursuits, and predicaments. Also, interelite consensus in protodemocracies may perform some of the functions of elite-mass congruence in stable democracies, because interelite conflict is often decided in favor of the leaders who can mobilize support from subelites and segments of the public. Furthermore, in emerging and consolidated democracies, interelite relations may be no more difficult to study than elite-mass relations, because counterelites are increasingly vocal and informed critics in the press and parliament, more subnational leaders are articulating demands and mobilizing support through the mass media, and more and more citizens are evaluating public officials frankly in public opinion polls and knowledgeably at the ballot box. Hence, governmental performance is much easier to assess in open or opening, rather than closed or closing, societies.

In addition, much greater attention needs to be paid to the interconnections between political and economic reforms. Lindblom's (1977) efforts to inject economic realities into democratic theory have stimulated surprisingly little follow-through in the last two decades. An important exception is the work of Haggard and Kaufman (1995b), who used the following theoretical orientation to analyze "the political economy of democratic transitions:"

The course of both regime change and economic policymaking is ultimately determined by the strategic *choices* of key actors—the supporters
and opponents of the incumbent government—as *constrained* by economic
circumstances and existing institutions. . . .

The inability to avoid or adjust successfully to *economic crisis* increases
the probability that authoritarian regimes will be transformed and reduces the capacity of authoritarian leaders to control the process of political change, including the terms on which they exit. Similarly, we expect
that the prospects for the consolidation of democracy will be better when
the government is able to successfully administer its economic
inheritance. . . .

In sum, we argue that the ability of both authoritarian and democratic
leaders to maintain power is partly a function of economic performance,
which in turn is dependent on the conduct of economic policy. Institutions affect the coherence of policy both in the initiation phase, when
executive authority is an asset, and during the consolidation phase when
success rests on building bases of *social support*. (1995b, 5, 10, 367–77, italics added)

It is much more difficult to create a democracy from a liberalizing
totalitarian polity and *noncapitalist* economy, such as Gorbachev's Soviet Union, than from a rigid authoritarian polity and *capitalist* economy, such as fascist Spain or apartheid South Africa. Although
Haggard and Kaufman only briefly compare democratic transitions
from market and nonmarket economies, they focus on the reciprocal
influences of political structures and economic performance. They emphasize that economic crises are important factors in weakening public
support for authoritarian regimes, widening splits within oligarchic
leaderships, and shaping the agendas of opposition groups. And they
insist that, in the early phases of transition, executive and legislative
institutions must formulate and implement a coherent economic policy
and must legitimize the difficult trade-offs among economic growth
and distributive justice. This calls for strong but cooperative executive
and legislative bodies, which can support or acquiesce in basic economic policies and policy-making procedures and can placate or respond to major political parties and interest groups. Haggard and
Kaufman (1995a, 8–9, italics added) draw important conclusions about
the desirable mix of political and economic variables at different
phases of democratic transitions:

Over the long term, the opportunities that democratic institutions provide
for debate and peaceful contestation offer the best hope for finding durable compromises for the social conflicts and economic policy dilemmas
[associated with economic crises and reform]. . . . Where underlying economic conditions are relatively favorable—as they were, for example, in

Spain—it may be feasible to give the right-of-way to the building of a democratic consensus. Where crises are deeper, however, democratic institutions may suffer as much from the *failure* to take swift and effective action as from the *temporary* exercise of discretionary authority. In many instances, such authority has pressed against constitutional limits; however, it should not be assumed that strong executive action implies that the legislature and other representative institutions have abdicated their responsibility for oversight. (See also Diamond and Plattner 1995, 1996)

Such conclusions are very pertinent to post-Stalinist and post-Soviet Russian experience. Khrushchev was the first Soviet leader whose power was dependent on the Politburo's assessment of the success of his domestic and foreign policies and of the legitimacy of his policy-making and administrative procedures. Declining socioeconomic performance, especially as perceived by reformist national and republic Communist Party leaders, played a major role in the gradual decentralization of the Soviet political system under Khrushchev and Leonid Brezhnev. Clumsy attempts to improve economic growth and productivity, coupled with increasingly candid information about social injustices and inequalities, contributed significantly to the polity's rapid disintegration under Gorbachev. Socioeconomic grievances spawned national independence movements, which co-opted local party elites in the non-Russian republics and hastened the Soviet Union's demise. Like Gorbachev, President Yeltsin found that his de facto power and authority, as well as the legitimacy of his formal and informal metapolicies, were highly dependent on the outcomes of his domestic and foreign policies, as seen through the eyes of competing elites and disaffected masses.

What *is* the best combination and sequencing of democratic political reforms and market economic reforms in postcommunist societies, and has Russia approximated this ideal? It is essential to avoid the Scylla of an authoritarian president who will not relinquish "temporary" powers granted him by the parliament and who makes far-reaching economic decisions virtually unilaterally, thereby weakening greatly all national governmental institutions and reducing dramatically the living standards of the vast majority of citizens (e.g., Yeltsin). Also, it is essential to avoid the Charybdis of an aggressive and uncompromising legislature, which cannot agree on decision-making rules with other branches and levels of government, which is preoccupied with professional perquisites and property redistribution and which thereby increases the likelihood of presidential co-optation of top parliamentary leaders and parliamentary support for communist rule (cf. Yeltsin's relationships with Ruslan Khasbulatov and Aleksandr Rutskoi, Ivan

Rybkin and Vladimir Shumeiko, and Gennady Seleznov and Igor Stroyev, respectively).

For democracies to take root, polities must foster and disseminate the attitudes and behaviors associated with the concepts of "civil society," "civil economy," and "civic culture"—in that sequence, if not simultaneously, and with immediate emphasis on "power sharing," "loyal opposition," "rule of law," "responsive leadership," and "responsible citizenship." A mix, not necessarily a balance, of executive, legislative, and judicial powers, as well as national, regional, and local powers, must be palatable to a broadening circle of political, economic, military, ethnic, and media elites. Interelite acquiescence in the metapolicies of democratic transition is especially important because of the need to transform power into authority and to share responsibility for the almost inevitable economic dislocations (e.g., skyrocketing inflation, elimination of price controls, vast property redistribution, and environmental pollution) and mass discontent (e.g., financial, professional, physical, and emotional insecurities).

To understand the reciprocal influences of the emerging state and society in contemporary Russia, as well as the impact of the world economy and transnational relations on Russia's development, are the central tasks of post-Sovietology. The presuppositions and findings of comparative political economists, together with a concerted effort to test their theories with data from the former Soviet Union and Soviet bloc, can help us compare transitions from totalitarian polities and command economies with transitions from authoritarian polities and market economies. Such comparisons will augment our knowledge of various kinds of democratic and nondemocratic transitions, especially if we focus on elite-mass linkages and their growth, retardation, or demise at successive stages from authoritarian withdrawal to democratic consolidation.

How can democratization and marketization be kept on course? Coleman's (1990, especially chaps. 8 and 12) concepts of "social capital" and "systems of trust" might hold the key. In post-Soviet Russia, these concepts must be applied to *interelite* linkages, to *elite-mass* linkages, and—most important—to the *balance, synergy, or feedback loops* between the two. Also, Coleman's concepts strengthen Walder's (1986) theory of "communist neo-traditionalism" and increase its relevance to postcommunist transitions, especially because of its focus on the adaptability and durability of socioeconomic networks such as clientelism, particularism, and familism. Stoner-Weiss (1997) and Kullberg and Zimmerman (1996) likewise stress the significance of continuity as well as change in the political economy of Russia's transition from Soviet rule. And these authors rightly warn that insufficient social capital will seriously weaken the effectiveness and legitimacy of Russia's polity and may produce greater unrest and violence in Russia's society. In other words, insufficient congruence of interests among the elites and between the elites and masses bodes ill for Russian democratization.

It is essential to recognize that elite-focused and mass-focused research on democratic transitions are complementary and that post-Sovietologists can profit from the insights of democratic theorists such as Eckstein and Putnam, sociologists such as Coleman and Lipset, and economists such as Lindblom, Haggard, and Kaufman. Cautious integration of these scholars' research suggests three key hypotheses on different aspects of congruence:

1. Trust, collaboration, compromise, and even stalemate among regime-founding elites are crucial for the launching of legitimate and effective governance and markets in protodemocracies moving toward democratic consolidation (interelite congruence).
2. Law-based cooperation between national political and economic elites, between national and subnational governments, and between subnational governments and socioeconomic networks is essential for the institutionalization of interest representation, especially the emergence of associational lobbies, broad-based political parties, and a meritocratic civil service (a mix of interelite and elite-mass congruence).
3. The lack of governmental responsiveness to associational interest groups and the paucity of feedback links between elite coalitions and mass organizations, as well as the huge gap between elite and mass priorities, resources, and worldviews, are significantly weakening the stability and performance of national and subnational governments and may eventually derail democratization and marketization (the lack of elite-mass congruence).

In addition, why not place more emphasis on the diversity of cultural and social legacies and their highly differentiated impacts on groups of elites and ordinary citizens in the multinational Russian Federation? Why not pay much greater attention to the interaction among the national, regional, and local governments, especially in the spheres of regional economic development and fiscal federalism? Why not underscore the problems of creating viable constitutionalism and a democratic legal ethos? Why not stress the importance of generational continuities and differences? And why not focus on the pressures for institutional and attitudinal changes generated by the global revolution in information technology and by the increasing permeability of national borders to world markets, ethnic rivalries, environmental haz-

ards, and Western culture? In a word, the countries of the former Soviet Union and the former Soviet bloc are living laboratories for
students of incremental and revolutionary change. The shortage and
shortcomings of applicable theories do not reduce the importance of
theorizing, in order to impart meaning to data, gain cumulative knowledge, explain current developments, predict Russia's future, and tailor
Western responses accordingly.

The Theory and Practice of Authoritarian Withdrawal (1991–1993)

Western and Russian Perspectives

Post-Sovietologists and Russian reformers can read Eckstein and be
reminded that stable democracies are difficult to establish in countries
without liberal religious traditions, without high levels of economic
entrepreneurship, and without "a vigorous associational life"—all of
which foster congruent authority patterns throughout the society and
balanced disparities between "governmental autonomy and dependence, 'democracy' and 'authoritarianism' " (Eckstein 1980, 219, 221).
But is congruence more likely to emerge out of a full-scale attack on
old institutions and beliefs in a bloody revolution or out of the structures and values of a totalitarian regime that survived intact after a
virtually bloodless transfer of power? How can political disparities be
balanced when key actors have little will and ability to do so, and when
corruption and money dominate the policy process? How can representative institutions develop when a presidential apparatus ignores
or manipulates the parliament, courts, and public opinion in formulating key domestic and foreign policies? How can free markets emerge
when huge bureaucratic lobbies refuse to be taxed and when certain
regional governments cut special deals with central authorities? How
can new freedoms strengthen the rule of law and distributive justice
rather than spur ethnonationalism, crime, greed, and territorial expansionism? And how important are diverse mass perspectives on the
linkages among representative democracy, rule of law, economic prosperity, and social justice? Existing theories have not satisfactorily resolved such issues, and it is to be hoped that postcommunist
experiences can help to produce much better explanations and data.

To begin with, more attention needs to be placed on the remarkably
peaceful nature of the anticommunist coups d'état in the Soviet Union
and Eastern Europe and on the resilient adaptation of old institutions
and attitudes to new problems and opportunities. Communist one-

party systems died with neither a bang nor a whimper. In Russia, there have been some political and economic policy "shocks," such as the tragic war in Chechnya, the president's bombing of the parliament building, the privatization of nearly sixteen thousand sizable enterprises in a year and a half, and the abrupt consumer price liberalization in January 1992. But Russia's postcommunist transition has generated unexpected entrepreneurial skills, especially among young and middle-aged people, as well as unprecedented independent-mindedness in the mass media, especially newspapers and magazines. Also, the assertiveness of regional and local governments has accelerated dramatically in both the ethnically mixed and predominantly Russian regions.

The Soviet Union's successor countries are fostering continuity as well as change in political, economic, and social authority patterns. A president can abolish local governments, a popularly elected legislature can perform various representative functions, and a constitutional court can interpret a new constitution. But ethnic and family bonds, local and departmental loyalties, and patron-client relations in the bureaucracies and workplace are all changing much more slowly than governmental institutions, economic policies, and social services. For both the self-reliant entrepreneur and the self-effacing citizen, "know-who" is still much more important than "know-how," and proven patterns of exchange are much more reliable than untested ones.

Reminding us of the Harvard Project's findings over four decades ago, Millar (1995, 9–12) argues that the USSR's demise did little to weaken the cohesiveness of Soviet "company towns" and the reciprocity of nomenklatura, kinship, and friendship "networks." Many old socioeconomic networks are being strengthened or enlarged to help their members thrive or survive under the uncertain, sometimes chaotic, conditions of postcommunism. Walder (1986, 252) concluded his study of Chinese industrial modernization with the following generalization: "Leninist forms evolve, by their own logic, into a form of clientelist rule. The particularism remains embedded in 'decayed' Leninist institutions . . . [and] does not melt away with the demands of industrialization." One can hypothesize that Walder's "patrimonialism," "organizational dependence," "institutional culture," and "cross-cutting networks of allegiance" are also core elements of *postcommunist* polities, surely in the short run and probably in the long run as well.

Given Lenin's and Stalin's extraordinary influence on the Soviet system, in addition to the millennium of primarily but not exclusively authoritarian rule since Kievan Rus, it is hardly surprising that elite responsiveness to mass preferences did not spring up overnight after the "velvet" revolutions of 1989 and 1991. But anticommunist and antitotalitarian impulses emerged from within these regimes, and elite aspirations and actions and their unintended consequences played a decisive role in the disintegration of the USSR. Khrushchev's domestic and international policy innovations in the mid-1950s, especially his denunciation of Stalin's "crimes" against the Communist Party and his rejection of the "inevitability" of nuclear war, laid the foundation for Mikhail Gorbachev's glasnost, perestroika, "democratization," and "new thinking" about foreign affairs, which were the primary catalysts for reform of the Soviet internal and external empires. Moreover, regional and local party cadres increasingly circumvented directives from national leaders during the Brezhnev period, especially in the all-union and autonomous republics with sizable non-Russian minorities. After the USSR's collapse, the national, regional, and local elites' personal ambitions and coalitions were key variables in the politics of transition. Although newly elected officials and newly formed interest groups were assertive on some policy issues, many average citizens became apathetic about voting, disheartened about lobbying, and skeptical about the fairness and efficacy of governmental programs, especially at the national level.

Congruence theories of democracy may help to explain the shifting relationships among Russian legislative and executive bodies as well as between elite and mass authority patterns. Sergeyev and Biryukov (1993, 207–8 ff.), after extensively studying the rhetoric and behavior in the Supreme Soviet before and after the August 1991 putsch, conclude:

> [T]he most important single obstacle to the transition from a totalitarian to a democratic society is the incompatibility of the new forms of social life and the new political institutions with the political culture of the nation. . . . The lesson of Russia's history must be learned: namely, that a modern democratic society will not emerge unless the political mentality of *sobornost* is overcome.

Sobornost refers to a political culture of organic collectivism, popular will, and quest for objective truth. It is based on a model of inclusive representation and consensual decision making that was formulated and developed in the protoparliamentary assemblies (*zemskie sobory*) of the sixteenth to seventeenth centuries and was adapted and used by Soviet leaders from Lenin to Gorbachev (e.g., in the 1921 resolution "On Party Unity" and 1989 Congress of People's Deputies as well as in the legitimizing functions of the Communist Party Central Committee and Supreme Soviet).

A *zemskii sobor* included representatives from all regions and estates (mostly boyar nobles, ecclesiastical leaders, service gentry, and affluent townspeople as well as a few peasants), and its decisions (mostly petitions and recommendations to the tsar as well as some local initiatives) were taken only if votes were unanimous. An autocratic ruler easily dominated a *zemskii sobor*, because it lacked the constitutional or legal right to share power. Unlike Western parliaments, which function as arenas of compromise, bargaining, and coalitions, the *zemskii sobor*

> is to represent the people in its intercourse with the authorities; its function is to confirm (or deny) the latter's legitimacy. It is, therefore, convened only when this legitimacy has, for some reason, been lost and is to be re-established. In this capacity it is expected to say either "yes" or "no," thereby assuming a markedly plebiscitary character. (Sergeyev and Biryukov 1993, 147)

If Sergeyev and Biryukov are right about the persistence of *sobornost* in the thinking of executive, legislative, and judicial leaders and average citizens throughout Russia, including many who consider themselves to be democrats, then congruence theories may help to explain the behavior of both President Yeltsin and his parliamentary adversaries. Yeltsin has wisely insisted on direct elections for the presidency of the Russian Soviet Federated Socialist Republic and post-Soviet Russia, but he has less wisely relied on plebiscites to reconfirm his authority, policies, and metapolicies and has persistently weakened the independent mass media, political parties, and other associational organizations common to civil societies. Beginning no later than his years as a top production executive in Sverdlovsk, Yeltsin developed a populist theory of democracy that was shaped by or, at the very least, reflected the legacy of *sobornost*.

Moreover, confrontation between the executive and legislative branches escalated sharply after the Soviet Union's demise. Supreme Soviet head Khasbulatov sought to discredit the president and to reverse his socioeconomic policies, and Yeltsin responded in kind to Khasbulatov. Eventually Khasbulatov tried to emasculate the presidency, Vice President Rutskoi appealed to the masses to overthrow the president, and Yeltsin responded by bombing the national legislature. Khasbulatov's *zemskii sobor* denied the legitimacy of a strong presidency, and Yeltsin's "tsarist" bureaucracy rebuffed the challenge. Both groups of rivals defined situations and chose tactics from perspectives compatible with *sobornost*; this concept sometimes motivated behavior, consciously or subconsciously, and at other times was used to justify behavior, often with appeals for broader elite and mass support.

Furthermore, Yeltsin's constitution has sought to legitimize a presidency and a burgeoning presidential apparatus that operate virtually unfettered by the executive as well as the legislative and judicial branches of government. As "head of state," only the president is the *"guarantor* of the Constitution of the Russian Federation and of human and civil rights and liberties"; only the president *"ensure[s]* the coordinated functioning and interaction of *[all]* the bodies of state power"; only the president *"determine[s]* the basic guidelines for the state's domestic and foreign policy"; and only the government, led by a chairman or premier, exercises *"executive power"* (Articles 80/1, 2, 3 and 110/1, italics added).[6]

Batkin (1995, 120), a cultural historian and democratic activist, affirms that "[t]he Russian president is clearly elevated above the three branches of government. He is like a fourth branch, or to be more accurate, the first and chief branch and in some sense, even the only branch." For instance, the president can grant or withhold membership in the Security Council to the chairmen of the State Duma and Federation Council, and he has exercised both options depending on the malleability of various parliamentary leaders. Oleg Lobov, former chief of the Security Council, offers a revealing comparison of the powers of the post-Soviet Russian president and those of the oligarchic Soviet Politburo. Notwithstanding the new constitution, Lobov confirms the current potential for autocratic rule: "The Politburo's decisions were binding. They were supposed to be put into effect automatically, while the Security Council is an advisory body whose resolutions can only be put into action by presidential decree. That is an important difference" (*Daily Report*, September 21, 1995, 35). Even Aleksandr M. Yakovlev (1995, 230, italics in original), Yeltsin's former personal representative to the parliament, acknowledges that Russian democracy is endangered by the *"paterfamilias* factor."

Will centuries-old traditions of autocratic ties between the tsar and his bureaucrats, village elders and their peasants, and fathers and their families induce post-Soviet Russians, especially in times of crisis, to look to their president as a father substitute? Or will a new-found belief in the separation of church and state and in the paramountcy of law—"the belief that God and the Law are above the president"—take root? Yakovlev (1995, 230–1) does not answer his own questions, prudently implying that the proverbial jury is still out on this crucial issue.

Significantly, the 1993 constitution not only gives the president virtually unlimited decree-making powers but was adopted in a very authoritarian manner. The Constitutional Assembly, which Yeltsin had established shortly after his electoral triumph in the April 1993 referendum, actively debated key provisions of the July 1993 draft constitution. However, when the Constitutional Assembly was reconvened, after Yeltsin's Pyrrhic victory in the October 1993 bombing of the "Rus-

sian White House," the president's staff did not consult assembly dele-
gates or top regional officials about major constitutional amendments.
Not surprisingly, many provisions concerning the separation of powers and federalism were weakened or deleted entirely. And the public
had little opportunity to read the document or hear unofficial commentary on it before the constitutional referendum of December 12. As
Dragunskii (1995, 149, italics in original) emphasizes,

> The reformers themselves have chosen to introduce democracy by highly
> undemocratic methods. Thus, in the context of present-day Russia, de-
> mocracy, rather than providing the *norm* (that is, the rules of political
> conduct), is a *value* (that is, a matter of conviction and sympathies) shared
> only by certain social groups. The democratic values of some groups are
> imposed as universal norms on other groups that actually share a differ-
> ent set of values which they, too, consider to be democratic.

After the plebiscite that ratified the 1993 constitution, President Yeltsin has selectively adjusted his old priorities and predispositions to
match the new political, economic, social, and cultural realities. Yeltsin
has tried to strengthen the citizenry's respect for constitutional law,
especially the powers of the presidency, and to institutionalize execu-
tive/legislative collaboration, especially by co-opting the top leaders
of the Duma and Federation Council. Also, he has created a Constitutional Court with ample de jure authority to resolve disputes between
national government institutions, between national and subnational institutions, and between top subnational institutions. And he eventually
approved a lengthy and detailed Civil Code, which guarantees on
paper, but which the current court system cannot enforce, many property rights and contractual obligations essential to the further development of private enterprise and foreign investment in Russia. Such
political innovations have weakly fostered the rule *of* law, procedural
democracy, popular consent, and governmental effectiveness, while
adapting rule *by* law and the traditional political culture of *sobornost.*
    Serious impediments to democratization include the venom and vin-
dictiveness of political rivalries throughout the Russian Federation; the
consolidation of power in "Red-Brown" regions and parties; the extraordinary concentration of wealth and access in about a dozen economic conglomerates; the weakness of democratic parties and
movements and of trade unions and associational interest groups;
and—perhaps most important—the pervasive corruption, crime, and
moral decay throughout government, business, and society as well as
the widespread public cynicism, anger, and angst in an alienating,
hardening, and unsettling ethos. Mafia penetration of political institu-

tions, kickbacks for rigged "auctions" of valuable state property, and bribes for large and small bureaucratic transactions have become the norm. Indeed, the very concept of "corruption" is problematic, because of the weakness of legal and ethical norms (Sergeyev 1998).

Such conclusions invite comparisons of the Soviet and post-Soviet political systems. Core elements of the Soviet polity included the top national leaders' power to determine public policies and policymaking procedures; to implement the state's priorities by mobilizing vast human and material resources, and to control all political, military, security, judicial, economic, social, educational, scientific-technological, mass media, religious, ethnic, and cultural (even avocational) institutions and organizations. Another core element was the arbitrary power of governmental ministers and provincial bosses, who were protected by their patrons in the Politburo and Central Committee apparatus and whose word was law in their functional or geographical fiefdoms.

In post-Soviet Russia's first two years, however, the stalemate between the president and the Supreme Soviet, the politicization of the Constitutional Court, the industrial and consumer price liberalization, and the precipitous economic decline for over half of the population all considerably weakened the national government, giving much greater leeway to regional and local leaders. Subsequently, more periodic or selected cooperation developed among the executive, legislative, and judicial branches of government at the national level and among the national, regional, and local governments, together with more dramatic privatization and marketization of the economy in many sectors and localities. But the ad hoc nature of these political agreements, the obvious favoritism to various regions, bureaucracies, and businesses, and the deterioration of basic social services and life expectancy remained sources of deep concern across the political spectrum.

The Theory and Practice of Emerging Democracy (1994 to the Present)

Western Perspectives

In the West, liberal politicians and political parties often try to concentrate power in the national executive branch and expand the public sector, and conservatives often try to disperse power among various governmental branches and levels and strengthen the private sector. In Russia, however, cross-cutting cleavages were produced by the concentration of leftists in the national parliament and rightists in the national government. The net result was a Russian state ruled, de jure, mostly by presidential decree and, de facto, mostly by regional and local governments, whose leaders ranged from market social democrats to "Red-Brown" reactionaries. The president's apparatus, the prime minister's bureaucracy, and the two chambers of the national legislature had considerable difficulty agreeing on metapolicies and substantive policies, implementing programs, allocating budgets, collecting taxes, paying civil servants, combatting rampant crime, providing basic social services, and equipping the demoralized armed forces. NATO expansion and Western influences, loss of the internal and external empires, and national pride and international respect became politically explosive issues. The desire to preserve great-power status was shared by most Russians, but "national-patriotic" appeals to reunite the Soviet Union, or to reimpose hegemony over parts of the Soviet bloc, resonated chiefly among older and rural segments of the population.

Succinctly put, there is nothing inevitable or unidirectional about "de-Sovietization" and "desatellitization." Both processes have been shaped by international pressure, national leadership, regional planning, local initiatives, and citizen activism. But both processes have amply demonstrated their resistance to these influences. Most important, de-Sovietization and desatellitization are not synonymous with democratization.

During the past two decades, dozens of authoritarian countries and former colonies have become more democratic, and some have even established stable democracies. Burgeoning theories and data exist about the dismantling of authoritarian and monarchical regimes, the building of viable constitutionalism and vibrant capitalism, and the development of a civil society and civic culture. Analysts of democratic transitions in Latin America and the Iberian peninsula have found high correlations among stable interelite ties, joint manipulation of malleable publics, and successful government performance as measured by socioeconomic outcomes. With notable exceptions, this literature has minimized the grassroots politics and socioeconomic prerequisites of emerging democracies, underscoring instead national political and economic initiatives as well as international and transnational socioeconomic linkages. The rule of law, minority rights, broad-based political parties, independent mass media, a large middle class, economic security for blue-collar workers and farmers, and tolerant mass and elite political cultures are deemed to be overly ambitious goals in the initial phase of transition but are presumed to be achievable in later phases leading to democratic consolidation.

Transitologists would not be at all surprised to observe that President Yeltsin has refused to align himself with any political party and that the new party formed by Prime Minister Chernomyrdin (with Yeltsin's blessing) consists predominantly of regional bureaucratic elites who are former Communist Party *apparatchiki*. Indeed, Yeltsin's and Chernomyrdin's concept of stability seems grounded on Brezhnev's discredited maxim "trust in cadres." A Russian journalist, Svetlana Shipunova, notes that when Chernomyrdin "launched the slogan 'Stability!', the economic managers and administrators understood him well: He was talking primarily about the stability of cadres, about ensuring that the next change of power did not involve a new reshuffle of leaders, and this is why they rushed to join Russia Is Our Home" (*Daily Report*, June 21, 1995, 16).

Many students of post-Soviet Russia are focusing on elite behaviors and attitudes. Stoner-Weiss (1997, 173–4), for one, stresses that close cooperation among regional political and economic elites promotes effective and legitimate policy making. In a well-documented study of four diverse localities, she found that a region's high "economic concentration" leads, in turn, to greater "collective action of economic actors," "collective action between political and economic actors," "consensus," and "higher performance." That is, the executives of sizable and similar enterprises tend to collaborate with one another and local government officials. Also, these enterprises are the nuclei of sizable and stable socioeconomic networks, which include farms, health clinics, and child care services to benefit factory workers and their families.

Stoner-Weiss (1997, 191–203) concludes that Putnam's ideas about civil society and civic culture, and by implication Eckstein's theory of congruence and balanced disparities, do not fit well in the initial phases of Russia's postcommunist transition but might become important in the longer run. She observed much greater trust, cooperation, and communication between some political and economic elites than between the elites and masses. Also, there were no significantly different mass authority patterns or intermediary organizations to explain significantly different governmental performance and legitimacy. The policies and policy-making procedures of top local politicians and enterprise directors were the key variables, and these explained quite well the wide differences in local government accomplishments and popularity. In short, constituents supported or accepted elite coalitions that produced tangible benefits.

Interelite bonds seem more important than congruent elite-mass authority patterns, and interest aggregation seems more important than interest articulation, during the initial phase of post-Soviet transition. Some analysts have reached these conclusions by focusing on the congeries of interelite and elite-mass networks, especially the ties between local politicians and enterprise directors and between a director and ordinary workers in a large factory or collective farm. Such traditional socioeconomic networks are behavioral and attitudinal and, while not impervious to change, act more as brakes on democratization than accelerators. Indeed, many old professional, departmental, and ethnic networks are becoming *more* important to financial success and physical survival in the free-wheeling and largely lawless economy of post-Soviet Russia. The broadening and deepening of mass commitment to democratic institutions (especially the rule of law, free elections, and competitive parties and interest groups) may depend heavily on the prior stabilization of elite interactions (especially conflict management) and socioeconomic outcomes (especially food supplies, good education, affordable medical care, and law and order). And, in Russia's civic and noncivic localities, collaboration between political and economic elites is being grounded on the authority patterns bequeathed by the Soviet regime.

Other observers have vigorously denied that "elites are central and publics peripheral" in postcommunist Russia, Ukraine, Belarus, and the Baltic and East-Central European countries. Bunce (1995b, 124ff.) affirms that the core concepts of "democratic transition," "democratic consolidation," and, "uncertainty" undergird primarily the elite interaction approach. Although she acknowledges in a footnote that "the key to democracy might be mass culture [or] elite political culture," she consistently highlights the significance of elite-mass linkages and bottom-up democratization. Also, Friedgut and Hahn (1994) have documented the development of grassroots politics in the post-Stalin era, and they underscore the increasing importance of local initiatives and self-reliance in the post-Soviet period. And Fish (1995b, 17 ff.) has focused on current informal groups and "democratic movement organizations," while placing heavy emphasis on "political opportunity structures and political entrepreneurship."

Bunce (1995b, 123–4, italics in original) lists many "crucial factors that are missing" in elitist theories of transition. These include "the centrality of national identity and nationalism in the process of democratization, the importance of the left as well as the right in shaping democratic prospects and, finally, all those thorny issues having to do with the state, its boundaries, its strength and its place within the international order." But even Bunce acknowledges that "pacted versus mass mobilization modes of transition do *not* explain patterns of success in democratic consolidation in the postcommunist world."

What, then, does explain such patterns? Post-Sovietologists have only begun to address this crucial question, and democratic theories do not seem likely to provide easy answers. For an important example,

Hough (1994a, 60) and others sharply distinguish between "democracy (majority rule) and constitutionalism (limitations on government and the majority)," and they contend that constitutional restraints on politicians and administrators must be imposed *before*, or at the very latest simultaneously with, free elections and fair campaigns. Hough (1994a, 61–62) laments that "Gorbachev and Yeltsin were both so contemptuous of the constitutional rules of the game and that both Russian and Western theories did not speak more of constitutional democracy than simply of democracy and democratization" (see also Hough 1997, 140–41 ff.). Influential advisers to Gorbachev and Yeltsin, in contrast, have argued that authoritarian leadership is necessary in the initial phases of liberalization or democratization, especially to control destructive conflicts arising from new "spiritual" freedoms, ethnic identities, and economic ambitions and deprivations. Elected executive leadership, not constitutional restraints and divided powers, is the quasi-democratic ideal.

For another example, scholars are just developing a theory about the types of constitutions that strengthen constitutionalism at successive stages of democratization. Holmes (quoted in Fischer 1996, 193) declares that the "optimal moment to draft and ratify a constitution . . . is the period when the memory of autocracy is balanced by the experience of chaos." But under perestroika and postcommunism most Russians quickly associated democratization and constitutionalism with economic deprivation and governmental corruption, as well as with intensifying lawlessness and insecurity throughout the society. The current Russian constitution is weakly grounded on elite-mass and interelite theories of representative democracy, and heavy emphasis is placed on presidential decrees and plebiscitary legitimation of presidential power. The enforcement of new constitutional and civil laws has been even weaker, especially in privatizing state property, taxing new business ventures, and creating a law-abiding citizenry.

Ironically, democratization in post-Soviet Russia was probably impeded by President Yeltsin's *insufficient* use of presidential power and by his *premature* efforts to establish a consensual policy-making process. After the August 1991 putsch, Yeltsin possessed charisma, electoral authority, and international acclaim, and he had enormous power to exercise transformational leadership. The president could have ordered new parliamentary elections to weaken further the reeling Communist Party and to bring many more democratically inclined deputies into the national, regional, and local legislatures. And he could have convoked a constitutional convention, representing disparate albeit predominantly noncommunist elements in society, and promulgated a real constitution, safeguarding individual liberties and limiting the powers of governmental bodies vis-à-vis one another and the citizenry. But Yeltsin tried unsuccessfully to collaborate with the Supreme Soviet deputies, who had been elected under reasonably democratic procedures in 1990. His draft constitutions differed considerably from the legislature's drafts, especially in the balance between executive and legislative powers. Political polarization and parochialism quickly gained the upper hand and, to make matters worse, were justified in the name of "constitutionalism."

Consequently, interelite confrontation and elite-mass dissonance were the chief legacies of "the first Russian republic" (1991–1993). Its successor (1994 to the present) was grounded on a shaky constitutional foundation, compounded by the despicable politics and economics of Moscow's military misadventure in Chechnya. Unbalanced disparities deepened political fragmentation throughout the Russian Federation, and subnational and associational institutions adjacent to national policy-making bodies were extremely self-serving or ineffectual. Only the promotion of Boris Nemtsov (from governor of Nizhnii Novgorod to first deputy prime minister) demonstrated that considerable democratic and capitalist skills could be brought to a high national office.

When all is said and done, Eckstein's theory of stable democracy is of enormous heuristic value but does not contain propositions easily testable in the current unstable Russian context. The past decade has produced a "permanent revolution" in Russia's political "superstructure" and socioeconomic "base," and the search for congruent authority patterns can be frustrating under such conditions. Propositions about balanced disparities are especially difficult to operationalize because of the revolutionary changes in social organizations, professional incentives, and income distribution, as well as in policy-making institutions, public policies, and the power of the state.

But the comprehensiveness and parsimony of Eckstein's theory are major strengths, particularly when confronting a highly complex and unstable configuration of variables and when juxtaposing middle-range theoretical frameworks with a wealth of new data. Minimally, Eckstein's basic concepts and hypotheses will enable post-Sovietologists to ask more penetrating questions in our archival, interview, and public opinion research. Maximally, Eckstein's ideas will help us to focus more clearly on state-society and elite-mass linkages and to identify key factors and relationships that are spurring or impeding Russia's democratization and marketization.

Russian Perspectives

Whether the public statements of government leaders reveal their real beliefs and motivations is always debatable. But the pronouncements of pragmatic Russian politicians and analysts, in addition to the results of elite and mass opinion surveys, can be elucidated by selected democratic theories. Consider the clear exposition and forceful advocacy of Eckstein's theory of balanced disparities by Moscow mayor Yury Luzhkov in an interview with journalists.

> Generally speaking, it is difficult to work with people we do not like. But although it is difficult for us personally, we have to think of the task itself. When I was leaving a large enterprise where I had been director, I told my colleagues: Under no circumstances get rid of people with nonstandard thinking. If you throw these uncomfortable, abnormal, or semi-normal people out of your system, you will immediately feel relief. Life will become easier for you, because these people always stir things up. These are people who always are unhappy with something, always looking for faults. But if you get rid of nonstandard people—that is it, forget it. In a couple of years the company will go downhill.
>
> The same is true here [in Moscow city government]. Therefore, I consider the symbiosis of experienced cadres with our revolutionaries the most effective mix. (*Daily Report*, August 8, 1995, 16)

Luzhkov's conception of democracy places heavy emphasis on inter-elite collaboration but also includes elite-mass congruence, governmental responsiveness to the electorate, and the independence of the mass media. "The task of the authorities is not to command or govern—it is to serve. And the principles of interaction between the people and the authorities must be strictly defined by the tasks the people (voters) delegate to the authorities. . . . The mass media must serve as an intermediary that determines the people's reaction to the authorities' fulfillment of their functions" (*Daily Report*, August 8, 1995, 17).

Consider also four Russian theories of congruence, the first eloquently voiced by longtime democrat and human rights activist Sergei Kovalev (1995, 2):

> In a truly democratic and law-abiding state the ruling regime is so wise that it deliberately limits itself—not only with the help of specially promulgated laws, but also by instituting independent bodies to control the regime. One such instance is the control over the observance of human rights that exists in many countries. . . .
>
> Freedom of the press is not merely a fundamental human value, but is the key guarantor of all other liberties. It is impossible to combat violations when it is impossible to say anything openly. . . .
>
> [The Russian people must reject] the idea that is very popular among the top state apparatchiks: that there is no straight road from totalitarianism to democracy, that Russia "which is not yet ripe for democracy" must first live under authoritarianism.

In this situation it will hardly be possible to advance liberal and democratic ideas from above, let alone from organizations that function "under the president." There is a need to build strong, professional social structures that are able to force the state to take responsibility for its actions. In short, it is necessary to build a civic society that has never existed in Russia, and without which genuine democracy is impossible.

Kovalev's vision of constitutional democracy is grounded on Western ideals. He insists that stable democracy can be achieved only by democratic methods. It is almost as if Kovalev keeps the Leninist experience in the forefront of his mind, underscoring (like Bertrand Russell and Barrington Moore) that the pursuit of humanistic ends by authoritarian means is a path to disaster: the means will subvert and eventually swallow up the ends. Also, Kovalev implicitly distinguishes between constructive and destructive forms of elite-mass congruence, contrasting a citizenry's active participation in public life with its passive acquiescence in a leadership's usurpation of power. And Kovalev would surely support the Russian people's increasing linkages with their regional and local institutions and leaders and would encourage civic organizations to make demands on all three branches and all three levels of government, holding them accountable for their actions and inaction.

Vladimir Shumeiko—former head of the Council of the Federation and a man with strong ties to the old and new nomenklatura elites—emphasizes the difficulties and risks of rapid democratization, especially with insufficient channels for citizen participation and government accountability:

The creation of a full-fledged democratic society in Russia is impossible in the nearest future. Under conditions of underdevelopment of the institutions of civil society, the low level of civic culture, and the long absence of the capacity of the Russian people to play a decisive role in public life, an abrupt transition to "democracy without limits," forced restructuring of the economy on a market basis, and harsh decentralization of social administration—all this taken together has already created a social and ideological vacuum, which may once again lead to serious economic and sociopolitical shocks.

In order for society to function in a stable manner on democratic principles, it is not enough to introduce the external attributes of democracy: openness, freedom of speech, freedom of assembly, elections, and the creation of political and civic organizations. The main thing is to create a system of management of society, in which its citizens play the decisive role. Only such as system is capable of limiting the omnipotence of the bureaucratic state apparatus and subordinating it to a mechanism of people's power, which is democratically formulated, controlled, and changed at the will of the citizens. (*Daily Report*, June 1, 1995, 16–17)

To a Westerner, however, Shumeiko's distinction between "external" and presumably "internal" components of democracy is problematic, and there are lingering Soviet connotations to his concepts of "democracy without limits" and "a system of management of society."

Yury Levada's public opinion polls are probing "the canon of Russians' social consciousness" and are identifying huge divergences between elite and mass authority patterns and political expectations. He affirmed in 1995, italicizing and quoting important concepts:

> The acute tension and mutual criticism between the ruling structures and the "public" is an unprecedented phenomenon in contemporary [Russian] domestic history, at least since 1917. The situation of practically free expression of opposition toward the authorities' actions in a setting of militarized tension is an unquestionable sign of the formation of some elements of a civil society. . . .
>
> However, public criticism of the authorities' actions and the particular actors has had no tangible effect. . . , since there are no mechanisms in society to convert the energy of criticism into real force.
>
> Events in late 1994 and early 1995 showed with excruciating clarity that there is no democratic *order* presupposing mass *participation* in the activity of power structures and mass *influence* on their decisions operating in Russia. Practically all elements or rudiments of democracy which appeared and took root in society after the collapse of the Soviet regime are part of *"symbolic"* democracy. . . . [This] is a "democracy of chaos [disorder]," and one which is strong enough to make it difficult to mobilize public sentiments under the old or slightly updated great-power banners, but too weak to take shape in organized structures, political or state. In the conflicting configuration of Russia's forces and structures in society and on the political stage, "democratic chaos" is doomed to play an important role for a long time. (*Daily Report Supplement*, May 11, 1995, 18–19)

But note that Levada's "democracy of order" and "democracy of chaos" might create expectations of a strong-armed presidency and plebiscitary democracy, rather than of legally based metapolicies and governmental responsiveness to myriad associational organizations.

Contrast the ideals expressed by Luzhkov, Kovalev, Shumeiko, and Levada with those *deleted* from the final draft of the Yeltsin constitution, and it becomes clearer why authority has devolved so rapidly from the national to the local level in Russia. As Rumyantsev (1995, 26 ff.) notes, "The new Constitution does not set the limits and purposes of the state" and fails to ensure "public control" over the executive branch or "legal control" over the legislative and judicial branches.

These principles were included in earlier drafts, which declared that "the state is an official representative of the society and expresses its will within the framework of the Constitution. The state, its organs and officials serve the whole of society and not any part thereof and are responsible to society and the citizens."

Of course, Luzhkov, Shumeiko, and other politicians may not always practice what they preach, and Kovalev was forced to resign as head of the president's human rights commission, after reporting atrocities from Chechnya and accusing Yeltsin of committing "a constitutional crime." Also, Kovalev, Rumyantsev, and other democratic activists may have a somewhat idealized view of functioning democracies, especially in their early phases of development. Recall, for example, that over six hundred thousand Americans died in a civil war contesting the territorial integrity and constitutional principles of the nation, that American federalism produced sharp conflicts between states' rights and civil liberties for a century thereafter, that a mounting tide of American opposition to the Vietnam War went unheeded for almost a decade by two presidents of different parties, and that campaign financing laws continue to be violated or circumvented by Democrats and Republicans.

But the five very different Russians quoted earlier have unequivocally supported several or many core elements of democratic theory. They have vividly described the impact of insufficient elite-mass congruence and imbalanced disparities on the disjointed development of democratic governance in post-Soviet Russia, on the erratic performance of its national government, and on the disappointments of ordinary citizens. As Levada reported in October 1994, nearly half of the Russian electorate agreed that Western democratic principles are "incompatible" with Russian traditions. Also, in a 1995 poll conducted by the Sociological Research Center of Moscow State University, Muscovites were asked to identify the main element of democracy; only 10.1 percent chose "power of the people" and 16.8 percent "freedom of the individual," but 51.2 percent chose "legality, law and order"—not to be confused with effective legal limitations on the president, separation of powers, federalism, or checks and balances (*Daily Report*, August 24, 1995, 53). And, as Richard Dobson's survey found in September 1993, a remarkable 71 percent of Russians identified the chief characteristic of democracy to be either "economic prosperity," "a judicial system that treats everyone equally," or "a government that provides for citizens' basic needs"—not a strong multiparty system, market economy, freedom to criticize politicians, minority rights, or free elections (cited in Millar 1995, 13).

In short, the Russian people seem much less interested in procedural democracy than substantive outcomes. Their primary concern is not the amount of Yeltsin's power but his inability to use it effectively, thereby squandering authority and creating counterproductive tensions with the other branches and levels of government. Very few Russians are pleased with the performance of their national government, including the directly elected president and legislators. Many more Russians are satisfied with the performance of their subnational governments, which have been left to their own devices and have employed a wide variety of methods to cope with pressing problems. In many regions and localities there may be a good fit between elite and mass authority patterns, and stable civic and noncivic subsystems include diverse combinations of authoritarian and democratic patterns.

The Prospects for Democratic Consolidation

One hopes that Russia can participate in the worldwide "tsunami" of democratization since the 1970s and that Russia will quickly progress toward the expansion of political rights and civil liberties. But neither the intraelite nor elite-mass theories of democracy offer much encouragement for democratic consolidation in Russia in the foreseeable future. Democracy without constitutionalism can easily revert to liberal authoritarianism. And reasonably free and unrestricted voting as well as a largely unchecked and unbalanced division of governmental powers are Russia's main accomplishments to date. Viable constitutionalism, checks and balances, fair election campaigns, effective political parties, interest group access to the policy process, citizen participation in decision making, and an ideology of "democratic patriotism" often take generations to embed in a polity. As Eckstein reminds us, unstable democracy is much more common than stable democracy.

Yanov (1987) observes that thirteen attempts at reforms have been made in Russia since the sixteenth century, and all have been reversed by force or faded away. He argues that the coming counterreform may be the worst of all, because the breakup of the Soviet military superpower will spur weapons proliferation, nuclear terrorism, environmental degradation, and ethnic cleansing and will thereby harm the West and weaken international organizations (Yanov 1987, 193–5 ff.). But public opinion polls and studies of actual behavior support a more optimistic view. Filatov and Vorontsova (1995, 227) conclude:

> The West has yet to realize that paralleling the peaceful political evolution of post-Soviet Russian society, the worldview (*mirovozzrenie*) of the Russian people has undergone a change no less radical in scope than that

caused by the 1917 Revolution. It has taken most Russians just a few years to cast aside values that traditionally have been regarded as inalienable features of their national mind-set: an omnipotent state possessing quasi-religious authority, disdain for wealth, egalitarian beliefs about property, conformity of opinion, collectivism, anti-Western attitudes, and the rejection of democracy and liberalism.

Whether this "psychological revolution" will deepen and broaden, and whether it will be easily reversed by socioeconomic crises or political movements, will be determined by contemporary Russian leaders and citizens. Notwithstanding the powerful authoritarian legacies from centuries-old Russian traditions and from the traumatic Soviet *Gleichschaltung*, Russians can choose to eschew historical determinism or any other kind of determinism (e.g., cultural, economic, or technological).

Why? Because some genies just cannot be put back in a bottle. Glasnost cannot be reversed. Russian borders will remain permeable to instant telecommunications, space satellites, and information technology. And many Russian media professionals, in addition to a sizable segment of the public, will continue to value *their* free access to the media, if not the general principle of a "fourth estate."

Moreover, individuals, groups, and even nations occasionally learn from their mistakes and gradually or abruptly change course. True, the war in Chechnya followed the bombing of the White House, which followed the Russian army's active participation in Georgia's civil war and overt intimidation in Moldova. And the performance of Russia's national government and the difficulties of everyday life are deemed to be unacceptable or intolerable by the overwhelming majority of citizens. But Russians are proposing a wide variety of solutions to their problems and are comprehending the importance of local and individual initiatives. There seems to be lessening disagreement about the nature of Russia's material and spiritual ills, and Russians' traditional capacity for suffering and delayed gratification may be diminishing.

Furthermore, freely elected former Communists are usually more responsive to their constituents than nomenklatura-appointed *apparatchiki*, and the privatization of municipal property can sometimes lead to creative decisions and effective implementation that benefit the entire locality. True, we are witnessing a self-serving quest for stability among certain elites who have benefited greatly since perestroika and the USSR's disintegration. And rule *by* law does not necessarily lead to the rule *of* law. But law and order are surely preferable to Russia's flirtation with anarchy during the 1990s.

De-Stalinization and desatellization will be completed when and if the Russian Federation fully disbands the Soviet Union's internal and external empires, immense military-security complex, and centrally managed economy and abandons all vestiges of cultural and ideological chauvinism at home and of geostrategic and commercial expansionism in the "near abroad." Democratization will develop when and if the different branches of levels of government, national and regional constitutions, electoral laws, political parties, and interest groups can establish legitimate and effective policy-making procedures, which in turn can produce feasible socioeconomic policies that are implemented and accepted by the citizenry, especially the voting public ("new institutionalism" in the broadest and deepest sense).

Yet the most important components of Russia's democratization may be the gradual resolution of the national identity, minority rights, and distributive justice issues. It is hard to conceive of a stable democracy in the Russian Federation without a widespread consensus about Russia's territorial boundaries and administrative subdivisions, a legal system that protects the civil liberties of all nationalities and strata, and official secular and religious support for an inclusive interpretation of the concept of "a Russian" (*rossiianin*, citizen of the Russian Federation, rather than *russkii*, ethnic Russian). In both the Soviet and post-Soviet periods the "Russian (*Russkaia*) Orthodox Church" has differed from its tsarist counterpart, the "Orthodox Russian (*Rossiiskaia*) Church." And the current name is likely to be retained, because church leaders are loathe to abandon their parishioners and property in the former republics of the Soviet Union (Kavrus-Hoffmann 1997, 7). Also, all Russian political leaders, especially ultranationalists, have taken a keen interest in the treatment of the twenty-five million ethnic Russians living outside Russia. This highly charged issue might become as important as socioeconomic stratification in retarding the development of a genuine democracy in Russia and a genuine commonwealth of Soviet successor states. Unfortunately, the loudest voices supporting Russian rights abroad are usually the quietest voices supporting non-Russian rights at home. But it would surely spur democratization to agree to disagree about the meaning of being "Russian" in all countries of the former Soviet Union. "Social capital" and "systems of trust" must be nurtured within and among these countries.

Some of the core elements of a viable constitutional order have begun to take root in Russia, but none is flourishing and all are perishable. A democratic legislature, judiciary, and political party system are in a very early stage of development at the national level, and democratic governance is progressing very unevenly in the regions and localities. To be sure, the disintegration of the Soviet Union has brought Russians considerable freedom from governmental intrusiveness and a state that used law as an instrument to control society. But the post-Soviet Russian government has hardly begun to bring citizens freedom *within* a democratic policy process, and neither the state nor society seems to respect or be restrained by law. Yeltsin himself declared in August 1995, "Until we have a strong rule of law, until we have a developed system of legal protection for human rights (including protection against the arbitrariness of officials), until we have a middle class (the bedrock of stability), and until constitutional values become part of people's self-awareness, we will not be able to talk seriously about democracy" (*Daily Report*, August 21, 1995, 24). Fine words, of course, but they come from an elected president whose view of his mandate retains elements of tsarism and *sobornost* and whose view of a law-governed state sometimes seems more Soviet than democratic.

In fact, some core elements of the Soviet polity are lingering or even thriving in post-Soviet Russia. Most important are oligarchic rule at the national and subnational levels; a self-serving symbiosis between political and economic elites; a rather weak and still politicized judiciary; a fairly strong and independent security police; environmental degradation; male chauvinism; Russian discrimination against non-Russians; and, throughout the population, an inability or unwillingness to distinguish between rule *by* law and the rule *of* law. As Rosenberg (1995, 407) forcefully concludes, "The opposite of communism is not anti-communism, which at times resembles it greatly. The opposite is tolerance and the rule of law."

Russia's constitution generates portentous pressures by mixing rhetoric about a strong democratic state with the political realities of a weak authoritarian state. According to the constitution, the president has more than enough power to shape his own programs, and the people have the right to hold him accountable for the consequences. In practice, Yeltsin lacks the power to implement most of his policy initiatives and disclaims accountability for most negative outcomes. Amorality, avarice, aggressiveness, and anxiety among the citizenry have their counterparts in the executive and legislative branches of government, perhaps especially at the national level, and have greatly reduced the chances of enforcing anticrime, tax, and election laws in the public interest. As Yeltsin openly acknowledged in February 1995, "All state activities are in need of radical reformation, first and foremost the decision-making process and personnel policy. What we are talking about is the observation of laws and ethical standards by the representatives of state power, and of getting rid of corrupt persons in a decisive manner" (*Daily Report*, February 16, 1995, 8).

Some prominent Western economists argue that a market economy has already been created in Yeltsin's protodemocracy (e.g., Aslund

1995). True, the new Civil Code is an important step in that direction. But the elastic legal distinctions between corruption and entrepreneurship, as well as the pervasiveness of economic crime and the weakness of judicial enforcement of the Civil Code, make this argument hard to sustain. Marketization and privatization must be grounded on the rule of law. If business contracts, property rights, and tax obligations can be easily flaunted or circumvented by bribery, and if these basic legal norms cannot be upheld in independent courts of law, it is impossible to construct a stable and broad-based capitalist economy. Private ownership of urban land and private sale or purchase of rural land are still not guaranteed by law. Also, surveys of Russian public opinion confirm that "the overwhelming majority of both elites and masses continue to favor state ownership of *all* heavy industry" (Kullberg and Zimmerman 1996, 19, italics in original). And, in a commissioned report to the president's staff, sociologist Olga Kryshtanovskaya (1995, A27) concluded: "I think we can describe today's Russia as socialism for the elite and capitalism for the people. . . . The political elite gets economic privileges, and ordinary people are free to sell goods in kiosks."

Russian democrats are sharply divided in their assessments of economic performance and in their prescriptions for remedying economic dilemmas. Yavlinsky (1995, A1) asserts that democratic political reforms "have become associated in too many minds with robbing the people and imposing hardship on the many for the benefit of the few." Former Prime Minister and rival democratic party leader Yegor Gaidar (quoted in Yavlinsky 1995, A2) contends that "the market will break up monopolies, create private property, and allow individuals to start new businesses." Yavlinsky (1995, A2) disagrees: "only real Government leadership can accomplish these goals." Kovalev, in a clear signal to Russian democrats, chose to join Gaidar's political party rather than Yavlinsky's.

Significantly, many Russians equate democratic reforms not only with greater freedom of speech and religion but with the loss of the external and internal empires, domestic political stalemate, economic hardship, ethnic rivalry, rising crime rates, and a wide range of professional and personal anxieties. Because of the surprisingly peaceful breakup of the Soviet Union and the Soviet bloc, most of the former bureaucratic elites have been able to preserve or increase their power and wealth in a freer and more chaotic polity, economy, and society. However, the prospects of the peasantry, factory workers, and cultural, technical, and military intelligentsias are deteriorating. The same is true for entire ethnic groups and geographical regions. Sergei Fateyev, head of the Reforma International Fund's Strategy Department, reported the results of a comprehensive and multiyear survey in 1995:

THE STANDARD OF LIVING OF MORE THAN HALF OF THE POPULATION HAS FALLEN SIGNIFICANTLY over the last few years, it has become relatively stable for approximately a fifth of the population, and it has risen for about 15 percent of the population. . . . For the bulk of the population, the perestroika and transformations of 1992–1994 have produced nothing good in the social sense. (*Daily Report Supplement*, May 31, 1995, 17, emphasis in original)

The Russian researchers concluded that the country is undergoing "a unique stratification revolution," in which social and demographic groups have exchanged places with respect not only to incomes but also to status, power, and access to information.

These socioeconomic upheavals have destabilized virtually all physical and psychological elements of daily life and work, thereby weakening the efficacy and legitimacy of the state. Yes, some citizens, especially young urban males, have welcomed the new freedoms and entrepreneurial opportunities. However, the nonpayment of wages and the drop in the standard of living of most Russians have generated considerable resentment among salaried workers and occupational associations, as well as antipathy toward governmental institutions and officials, especially at the national level. And many Russian citizens have been quick to blame democratic politicians and market reformers, as well as non-Russian ethnic groups and Western businessmen, for unemployment, bankruptcy, hyperinflation, increased crime, and reduced social services.

In contrast, American citizens esteem the ideals, if not always the operation, of their political and economic systems. Separation of powers, federalism, checks and balances, rule of law, minority rights, and free enterprise are laudable goals, given the American proclivity to limit governmental power and not to rely on governmental institutions. We want these structures, procedures, and predispositions to fragment power and to generate the compromises, coalitions, and comity that ensure responsive leadership, as well as the opportunities, restraints, and guarantees that foster responsible individualism.

Such ideas about democratic governance and citizenship have never been an integral and durable part of Russian political theory or practice, although Russian variants of these ideas have surfaced and been temporarily institutionalized over the past millennium. Nascent democratic structures began with the elements of direct democracy in Kievan Rus, notably the *veche* or open town meeting for key decisions, and included the occasional enlightened restructuring, protodemocratic bodies, and protest movements thereafter, especially the legal and local government reforms of Alexander II, the dumas and constitution of Nicholas II, and the coalition Provisional Government and elected Constituent Assembly of 1917–1918. Emphasizing the periodically emerging and unsuppressible democratic tendencies in Russian politics, Peter Juviler (personal correspondence, 1996) rhetorically and perceptively inquires, "Was there not revealed twice this century a fatal rigidity of absolutism, and then of communism, no less telling than was the absolutist history of less-modernizing Russia before that?" (see also Petro 1995). To be sure, a sizable majority of Russians have exercised their right to vote in contested national, regional, and local elections since 1989 (White et al. 1997). But only a tiny number of dissidents in post-Stalin Russia and only a small segment of the electorate in post-Soviet Russia have strongly supported the democratic principles of majority rule and minority rights, and the current democratic parties are badly divided over the practical applications of these principles. In addition, public opinion polls show that elite and mass support for democracy has been shaken by the political, economic, and social traumas of the Yeltsin presidency (e.g., Fleron 1996b).

Approaching the year 2000, the Russian Federation's peoples have never been more demanding of their governmental institutions and never more capable of ignoring them. The cleavages among structures of the state and among strata of the society, and between state and society, are numerous and could easily deepen. There is a corrosive political apathy, cynicism, and hostility toward government—especially among older and rural wage earners toward the presidential apparatus and its privatization programs. To be sure, free elections, freedom of speech, and freedom of association have facilitated more direct and indirect public representation in the policy process, especially in subnational governmental bodies. But democratic participation can flourish only if Russian elected officials are much more responsive to the needs of all of their constituents, and only if a multiparty system, independent interest groups, and civil service bureaucracy, as well as the separation of powers, federalism, and checks and balances, become constitutionally grounded at the national, regional, and local levels. These are very big "ifs." For the foreseeable future, Russian democrats will find it exceedingly difficult to pursue successful political careers, to implant the institutions of viable constitutionalism, and to nurture the traditions of a civil society, civil economy, and civic culture. The transformation of democratic *forms* into democratic *norms*—especially the constitutional, civil, criminal, electoral, and tax laws—is crucial for democracy to take root throughout Russia.

Western countries can influence post-Soviet Russia's development only at the margins, and Western diplomacy, economic pressures, and technocratic counsel have already begun to generate more resentment than gratitude. But the United States, Western Europe, and Japan, as well as the would-be democracies of Eastern Europe, the Baltics, and the Commonwealth of Independent States, have an immense stake in Russia's democratization and marketization. Our national, regional, and local governments should expand their bonds with Russia through diplomatic, economic, and "sister city" ties, respectively. Moreover, our legal, educational, commercial, and not-for-profit institutions and organizations should double their efforts to help Russians create a stable constitutional democracy and a prosperous market economy. And it is to be hoped that such collaboration will produce a theory of democratization and marketization that incorporates the realities of Russian experience.

Notes

An earlier version of this essay was presented at the 1995 Annual Meeting of the American Political Science Association, Chicago, August 31–September 3, 1995. I wish to thank Frederic J. Fleron Jr., Peter Juviler, Nadia Kavrus-Hoffmann, and Robert Sharlet for their very helpful comments on an earlier draft of this chapter.

1. But note the increasing emphasis on elite-mass bonds in the writings of some theorists. For example, cf. Dahl's *A Preface to Democratic Theory* (1956) and *Democracy and its Critics* (1989), and cf. Huntington's *The Third Wave: Democratization in the Late Twentieth Century* (1991) and *The Clash of Civilizations and the Remaking of World Order* (1996).

2. For thoughtful "checklists" of political rights and civil liberties, see Freedom House (1996, 530–44). The accurate measurement and annual reassessment of these rights and liberties, however, pose formidable data gathering and analytical problems, which demand a much larger staff of full-time researchers and many more on-site investigations than those supported by the limited resources of Freedom House.

3. See especially Eckstein, "Congruence Theory Explained," chap. 1 in this volume; see also Eckstein (1992b; 1980; 1969, 269–325; 1971); and Eckstein and Gurr (1975). According to Eckstein and Gurr (1975, 22, 403, italics in original), "An *authority pattern* is a set of asymmetric relations among hierarchically ordered members of a social unit that involves the direction of the unit," and "Congruence is a 'relational' property of a set of authority patterns." Authority patterns and governmental performance are viewed as either causes or effects, and the relationships between performance variables (e.g., allegiance, conflict management, efficacy, efficiency) and authority variables (e.g., dimensional and configurative) are explored (see overview table, Eckstein and Gurr, 1975,

469). Note that Eckstein and Gurr focus on authority rather than power relations, thus incorporating the concept of legitimization (and conceivably elite self-legitimization) into their theory. And note that authority patterns are policy-making practices rather than policy outcomes, thus underscoring the synergistic interaction between procedural democracy and substantive democracy, and the need to establish the former before the latter in democratic transitions.

4. On the important but underutilized concept of "civil economy," see Rose (1992, 1993). Distinguishing between "civil" (legal) and "uncivil" (nonlegal) market economies, he defines the former as a market that operates "within a framework in which public officials act according to the rule of law as laid down by a properly elected government, and individual citizens and private enterprises obey the law, including obligations to pay taxes" (Rose 1993, 2).

On the familiar but often misunderstood concept of "civic culture," recall that Almond and Verba (1963, 30) define it as "a mixed political culture" in which "participant political orientations combine with and do not replace subject and parochial political orientations." This conceptualization is highly compatible with Eckstein's concept of "balanced disparities."

5. See also Colton (1995), especially the analysis of Yeltsin's "mismanagement of economic reform" and "the near absence of . . . the harnessing of mass support" (60–65). And see Brudny's (1995, 75–101) essay on the consequences of irreconcilable disputes over metapolicies in a "regime founding coalition."

6. Probably the best English translation of the 1993 constitution is in *Current Digest of the Post-Soviet Press* 45 (December 8, 1993): 4–16. For the official Russian and English versions under one cover, see *Konstitutsiia Rossiiskoi Federatsii: The Constitution of the Russian Federation* (Moscow: Iuridicheskaya Literatura, 1994).

5

Congruence Theory as a Perspective on Russian Politics

William M. Reisinger

It is to the good that debates continue about how we study transitions away from communist rule. The changes that have occurred and will occur in a society such as Russia can make sense only with the help of theory. Similarly, theories of democratization and other political change need to confront postcommunist developments to become more sophisticated. Those who start from an interest in the transitional societies and those who start from an interest in the theories are both hard at work, sometimes clashing over what forms research should take (e.g., Terry 1993; Schmitter and Karl 1994; Bunce 1995a, 1995b). Yet debates about theory, method, and findings should be combined, as this volume attempts to do. In this chapter, I address the question that sets this volume off from other discussions of postcommunist change: How well does Eckstein's congruence theory illuminate Russian political change, in particular Russia's prospects to achieve stable democratic governance?

As Eckstein explains in chapter 1, congruence theory comprises a complex tapestry of arguments extended from the postulate that, to paraphrase, polities will be effective and long-lasting if and only if their operating principles (their "authority patterns") are basically similar to (i.e., are congruent with) the operating principles that guide the country's political parties, civic groups, local governments, even churches, PTAs and other social units. Eckstein persuasively argues that much good flows from such congruence and that in its absence, the machinery of government is likely to get out of whack.

A split second's reflection about today's Russia brings to mind many ways in which congruence theory could provide insight into what underlies Russian politics. Yet, as Eckstein discovered when he set up the Princeton Workshop to apply congruence theory to numerous countries in the late 1960s and early 1970s (Eckstein and Gurr 1975), it takes enormous work to measure the concepts of congruence theory. Is such effort worth undertaking in Russia and, by extension, in other new democracies? I answer a tentative yes. I will first discuss Eckstein's congruence theory, then examine how it pertains to current Russian political developments, especially the quest for a stable democratic order.

Congruence Theory as a Perspective on Politics

Congruence theory directs one's attention to whether a country's governmental authority pattern is similar in its important aspects to the authority patterns that characterize nongovernmental spheres in the society. Eckstein theorizes that countries exhibiting this similarity will be more likely to exhibit stability in their systems of rule. If true, this view matters greatly for contemporary efforts to strengthen the institutions and practices of democracy in formerly authoritarian systems. Instances of democratic institutions that fail to be stable outnumber instances of democratic institutions that have survived for, say, fifty or more years. Scholars of "democratization" typically use that term to denote a process with stages: (1) undermining the authoritarian regime, (2) establishing democratic institutions and (3) (the longest, most difficult stage) the consolidation of those democratic institutions (see, e.g., Rustow 1970). Eckstein's congruence theory began as an effort to understand *democratic* stability, the most vexing issue in the study of democratization, and his treatment (1992b) of Weimar Germany reflects that case's importance as a failure of democratic institutions to become consolidated (to evince stability).

Where does congruence theory fit, then, in the panoply of theories of democratization? I have sought elsewhere (Reisinger 1996) to cluster democratization theories. The first cluster consists of those scholars who examine one or another aspect of the society in question—the level of economic development (e.g., Lipset 1959) or public attitudes (e.g., Almond and Verba 1963; Inglehart 1990), for instance—as a requisite condition for the development of democracy. The second cluster uses historical case studies to identify the factors influencing the sequencing of political change (e.g., Moore 1966a; Skocpol 1979; Rueschemeyer, Stephens, and Stephens 1992). The third cluster consists of those focusing on the choices and strategies of key political elites during (short-term) struggles over the shape of political life in a given country (e.g., O'Donnell, Schmitter, and Whitehead 1986; Przeworski 1988). The final cluster examines the nature of the democratic institutions established in order to judge how likely it is that those institutions will survive the challenges they will inevitably face (e.g., Lijphart 1984; Grofman and Lijphart 1986; Linz 1990a). Each of the four has been developed by numerous scholars and includes as much diversity as it does unity. Those in the first two clusters stress long-term developments within a society and downplay the actions and decisions made during the process of transition away from authoritarianism.[1]

Congruence theory is fascinating and merits a revival among theorists of democratization because it spans almost all four of these clusters without fitting snugly into any. Like those scholars in the first cluster, congruence theory points to the importance of societal characteristics. Yet, it does not focus on masses of individual values, income levels, or whatever else serves as a "prerequisite" or even just as a "requisite" of democratic stability. Instead, it focuses on a specific type of *relationship* among individual members of the society (i.e., on authority patterns). To apply congruence theory to a given country, one must know something about long-term historical developments and how those influenced the rise of certain authority patterns throughout the society. Congruence theory does not, however, call for process tracing of key turning points in the country's past. It suggests that prospects for elites to make choices during the key transition period that will eventually result in stable democracy cannot be specified a priori without knowledge of that society's authority patterns. It also highlights that the question of how to "transplant" democratic institutions, which may work quite well elsewhere, into new democracies depends on existing authority patterns. Some hosts may reject the foreign invader, while others may engage in a process of mutual adaptation with the foreign institutions, resulting in a successful transplant.

Many of those interested in democratic consolidation posit that the key is the *endurance* of the democratic institutions for a sufficiently long time (or, in any case, that endurance reflects the achievement of other things so that endurance can be used as an indicator of success). Huntington (1991) proposes what he calls the "two-turnover test": we can judge a set of democratic institutions to have endured sufficiently long to be considered consolidated when competitive elections have produced two genuine changes of governing party. The two turnovers might occur rather quickly, in which case this would be a sign that elites and the public had already learned at a minimum how to use democratic institutions to "throw the bums out."

While this does seem a significant milestone, Eckstein gets at the more intriguing issue, it seems to me, by making endurance only one part of his understanding of "stability." Besides enduring, a stable system of governance "implies effective decisionmaking—'effective' not in the sense of right action on the basis of some particular scheme of values, but in the basic sense of action itself, any sort of action, in pursuit of shared political goals or in adjustment to changing conditions. . . . A government must govern." (Eckstein 1992b, 184; see also 209).

This leads to Eckstein's treatment of the state in his writings. Frankly, I find puzzling Eckstein's animosity toward the importance in twentieth-century political science of the state (see Eckstein 1992b, 182–183; Eckstein and Gurr 1975, chap. 1) and his preference for the term *government*.[2] I see no reason that advocating greater attention to society requires denigrating the analytic utility of the concept of a state. (This is not to say that every society must have a state, but why ignore that some do?) I further see little fundamental difference between Eckstein's use of the term *government* and what others would call *the state*. The term *government* can have several meanings among political scientists, though some clearly are not what Eckstein means: Given the major variables of congruence theory, it cannot be that Eckstein understands government to mean the executive agencies of a polity (the cabinet or the council of ministers, what the French Constitution specifies as the *gouvernement*). It also cannot be that Eckstein understands government to mean one set of leaders, since it would not fit the macro purposes of congruence theory to analyze how congruent "the Clinton administration's authority pattern" is with authority patterns in American society. Clearly, he uses the term in the colloquial American sense to mean "every official in Washington D.C.," or "Moscow," and so forth. "The government" of Britain for purposes of congruence theory did not change when Major replaced Thatcher. "The government" of Russia for purposes of congruence theory includes Yeltsin and his advisers, the executive branch ministries (which Russians refer to as "the government"), the legislature, the Supreme Arbitration and Constitutional Courts, as well as interbranch agencies.

In fleshing out his conception, Eckstein (Eckstein and Gurr 1975, 24–26) proposes that what is really of most import is the authority pattern of "the most inclusive (or most extensive) social unit," and he uses the term *government* as shorthand for this. Yet this is not satisfactory because Eckstein wants to privilege the authority pattern that he refers to as the government. It is, after all, the stability of the *governmental* authority pattern that is the main dependent variable for congruence theory (this is true even given Eckstein's broadening of the dependent variable away from democratic stability to governmental stability by the 1970s). On what basis does it receive preeminence? Surely not its inclusivity or extension per se. If so, why did Eckstein study Norway, not the United Nations?

Since, as Eckstein stresses in several places, "a government must govern," he has in mind that this most inclusive authority pattern has to accomplish some things. Various "things" vital to governance are accomplished (i.e., various functions are fulfilled)[3] by different levels of authority (as Eckstein lucidly discusses). Even the United Nations in some small way is part of what governs me, as is the U.S. government, as is the Iowa government, as is Iowa City's government, as is the University of Iowa's administration. Are all these of equal importance, however? Clearly not, and congruence theory (quite properly) gives centrality to only one of those—the U.S. government in the example I use. That choice is appropriate because the U.S. government is a "state" government in the international legal (and Weberian) sense.

When Eckstein (1969, 287) discusses the importance of governmental performance, the tasks that he lists strike me as little different from what others might describe as core state tasks. Democracy in the modern sense—and hence democratic stability, Eckstein's interest in which got congruence theory started—is even more recent than the Treaty of Westphalia. Eckstein's (Eckstein and Gurr 1975, 5) observation that focusing on the state limits one to the post-Westphalia West is therefore not such a problem given the topic at hand. All the societies that successfully or unsuccessfully created "democratic" institutions (in our century, this includes societies outside the West) have sought to create democratic states. I prefer to understand the phrase "a democracy" as shorthand for "a democratic state." A democratic state must succeed as a state, not simply as a governmental selection mechanism. A successful democracy is a polity that not only provides civil liberties, protects minority rights, and produces representative governments but does these things while adequately fulfilling such state tasks as defending its territory from outside attack, preserving internal order, and promoting economic prosperity. So, in the early years of a formally democratic polity, developments such as high inflation, unemployment, rising crime, poor health care provision, and tension from abroad will reduce the development of individuals' attachment to democratic institutions. How could it not? If a state with democratic institutions is failing as a state, support will grow for its replacement. *This* is the lesson of Weimar, and phrasing it as "too much democracy" is misleading. If one lets the term *state* back into polite company, I believe congruence theory becomes *more* pertinent for assessing the prospects of democratic consolidation not less.

I want at this point to turn to an aspect of the original formulation of congruence theory that was dropped by the 1975 Eckstein and Gurr volume. Yet given this volume's focus on Russia's future as a democracy, the arguments deserve revisiting. In the original formulation, congruence theory was designed to explain democratic stability, as opposed to the more general focus on governmental stability that emerged during the Workshop in the late 1960s. In examining stable democracy from the viewpoint of congruence theory, Eckstein (1992b, 207) poses the perhaps unexpected but significant insight that a stable democracy is unlikely to be a pure democracy. (See chap. 1 for more on this point.)

The terminology Eckstein uses to amplify on this important claim, however, deserves exploring. He speculates (1992b, n. 9, italics in original) that authority patterns can be categorized into democratic, authoritarian, and constitutional:

> *Democracy* in this case refers to the rule of numbers. . . . *Authoritarianism* refers to limited participation in decisions by the mass and to a high degree of autonomy and a low degree of formal precariousness of position on the part of the elite. *Constitutionalism* refers to the subjection of the elite to a broad and highly explicit impersonal framework of rules, procedural and substantive, where this framework of rules operates as the principal limitation on the autonomy of the elite.

While it is clear why one would counterpoise democracy and authoritarianism, it is unexpected to see constitutionalism set off as a different category of authority relations entirely. Although not every democracy is a constitutional one, and although a prominent branch of democratic theory finds fault with any framework of rules that hems in a properly elected elite (e.g., constitutional review by a court), still constitutional democracies comprise the vast majority of successful democracies. Indeed, some argue (see, e.g., Elster 1988; Ackerman 1991) that the very limitation of the powers of temporary majorities strengthens democracy over the long run. I prefer, therefore, to reserve the term *democracy* for a complex of institutions and behaviors that includes the election of elites through mass suffrage but is not limited to it. Polities that have not produced a number of conditions beyond elections cannot be properly labeled a democracy. Eckstein's treatment of Weimar supports this, I believe, and it fits with my argument in favor of treating democracies as democratic states.

If we accept, though, that Eckstein has in mind the very narrow sense of democracy as elections and majority rule, the odd term in the trilogy becomes *authoritarianism*. Authoritarianism is also most commonly thought of as a type of polity. It certainly is not a label that someone positive toward Britain, as is Eckstein, would apply to that country.

Yet, in explaining why Britain has democratic stability and Weimar Germany vanished, he stresses (1992b, 208) that Britain mixes democracy, authoritarianism, and constitutionalism: "British government and British authority beliefs, as already pointed out, are a mixture of all the elements out of which governmental authority can be concocted: popular government, the government of an autonomous elite, and government under an impersonal law." It is "the government of an autonomous elite" that Eckstein has in mind as British authoritarianism—in other words, Britain's executive agencies! The other two, clearly, refer to parliament ("popular government") and to the judiciary ("government under an impersonal law"). Eckstein has given new labels to Montesquieu's divisions of governmental functions.

This matter raises two points. First, effective executive branch bureaucracies should not be tarnished with the derogatory term *authoritarianism*. There is nothing authoritarian or antidemocratic about having laws executed, and the failure to implement legislation will soon discredit the most procedurally pure electoral process.

Second, treating different governmental functions as types of authority patterns does not seem to me to fit well with the general thrust of congruence theory. This theory stresses the congruence between the governmental authority pattern and others in society, with an authority pattern defined (Eckstein and Gurr 1975, 22) as "a set of asymmetric relations among hierarchically ordered members of a social unit that involves the direction of the unit." Those who struggle over the direction of a country's entire social unit include officials in all three branches of government. In other words, we should expect to find that authority relations within the U.S. Congress, the White House and cabinet, as well as in the judiciary, all exhibit congruence with societal authority patterns (since the United States is the most stable democracy). We surely do not want to look at each as an example of a different authority pattern.

As I noted, the democracy-authoritarianism-constitutionalism trilogy does not appear in Eckstein and Gurr (1975). So, perhaps this critique is not needed, but it raises important issues of democratic theory and how congruence theory relates to it. Given the implicit logic that there is a single governmental authority pattern (no matter how mixed and multivariate its characteristics might be) with which societal authority patterns can be compared, what is one to do about the complexity of modern multibranch polities?

A final comment regarding congruence theory relates to the political culture approach to comparative politics. A huge literature got under way in the 1960s consisting of works that describe the political cultures of one or more countries by measuring the average levels of support for certain propositions through surveys of (one hopes) representative samples of the population of the country(ies). Eckstein himself (1988) has written a thoughtful defense of political culture theory against rational choice theory. For the most part, this defense seems to understand political culture and how to measure it in a manner that is quite compatible with the approach used by Almond and Verba, Inglehart, and others: if one looks for cross-national differences in the mean scores of certain variables, one has found out something important about a country's political culture. This approach, however, has conceptual shortcomings and a large gap between the concept and what gets measured. As a result, the Almondian conception of political culture fell into disrepute in the 1970s. Despite recent claims of a "renaissance of political culture" (Inglehart 1988; Almond 1990b), the shortcomings remain (Reisinger 1995).

I therefore find it important that Eckstein's congruence theory is *not* compatible with the Almondian survey approach to political culture. Congruence theory directs the scholar's attention away from the prevalence of certain values, focusing instead on "authority patterns," something quite different indeed. Eckstein (1992b, 187, italics in original) depicts an authority pattern in the following way:

> In every society we can discover numerous authority patterns, both attitudes regarding authority and, to use Lasswell's terminology, authority "practices." . . . [A]s the term is used here, authority in some form is a characteristic of practically any persistent social aggregate at least in that certain actual practices of subordination and superordination will be found in such aggregates, and probably also in that there will exist in the society as a whole and in its subunits certain dominant notions as to how such practices *should* be conducted.

(Note, by the way, that this definition incorporates individuals' *behavior*, which those in the Almondian tradition choose to exclude from their definition of political culture so that the latter can be used to explain behavior.) The congruence theory conception of the object of inquiry is, in my opinion, likely to be much more profitable for cross-national comparisons than when political culture is defined as the mean score for the measure of one or more values. (Eckstein himself critiques the survey-based approach to pursuing knowledge of "cultures" in a recent work [1992a, chap. 8].)

Besides wanting to praise this aspect of congruence theory, I stress its departure from typical political culture work to make the following point: it is not relevant to an examination of congruence theory to ask whether current research into Russians' values are really getting at what they purport to. As one engaged in surveys of Russians' values, I believe that such work has merits but does not engage congruence theory very directly. What would we know, for example, about authority patterns in Russian society even if we had a perfect measurement of the distribution of tolerance? Not much, by itself.

Despite congruence theory's seemingly high potential utility for comparing societies, however, I must point out that its call for comparing the congruence of authority patterns shares some of the key difficulties facing Almondian political culture theory. Congruence theory wants to come up with propositions that apply to the entirety of a country. It is a daunting task to assess the depth and breadth of congruence even for a single country, especially a huge one such as Russia. Beyond that, any country almost certainly has more than one "authority pattern" coexisting in it, and issues of generalizing from complexity become sharp. For example, even the Russian "government" is not a single entity, composed of many different institutions, agencies, and so forth, so does one want to search for only a single governmental authority pattern?

Congruence Theory and Contemporary Russia

The sum of the preceding comments is that congruence theory has much to recommend it as an approach to understanding comparative politics, especially the prospects for democratic consolidation in countries under authoritarian rule until recently. It is not, however, a theory that fits straightforwardly with the some common notions of democratization, so one must apply it with care. With regard to Russia as a case, congruence theory asks us to consider aspects of Russian life that remain little studied. These aspects of Russian life, moreover, are not simple to extract from news reports emanating from that country.

For example, one may be tempted to take Eckstein's discussion of strain and anomie, look at Russia, and say "Aha—Russians are facing strain, they have anomie, that must mean that Russia's nongovernmental authority patterns are incongruent with the current governmental authority pattern (putatively, a democratic one). Russians, whether they know it or not, don't want democracy. Hence, Russian democracy, like Weimar's, is in deep trouble." Yet the strain in Russian society flows so directly from poverty, crime, and rapid change that any possible incongruence between governmental and societal authority patterns becomes unnecessary for explaining it. Moreover, I am not making an assertion about "Russian culture" when I state that Russians experience strain because life for many is poor, dangerous, and uncertain. Although a Russian cultural affinity for stability and order may well enhance strain when the state is unable to fulfill its duties, any society, regardless of culture, will experience increased strain under similar circumstances. In other words, the strain and potential anomie come from the Russian state failing to fulfill key state functions more directly than from Russian political culture.

Nevertheless, if applied with the care it requires, congruence theory strikes me as quite likely to enhance the discussion of Russia's prospects for stable democracy. This discussion, at present, too often turns on such issues as whether the "democrats" can win in the coming elections (even though those so labeled are a small minority with certain ideological positions), whether the Communist Party of the Russian Federation has gained increased support (even though that party seeks to operate within the current system), or how big a proportion of the Russian people praise the word *democracy*. Congruence theory, by contrast, draws our attention to phenomena that are almost certain to be more useful in studying Russia's transition away from communism: the behaviors (authority relationships) and the orientations toward such behaviors of the actors within numerous key social units, some within and some without the Russian state. As I understand Eckstein's work, employing congruence theory in the study of Russian politics poses several (difficult) tasks. Within each of various social units one would seek to determine such things as (1) whether recruitment is regulated or unregulated (and, I presume, how the regulation is accomplished), is closed or open, and involves selection or election; (2) whether decision rules are monocratic, by majority vote, or by consensus; (3) the degree of directiveness; (4) whether participation in decision making is by suffrage or sufferance; and (5) whether responsiveness by officials to concerns and criticisms from below is discretionary or obligatory (Eckstein and Gurr 1975, passim).

Given that pertinent studies of such matters in contemporary Russia do not abound, it would be relevant to turn to earlier works for clues. This approach might include examinations of Russian society during the pre-Soviet period. White's (1979) study of Soviet political culture is a leading example of using information on imperial Russian politics to interpret contemporary (at that point, Soviet) outlooks and practices. Keenan (1986) attempts to show continuities in Russian elite authority patterns over several centuries. Yet historians' findings about authority patterns in tsarist Russia must be examined carefully for their current utility. First, much time has passed, and virtually every Russian citizen now alive grew up dealing with Soviet-era political and social institutions rather than imperial institutions. Second, the demographic, educational and other aspects of Russia's populace shifted fundamentally from the late 1920s to the 1960s (Hough 1988; Lewin 1991). The authority patterns within the Russian peasant *mir* should be expected to be only partially reflected in post-Soviet realities, even among collective farm workers. We should expect that Soviet-era experiences reinforced some of the *mir's* authority patterns, gave different meanings to others, and eliminated still others.

Evidence of authority patterns toward the end of the Soviet period is likely to prove most helpful, because of its temporal proximity, for assessing contemporary Russian authority patterns. There actually exist many excellent studies of authority patterns (or of one or another aspect of authority patterns) in the late Soviet period *with regard to Soviet elites*. Let me just mention the research into Soviet recruitment of elites (e.g., Harasymiw 1969; Fleron 1970; Moses 1981; Clark 1989; Urban 1989), decision making and consultation (e.g., Hough 1969; Skilling and Griffith 1971; Cocks 1976; Gustafson 1981; Hodnett 1981; Löwenhardt 1981; Breslauer 1982; Hoffman and Laird 1982), and the leadership's responsiveness (e.g., White 1983).

Willerton (1992) has used innovative methods to document the salient role that personalistic, patron-client ties played in Soviet elite politics. To return to Eckstein and Gurr's (1975) terminology, relations between "supers" and "subs" in a setting governed by patron-client norms will differ from those in settings governed by bureaucratic norms and by established regulations concerning the hierarchy of offices. Also, Soviet elite politics flowed in part from the competition among different "chains" of patrons and clients linked by personal ties. The colloquial term for a number of officials in a chain was a *mafia*—for example, Brezhnev's cronies were dubbed the "Dnieprpetrovsk mafia" from his first major governing post. This point has particular interest given the extent to which observers decry the tendency for Russian officials to circumvent formal regulations in favor of building coalitions that depend on trust gained through personal ties. In other words, many fear that Russia is governed by mafias rather than exhibiting the strict adherence to the rule of law that seems a vital concomitant to democracy in the West. Congruence theory, however, calls on us to ascertain whether Russia's state authority pattern might incorporate relations between supers and subs with which Russians feel comfortable and remain democratic nevertheless. Rather than lamenting that Russians do not seem to follow formal procedures in the same way as Germans (stereotypically) do, congruence theory suggests that Russia must develop a form of democracy that allows personalistic ties to continue and yet does not undermine genuine democracy.

Unfortunately, I am not aware of equivalent knowledge about authority patterns among the Soviet-era Russian mass public. Only since

1987 or so did it become possible to undertake "fieldwork" of the type necessary to observe the authority patterns of one or more societal units. Such work remains sparse a decade later. Fortunately, much of relevance will be appearing over the coming years as current dissertation research gets published.

Conclusions

This discussion supports, I hope, the utility of investigating Russian authority patterns within and without the Russian state. Yet it may not be best to advocate any scholar or group of scholars setting out to "test" congruence theory in Russia. To gather from scratch sufficient information to credibly assess the theory's propositions is daunting. So, too, would be the task of extracting from others' research sufficient knowledge relevant to congruence theory. Perhaps a more appropriate goal would be to broadcast as widely as possible within the field the advantages of bearing congruence theory in mind so that the work of many different scholars becomes more likely over time to produce a body of knowledge that permits an assessment of the congruence of different authority patterns in Russia. Congruence theory could well provide conceptual links to bridge the findings that have recently begun to emerge, and will continue to emerge, from survey work, documentary studies, informal interview-based research, participant observation, and other methods.

Notes

An earlier version of this essay was presented at the 1995 Annual Meeting of the American Political Science Association, Chicago, August 31–September 3, 1995.

1. Eckstein (1969, 275–76) has broken down theories of democratization into only two categories. His two categories correspond roughly, I believe, to my first and fourth categories. Most of the work in the second and third categories had not been published by 1969, of course.

2. When citing the 1961 essay in which Eckstein laid out the original formulation of congruence theory, I use page numbers from its reprinting in Eckstein (1992b).

3. It is therefore puzzling that he dismisses (Eckstein and Gurr 1975, 6–7) functional approaches rather than incorporating them.

6

Survey Research and Authority Patterns in Contemporary Russia

William M. Reisinger

As chapter 11 by Fleron and Ahl will demonstrate, sophisticated surveying of Russian public opinion can be a significant step forward. Contemporary Russian society is better understood than was Soviet Russian society, and recent survey analyses get part of the credit. A careful examination of the literature, such as Fleron and Ahl's, also shows the pitfalls that can occur in planning and interpreting survey data. Survey researchers must thus be careful in the claims they make about how definitive are their survey-based findings. Nevertheless, surveys of mass public opinion will and should continue to be an important research tool.

A different question, though, concerns what role survey research should play in investigations that aim to shed light on one or more countries' authority patterns. As discussed more fully in earlier chapters, an authority pattern is "a set of asymmetric relations among hierarchically ordered members of a social unit that involves the direction of the unit" (Eckstein and Gurr 1975, 22). For each authority pattern, one needs to distinguish and acquire information on its *forms, norms* and *practices* (Eckstein and Gurr 1975, 261–2). Obviously, studying authority patterns in any society poses significant challenges. Survey research is not necessarily the best way to produce the necessary information, and it is certainly not the only way. Survey data must at least be combined with other forms of information. Survey data do have a place, however, in the study of authority patterns. In this chapter, I attempt to identify this place and provide illustrations concerning Russian authority patterns.

Survey Data and Methods of Analysis

Two related but distinct issues influence how useful survey data can be in the study of Russian authority patterns. The first arises because of the association between survey data and large-*n*, quantitative statistical analyses. If one believes that statistical analyses are not the appropriate means to reveal authorities patterns—or, at least, must be combined with other types of information—then survey data may seem to have little utility. The second arises because of the nature of question wording in many survey questionnaires. To address the first issue, I will discuss alternative methods for analyzing questions of interest to comparativists (and others) and then discuss how survey data relate to these methods.

Broad Methodological Choices in Comparative Research

Collier (1993) has recently updated and extended a categorization of research approaches proposed and defended in the early 1970s by Arend Lijphart (1971, 1975).[1] These categories provide a useful starting point for thinking about how to approach the study of Russian (or other postcommunist) authority patterns. The four research approaches are the case study method, the statistical method, the experimental method, and the comparative method.

In an experimental design, of course, the researcher manipulates something in a carefully controlled fashion so that the impact of a single factor can be separated from other possible influences. The predominant method in the hard sciences, experimentation is impractical for many topics of interest to social scientists. Among social scientists, a basic methodological choice was therefore between case studies and statistical analyses. In Singer's (1969) words, the two approaches differ on the magnitude of the "*n/v* ratio." That is, a case study has a small number of cases (*n*) and a large number of variables (*v*) that are brought into explaining the case or cases, hence a low *n/v* ratio. A statistical analysis manipulates a large number of cases for a relatively small number of variables. In a statistical analysis, it is possible to control for (i.e., to remove from active consideration) extraneous potential influences on the matter of interest. Statistical control is less desirable than experimental control but better than no control at all under certain conditions. First, the theoretical questions at issue must lend themselves to formulation as a statistical relationship. Second, both the theory and the data must match the assumptions necessary for the statistical procedures to produce interpretable results. Each statistical procedure—Pearson's correlation coefficient, least-squares regression, or whatever—demands that the researcher start from certain assumptions about the data and the processes that produced the data.[2] Because much that interests social scientists is not best studied by experimental or statistical techniques, case studies have been and remain an important approach for social scientific investigations.

Case studies, experiments, and the statistical manipulation of data were standard techniques in the social sciences long before the early 1970s, as were debates about which was preferable. Lijphart, however, sought to distinguish a fourth approach from these, an approach of particular relevance to scholars attempting to study more than one polity or social system. He dubbed it the comparative method. The comparative method involves analyzing more cases than in a typical case study (say, five to fifteen) but fewer than are necessary for statistical controls. As Collier (1993, 106) paraphrases Lijphart, "Despite the constraint of addressing more variables than cases, the comparative method allows systematic comparison that, if appropriately utilized, can contribute to adjudicating among rival explanations."

In 1975, Lijphart amplified on his category of the comparative method by distinguishing between two strategies. One strategy is to incorporate as many cases as possible in the analyses, while still choosing variables and cases carefully. This allows the researcher to draw conclusions in a quasi-statistical manner based on the relationships found across the cases. The second strategy is to select cases that are as similar as possible with respect to as many as possible of the factors not being directly considered by the theory in use. Then, the differences across the cases in the explanatory factors can be used to explain differences in the factor needing explanation.[3] This latter strategy, called the "comparable-cases strategy," represents the method that is most clearly distinct from the experimental, statistical, and case study methods.

So, four methods or logics for testing theoretical propositions have been identified.[4] All four are valid ways to produce insights into authority relations. Moreover, as Collier (1993, 108–17) discusses, innovations in each of the four methods have appeared since Lijphart's original articles. Among other things, new techniques for making case studies valuable as tests of theory have appeared, additional reasons have been put forth for valuing small-*n* research, the use of key events as "quasi-experiments" has become more viable, and methodologists have developed new statistical techniques for dealing with small numbers of cases.

Survey Research and Different Methods of Comparative Inquiry

Large-scale surveys represent one data-gathering technique, not a method like those already discussed. Survey data, however, are usually associated with the statistical method. The interviews conducted for a survey are deliberately kept shorter and less flexible than might otherwise be possible. In return for the loss of depth and flexibility, it becomes feasible to interview hundreds of people across a country rather than, say, a couple of dozen elites. Producing statistically analyzable samples is, in other words, its raison d'être.

Despite this, the data produced by a large-scale survey can be part of quasi-experimental approaches, case studies, and the comparative method. Given the large investment that has been made in the 1990s to produce a storehouse of survey data from the formerly communist countries of Eastern Europe and the Soviet Union, it is worth keeping multiple uses for the data in mind. Follow-up analyses of these data in coming years could reveal insights into authority relations in these societies. Moreover, support for social-scientific surveys of these populaces seems likely to continue. Those with an interest in analyzing authority relations should seek to design future surveys in ways that produce relevant data.

A "quasi-experiment" occurs when a researcher utilizes data that were not produced in a laboratory setting but which nevertheless provide controls for one or more potentially confounding factors, thereby approximating an otherwise impossible experiment. The unexpected development that changes an existing situation, perhaps only for a time, is usually dubbed an "intervention." When newspapers in Pittsburgh went on strike in 1991, for example, Mondak (1995) had an opportunity to assess how the flow of information in a community influences political discussion. Survey data can serve as part of a quasi-experiment of this type. Mondak was able to contrast survey data before and during the newspaper strike. One can imagine that, when comparable samples across multiple years are available and there is an appropriate "intervention," many other research questions and settings would make it possible to employ survey data as part of a quasi-experiment.

It might seem strange to argue that case study approaches should take advantage of survey data, since the one minimizes the "n/v ratio," and the other maximizes it. Yet, the data from surveys are nothing more than many people's answers to a series of questions. Even though the answers are frequently constrained by closed-ended question formats, the nature and range of those answers should remain of interest to many scholars pursuing a case study. Whether by examining the range of different responses or by keeping some societal mean score in mind as a counterweight to the researcher's personal observations, nonquantitative uses of survey data are several.

Pursuing Lijphart's comparable-cases method in search of authority patterns might also benefit from the analysis of survey data. In fact, much of the major work using cross-national survey data has done so in a fashion closer to the comparable-cases method than to the large-*n* statistical method. Inglehart's (1990, chap. 1) recent defense of political culture is an example. Using data from a small number of countries (about the number Lijphart had in mind), Inglehart uses national mean scores on various variables. The countries surveyed are all developed Western democracies and, in that sense, comparable on many dimensions. Primarily, Inglehart supports his arguments by asking the reader to inspect the mean scores visually. Although Lijphart tended to assume that, after carefully selecting a small number of comparable countries, the researcher would then use historical or nonquantitative forms of evidence, the logic of his comparable-cases method does not require that such be the case.

Survey Question Wording and the Study of Authority Patterns

Whatever the research method employed, survey data will not shed light on a society's authority patterns unless appropriate questions are in the survey questionnaire. A team of faculty and graduate students, working in the late 1960s and early 1970s under Eckstein's direction, was able to flesh out the general definition of authority patterns into nine categories of information worth knowing about a given society (Eckstein and Gurr 1975, passim): directiveness, participation, responsiveness, compliance, relations between leaders and led, decision rules, decision behavior, recruitment, and bases of legitimacy. Eckstein elaborates on several of these in chapter 1, but a brief definition of each is merited.

"*Directiveness* refers to the extent to which activities in a social unit are subject to directives, rather than being left to the free discretion of members" (Eckstein and Gurr 1975, 53, italics added).

Participation refers to acts by which subordinates attempt to influence the directive activities of their superiors (Eckstein and Gurr 1975, 60). One wants to know whether participation involves (1) group activity, (2) direct personal actions, (3) indirect personal actions, or (4) impersonal actions. Is participation by suffrage or sufferance?

Is *responsiveness* by officials to concerns and criticisms from below discretionary or obligatory? (Eckstein and Gurr 1975, 67–69).

The complement of directiveness by a superordinate is *compliance* to the directives by a subordinate (Eckstein and Gurr 1975, 71).

Relations between leaders and led: The extent of leaders' superiority

(Eckstein and Gurr 1975, 80), includes subdimensions of distance, deportment (arrogance/familiarity) and proximity.

Decision-rules: Rules that provide the basic criteria under which decisions are considered to have been taken (Eckstein and Gurr 1975, 121).

Decision-Behavior: How leaders interact in working out directives (Eckstein and Gurr 1975, 132).

The *recruitment* of leaders (superordinates): "Are positions of authority open to competition? To what proportion of a unit's members, and what particular kinds of people? And what are their intrinsic chances for converting eligibility into incumbency?" (Eckstein and Gurr 1975, 151–2).

"*Bases of Legitimacy* are values which govern perceptions that authority patterns are rightly constituted and therefore worthy of support" (Eckstein and Gurr 1975, 198, italics added). "Although certainly a 'variable' (they vary), the bases on which the perceptions of legitimacy rest do not constitute a continuous dimension" (198).

Recall that, for each of these nine categories, a complete analysis must seek to ascertain the relevant norms, forms, and practices. For example, with regard to directiveness, three questions become relevant: What do members of the society see as the desirable level of directiveness? What institutional forms exist to produce and regulate directiveness? How do members of the society actually behave in reaction to those forms?

Many potential sources of information can quickly be proposed. The researcher might analyze texts of various sorts. Or, he or she could spend a lengthy period living in the society, observing and interacting with the native members of the society. With regard to understanding formal rules, textual analysis ought to be a primary technique. It cannot suffice, however, given the importance of unwritten rules that can be as institutional as written rules. For practices, observation would seem to be the primary technique. Yet, what observer would resist the opportunity to ask natives of the society to explicate what they are doing and why? With regard to both forms and practices, an important supplement to other information-gathering techniques is to ask questions of the members of the society under study. With regard to norms, moreover, asking questions is the primary technique: who better than an individual member of the society to provide information on his or her preferences?

Because surveys are, to repeat, a form of asking questions, they ought to be able to serve as valuable supplements to other information-gathering techniques. When surveys are gathered for social-psychological purposes, the goal is to learn about how each interviewee sees the world, the connections among ideas, affect toward various symbols, and so forth. Each interviewee is, in jargon, a respondent. Questions designed to tap what Eckstein and Gurr call norms will take this general form. Questions designed to elicit information about forms and practices, however, will be using the interviewee as, in effect, a video camera that has spent a long time in the society and gone to more places than could the researcher. In jargon, the interviewee is an informant, not a respondent.

Surveys routinely incorporate questions that call upon the interviewee to be an informant as well as those for which the interviewee is a respondent. Examples relevant to the nine categories of authority patterns are easy to imagine: "If the residential council in the apartment complex where you live wanted residents to make some change to their apartments, what would the council do to get residents to follow its wishes? What would the council do if it wanted the courtyard of the apartment complex to be kept cleaner and the landscaping to be protected?" "Now, what if your district or city council issued a ruling concerning the apartment complex where you live and this ruling was very unpopular among people living there. Please tell me whether most, some, a few or almost none of the people living in your apartment complex would do each of the following: (1) Contact the council or one of its members to try to get the ruling changed; (2) sign a petition protesting the ruling; (3) create a group to organize opposition to the ruling; (4) comply with the ruling even if it is unpopular; (5) ignore the ruling if they were not likely to get punished; (6) ignore the ruling on principle even if they might be fined or punished." "How often do the foremen/administrators where you work check up on the way workers carry out their prescribed tasks—very closely, somewhat closely, somewhat loosely, or very loosely/not at all?" Those participating in Eckstein and Gurr's (1975, 270) effort to operationalize the study of authority patterns did, in fact, develop survey questions along such lines.

With regard to post-Soviet Russia, I can offer a few examples of findings relevant to the task of building knowledge about that society's authority patterns. What are, for instance, Russians' orientations toward styles of leadership? Do they look for technical expertise, procedural skill, strength of personality, decisiveness, or entirely different qualities? Surveys, even given that the interviewees are responding to the situation of being surveyed, can shed light on the distribution of this orientation. The surveys with which I have been involved (Reisinger et al. 1994) indicate that Russians seek leaders who are "strong" but benevolent. This desire for strong leadership does *not* equate to a desire for an authoritarian government. "From all indications, public opinion does not identify the concepts of 'firm order' and an 'iron hand' with a dictatorship" (Levada 1995). The adjective *strong* seems, instead, to mean competence in producing the outcomes necessary to fulfill state tasks. In contemporary Russia, that means public order and an improving economy above all. A large degree of public consultation in the policy-making process is not necessary as long as the power to throw out the government remains in public hands.[5]

The same surveys shed additional light on Russians' outlooks on whether public participation should be "by suffrage or by sufferance" (Eckstein and Gurr 1975, 378). In a study examining the reactions of elites and the public to a question asking them to agree or disagree with the statement that "A legislator is obligated to follow the wishes of his constituents even if he thinks his constituents are mistaken," we found that the question

> provides an intriguing contrast in perspective between elites and masses. It measures whether the respondents see legislators as trustees or as delegates. The question is not written to provide an obvious "right" answer, not from question wording and not because one answer is more clearly "democratic" and thus the socially approved way to answer. Also, the question does not easily relate to a pro- or anti-reform position. The Russian elites pretty consistently disagreed with the view that they should act as delegates, following only their constituents' wishes. This accords with findings that legislators even in established liberal democracies tend to stress their trustee role (Welsh 1979, 150; Converse and Pierce 1986, 498, 687). In other words, elites see themselves as having been placed in a position of public trust and responsibility and consequently feel that they are the proper ones to make decisions on behalf of the public. Russian citizens, by contrast, are more likely to see themselves as able to play a continued role between elections and as justified in doing so (though the distribution of answers is wider than in the elite sample). (Reisinger, Melville, Miller, and Hesli 1996, 89)

Given frequently heard arguments that Russian authority patterns are strongly influenced by personalistic ties, a question we have asked concerning the importance of personal contacts in getting things done is pertinent. Few Russians believe that one can get by if they only work through official, legal channels. The vast majority agree with the proposition that personal contacts are needed to get things done—82 percent either agreed or fully agreed in 1995 (Reisinger, Miller, and Hesli 1997). Knowing how to interpret such patterns is, of course, difficult. For example, while the data show little change from 1991 to 1995, they do show a reasonably linear relationship between this view and one's age: the younger individuals are more likely to believe that they can succeed without necessarily having strong "connections."

Because authority patterns incorporate practices as well as norms and forms, it directs us to learn more about the extent and variety of Russians' political behavior. Survey research is beginning to provide a detailed picture of the levels and modes of Russians' political and social behavior (Bahry 1993; Kaplan 1993; Bahry and Way 1994; McAllister and White 1994). In a study using our surveys (Reisinger, Miller, and Hesli 1995), we found that former Soviet citizens are more participatory than totalitarian images of the Soviet period would suggest. With regard to electoral and protest activities, the level of participatory Russians generally approximates or exceeds levels found in established democracies. With regard to associational activity, however, the picture is more gloomy. We asked whether the respondent belongs to a social organization or initiative group. This formulation reflected our interest in the phenomenon of *neformalniye*, the informal organizations that began forming at a phenomenal rate in the late 1980s for social, political, or even just recreational purposes. The "social organization/ initiative group" formulation is less likely to have been seen as referring to membership in the regime-sponsored socially oriented bodies such as housing commissions (in which 2.5 percent of Soviets were found to be active in the SIP data), parents' commissions (10.6 percent), and people's militia or comrades' court (10.9 percent) (Bahry and Silver 1990, 831). Social organizations and initiative groups are reasonably comparable to the type of voluntary association examined in other countries—membership is voluntary, communal, directed most commonly at local issues or problems, and often only indirectly "political" (including athletic clubs, professional associations, neighborhood groups, and others). The membership levels that we found represent a smaller portion of society than was the case for contacting, petition signing, and demonstrating: 6 percent of Russians reported belonging in 1992. Moreover, membership in a political party was extremely rare (about 1 percent). Even if we assume that the levels of public involvement in the civic groups that Bahry and Silver documented, and about which we did not ask, have stayed steady into the 1990s, communal activity is low.

Conclusion

The growing body of high-quality survey data drawn from post-Soviet Russia and other postcommunist societies constitutes an important resource for social science researchers. Its value is not limited to those pursuing large-*n* statistical analyses of social-psychological questions. Interviews with randomly selected citizens can contribute to quasi-experimental, case study, and qualitative approaches as well as to statistical analyses. The answers to closed-ended questions (the majority of questions for most surveys) are coming to have increased value to a wide range of researchers. The diversity of topics covered has grown, and it is now possible to examine trends in a society's answers over time. In addition, open-ended questions, in which the respondent's verbatim reactions to a question are recorded, are being included in most surveys. The answers to such questions promise to shed considerable light on the meaning of citizens' answers to other questions.

The investigation of authority patterns in Russia can likewise benefit from examining results from surveys. Depending on the form of the question, survey results can shed light on the forms, norms, and practices of authority in a variety of settings. When the survey has been properly conducted, the pattern of answers can be inferred to represent the pattern of answers characteristic of the entire society. This makes survey data especially pertinent as a check on—though certainly not a substitute for—personal observations, documentary evidence, and other sources of information.

Existing survey results have been little studied with an eye to authority patterns per se. An effort is needed to determine what insights into Russian authority patterns emerge from the data that has now been gathered by several Western and Russian research teams (see chap. 11 for a useful first effort at this task as well as for details on different teams and their projects). In addition, there is a need for questions specifically designed to reveal citizens' views on directiveness and the other categories of authority relations in a variety of social units. To better understand Russian authority patterns, then, researchers should work to incorporate such questions into surveys or to design entire surveys around them.

Notes

1. Please see the cited articles by Lijphart and Collier for more details about the four methods than I can provide here.

2. Much of what methodology texts do, of course, is to outline which assumptions are necessary for given statistical techniques, why and which types of questions and data are typically well studied using a particular technique. So, any of the numerous books on statistics or quantitative methodology for social scientists will elaborate on this. With regard to linear regression, the

most common statistical technique among political scientists, see Lewis-Beck (1980) and Berry (1993).

3. As Lijphart notes, others had earlier discussed this same approach, in essence, including Przeworski and Teune (1970), who call it the "most-similar systems design."

4. Lijphart and others who investigate the comparative method or "the logic of comparative inquiry" generally presume that the analyst is interested in comparisons among countries. Yet the same four-way categorization of methods is relevant for attempts to learn about social phenomena within a single country.

5. I find it intriguing that the British system of democracy is justified on similar grounds. A government backed by a majority party in Parliament has tremendous power to execute its laws. It also is much less open than, say, the U.S. government. Public control over the government comes through the ability to vote the government out of power if overall performance is deemed unsatisfactory, not through public involvement in or influence over the making or implementing of individual policies.

III

STATE-CENTERED VERSUS SOCIETY-CENTERED APPROACHES

7

Political Culture, Authority Patterns, and the Architecture of the New Russian Democracy

Russell Bova

The "third wave" of democratization has given rise to a resurgent debate over the relative contribution to democratic stability of different kinds of democratic institutions. Controversy over the relative merits of presidentialism versus parliamentary democracy has been stimulated anew, as has discussion of the relative strengths and weaknesses of proportional versus majoritarian electoral systems. Meanwhile, as the "new institutionalists" compare and contrast the virtues and deficiencies of the various institutional choices that present themselves, others wonder whether all of the attention given to the question of institutional craftsmanship really matters all that much in the end. Thus, while noting the frenzy of activity related to institutional choice and design, Fukuyama (1995) has suggested that prospects for democratic consolidation and stability in third wave democracies will rest primarily on considerations of culture. Alternatively, Rowen (1995) has suggested that the third wave of democratization rises on a "deep tide" of economic development and its resulting increases in levels of income and education. While neither analysis precludes some significance for matters of institutional choice, the rise, consolidation, and stability of democratic institutions is seen as primarily dependent on exogenous variables such as culture and economic development.

These issues and debates all find an echo in the context of contemporary Russia. Throughout much of the spring and early summer of 1995, the two houses of the Russian legislature along with the Russian president were locked in a political struggle over the proportion of seats to the State Duma to be elected from party lists as opposed to single-member districts. In early 1997 as Boris Yeltsin lay ill with double pneumonia, leading members of the Russian legislature were pushing for constitutional changes that would redistribute some power from the executive to the legislative branch. Quite apart from the individual interests at stake, the larger question is which institutional arrangements are most likely to contribute to democratic stability. Does, in fact, the choice really matter? Are decisions made regarding the electoral system or the distribution of power between the executive and legislature fundamental in determining the future stability of Russian democracy? Or is all the debate and fuss over such issues equivalent to struggles over the rearrangement of deck chairs on cruise ships— perhaps important to those looking for the best view but irrelevant when it comes to determining the fate and fortune of the ship itself?

The central thesis of this chapter is that institutional choices can make a difference, but that the question of the appropriateness of the available alternatives cannot be divorced from the context in which they will be implemented. When it comes to the selection of democratic institutions, one size does not necessarily fit all. This argument is rooted in an analytical approach that has been labeled congruence theory.

Congruence Theory and Democratic Stability

Congruence theory is a promising approach to the question of democratic consolidation and stability whose virtue is to be found precisely in its potential to bridge the gap between institutionalists and their critics. To the question of whether it is context or institutional design that matters most in producing political stability in general and democratic stability in particular, the response of congruence theory is "both of the above." To be specific, congruence theory is concerned with the "fit" between institutions and their context. Thus, to those who would ask whether it is presidential or parliamentary democracy that is "best," congruence theory might answer that it depends once again on the specific historical and cultural context.

A distinction between what one might call "soft" and "hard" theories of congruence will help define the approach. The soft theory of congruence is concerned with the general fit between the values embedded in the political culture and political institutions. In this sense, all those who emphasize the importance of political culture are implicit congruence theorists of a type. For example, in arguing that democratic values run counter to the deeply entrenched values of Russian culture,

Jonathan Steele (1994) is, in effect, applying the soft theory of congruence. The instability of new democratic institutions in Russia is traced to a fundamental incongruence with Russian political culture.

In its "harder" or more specific form, congruence theory is primarily associated with the work of the political scientist Harry Eckstein. According to Eckstein (1992b, 188, italics in original), *"a government will be stable if its authority pattern is congruent with the other authority patterns of the society of which it is a part."* Thus, for Eckstein, congruence (or the lack thereof) is measured by comparing authority patterns in government and those that exist in any number of societal institutions and relationships. Perfect congruence could be said to exist when all governmental and nongovernmental authority patterns are identical. However, Eckstein recognizes that congruence on such a high level can never exist. Thus, he suggests that the minimum condition of congruence could be said to exist "if a high degree of resemblance exists in patterns adjacent to government and one finds throughout the more distant segments a marked departure from functionally appropriate patterns for the sake of imitating the government pattern or extensive imitation of the government pattern in ritual practices" (Eckstein 1992b, 191).

Eckstein introduces additional complexity into the argument in noting that primary-level authority relations in the family, schools, workplace, and elsewhere have traditionally and perhaps inevitably contained strong authoritarian elements. From this observation, Eckstein draws two conclusions. First, democratic stability requires vigorous "intermediate associations" that give citizens a chance to learn and develop democratic authority patterns as a counterpoint to the more inherently authoritarian character of authority in the home, school, and workplace (Eckstein 1992b, 220). Second, because all societies, even the most democratic, combine disparate forms of authority, Eckstein (1992b, 207) concludes logically that "governmental democracy will tend to be stable only if it is to a significant extent impure—if, in short, the governmental authority pattern contains a balance of disparate elements, of which democracy is an important part (but only a part)." The same may be said to apply in the opposite case of societies where authority patterns are generally nondemocratic but where some nonhierarchical, democratic patterns coexist with the predominant authoritarian pattern. As Eckstein (1992b, 206) suggests, the apparently irrational efforts of totalitarian regimes to redesign all social relations may in fact be explained by an intuitive grasp by totalitarian rulers of the importance of congruence.

Short of such ultimately futile efforts to reshape totally societal relationships to fit the preferred governmental pattern, Eckstein argues that all governments, if they are to be stable, must necessarily be characterized by a mix of authority patterns. It is differences in the relative mix of "balanced disparities" rather than pure and absolute distinctions in authority patterns that thereby constitute the difference between stable democracy and stable authoritarianism.

Applied to the Russian case, congruence theory suggests at least four perspectives on the question of political and, specifically, democratic stability. The first three find at least implicit representation in the existing literature on contemporary Russian politics. The fourth will be developed in this chapter.

The first view is *incongruence between a political culture that remains fundamentally authoritarian and newly imported democratic institutions.* Represented, for example, in the aforementioned book by Jonathan Steele (1994), this perspective is very pessimistic regarding the prospects for democracy taking root in an inhospitable Russian political culture. From this perspective, debates over the specifics of electoral systems and institutional design are largely beside the point. The impact of these institutional choices is overwhelmed by larger cultural factors.

Second is *congruence between a Russian political culture in flux and democratic institutions.* Without necessarily comparing authority patterns specifically, some literature argues that the authoritarian elements in traditional Russian political culture have given way, at least partially, to a new political culture more in keeping with democratic values and institutions. Representative of this view is the work of Jeffrey Hahn (1993b, 323), who has argued that the democratization that has occurred in the USSR and Russia since 1987 is *"congruent* [italics added] with a relatively participant political culture already present." Driven perhaps by economic development and social change, these changing values allow for and, some might say, even require democratization if congruence and stability are to be maintained. Once again, debates over specific democratic institutions matter much less to the future of Russian democracy than does large-scale social and cultural change.

The third view is *congruence between a political culture that remains fundamentally authoritarian and a version of democracy that is heavily adorned with authoritarian features.* Unconsciously applying Eckstein's notion of "balanced disparities," the implicit assumption of this perspective is that democracy is a continuous rather than a dichotomous variable. Thus, it is possible to introduce authoritarian elements into a democratic regime while retaining its essentially democratic character. The most common expression of this view is that the broad powers given to the Russian president by the new Russian Constitution, including the ability, under some circumstances, to dismiss the legislature and to rule by decree, are most appropriate for a country not quite ready to absorb democracy in a purer form. Some versions of the idea of "soft authoritarianism," popular among many Moscow intellectuals and political figures alike, sound very much like a call for a mix of democratic and authoritarian authority patterns (see Sautman 1995). Note that in this perspective, unlike the first two, questions of institutional design and constitutional engineering are crucial for stability insofar as they are seen to interact with Russian political culture. (Of course, critics—even those who implicitly appreciate the concept of balanced disparities—might argue that the quest for congruence has gone so far as to undermine democracy altogether. There comes a point at which the introduction of ever more authoritarian elements comes to dominate the entire project [see Tolz 1994]. In that case, one would be back to perspective 1 above.)

The fourth perspective is *incongruence between, on the one hand, a political culture that is potentially receptive to democratic authority but that continues to value effective authority and governability and, on the other hand, a set of democratic institutions that have been selected and mixed in a way that appears almost designed both to inhibit effective authority and governability and to thwart the development of key intermediate associations.* The basic assumption of this view and a central argument of this chapter is that the one constant in Russian political culture is the value placed on strong and effective government. Throughout most of Russian history, authoritarian authority patterns were the means adopted to achieve this end. More recently, as Russian society has become more complex, democratic authority patterns have begun to emerge as an alternative and potentially more effective form of governance. However, the particular institutions of democracy adopted have served to minimize governmental effectiveness to a degree that democracy itself may be discredited. Moreover, the development of key intermediate associations, most notably political parties, has not been most effectively facilitated by the particular institutional choices that have been made. Note that like perspective 3, this view also sees matters of institutional design and constitutional engineering as important. However, unlike that previous perspective, the argument here is that the Russians have made the wrong choices.

In developing this argument, the rest of this chapter will first briefly examine and consider our assumptions about Russian political culture and then proceed, on that basis, to analyze the architecture of the new Russian democracy.

Russian Political Culture and Patterns of Authority

A number of interrelated assumptions about traditional Russian political culture and authority patterns have long taken center stage in both the scholarly and popular literature on the subject. Stated most generally, Russian authority patterns tend to be described as autocratic, authoritarian, and premised on the overwhelming priority allocated to order *(poryadok)* over freedom. Given such characteristics, democratic institutions would seemingly find it difficult to take root (see perspective 1 above) unless the political culture can be shown to have changed (perspective 2) or unless those democratic institutions can be customized to a degree necessary to allow their development in the Russian setting (perspective 3). However, though the conventional view of Russian political culture may be largely accurate, it is also a bit oversimplified, and it is, therefore, necessary to look more closely in search of a bit of the complexity behind these very simple assumptions about Russia.

Russian Autocracy and Personalized Authority

It is commonly asserted that Russians need a powerful leader willing and capable of taking the fate of the country and its people into his or her hands. According to White (1979, 22), Russia has been predisposed by geography to rule by "a succession of strong, autocratic monarchs." He further notes "a highly personalised attachment to political authority" that corresponds, inversely, to a very low level of attachment to more impersonal political institutions (White 1979, 30–33). As a Russian soldier is reported to have told the British ambassador to Russia in 1917, "Oh yes, we must have a Republic, but we must have a good Tsar at its head" (White 1979, 31).

In fact, however, if one looks at authority patterns in the post-Stalin era USSR, one finds that the predominant pattern is less autocratic than oligarchic. Post-Stalin Soviet leaders stressed "collective leadership," and Western, posttotalitarian approaches to the study of the USSR all stressed the significance of the constraints on the powers of the General Secretary (see, e.g., Hammer 1990). This governmental pattern was, moreover, congruent with the pattern of authority relations in other key institutions. Perhaps most important, one sees this oligarchic pattern manifested in the work collective. Despite the emphasis on the autocratic-sounding principle of "one-man management," studies of Soviet-era management practices indicate a more complicated reality in which a troika of management, party, and trade union officials jointly and collegially governed workplace affairs (Ruble 1982;

Grancelli 1988; Yanowitch 1977, 134–64). Though the factory director was the symbolic leader of the enterprise and was burdened with ultimate formal authority and responsibility for enterprise affairs, he or she was both constrained and assisted by the enterprise oligarchy.

Oligarchic authority patterns can also be detected at earlier points in Russian history. For example, studies of the Russian peasant commune or *mir* suggest that the predominant authority pattern was collective decision making (Hosking 1990, 22–24). The heads of the peasant households would meet in a gathering called the *skhod* to make decisions to which individuals would be bound. When peasants moved to the newly industrializing centers of Russia in search of work, they brought with them this same pattern of authority. The *artel'* or workers' cooperative was an attempt to reproduce organizational and authority patterns learned in the *mir* into a new setting.

Perhaps the most radical statement of the oligarchy perspective comes from the historian Edward Keenan. According to Keenan (1986, 118), "the Muscovite, and later Russian, systems tended to prefer oligarchic and collegial rule, to avoid the single leader, and to function best when the nominal autocrat was in fact politically weak." Like others, Keenan sees this pattern in the political culture of the Russian peasant commune. According to Keenan, the pattern was one of collegial decision making in which heads of households would express their interests and views in an effort to influence decision making. Once a decision was made, the leadership group (in a fashion consistent with what Lenin would later term "democratic centralism") would close ranks and present a unified front for the community at large (Keenan 1986, 128).

More controversial is Keenan's (1986, 36–45) view of a high level of congruence with the peasant model in the political culture of the Russian court where a corporate form of decision making was also emphasized. This is not to suggest that the nominal autocrat or tsar was unimportant. On the contrary, Keenan argues that the system could not handle "tsarlessness" (*bestsarstvie*). Nonetheless, he argues that it was the *"idea* of a strong tsar" rather than the reality of strong autocratic power that was essential for systemic stability (Keenan 1986, 142).

Keenan's radical attempt to rethink our traditional understanding of Russian political culture has been received with both skepticism and even a degree of hostility (see Crummey 1987; Daniels 1987; Hellie 1987; Wortman 1987). However, in a more cautious fashion, other scholars have also begun to look closer at the political system of the Russian autocracy and, in the process, to adopt a more "balanced" view of the relationship between the tsar and the boyar class (Kollmann 1987; LeDonne 1991). Even some critics of the "oligarchy" school have accepted that it is a useful corrective to interpretations that "place far too much emphasis on the unlimited personal authority of the ruler" (Crummey 1988, 111–12).

Russian Authoritarianism

One might argue that the issue of autocracy versus oligarchy is, for purposes of establishing the odds for Russian democracy, largely beside the point. Either way Russian authority patterns look authoritarian. Shaped by centuries of geopolitical insecurity, a harsh natural environment, and a host of man-made tragic experiences, the Russians are seen as a people who have willingly accepted and internalized the need for authoritarianism (see, e.g., Szamuely 1974). While historians debate the relative importance of subcultural variations from this dominant theme, there is, as one Western observer put it, "no getting away from the predominantly authoritarian political nature of Soviet and Russian political experience" (Brown 1989, 18).

Thus, collective leadership of the Soviet party/state and of the Soviet economic enterprise should not obscure the undemocratic, hierarchical nature of the system. Nor should the collegial governance of the *skhod* obscure the fact that the heads of the peasant households collectively exercised "almost despotic authority" in the peasant community (Le-Donne 1991, 15–17). As one observer has argued, traditional Russian society was based on a command structure from the traditional "power assertive relationship" between Russian parents and their children to the level of the Russian government (LeDonne 1991, 15–17).

Notwithstanding this tradition of pervasive authoritarianism in authority relations in both Russian government and society, the question of change in those authority relations remains an open question. Surveys that seem to show public support for democratically constituted authority among many Russians provide one source of evidence of change in Russian political culture (Hahn 1993b; Reisinger, Miller, Hesli, and Maher 1994). In addition, developments in Soviet society in the post-Stalin era gave a hint of changing authority patterns long before democratization was to become an official political slogan. Though the kind of vigorous intermediate institutions emphasized by Eckstein were stifled in their development by the nature of the Soviet regime, subtle changes in authority patterns in primary-level institutions are worth noting. Thus, a 1971 study of family authority patterns pointed to a shift from an autocratic to a democratic pattern (Yanowitch 1977, 182). In the work collectives, Taylorite notions of industrial management that viewed workers as appendages to machines and that

Lenin had so enthusiastically embraced began, by the 1970s, to give way to a Soviet version of the "human relations" school that stressed the need to take account of psychological needs of the labor force. Even more to the point, crude, command forms of management were questioned by those who advocated broader participation in management by workers (Yanowitch 1977, 141 ff.). To be sure, the inherently hierarchical nature of the workplace hardly makes it the most promising starting point for democratization of authority. Moreover, none of these new ideas would fundamentally overturn the authoritarian character of Soviet workplace politics. However, the fact that the command system was even symbolically questioned in this manner in the work collective—the key nongovernmental institution in Soviet society— suggests some straining against the limits of existing authority patterns.

The Russian Emphasis On Order

Change in Russian political culture involving receptivity to less authoritarian patterns of authority may be partly explained in connection with a consideration of the traditional Russian emphasis on security and order. The Russian fear of chaos and disorder has been noted by many observers, both Russians and outsiders alike (see Brown 1989, 19–20). Strictly speaking, the priority allocated to *poryadok* and to government that is effective in achieving that end is not an authority pattern per se. Instead, this emphasis on order represents a larger societal value that has conditioned the construction of specific patterns of authority in Russian government and society. In particular, the consensus of the literature seems to be that it was the goals of security, order, and survival in a harsh context that gave rise to the tradition of Russian authoritarianism (Crummey 1987, 160). In effect, authoritarianism is best viewed not as a fundamental but as an instrumental value of the political culture, and nondemocratic, hierarchical patterns of authority might be said to be the empirical manifestation of the primary importance attached to order.

This emphasis on order appears to remain a constant in contemporary Russia. For example, a November 1994 survey found that 81 percent of respondents agreed, either completely or for the most part, that order needed to be established "at any price" (Levada 1995). Support for Zhirinovsky in the 1993 parliamentary elections was attributed largely to voters' concern with weak government (Teague 1994, 5). More recently, Alexander Lebed has been the prime beneficiary of the Russian desire for what is variously termed "strong leadership" or a "firm hand." His emphasis on the restoration of order to the chaos of Russian economic and political life resulted in his status as the most popular Russian political figure according to early 1997 public opinion polls ("Poll Shows Russians" 1997).

The continued desire for order does not, however, always or necessarily imply a desire to return to authoritarian rule. The Zhirinovsky and Lebed phenomena notwithstanding, some of the data appear to suggest that Russians have been able to divorce the concepts of authoritarianism and effective authority. Support for the idea of strong government remains high even among Russians who support democracy, and less than a quarter of those polled in one survey believed that dictatorship was the only solution to the problem of disorder ("Poll Shows Russians" 1997; also see Reisinger, Miller, Hesli, and Maher 1994). Citing a public opinion poll in which Russians ranked former British Prime Minister Margaret Thatcher very high on a list of "ideal leaders," Igor Klyamkin, one of the early Russian proponents of a "firm hand," suggested that for many Russians the ideal of strong leadership is better reflected in the "Iron Lady" than in a Pinochet or Stalin-type figure (*Izvestiia*, November 4, 1993, 4). Klyamkin concludes that in the eyes of most of its supporters, the "firm hand is not an alternative to democracy" (*Izvestiia*, November 4, 1993, 4). On the contrary, a May 1996 survey showed that a large majority of Russians believed that a strong state is a requirement for improving human rights and freedoms and for raising the general level of well-being of Russian citizens (Kutkovets and Klyamkin 1997). There is, moreover, no logically necessary inconsistency in such a position insofar as many established democracies have a record of strong, effective government.

This apparent ability of some Russians to distinguish the concepts of authoritarianism and effective authority may be partly explained by several decades of post-Stalinist stability in which Russians were largely free of such immediate threats to their physical security as war and famine. In this new, relatively more secure context, the meaning of order and security for Russians was subject to change. Whereas the emphasis on strong government and order may have once implied a concern with avoiding basic threats to survival, the Russian attachment to the "firm hand" now, according to one survey, seems to be primarily related to higher order dimensions of security such as economic security and protection from governmental "high-handedness and lawlessness" (*Izvestiia*, November 4, 1993, 4). It is not at all clear that authoritarianism is the most effective means of realizing this new and more demanding set of expectations.

Implications for Russian Democracy

From the view of Russian political culture and authority patterns discussed earlier, a number of implications for Russian democratization follow. First, the obstacles to democratization inherent in the political culture may be less than is often assumed by the most pessimistic observers. Those observers assume that the Russian penchant for authoritarianism and for powerful, autocratic leaders makes the attainment of stable democracy difficult at best. However, to the extent that Russian authoritarianism is seen as an instrumental value and to the extent that the Russian predisposition to autocracy is even partially overstated, then the possibility for congruence between democratic institutions and Russian political culture seems brighter.

Second, democratic stability in Russia will be dependent upon institutional choices that maximize the level of governability. Of course, the political stability of any political system will be dependent on the attainment of a minimum level of effective governance. However, in the course of institutional design there are trade-offs to be made, for example, between governability and responsiveness, and even within the parameters of what one would consider democratic government, there is a wide combination of institutional choices which can be made. Given the continued Russian emphasis on the "firm hand," choices that maximize governability in the pursuit of both the traditional and the newer Russian view of order will be particularly important.

Third, the common view of a Russian need for a president with autocratic-like power is probably exaggerated. As has been suggested, oligarchic authority patterns are at least as common in Russian political culture as are autocratic patterns, and in post-Stalinist Russia oligarchic patterns appear dominant. Thus, constitutional design that promotes corporate decision making among key institutions and leaders would tend to be most congruent with that political culture. At the same time, a symbolic leader (president or otherwise) who can represent the nation and its interests would be congruent with the Russian "tendency to conceive of political authority in personalised terms" (White 1979, 31) and with the consequent need to avoid "tsarlessness."

Finally, the new democratic institutions will tend to be most congruent with the political culture to the extent that they provide for at least the perception of a degree of consensus and shared purpose in governing. As was previously noted in discussing the political culture of the peasant commune, the Leninist principle of democratic centralism with its emphasis on at least the appearance of unanimity among leaders is unique neither to the Soviet period nor to the highest levels of Russian government.

In short, while democracy in Russia may not be precluded by considerations of political culture, it is not guaranteed either. Much will depend on making the right institutional choices. The extent to which the design of Russia's new democratic institutions meets the requirement of congruence with the political culture is the subject of the next section.

Russia's Democratic Architecture

Newly established democracies such as Russia are faced with a large number and range of choices to make in the design of democratic institutions. Included here are choices related to the distribution of powers between the legislature and executive, the design of the electoral system, the vertical division of power between the central government and local political units, and the role and powers of the judiciary. In making these choices, the issue of governability will be one important criterion guiding democratic craftsmanship, but it will not be the only one. Also important are considerations of democratic responsiveness, the legacy of past institutional arrangements, the advice and experience of nations providing support, and calculations of interest by participants in the process. Thus, there is room for considerable variation in the overall package of choices made, and the outcome of this process of democratic craftsmanship will often differ considerably from one democratizing regime to another.

The concern here is with the choices that the Russians have made and with their fit (or lack thereof) with the patterns of political authority found in the larger political culture. Specifically, the focus will be on what are perhaps the two most crucial choices made in the design of democratic institutions: the division of powers between the legislature and the executive and the nature of the electoral system.

Executive–Legislative Relations

As most observers of Russia have noted, the Russian semipresidential system created by the 1993 constitution tilts strongly in the direction of presidential power.[1] The power advantage of the Russian president stems, in large part, from two constitutional provisions. First, the president appoints the head of the government with the consent of the lower house of the legislature, the State Duma. However, if the president's nominee is rejected three times, then the president appoints the head of government, dissolves the Duma, and schedules new legislative elections (Russian Constitution, articles 83 and 111). Second, the

Duma has the right to adopt a vote of no confidence in the government. After the first such vote, the president can either dismiss the government or ignore the no confidence vote. If a second vote of no confidence is taken within three months, the president has the option of either dismissing the government or dissolving the Duma and scheduling new elections (Russian Constitution, article 117).

These two aspects of the Russian constitution give the president strong control over the prime minister and, indirectly, over the government, thus causing the formally semipresidential system to operate, in normal times, much like a presidential system in that respect. At the same time, unlike pure presidentialism in which both the legislature and president are elected to serve fixed terms that (impeachment aside) cannot be cut short, semipresidentialism allows, as we have already seen under the circumstances previously described, the president to dissolve the Duma. Yet, the president remains out of the reach of a legislature (again excepting the difficult impeachment process) that might want to cut the president's term short. Thus, the Russian president appears to have the best of both worlds.

When one factors into the power equation the broad and only vaguely circumscribed right of the president to rule by decree in both normal and emergency situations, the advantage of the Russian presidency appears even more lopsided (Russian Constitution, articles 88 and 90). Some of the most significant policies of the postcommunist era in Russia, including industrial privatization and the war in Chechnya, were conducted almost entirely via the mechanism of presidential decrees.

These features of Russia's presidentially oriented democracy suggest a very close resemblance to what O'Donnell has called "delegative democracy." According to O'Donnell (1994, 59), delegative democracy is premised on the assumption that, "whoever wins election to the presidency is thereby entitled to govern as he or she sees fit, constrained only by the hard facts of existing power relations and by a constitutionally limited term of office." In such a system, the president sees himself as the embodiment of the nation and its interests and seeks to stand above politics. Institutions such as parties and legislatures are treated as nuisances, whereas the president and his close advisers are "the alpha and the omega of politics" (O'Donnell 1994, 59–60). Yeltsin's reluctance to attach himself firmly to any political party, his penchant to rule through what Latin Americans call *decretismo*, his past dealings with the legislative branch (most notably the October 1993 use of the military to shut down the old Supreme Soviet), and his reliance on a small circle of advisers are all textbook indications of delegative democracy.

Though some have worried that the powers granted to and exercised by the Russian president threaten to subvert democracy in favor of what might, at best, be considered a constitutional dictatorship, there is also an understandable temptation to interpret the Russian constitution and the impressive formal powers it grants to the president as providing for an appropriately customized version of democracy that is congruent with the political culture. A strong and largely nonaccountable Russian presidency might be viewed as congruent with the Russian penchant for strong, personalized leadership and with the emphasis in the political culture on order and effective government. In fact, until recently, the common assumption in the literature on democratic systems was that presidentialism was the system most "conducive to strong and effective government" (see Sartori 1994, 88). Therefore, a strongly presidentially dominated system with significant autocratic features might be said to provide that "healthy element of authoritarianism" that Eckstein argued was required for democratic stability in any country and that one might argue is particularly important in the Russian case.

However, this view that Russian political culture requires a strong presidency for democracy to succeed is mistaken on three different counts. First, as was previously discussed, the Russian need for strong *individual* leadership may be overstated. Second, the "personalist" style of leadership characteristic of delegative democracy is not likely to contribute to the effective development of strong political parties and other intermediate associations that Eckstein sees as crucial to democratic stability. On the contrary, it appears to promote what he terms "mass society"—that is, a society in which leaders and the masses have a direct and unmediated relationship to one another, in which people are atomized, and which is thereby prone to instability and political extremism. Furthermore, the absence of those intermediate institutions means a lack of opportunity to develop the habit of nonauthoritarian authority patterns that tends to be absent from primary level institutions such as the workplace.

Third, and perhaps most important, the Russian desire for order and effective government may not, in the final analysis, be best served by a strong and independent presidency. On the contrary, the consensus in the most recent literature on the subject is that strong leadership in presidential systems is more an illusion than a reality (Linz and Valenzuela 1994; Stepan and Skach 1993). This conclusion is based on a number of observations about the nature of presidential democracy.

Most significant is the fact that the fundamental characteristic of presidentialism is dual authority. Both the legislature and the executive are popularly elected, and each can thus rightfully claim to represent the popular will. When presidents enjoy the support of legislative majorities, strong, effective government can be the result. But a survey of presidential democracies between 1973 and 1987 indicated that presidents enjoyed such majorities less than 50 percent of the time (Stepan and Skach 1993, 18). Thus, presidentialism can be a recipe for stalemate, gridlock, and confrontation without any democratic means of resolution. The frequent result is nondemocratic resolution through presidential dictatorship and/or military intervention in politics.

In Russia, the semipresidential nature of the system does, theoretically, allow for such stalemates to be brought to a head through the mechanism of the no-confidence vote. However, compared to the situation in parliamentary systems, the no-confidence vote in Russia is much less likely to deal effectively with the problem of stalemated government. For one, the no-confidence vote can only challenge the president indirectly by attacking his government and prime minister. The president himself cannot be removed from office in this manner. In addition, as previously noted, the president's response to a second no-confidence vote can be to dissolve the Duma instead of the government. Thus, it is much less likely that the legislature would actually follow up on threats to carry through with a second such vote, as witnessed in the summer 1995 decision of the Duma to back away from a threatened second vote of no confidence in the Chernomyrdin government. At the same time, the need for an effective mechanism of no confidence as a means of clearing away gridlock is greater in the Russian system than in parliamentary systems precisely because the legislature in Russia had less control over the formation of the government in the first place. The odds of a government out of tune with legislative thinking are therefore greater in Russia than would be the case under a parliamentary system. In fact, with the exception of a brief honeymoon period during the early months of the postcommunist era, the record of relations between Yeltsin and the Duma has been one of largely unremitting conflict and tension.

To the extent that formal presidential power is so great as to allow the president simply to ignore a legislature with which he is at odds, then the lack of an effective mechanism for dealing with apparent gridlock would be of little consequence. However, even in the Russian case in which the balance of constitutional authority clearly favors the president, ignoring the legislature does not necessarily come without a price. First of all, the Russian Duma does have negative powers that allow it to block presidential initiatives in some areas and to complicate, at the least, presidential plans in others. For example, the Duma's refusal to ratify START II and its decision to override a presidential veto of ''trophy art''[2] legislation have complicated Yeltsin's foreign policy. Second, even where the president is able to thwart legislative opposition, the legislature retains the ability publicly to question presidential initiatives. Outspoken legislative opposition to the war in Chechnya and constant criticism of Yeltsin's economic policies each contributed to the sense of a presidency under siege and of a government working at cross-purposes. Even the theoretically strongest of presidents needs the legislature and the parties represented therein to provide some public support for presidential initiatives and to share publicly some of the responsibility for the implementation of difficult policy decisions.

In presidential systems in general and in delegative democracies in particular, there is strong incentive not to provide presidents with this support. A weak legislature without much ability to shape public policy is an invitation to political grandstanding precisely because the legislature does not have real responsibility for governing. It also encourages voters to cast protest votes in parliamentary elections insofar as real power is found elsewhere in the presidency. The success of Zhirinovky in the December 1993 parliamentary vote and of Zyuganov and his Communist Party in December 1995 might have been augmented precisely by knowledge that the power of the Duma was more symbolic than real. Moreover, the winner-take-all character of presidential elections mitigates against compromise and coalition building. In keeping their eye on the larger prize of the presidency, parliamentary and party leaders will tend to distance themselves rather than to rally behind the president in difficult times. This is particularly true of delegative democracies such as Russia where the president's lack of a base in any political party can deprive him of the dependable support of a party of his own. For example, Russia's Choice, the closest one came in Russia to a presidential party in the 1993 elections, openly broke with Yeltsin over the issue of Chechnya, leaving the president politically isolated.

Meanwhile, the fixed terms of office of presidentialism prevent an immediate electoral solution to the problem of declining presidential popularity that can result. In early 1995, in large part because of the Chechen fiasco, opinion polls indicated that public confidence in Yeltsin was extremely low (Sedov 1995). Yet despite that fact, any question of a change in leadership had to await the summer 1996 presidential elections. Likewise, Yeltsin's poor health following his reelection left much of the country feeling rudderless. The combination of a constitutionally weak legislature and a physically and politically weak president led many, as of early 1997, increasingly to question the future of Russia's democratic experiment. Poll results published in May 1997 indicated that close to three quarters of Russians did not approve of the activity of Yeltsin as president and that only 5 percent of eligible voters would support him in the first round of a presidential election (Savelyev 1997; "Poll Shows Standing" 1997). Yet another presidential election is years away.

In short, the powers granted to the Russian president, though justified by some on the grounds of congruence with a political culture and a set of authority patterns that emphasize both authoritarianism and order, have produced neither. On the contrary, a majority of Russians surveyed in 1995 indicated that the defining characteristic of contemporary Russia is neither democracy nor dictatorship but, rather, anarchy (Levada 1995, 5). Since then, according to yet another survey, things have gotten still worse as public confidence in state institutions has continued to plummet in response to a growing perception of a crisis of state power (Gorshkov 1997b, 1–2). These trends seem to confirm an observation once made by a scholar of Latin America to the effect that, "the stronger the president, the weaker the presidential system" (Valenzuela 1995, 97).

The Electoral System

Further complicating and detracting from the performance of Russia's semipresidential democracy is the electoral system that has been in place since the time of the December 1993 parliamentary elections. The electoral system is spelled out by law rather than in the constitution, but its impact is potentially so fundamental to the performance of a political system that it might be considered of greater consequence than many a constitutional provision.[3]

In designing an electoral system for the purpose of filling the State Duma, the Russians, after much debate, opted for a hybrid system. Half of the 450 seats were to be filled through elections in single-seat districts and the other half through proportional representation (PR) based on a single national constituency with a 5 percent threshold. Part of what shaped this set of choices were considerations of political self interest. It was, for example, commonly assumed at the time that the Communists, with their countrywide organization, would benefit from single member districts more so than newer reformist parties. At the same time, the choice of electoral system would have larger implications for the overall development of democratic stability.

In particular, the goal of many democrats was to use the electoral system as a means to engineer an effective party system. On the one hand, this meant stimulating party development. As Eckstein and others have (for varying reasons) emphasized, mediating institutions such as political parties are crucial for democratic stability. Yet, after more than seventy years of one-party rule, parties in Russia were embryonic and weak. The party list vote was, thus, intended in part to stimulate the further development of Russian political parties. On the other hand, an effective party system requires keeping the number of relevant parties limited. Too many relevant parties inhibits governability and runs the risk of what Sartori has called "polarized pluralism" in which parties flee the political center in an attempt to outbid one another in the quest for political support (Sartori 1976). Thus, in Russia, the 5 percent threshold on the party list vote and the 50 percent of seats to be selected from single member districts might have been expected to keep the number of relevant political parties limited in the effort to promote governability.

As measured by the results of the 1993 Duma elections, the hybrid Russian electoral system seemed to have produced a paradoxical result in which there was simultaneously both too much and not enough party development. The PR vote for party list seats, despite the 5 percent threshold, gave seats to eight parties, too many under most circumstances for effective government (*Election Observation Report* 1994). Moreover, the largest vote getter was Zhirinovsky's extremist Liberal-Democratic Party, which was allocated about one-quarter of the party list seats.

Meanwhile, despite the proliferation of parties and the breadth of party representation in the Duma, the depth of party development remained shallow. The party development stimulated by the party list vote was more apparent than real. In many cases, Russian political parties proved to be little more than labels placed on the political ambitions of individual politicians. Thus, the Liberal-Democratic Party's success in the party list vote had more to do with Zhirinovsky's personal appeal than with party organization and development. That this was generally the case was reflected in the electoral results in the single-member constituencies. In those contests the continuing weakness of parties in general was made clear as more than half of the seats were won by candidates running without a firm affiliation with any party (*Election Observation Report* 1994).

Many Russian observers, most notably Yeltsin himself, seemed to appreciate the problem of political fragmentation manifested in these electoral results. Note in this regard that Yeltsin in early 1995 was urging the formation of two centrist political blocs, one right of center to be led by his Prime Minister Viktor Chernomyrdin and the other left of center to be led by then Duma chairman Ivan Rybkin. Yet the December 1995 parliamentary elections gave little indication that the Russian political system was moving in that direction.

In those elections, the number of parties that exceeded the 5 percent threshold fell to four and the Russian Communist Party's overall representation in the Duma constituted a plurality of more than one-third of all Duma seats. To some extent, the 1995 results thereby showed some modest degree of party consolidation. Still, overall, the Duma remained an excessively fragmented body. It was, in fact, the single member districts that produced most of the fragmentation, with candidates elected from two dozen different parties. In addition, some seventy-seven seats in the individual districts were won by independents not formally affiliated with any political party. Meanwhile, the Russian Communist Party, the single most successful party in the district races, had only fifty-eight of its candidates elected in that fashion ("Results" 1997).

Those results made it clear that one cannot simply will a two-party system into existence. Especially given the fragmentation that characterized postcommunist Russian society, it would have been naive to expect that a strong party system based on two or three well-developed parties could be made to appear in Russia overnight. Still, the specific choices made by Russia in designing its electoral system did little to promote the process of party development and consolidation.

The problem with the Russian electoral system is twofold. First, the election of half of the Duma deputies via the national party list vote reduces the incentive for party organization in each of Russia's eighty-nine regions (see Ordeshook 1995, 56–57). Instead, it puts a premium on national personalities to which party labels are, as an afterthought, then attached. Development of a truly national party organization is thereby stifled. As Yeltsin aide Georgy Satarov has argued, instead of promoting the development of strong parties as originally intended, the party list vote has served only "to encourage the proliferation of political clubs" ("Is the Kremlin" 1997).

Second, the combination of this national party list voting with single-member districts reduces the likelihood that the latter will have the hoped-for reductive effect on the number of parties that achieve representation. Since only half of the seats will be elected in this fashion, the incentive for regional party organization is thereby diminished by half. The result is to leave the field open to local notables running as independents, allowing a host of minor parties to succeed in various localities. Instead of helping to promote the development of a "structured party system," the mix of choices reflected in Russia's electoral system seems almost designed to thwart any hope that such a goal can be accomplished.

As Steven Fish (1997, 201–3) has argued, Russia's "liberal" parties have been the primary casualties of this lack of party organization. He argues that their less than stellar electoral performance to date may have less to do with any fundamental incongruence between liberal values and Russian culture than with weak party organization and poor quality electoral campaigns. But although he sees party organization as a factor "strictly endogenous to the liberal parties themselves" (Fish 1997, 201), it may be the case that the liberal parties have been simply responding to the structure of incentives established by the electoral system. At the very least, the electoral system provided the illusion that one might succeed without extensive party development. Ironically, a system based entirely on single-member districts, which was once assumed to be of primary benefit to the Communist Party given its countrywide organization, might actually have been in the interest of Russian liberals if only because it would have induced an earlier and more active effort to create nationwide party organizations of their own.

Perhaps in recognition of this logic, in 1995 Yeltsin proposed, without success, to change the electoral system to allow for a greater proportion of seats elected from single-member districts. In spring 1997 the notion of eliminating the Duma's party list vote and replacing it with single-member districts was raised again. The Saratov region had already switched to single-member districts in elections for its regional legislature and was being touted by some as a model for electoral reform at the national level ("Is the Kremlin" 1997). Under such a system, national politicians seeking to support their ambitions would have no choice but to develop a party organization which was truly national in its scope (i.e., organized throughout Russia's eighty-nine regions). In addition, single-member districts would give Russia's developing parties greater incentive to form coalitions or even to merge to acquire the majority or plurality required for election. Alternatively, a party list vote based on regional constituencies rather than on a single national constituency would, by itself or in combination with single-member districts, have also required the development and organization of truly national parties whose reach extended far beyond Moscow. However, any electoral reform proposal will be contentious and will have to contend with the inevitable difficulty involved in persuading a sitting legislature to change the voting rules under which its members were originally elected.

When one examines the nature of the Russian electoral and party system in conjunction with the previous consideration of presidential power, the problems with Russia's institutional choices become even more apparent. On the one hand, the dominant role of the Russian president in the formation of the Russian government reduces the incentive of Russian political parties to merge or form coalitions, either in the election campaign or in the Duma, for the purpose of being able to constitute a governing majority. The inability of Russian democrats to close ranks and form a unified bloc has been due in large part to the fact that the leaders of the various democratic parties all had their eyes on the larger prize of the presidency.

On the other hand, to the extent that the electoral system has allowed for the development of a fragmented, multiparty system, it reduces the likelihood that any Russian president will be able consistently to maintain majority support in the legislature (see Mainwaring 1993). The impressive powers of the presidency notwithstanding, the system is likely, under these circumstances, to continue to lurch from one crisis of executive-legislative relations to another. That is neither symbolically nor substantively conducive to effective or stable democratic government.

Conclusion

Issues of institutional craftsmanship of the kind discussed here are arguably more crucial to the development and consolidation of democracy in Russia than they are in many other postcommunist regimes. In the more Western-oriented countries of the postcommunist world, most notably the nations of Central Europe and the Baltics, the cultural foundations of democratic government appear deeply enough rooted to survive irrespective of institutional design. In other cases, most notably former Soviet Central Asia, democracy appears so foreign to the local political culture that the question of parliamentary or presidential democracy is an irrelevant issue. It is precisely in culturally more ambivalent cases such as Russia, however, where such matters have the potential to make the greatest difference. In such cases the future of democracy appears most difficult to predict, and it is there that the design of democratic institutions can tip the balance between democratic consolidation and authoritarian revival.

To this point, however, many of the key choices that have been made in crafting Russia's democratic institutions have been "wrong" choices. They have served to minimize the chances for effective government in a political culture where the preference for order and "governability" has always been and continues to be a central political and social value. Left uncorrected, Russia's drift in the direction of a weak democratic state may lead to increasing support for a strong authoritarian alternative. To counter that tendency, *Russian democrats must be able to demonstrate that democratic states can also be strong states and the basis of effective government.* At least in part that will require institutional reforms that provide a new system of executive-legislative relations that both reduces the dependence of the Russian polity on the political and physical health of the president and provides greater incentive for cooperation between the legislative and executive branches. At the same time, electoral reforms that more effectively stimulate the emergence of a structured party system, most notably an end to national party list voting, would also be a step in the right direction (see Ordeshook and Shvetsova 1997).

Fears of some Russian democrats that strengthening the power of the legislature and shifting from party list voting to single-member districts would primarily benefit the Russian Communist Party are overstated. First, abandoning party list voting or at least switching from a national to regional lists would once and for all destroy the illusion that one can win elections and govern entirely from Moscow. It would force Russian liberals, who Fish (1997) sees as particularly disadvantaged by a lack of strong national organizations, to remedy that deficiency. Second, a strengthened legislature would tend to induce changes in voting patterns that could reduce the tendency of some citizens to use legislative elections as a means to send a message of protest to the Russian government. Finally, both strengthening the legislature and initiating electoral reform will tend to induce and reward greater moderation and political consolidation on the part of key political figures and their parties. Such a result is a product both of the necessity to achieve the requisite pluralities of votes in the single-member district races and of the greater responsibility of the legislature for actual governance of the country.

To be sure, no such institutional reforms will themselves guarantee the success of Russia's democratic transition. Economic performance or international developments can also serve to tip the balance in one direction or the other. Still, the design of institutions remains one of the few areas in which leaders can, within the parameters established by the political culture, intervene to help determine the odds of success.

Notes

An earlier version of this essay was presented at the 1995 Annual Meeting of the American Political Science Association, Chicago, August 31–September 3, 1995.

1. Newly democratizing nations have three essential choices in defining the nature of the executive-legislative relationship. They are: presidentialism, parliamentarism, and semipresidentialism (see Sartori 1994). Presidential systems are those in which one finds a popularly elected president who directs the executive branch of government and who serves a fixed term of office that

(except for the extreme case of impeachment) cannot be cut short by legislative action. Presidential systems are, thus, systems of separation of power between the legislative and executive branches. Parliamentary systems, in contrast, are based on the sharing of power. In such systems, the head of the executive is appointed by the parliament, serves with the continued support of the parliament, and can be dismissed via a parliamentary vote of no confidence. The executive, in turn, can dissolve parliament and call for new elections. Thus, unlike in presidential systems in which the executive and legislature have independent claims on authority, in a parliamentary system the authority of each branch is mutually interdependent.

The Russian constitution of 1993 provides for neither pure presidentialism nor pure parliamentarism but for a hybrid system of semipresidentialism. Semipresidential systems incorporate features of both presidentialism and parliamentarism. As in presidential systems, the president is popularly elected for a fixed term. However, the president must share the power of the executive with a prime minister who, as in a parliamentary system, is dependent on legislative support. Thus, the president is elected and serves independently from the legislature, but his will must be processed via a legislature-dependent prime minister. Whereas some observers see semipresidentialism as a third and genuinely distinct form of democratic government, others see it as a system that alternates between presidential and parliamentary phases according to political circumstances and the political will and character of whoever is elected president.

2. "Trophy art" refers to artifacts taken by Russian forces from Germany and other occupied nations at the end of World War II. The Duma has consistently taken a harder line on the question of returning trophy art than has Yeltsin.

3. Two essential choices are possible in designing an electoral system—majoritarian and proportional systems (see Sartori 1994). Majoritarian systems are typically based on single-member districts in which the winner takes all. There is room for some variation insofar as winning might require an absolute majority (in which case run-off elections will generally be required) or simply the largest plurality. In either case, the goal of such systems is to process votes with the intent of sacrificing pure representation in favor of limiting the number of competitive and relevant political parties. The winner-take-all format provides a disincentive to waste votes on "third" parties and thereby has a tendency to produce, on a constituency by constituency basis, two-party systems. However, as Sartori (1994, 36–37) has emphasized, it does not necessarily follow that this electoral system will produce a two-party system at the national level unless it is the same two parties that are most competitive in each of the country's single member districts. According to Sartori (1994, 37), the latter will not occur unless the party system is one that is "structured" (i.e., one in which the primary allegiance of voters is to the party label rather than to the local notable or chieftain).

Systems of proportional representation (PR), in contrast, seek to translate votes into legislative seats in a fashion that is in some sense proportional. In a pure system, the degree of proportionality might be very high, though again there are variations. There are differences in the translation rules that govern the mathematics of converting votes into seats—including differences in the vote thresholds required for representation. Potentially introducing even more variation is the size of constituencies. A single nationwide constituency in which citizens engaged in party list voting will produce a more purely representative outcome at the national level than would party list voting on a district by district basis.

8

Transitions from Communism: State-Centered Approaches

Philip G. Roeder

The last Soviet legislative elections, which began in January 1990, opened opportunities for democratization in the union republics of the USSR. Yet, starting with similar Soviet institutions and facing a common opportunity to develop democracy, the Soviet union republics and successor states have pursued diverging paths of constitutional development. Of fifteen successor states, fewer than half can be categorized unambiguously as democracies, and an equal number are ruled by authoritarian regimes. How can we explain this variation? In inviting me to contribute this chapter, the editors posed this problem as a competition between society-centered and state-centered explanations. I will take some liberties with their question and argue that it misses more important distinctions that cut across the state–society divide—specifically, distinctions among theories of democratization rooted in competing paradigms of political science.

In this chapter, the dependent variable is the *constitution* of each regime, which—whether accurately described in a written document or not—is a polity's most fundamental rules defining political roles and relationships. Most important, the constitution creates offices that exercise the policy-making powers of a political community and defines relationships of accountability (Finer 1971, 145; Maddox 1982, 806). The question that the editors pose concerns variation among regimes in different successor states (cross-sectional variation) and among regimes within individual states over time (longitudinal variation). In this chapter, I pool cross-sectional and longitudinal comparisons to analyze the twenty-one regimes that existed in the union republics and successor states between the 1990 elections and the end of 1996 (see table 8.2). The object of this chapter is to identify the independent variables that led to the adoption of either democratic or nondemocratic constitutions in these states. I will sketch a theory of democratization rooted in the realist paradigm; specifically, I will argue that the most immediate constraint on the post-Soviet outcomes was the balance of power among major politicians engaged in the bargaining process of constitutional design and that this balance was itself constrained by the preexisting Soviet institutional structure of each union republic.

This chapter is divided into three parts. In the first I make a case for theory rooted in political realism, comparing this with alternative paradigms—specifically, political economy and political sociology. In the second I develop a realist analysis of bargaining over constitutions. The third part very briefly presents a test of this theory, using the recent experience of the fifteen successor states of the former Soviet Union. The successor states provide a "natural experiment" in which to study the processes of democratization and "authoritarianization," for the states began with nearly identical institutions that were established in their common recent history. Moreover, their divergent constitutional development is in itself a significant phenomenon and needs explanation.

Explaining Democratization: Alternative Paradigms

Theoretically informed research on the sources of post-Soviet democratization must specify dependent and independent variables in ways that permit comparison of cases, even if the comparison is simply counterfactual (Fearon 1991; King, Keohane, and Verba 1994). The choice of variables will be conditioned by the paradigm—whether explicit or not—that informs one's research. The choice of paradigm—conscious or not—is prior to the choice of focus on the state, on society, or on the relationship between them.

Choice of Paradigm

Competing paradigms of comparative political analysis—such as political economy, political sociology, and political realism—are rooted in different epistemologies. In the study of democratization, the most important difference among these paradigms is their assumptions about the motivations of the primary actors in the process.[1] A paradigm describes fundamental variables that are common to all the theories that develop under its conceptual umbrella (Kuhn 1970). A paradigm defines certain questions as more central and others as more peripheral to its concerns; it provides the conceptual building blocks with which to construct middle-range theories, including theories of democratization.

Political economy typically explains politics by human relations of production, consumption, and exchange. For example, Frieden (1991, 7, 15–16), in defining modern political economy, argues that "political outcomes are the result of choices made by social groups . . . [and] the economic interests of social groups are central to their political choices." Political economists are a diverse lot, claiming such different precursors as Adam Smith, John Stuart Mill, and Karl Marx and today describing themselves with such labels as neoclassical, liberal-institutional, and Marxist political economists. Nonetheless, they share a common epistemology that sees politics as yet one more realm in which *Homo economicus* as producer and consumer pursues advantage (often called "utility") in the form of wealth and other consumables. This distinctive epistemology is seen in the political economists' explanations for the origins and institutional forms of the state. Marx's theory of the state as an instrument of class domination is well known to students of post-Soviet politics; his theory of the bourgeois roots of parliamentary democracy, equally so. Paralleling this is the positive political economists' view of the state as a system of material distribution (Heckathorn and Maser 1987) or as a monopolistic service provider engaged in exchange with other major economic actors. For example, Geoffrey Brennan and James Buchanan (1985, 25–27, 65) assess the value of alternative state rules by their relative contribution to the economy, based on their assumption that "market and political institutions are valued instrumentally for their capacity to produce goods and services that citizens want." They characterize their enterprise as analyzing *Homo economicus* in nonmarket settings. North (1979, 252) explains the particular institutional form of the state by the bargaining between a leader who seeks to maximize rents and subjects who want to procure the services of the state (protection and justice) at least cost:

> The basic set of services that the state would provide are the underlying rules of the game. Whether evolving as a body of unwritten customs (as in the feudal manor) or as a written constitution, they have a two-fold objective. (1) They are designed to specify the fundamental rules of competition and cooperation which will provide a structure of property rights . . . for maximizing the rents accruing to the ruler. (2) Within the framework of the first objective, they are designed to reduce transaction costs in order to foster maximum output of the society and, therefore, increase tax revenues accruing to the state.

Democracy prevails over alternative constitutional forms when its rules provide greater economic efficiency (North and Weingast 1988).

Political sociology finds the roots of political action in cognitive constructs such as beliefs, norms, and intersubjective meanings. Inspired by the writings of Émile Durkheim, Ferdinand Tönnies, Max Weber, and Talcott Parsons, the dominant tradition of political sociology finds the bases of human action in internalized norms that constitute shared meanings and define appropriate action. The bases of social equilibrium are role orientations that are learned through socialization, that shape an individual's conception of appropriate behavior in different contexts, and that may even come to shape the ways in which individuals impute meaning to events and order reality (see Hall and Taylor 1994; March and Olsen 1989; Steinmo, Thelen, and Longstreth 1992). The culturalists' hypothesis, in the words of Parker (1992, 58), is that a state is more likely to develop democratic institutions today when its traditions provide models for democracy: "In most recovering communist countries, reform is made easier by distant traditions of free-market democracy" (cf. Sneider 1991). These traditions may be found in the state, nonstate public practices, or the family. For example, Critchlow (1992, 12) predicts a bright future for democracy in Kazakstan, because "Kazakhs have notions of democracy stemming from their own nomadic tradition. The life-style of their ancestors engendered a certain practical, grass-roots democracy: it was necessary for a tribal chieftain to gain popularity among his followers; otherwise, given the living conditions of the steppe, members of the tribe would merely wander off." From Weber's taxonomy of legitimacy to Gabriel Almond and Sidney Verba's analysis of civic culture, an essential ingredient in the origins and stability of democracies is congruence between political culture and constitutions.

Alternatively, political realism approaches politics as the sphere of activity in which individuals seek to expand and to secure power. It begins from the political scientist's conceit that the political realm is not simply a manifestation of economic or cultural forces but enjoys considerable autonomy from these and, indeed, is a powerful, independent causal force in the economy and society. Precursors of modern political realism include Niccolò Machiavelli, Benedict de Spinoza, and Thomas Hobbes, who set down basic premises of subsequent realist analysis—that humans naturally seek power, that power relations are both cooperative (for joint gains) and competitive (for relative gains), and that the chief constraint on the pursuit of power is the balance of power. In this realist tradition, power is the ability to affect and effect outcomes by one's decisions, and, so, a central analytic concern for realism is the allocation of decision making in different polities. In the analysis of constitution making, realism begins from two assumptions: that constitution making is first and foremost about the allocation of decision-making powers and that each politician is a rational self-interested actor who seeks to design political institutions so as to maximize his or her own power. This has both static and dynamic aspects; that is, it concerns both the extent and the duration of their power. Power-maximizing politicians seek to maximize their effective decision-making domain, but they also seek to increase their chances of political survival.

The brief for the realist approach to constitution making is simply that compared with alternative paradigms, political realism more immediately addresses the core issues in that process. Realism configures constitution making as bargaining among politicians (whether state officials or not) over the allocation of decision-making powers; that is, the fundamental issue in constitutional politics is rules that define who gets to decide. Included in constitutional politics are ethnoconstitutionalism (allocation of decisions concerning policies affecting ethnic communities),[2] federalism (allocation of decision making between central and peripheral governments), and privatization (allocation of decisions concerning economic production and distribution between state and private actors) as well as democratization (allocation of decisions concerning the tenure of state officials).

Choice of Focus

The decision to begin research with a focus on state, society, or the state–society nexus should be a pragmatic choice influenced by one's dependent variable and empirical cases. Most important, an analyst must identify the primary actors who can affect the outcome. Once it has been made, however, this choice of focus should have a powerful impact on the structure of one's analysis. Although the *locus* of causes (what is implied by the distinction between state-centered and society-centered "approaches") need not be limited to either state or society, more rigorous theory should seek to cast these causes as variables with a single consistent *focus*. To illustrate: An analysis of the collapse of authoritarian regimes might identify state officials as the primary actors. Yet the constraints on their choices are not simply attributes of the state; these constraints may include, for example, performance of the economy or shifts in public attitudes. Analysis that focuses on these state officials must include these societal causes but must keep in mind two admonitions: First, whatever the locus of these causes, they must be cast as variables and their causal effect explained in terms of the focus selected—in this illustration, as constraints on the choices of state officials. Second, the more remote the causes from the primary actors' choices and the longer the causal chain from constraint to choice, the less important the relationship. In this illustration, "mass" political culture might be one of the first constraints to be severed by Ockham's razor.

The choice of paradigm is prior to, but does not predetermine, the choice of focus. The distinctions between paradigm and focus are cross-cutting. Thus, in the political economic tradition classical Marxist historical materialism focuses on society and stresses the role of societal actors who design a political order to defend their class interests; the constitution is part of a superstructure erected on the material base of production. The model of a revenue-maximizing ruler found in positive political economy shifts the focus to the calculations of state officials, who design institutions to extract revenues more efficiently (Levi 1988). The contract theory of the state, however, focuses on the exchange between state officials and major economic actors (North 1979). In the political-sociological tradition, students of political culture have stressed the cognitive, normative, ideational, evaluative, affective, or subjective bases of democracy in both the populace at large (society-focused) and among state officials (state-focused). Although realist analysis is most commonly associated with an intrastate focus on checks and balances, it may also focus on the balance of power within society or between states and societies. A realist reading of Moore (1966a), for example, would stress his thesis that the balance of power between aristocracy and crown and between aristocracy and urban bourgeoisie gave rise to and sustained British democracy. A realist theory of civil society stresses not its cognitive elements, as political sociologists (de Tocqueville 1966; Putnam 1993) might, but the balance of power between state and society as a constraint that makes the costs of suppression too high for a government. Table 8.1 summarizes these points.

My own decision to focus on state actors in the analysis of the transition between Soviet authoritarianism and the constitutions of post-Soviet regimes from 1990 to 1996 reflects three factors that are empirical rather than paradigmatic: First, as suggested earlier, the primary actors on both sides of the bargaining table in this period were persons in official positions of power. In the post-Soviet drama that determined whether authoritarian regimes survived and whether democracies consolidated, the populace only infrequently played a major role and never was a primary actor at the bargaining table. Second, the associational ties of civil society, and particularly political society as Stepan (1988, 4) labels it, were extremely weak in this period—far weaker than in Latin America, let alone advanced industrial societies (Linz and

TABLE 8.1
Examples of Alternative Research Paradigms and Foci

Paradigm	Focus on Society	Focus on State-Society Nexus	Focus on State
Political economy	State as superstructure	Contracts between ruler and ruled	Revenue-maximizing state
Political sociology	"Mass" political culture	Cultural-institutional congruence	Elite culture
Political realism	Class balance	Balance between state and civil society	Institutional checks and balances

Stepan 1996a). In the space between the purely private lives of house-holds and the state, the policies of forced departicipation under the Leninist regime left a nearly atomized public sphere (Roeder 1989). The state's previous monopolization of economic and public life left organizations outside the state with few resources by which they can increase the costs of oppression to political leaders (Dahl 1971, 14–16). Although on the output (implementation) side these may have been weak states facing strong societies, to use Migdal's (1988) phrase, on the input side of the polity, society was very weak. Third, as a legacy of the Soviet period, the state played a predominant role in structuring the interests that dominated politics in this period. By virtue of the state's active role in the economy and the anemia of the nonstate sector, the state and posts associated with it were some of the most important sources of personal wealth. The state and organizations that live in a symbiotic relationship with it became the locus of the most important interest groups. The major actors formally outside the structure of the state were dependent on the state, resembling parastatals more than truly private institutions.

Realism does not predetermine the focus of analysis on actors in positions of power. It does, however, predetermine the level of analysis (Singer 1961). In positing that the dependent variable is an outcome of a bargaining process, realism establishes the process itself rather than the individual actors as the unit of analysis and comparison. That is, the variation that realism seeks to explain in constitutional politics is the outcomes of different bargaining processes. Both dependent and independent variables must be cast so as to describe this process rather than simply the individual participants.

A Realist Theory of Democratization

In the realist paradigm, a constitution is the resultant of bargaining among politicians who typically seek to design institutions that will maximize their control over the policy process and maximize their tenure in office. The outcome of this bargaining depends on the balance of power among them, which is principally created by the preexisting political institutions within which they operate. In this process, democracy emerges not because it is the object of the politicians' collective ambition but because it is a practical compromise among politicians blocked from achieving their particular objectives.

Variables: Constitutive Rules and Relative Leverage

The dependent variable distinguishes polities according to the structure of accountability in each. Democracy is a constitution in which any majority of the population can pose a credible threat of removing the effective policy makers (or can defeat such a threat). Authoritarianism, as the term is used here, refers to the broad category of nondemocracies—the set of polities in which those who exercise the policy-making powers of the state are accountable to only a segment of the adult population (Schumpeter 1975; Dahl 1971). In short, alternative constitutions are defined by the nature of the *selectorate*—the group that can pose a credible threat of removing the policy makers (or can defeat such an attempt) (Roeder 1993). On this basis, it is possible to identify four types of constitutions—autocracies, oligarchies, exclusive republics, and democracies—distinguished by the locus and relative restrictiveness of their respective selectorates. *Autocracies* are defined by the concentration of power in the hands of the executive; the inner circle of the leader (be it the monarch's court or the general secretary's politburo) constitutes the selectorate. In *oligarchies*, often found in military regimes, bureaucratic-authoritarianism, and caciquismo, policy makers are the agents of a broader political elite that may include generals, *apparatchiks*, regional governors, warlords, or others within the state. *Exclusive republics* make policy makers the agents of the private sector but, as in apartheid-era South Africa, of only a segment of the adult population, which constitutes an exclusive selectorate. *Democracies* expand the selectorate to include the entire adult population.

The major constrain on outcomes in the realist model is the balance of power or relative leverage of primary actors in the bargaining process. Leverage is a measure of the power losses each side can inflict on the other, relative to the existing power of the other side. It includes the ability to block implementation of laws passed by the other and so reduce the effect of the other's decisions—that is, leverage over the *extent* of the other's power. It also includes the ability to increase the risk that the other will not survive in power—that is, leverage over the *duration* of the other's power. Leverage may be thought of in probabilistic terms—the probability that the other's decision will be frustrated or the other incumbent will fall from power given one's own all-out effort to produce this outcome. The balance of power—the simplest and most fundamental comparison among cases—is a measure of the relative leverage exercised by participants in constitutional bargaining over one another. The primary constraint that shapes this balance is the preexisting state structure in which the bargainers operate.

Realism's core working hypothesis to explain democratization in different countries is as follows:

> The more heterogeneous in objectives and the more evenly balanced in relative leverage are the participants in the bargaining process of constitutional design, the more likely is the outcome to be a democratic constitution.

In bargaining among purely self-interested politicians seeking to maximize the extent and duration of their power, democracy emerges because they find it the best compromise among competing autocratic, oligarchic, and republican strategies. Heterogeneity increases the prospects that participants will engage in competitive expansion of the selectorate. Heterogeneity also increases the prospects that they will find any one leader threatening and so will seek to check authority. Balance in relative leverage among factions means that no one participant can impose its preferences on others.

Causal Nexus: Explaining transitions from communism

The link between the institutionally defined balance of power (as independent variable) and constitutions (as dependent variable) is the bargaining process among constitutional designers.[3] To reach agreement on constitutive rules, one party must make a sufficient concession to accept the proposal of the other side. Why would one side concede? Because it does not expect the other party to give in, and it expects that by holding out it will end up with less than by agreeing to the other's terms now. In other words, participants in constitutional bargaining reach agreement over rules for apportioning decision-making powers when two conditions hold: (1) each believes that the current proposal on the table is better than the conflict associated with disagreement, and (2) each believes the other is unlikely to accept a smaller allotment of decision-making powers in subsequent rounds of bargaining. Concerning the first condition, each side compares the power gains and losses associated with failure to reach agreement and with continued bargaining, on the one hand, against the power gains and losses of various agreements, on the other. One's assessment rests on an estimation of the power of the other side to cancel the effect of one's own decisions and to threaten one's own tenure during the bargaining and under various agreements. Since the power losses are a stream of losses into the future, this assessment also rests on one's estimation of the length of time that the other side can hold on to positions of power and continue to inflict these losses during bargaining and under various agreements. Concerning the second condition, each participant also assesses the likelihood that the other side will change its position. This assessment rests on the power gains and losses that the other will experience because of continued failure to reach agreement and the likelihood the other will fall from power.

Inherent Dilemmas

Although they may be divided by diverging preferences, the participants in constitutional bargaining, nonetheless, labor under two common constraints:

The dilemma of inclusion (oligarchs' dilemma). Each participant seeks to tailor the selectorate, giving greater weight to one's own supporters and less to one's opponents' supporters. On the one hand, in autocracies, oligarchies, and selective republics each leader is tempted—and knows others are tempted also—to expand the political game by including his or her own allies or partisans in the selectorate. For the individual leader this selective expansion of the selectorate will maximize the extent and duration of her or his power—as long as others do not also succeed at including their own partisans or allies. For each leader the worst outcome would result if other leaders mobilized their partisans while he or she does not. In the absence of guarantees that other leaders will not defect, each oligarch feels a compulsion to defect in anticipation of others' defections. Owing to the constant temptation to defect, the oligarchs' dilemma contains a threat of authoritarian collapse. On the other hand, in more democratic regimes the oligarchs' dilemma is manifest in attempts to exclude partisans of one's opponents; short of outright exclusion, it is manifest in various electoral schemes, gerrymandering, special seats, and so forth, that inflate the weight of some constituencies at the expense of others.

The dilemma of authority (Madison's dilemma). When creating leadership and delegating powers to it, designers of constitutions are often constrained by a second threat—those who create a constitution seek to create a terrible power that can subsequently be turned against them (Kiewiet and McCubbins 1991; Kubiček 1994). Autocracies, oligarchies, exclusive republics, and democracies all need leadership to solve their collective-action problems, yet individual leaders in possession of this power may use these institutional advantages to displace other members of the polity. Constitution builders must design institutional guarantees to protect themselves against becoming the victims of their own creations. To illustrate: designers of oligarchic constitutions often use institutions that disperse policy-making power (e.g., collective leadership or a rotating chairmanship) to reduce the threat that one member will use the power of a regime to exclude others from power. Designers of autocratic constitutions may develop checks on the leader's access to the terror machine—not only to increase the probability of continued empowerment for each member of the regime but also to minimize the costs of possible dispowerment.

Preferences of Different Participants

The preferences of individual participants in this process may be categorized by the type of constitution that will favor their partisans over others' within the selectorate.

Autocratic faction. Those who seek to build autocracy must establish strong control by the executive over the policy-making centers of the state and over the mechanisms of executive accountability. To achieve the former, the autocratic faction's strategy must transfer powers of legislation to the office of the chief executive. With this control, meaningful policy deliberations shift from the legislature to such decision-making centers as state councils that are dependent on the executive and beyond the control of the parliament. Executive decrees displace statutes as the mode of normal legislation.

Equally as important, the executive must gain control over the mechanisms of his or her own accountability, in particular by placing him- or herself beyond easy reach of the parliament or population. The creation of presidencies, for example, can remove the leader from direct accountability to the parliament. The power of impeachment can be qualified by requiring supermajorities that are improbable or by establishing executive control over the mechanisms of selecting the body that could possibly pose this midterm threat of removal. Control over the executive's own accountability has often meant removing the need to stand for popular competitive election: autocratic leaders often substitute referenda for competitive elections or deny other candidates the opportunity to participate. If elections are held, the autocratic faction may seek to establish an integrated electoral machine (called the circular flow of power in the Soviet period but found around the world in authoritarian polities) in which the executive subordinates the regional and local governments that in turn conduct the elections to parliament.

In addressing the dilemma of inclusion—that is, in order to guard against the political competition that might lead to competitive attempts to expand the selectorate—the autocratic faction must prevent the emergence of attractive alternatives to the leader. The autocratic faction may become particularly vigilant in preventing criticisms of the person of the chief executive, lest these become focal points for the emergence of alternative leadership. To limit the probability that alternative leaders will emerge, the presidential faction may seek to strip all other political forces of resources that can be used to mobilize political action.

In addressing the dilemma of authority, the autocratic faction faces the acute problem that its very strategy aggravates these threats—the strong leader that they seek to create may subsequently transform them into dependent clients or dispense with them entirely. Members of the faction may seek to check the powers of their leader by sharing or parceling responsibility for policy realms. (The faction might even select as its leader an individual with handicaps, such as advanced age and physical frailty, that would prevent consolidation of personal rule at their expense.) Members of the autocratic faction are torn between the essential role of the leader to autocracy and the threat such an individual can pose to each of them.

Oligarchic strategies. In constitutional design, the oligarchic faction seeks to institutionalize the representation of its varied bureaucratic and political interests and to establish the power of this body to remove the state's leadership. For example, a junta representing different bureaucracies may select and remove the president. Where democratic-appearing organs are adopted, oligarchies often prefer parliamentary over presidential institutions, so that the chief executive is selected by the legislature that represents oligarchic interests. A stable oligarchy must establish control of its own accountability. This can be accomplished by fixed rules that define membership in the selectorate, such as ex officio representation of armed services, ministries, or regional administrations in juntas, or by direct parliamentary control of the agencies that conduct elections to the parliament.

An oligarchy faces an acute dilemma of authority—that is, in order to solve its collective-action problem, the oligarchy typically must delegate powers to agents, but in doing so oligarchs give these agents powers that can be turned against them. Thus, oligarchies tend to favor dividing executive powers and assigning these to agents that the parliament can hold directly accountable to itself (such as a prime minister rather than a president). Oligarchies must develop mechanisms for monitoring and controlling agents and must conduct their own policing of executive agencies. The success of an oligarchy against threats of autocracy depends on its ability to control the mechanisms of its own accountability; the organ that represents oligarchic interests, be it a junta or parliament, must control the decision to call elections as well as the organizations that conduct elections. Delegation of this control would give that agent the means to become an autocrat.

The dilemma of inclusion in an oligarchy may also be particularly acute—the resources that can be used for mobilization of actors outside the oligarchy are dispersed among its several members. Competition among oligarchs may increase the temptation to defect. In response to this threat, oligarchies may develop very strict limits on political activity and establish verification norms that count any action to appeal outside the oligarchy as prima facie evidence of impending defection. In the context of this oligarch's dilemma, the logic of forced departication, which strips the subject population of the organizational resources essential to autonomous collective action, is to remove temptation from oligarchs.

Exclusive-republican strategies. Republicans seek to make the state accountable to society, but exclusionist republicans seek to limit the selectorate to some subset of social interests. Typically exclusionist republicans are politicians who find their greatest political advantage against other politicians not within the state itself, but in votes. They seek to establish or maintain their advantage in electoral politics by designing constitutive rules such as electoral schemes that advantage their followers against those of their opponents. This aim can be accomplished by excluding movements and parties on the basis of their programs or social groups on the basis of their characteristics.

In confronting the dilemma of inclusion, exclusive republics can dissolve into democracies under the threat of competitive defection. The temptation for parties to seek advantage by including excluded constituents is strong. In the face of open elections within the included segment, it is difficult to prevent strategies to reach out to the excluded. It may be particularly difficult to maintain exclusion based on programs, for the members of excluded movements can always reconstitute themselves or join other movements in order "to pass" as enfranchised. It may be easier to maintain exclusion based on ascription, for ascriptive "passing" can be more difficult. A stable exclusive republic may depend on successfully anathematizing the excluded population or establishing rules that require supermajorities to extend the franchise.

In facing the dilemma of authority, designers of exclusive republics must also take precautions to protect themselves against their own exclusion: those who join in the exclusion of segments of the population from the political process need assurances they will not themselves be excluded—for example, on grounds that they, too, are subversive or alien. Disqualification of movements or ascriptive groups on grounds that are qualitative rather than merely matters of degree may assure constitution builders that this cannot later be extended to exclude them. Nonetheless, the claims often used to exclude movements, such as the claims that they are agents of a foreign power, have shown themselves to be highly fungible standards.

Empirical Test: Comparing Post-Soviet Outcomes

In the Soviet successor states, development toward autocracy, oligarchy, exclusive republicanism, or democracy has been the resultant of intersecting strategies in the game of constitutional design. The relative leverage of the different factions in this game was initially allocated by political institutions created under the Soviet regime. At the moment of the 1990 elections, the state institutions were parliamentary in design: the citizenry voted either for a legislative body (the Supreme Soviet) or for an electoral college with powers to amend the constitution (Congress of People's Deputies) that in turn elected the legislative body. These bodies, which were constitutionally the highest authority within each republic (subject to the authority of the national, or "all-union," government), then elected the republic's government (council of ministers) and head of state (chairman of the Supreme Soviet).

The 1990 elections established the power configuration within the political institutions that determined the constitutional development of these states. These elections shaped the process of constitution building in that they determined who would sit at the bargaining table of constitutional design, and assigned various leverage advantages among actors. The outcome of this bargaining has been twenty-one different constitutional orders (see Table 8.2). In this context there are four significant patterns among the fifteen union-republics.

TABLE 8.2
Constitutions of the Soviet Successor States, 1990–96
(Inclusive Dates: Month/Year)

	Autocracy	Oligarchy	Exclusive Republic	Balanced Republic
Armenia				Ag/90-D/96
Azerbaijan	F/91-My/92 Je/93-D/96			My/92-Je/93
Belarus		My/90-D/96		
Estonia			Ap/90-D/96	
Georgia		Ja/92-D/96	N/90-Ja/92	
Kazakstan	F/90-D/96			
Kyrgyzstan	Ap/90-O/90			O/90-D/96
Latvia			My/90-D/96	
Lithuania				Mr/90-D/96
Moldova				Ap/90-D/96
Russia				My/90-D/96
Tajikistan	Ap/90-S/92 N/94-D/96	S/92-N/94		
Turkmenistan	Ja/90-D/96			
Ukraine				Jl/90-D/96
Uzbekistan	Mr/90-D/96			

Pattern 1: Unified Bureaucracies and Autocracies

Where a unified bureaucratic faction led by the Communist Party first secretary was able to control the 1990 election and win a controlling majority in the Supreme Soviet, it tended to work together to support creation of a presidential autocracy. The bureaucrats seemed to recognize that their special position in the polity depended on avoiding democratic elections. Their personal future within the party bureaucracy and the special position of the party apparatus vis-à-vis other bureaucracies depended on the first secretary's predominance in the state. Using their parliamentary majority, the bureaucrats and presidents established autocratic control over the policy-making centers of the state and the mechanisms of accountability.

This pattern prevailed initially in Azerbaijan, Kazakstan, Kyrgyzstan, Tajikistan, Turkmenistan, and Uzbekistan; it has survived in all but Kyrgyzstan, although in Azerbaijan and Tajikistan it has been unstable (Kangas 1994; Nissman 1994; Nourzhanov and Saikal 1994).

Three of the original autocratic presidents fell in the face of mounting extraparliamentary pressure that led the unified bureaucratic majority in parliament to jettison its leader in hopes of saving their own positions. In Azerbaijan, following the failed coup in Moscow, mounting pressure from the Azerbaijan Popular Front (AzPF) led the parliament to remove President Aiaz Mutalibov and transfer his powers to Etibar Mamedov, rector of the Baku Medical Institute. On May 14–15, 1992 the popular front seized power in a coup, named its own interim president, and transferred parliament's powers to a fifty-person National Council pending new parliamentary elections. Three weeks later, on June 7, the popular front leader prevailed in new presidential elections (TASS, October 30, 1991; Fuller 1992a, 1992b). Yet, by June 4, 1993, the unified bureaucracy had reestablished its predominance in another coup and the old parliament (purged of most popular front members) elected former Communist Party First Secretary Geidar Aliev as acting president. Similarly, in Tajikistan, following the August 1991 coup attempt in Moscow, demonstrations in Dushanbe organized by the Democratic Party, the Rebirth movement, and the Islamic Renaissance Party led the bureaucrats to force President K. M. Makhkamov's resignation, to declare a state of emergency, and to appoint Rakhmon Nabiev as acting president until elections on November 24, 1991. Nabiev began to exceed the Supreme Soviet's mandate, by reaching out to popular constituencies, but in September 1992 the Supreme Soviet abolished the presidency (Brown 1992, 1993). In November 1994 once again the Supreme Soviet permitted its chairman to validate his leadership role in elections to a newly (re-)created presidency. In Kyrgyzstan mishandling of ethnic demonstrations led the Supreme Soviet to remove Absamat Masaliev and appoint Askar Akaev as chief of state. The bureaucratic majority in Kyrgyzstan succumbed to dangers inherent in the authoritarian dilemma, for Akaev used his position to turn against the bureaucrats in the Supreme Soviet (Huskey 1995).

Pattern 2: Bureaucratic Coalitions and Oligarchies

Where the unity of the bureaucratic majority broke down (in particular, in response to the dilemma of authority) or where Soviet-era bureaucracies within a republic were not subordinate to a single union-republic chain of command (particularly, where the armed forces, security apparatus, and all-union defense industry were significant bureaucracies in the Soviet era), the bureaucrats were not as unified at the time of the 1990 elections as in the first pattern. The bureaucracies were able to dominate the legislatures, but no one bureaucracy could muster a legislative majority. The result was a parliamentary majority composed of a coalition of bureaucratic constituencies rather than a unified bureaucracy. These coalitions tended to adopt oligarchic rather than autocratic constitutions. To maintain their autonomy, the leaders of separate bureaucracies attempted to block the emergence of an autocrat and to establish stronger accountability controls over the executive. In the context of authoritarian regimes using democratic-appearing institutions, this strategy has meant a preference for parliamentary over presidential institutions.

Bureaucratic coalitions have emerged in at least three republics. In Georgia and Tajikistan they emerged temporarily following an oligarchic revolt against an increasingly autocratic leader: when the presidents attempted to strengthen their positions against the bureaucrats by bringing in nonbureaucratic allies, the bureaucratic factions in the parliaments toppled the presidents and reasserted their predominance. In both republics the need for leadership in the civil wars has led the parliaments once again to create strong leadership under their new leaders—Imomali Rakhmonov and Eduard Shevardnadze (Jones 1996). In Belarus the leadership of the party apparatus in the parliament was weaker at the start and the fall of party leadership after the failed August 1991 coup permitted the bureaucracies to establish their predominance. The Belarusian oligarchy initially sought to avoid the threat of autocracy by refusing to create a strong presidency, but with time it saw this as the only solution to its collective-action problems that were exacting an increasingly high price in economic and social decline. This may have been the oligarchs' undoing: President Aleksandr Lukashenka appears to have consolidated autocratic leadership at the expense of many bureaucratic interests.

Pattern 3: Fragmented Party and Exclusive Republics

Where the Communist Party fragmented internally during perestroika, competitive appeals to the public by its various factions expanded the political process (Ishiyama 1993; Nelson and Amonashvili 1992). Where this permitted a coalition of Communist Party dissidents and non-Party intelligentsia to establish its dominance within the Supreme Soviet during the 1990 elections, this coalition did not rush to establish democracy. Instead, it sought to cement its future electoral fortunes against the Communists by excluding segments of the population from politics. The weakness of the more orthodox Communist Party factions within the new legislature left them unable to defend themselves and their supporters from exclusion. The dominant exclusionist-republican coalition turned to one or another strategy—either

barring movements from politics on the basis of their programs or dis-
franchising individuals on the basis of their ascriptive characteristics.

The first strategy excluded political parties or movements by label-
ing these subversive or agents of a foreign power. For example, in
Georgia in December 1991 the Round Table majority that backed Zviad
Gamsakhurdia stripped Georgian deputies elected under the Communist Party label of their credentials, passing a law to reduce parliament
from 250 to 201 so as to avoid new elections to replace the deputies
(Fuller 1992a). This action nicely strengthened the Round Table's parliamentary majority.

The second strategy excluded voters on the basis of their ascriptive
characteristics. In Estonia and Latvia electoral exclusion took place
through restrictive definitions of citizenship. Citizenship was initially
granted only to those who were residents or descendants of residents
in the republics before incorporation in the Soviet Union in 1940.
(Gamsakhurdia had attempted to carry this principle to its logical extreme in Georgia, by proposing that citizenship should be extended
only to those whose ancestors had lived there before 1801, the year of
Georgian incorporation into the Russian Empire.) These laws had the
predictable effect of reducing the electorate. In Estonia, the new law
initially disfranchised about 45 percent of the electorate, which declined from 1.14 million to about 625,000. In Latvia the disfranchised
accounted for about one-third of the adult population.[4] For the groups
that dominated the process of constitution building, this exclusionary
policy ensured their electoral fortunes. In Estonia, as Kionka (1992, 17)
notes,

> given the political breakdown between supporters and opponents of ex-
> tending voting rights to non-citizens and the implications of the extended
> franchise for the power configuration in the new parliament, it is safe to
> characterize the voting-rights question in its current form as a thinly
> veiled political struggle rather than a battle of high ideals. The right to
> vote, in short, has come to symbolize the disputes between Estonia's Left
> and Right for predominance in the forthcoming political order.

Pattern 4: Political Balance and Democracy

Where the Communist Party divided internally, but the party itself
remained one of the significant players in politics, democracy was
strongest. This curious relationship was a reflection not of the Communists' abiding commitment to democratic values but of the balance that
this introduced into constitutional politics. The result was a legislature
mixed in its composition with both bureaucrats and non-Communist

Party politicians jockeying for power. The interplay of autocratic, oligarchic, and exclusive-republican strategies among self-interested factions led to a form of balancing and checking that prevented any single coalition from establishing its predominance and excluding the others from power. In Armenia, Kyrgyzstan under Akaev, Lithuania, Moldova, Russia, and Ukraine, balancing in this period prevented any one faction or coalition from establishing its hegemony (Bojcun 1995; Crowther 1994; Kubiček 1994; Rutland 1994; Sakwa 1993).

The major danger in these balanced polities was the threat of deadlock and coup d'état, but the remedy for the latter was greater balance. For example, as a result of deadlock, the period under President Abulfaz Elchibei in Azerbaijan was the republic's most democratic, but this came to an end as a result of extraconstitutional actions by one faction that the other faction was too weak to block. The continued strength and cohesion of the unified bureaucratic faction permitted it to impose a new autocratic constitution on Azerbaijan in 1993 and to bring back the former Communist Party first secretary to serve as president. Where there was greater balance, however, even coups did not lead to a break with democracy. In Russia the coup and countercoup of 1993 did not permit any one faction to establish its hegemony. Despite the president's success at imposing his constitution, Yeltsin was not able to exclude his opponents permanently from positions of power such as the Duma and provincial governments. This balance stayed his hand over the next three years, even as many of the autocratic faction within his presidential administration counseled exclusion of his opponents.

Recapitulation

The four patterns identified here reflect the following causal chain: First, where the Communist Party apparatus dominated the local administration in the late Soviet period and remained unified, it blocked other parties from offering serious challenges in the 1990 elections. Where this apparatus fragmented internally, it was unable to prevent candidates from scrambling to align with different parties in the elections (see Table 8.3). This initial configuration of political forces in the late Soviet period on the eve of the 1990 elections set in motion a chain of events that defined the constitutions in different successor states; that is, it constrained subsequent constitutional development, increasing the probability of certain outcomes over others (O'Donnell and Schmitter 1986; Bermeo 1987).

Second, elections to the Supreme Soviets of the fifteen union-republics in 1990 (or Congress of People's Deputies in Russia) varied greatly in the nature of the candidacies offered to the citizens. Unified bureau-

TABLE 8.3
Power Configurations on the Eve of the 1990 Elections

Unified Bureaucracy	Bureaucratic Coalition	Fragmented Party	Political Balance
Azerbaijan	Belarus	Estonia	Armenia
Kazakstan		Georgia	Lithuania
Kyrgyzstan		Latvia	Moldova
Tajikistan			Russia
Turkmenistan			Ukraine
Uzbekistan			

cracies favored nonparty elections; fragmentation of the Communist Party tended to favor party-based elections (see Table 8.4). Where the apparatus remained a powerful force but faced either internal disunity or competing bureaucracies, mixed elections were more likely. In four union republics, the elections to parliament were conducted on the basis of well-defined partisan groupings resembling parties, with almost all candidates carrying a partisan label and running on its platform. In five union-republics, alternative parties were effectively excluded from offering candidates. Between these extremes, in six "mixed" elections parties were able to field or endorse candidates, although only in some districts, and these parties faced such obstacles that only a few contests offered voters a fair choice between parties.

TABLE 8.4
Types of Union-Republic Parliamentary Elections, 1990

Nonparty Elections	Mixed Elections	Party-Based Elections
Kazakstan	Armenia	Estonia
Kyrgyzstan	Azerbaijan	Georgia
Tajikistan	Belarus	Latvia
Turkmenistan	Moldova	Lithuania
Uzbekistan	Russia	
	Ukraine	

Sources: Foreign Broadcast Information Service, *Daily Report (Soviet Union)*, February 1, 1990, 43-44; February 27, 1990, 96; April 6, 1990, 105-7; May 10, 1990, 103-4; CSCE, 1990, 128, 144.

For example, in Azerbaijan, the opposition Azerbaijan Popular Front ran under serious handicaps, including a state of emergency and arrest or disqualification of many of its candidates, while Communist Party workers, who constituted the largest cadre of candidates, often ran for uncontested seats. The Popular Front in Belarus was not permitted to register as a social organization and so could not nominate its own candidates but could only informally endorse candidates that had been nominated by other organizations. The Communist Party-controlled electoral commissions in Ukraine registered opposition Democratic Bloc candidates in only 29 percent of the districts; the opposition bloc was able to nominate or endorse candidates for less than half of the parliamentary contests (Commission on Security and Cooperation in Europe 1990).

Third, as a consequence of these elections, the Supreme Soviets differed in the extent to which Party *apparatchiks*, other bureaucrats, or nonbureaucrats dominated their membership. Four important bureaucratic constituencies were typically represented in the parliaments—Communist Party *apparatchiks*, central state bureaucrats, regional state leaders, and the directors of parastatals. Democratization depended on the extent to which these and non-bureaucrats balanced one another in the legislature. The figures cited here attempt to estimate the extent to which nonofficeholders broke into the legislature; these use a surrogate measure—the proportion of legislators who were not members of the Communist Party of the Soviet Union (CPSU)[5] (see Table 8.5). Where parties had played a greater role in the legislative elections, bureaucrats and officeholders were less prominent in the new Supreme

TABLE 8.5
Influence of Election-Types on Composition of Supreme Soviets, 1990

Type of Election	Proportion Non-Communist	
	Average (%)	Range (%)
Nonparty (*n*=4)	8.3	6-11
Mixed (*n*=4)	18.5	14-26
Party based (*n*=2)	42.5	42-43

Sources: Foreign Broadcast Information Service, *Daily Report (Soviet Union),* January 23, 1990, 93; February 27, 1990, 117; March 6, 1990, 117; March 7, 1990, 120; March 20, 1990, 112; April 4, 1990, 87; April 13, 1990, 98; April 18, 1990, 100-6; April 19, 1990, 115; June 5, 1990, 18; October 11, 1990, 115; October 18, 1990, 101; November 16, 1990, 89.

Soviets. For example, in Latvia none of the republic's five Central Committee secretaries ran for legislative positions; and in the countryside Communist Party secretaries largely failed. Communist Party workers held only about 8 percent of the seats; the combined corps of officeholders (including directors of parastatals) constituted only 39 percent of the legislature (*Sovetskaia Latviia* March 23, 1990, in FBIS April 18, 1990, 100–6). Alternatively, where parties were weaker, bureaucrats dominated the Supreme Soviets. In Kyrgyzstan and Turkmenistan, Communist Party *apparatchiks* alone constituted about one quarter of the deputies. Even in some mixed elections, the officeholders emerged supreme—most notably in Azerbaijan. According to the Azerbaijan Popular Front's estimate, the parliamentary deputies "are mainly party officials and major economic leaders. . . . 75 of the 81 secretaries of town and rayon . . . committees who ran for election have become members of the republic Supreme Soviet" (Moscow Television, October 5, 1990).

Fourth, the composition of the Supreme Soviet for the most part determined the nature of the executive branch and whether it could become the basis for autocracy. In the parliamentary structure of late Soviet political institutions, the executive was the agent of parliament: the parliamentary majority delegated powers to a chairman of the Supreme Soviet, who served as chief of state, and to a council of ministers, which served as government. Where the union-republic Communist Party apparatus (plus the agencies it controlled) constituted a majority in the legislature, the parliamentary majority delegated these powers to the first secretary of the Communist Party. Where a bureaucratic coalition dominated, the majority elected the incumbent Supreme Soviet chair as chief of state. Where another party (or movement) held a majority in the legislature, the parliamentary majority tended to delegate these powers to a party or faction leader who had held no bureaucratic post before the 1990 election. Political balance, however, introduced greater indeterminacy and real prospects for independent choice by the legislative bodies. Thus, in 1990 the power configuration on the eve of the elections was a good predictor of the outcome of the elections for chief of state by the parliament (see Table 8.6). In the legislative bodies constituted by bureaucrats or parties, the process of constituting the executive authority proceeded quickly and often without contestation. For example, in legislatures dominated by unified bureaucracies, the elections for chairman of the Supreme Soviet presented only one candidate. Similarly, in Georgia, Latvia, and Lithuania, the solid party majorities selected their leader for the chief executive position, who then nominated another party leader as the head of government.

TABLE 8.6
Influence of Initial Power Configurations on Selection of
Chiefs of State, 1990

Initial Power Configuration	Previous Post of Chief of State		
	CP Secretary	Supreme Soviet Chair	None
Unified Bureaucracy	6	0	0
Bureaucratic Coalition	0	1	0
Fragmented Party	0	1	2
Political Balance	1	1	3

In the republics with political balance, where the bureaucracy was not unified under Communist Party leaders and no party coalition constituted a majority in the parliament, the selection process was more indeterminate; it was often protracted and sometimes led to compromises. In Armenia the first three rounds of elections over two days did not produce a solid majority for either the candidate of the Armenian National Movement or the first secretary of the Communist Party (*Izvestiia*, August 5, 1990). In Moldova, the contest between the Communist Party first secretary and the chairman of the Supreme Soviet Presidium was the first decision of the Supreme Soviet session, but it came ten days after its opening because of the internal divisions in the body (*Izvestiia*, April 28, 1990). In Russia the election of Yeltsin by the Russian Congress of People's Deputies came after four days of deadlocked votes: On the morning of May 25, 1990, seven candidates stood for election, but the first round narrowed the choice to the nominee of the bureaucracy (Russian Communist Party First Secretary Ivan Polozkov) and the nominee of Democratic Russia (Yeltsin). When neither candidate won a majority in the run-off, new nominations and a third round of elections were held. According to *Izvestiia*'s correspondents, "This election proceeded with difficulty, in a bitter struggle of positions and opinions. The atmosphere in the hall became heated to the breaking point on the morning of May 28" (*Izvestiia*, May 29, 1990; also see *Izvestiia*, May 26 and May 27, 1990). In Ukraine the unexpected resignation of the Communist Party first secretary two weeks before the election of the chairman of the Supreme Soviet left the bureaucrats without a leader to whom to delegate the executive power: The first round produced twenty-seven candidates, but the run-off produced a victory for the parliamentary grouping that *Izvestiia* characterized as "Party officials, economic managers, and some Soviet officials" (*Izvestiia*, July 24, 1990).

Fifth, because the configuration of power within the union-republic on the eve of the 1990 legislative elections constrained subsequent constitutional development in each union-republic and successor republic, the former is a fairly good predictor of the latter. That is, the figures in the upper half of Table 8.7 show a perfect relationship (all 100 percent on the diagonal) between the configuration of power on the eve of the 1990 elections and the first constitutional order adopted in each repub-

TABLE 8.7
Influence of Initial Power Configuration in 1990 on Subsequent
Constitutional Orders, 1990–96

| Initial Power Configuration | Initial Postelection Constitutional Order, 1990 | | | | |
	Autocratic	Oligarchic	Exclusive-Republican	Democratic	*n*
Unified bureaucracy	100%	0%	0%	0%	6
Bureaucratic coalition	0%	100%	0%	0%	1
Fragmented party	0%	0%	100%	0%	3
Political balance	0%	0%	0%	100%	5

| Initial Power Configuration | All Constitutional Orders, 1990-96 | | | | |
	Autocratic	Oligarchic	Exclusive-Republican	Democratic	*n*
Unified bureaucracy	73%	9%	0%	18%	11
Bureaucratic coalition	0%	100%	0%	0%	1
Fragmented party	0%	25%	75%	0%	4
Political balance	0%	0%	0%	100%	5

lic after the 1990 legislative elections. The choice among constitutions depended on the ways in which the parliamentary majority saw various institutions as guarantees of their positions against expansion of the political process (as a solution to the dilemma of inclusion) and as assurances that the power of its agents would not be turned against them (as a solution to the dilemma of authority). Where the parliamentary majority was constituted by bureaucrats united in a single chain of command, it was more likely to support the building of autocracy. Where the majority was constituted by bureaucrats divided among several chains of command, it was more likely to demand stronger selectoral constraints on the leadership, leading to forms of oligarchy. Where the parliamentary majority was constituted by parties that depended on votes, the parliamentary majority sought to maintain popular enfranchisement but to exclude the opposition or to disfranchise the population from which the opposition drew its support. Where there was no solid majority in the legislature, the result was more likely to be checking and balancing within the legislature and between legislature and executive that encouraged development toward a democratizing compromise among factions.

The relationship is only slightly less perfect between this initial configuration and all subsequent constitutions adopted over the period 1990–1996; this is shown in the lower half of Table 8.7. This declining precision in predictions over time should be expected because the internal dynamics of these regimes (due to the dilemmas of authority and inclusion) opened prospects for constitutional change. Indeed, deviations from this pattern (the off-diagonal cases in Table 8.7) were due to the dynamics discussed previously in this chapter. That is, the ability of the autocratic, oligarchic, or exclusive-republican factions to turn a parliamentary majority into a coalition that would support a nondemocratic constitution was constrained by the dilemmas of inclusion and authority. Attempts by leaders to expand their power vis-à-vis their legislatures by expanding the selectorate led to democratization of the autocratic constitutions of Azerbaijan under Elchibei (1992–1993) and Kyrgyzstan under Akaev (after 1990). Yet, the revolt of bureaucratic interests against such attempts brought a return to an autocratic constitution in Azerbaijan under Aliev (after 1993) and the establishment of oligarchic constitutions to replace the autocracy in Tajikistan (1992–1994) and the exclusive republic in Georgia (after 1992). The collective-action problems of oligarchy have led Tajikistan to return to a more autocratic constitution (after 1994).

Consistent with our realist hypothesis on democratization, the initial power configuration predicts fairly well the likelihood that subsequent elections would give the population real control over officials; that is, the initial configuration that constrained subsequent constitutional development also constrained the probability that elected officials would be held accountable to a majority of the population. Drawing on the reports of international observers, we can categorize each presidential and legislative election according to the extent of democratization. This is operationalized with an answer to the question: Could 51 percent of the adult population have removed the incumbent president or majority in parliament? At one extreme, the probability of this is low $(p \to 0)$ because voters were given no choice in the elections. At the other extreme, the probability is high $(p \to 1)$ that the will of a slim majority would prevail against incumbents. Where elections were competitive but the incumbents engaged in widespread fraud and threatened that they would not step down even if they failed to win voter approval, the ability of a majority to remove the incumbents becomes more uncertain. At greatest uncertainty it is as if the elections were followed by a coin toss to determine whether the will of a majority will be enforced $(p = 0.5)$.[6] Table 8.8 shows the results of this assessment. It also shows the close association between initial power configuration and subsequent likelihood of democracy. In republics that began with political balance, over half of the subsequent sixteen elections provided a high probability that any majority of the population could remove the incumbents. In republics that began with a unified bureaucracy, 86 percent of the subsequent twenty-one elections provided virtually no

TABLE 8.8
Influence of Initial Power Configuration in 1990 on Subsequent
Accountability of Incumbents to Popular Majorities, 1990–96
(in 46 Presidential and Legislative Elections)

Initial Power Configuration	Probability that 51 Percent of Adult Population Could Remove Incumbents			
	Low $(p \to 0)$	Uncertain $(p \approx .5)$	High $(p \to 1)$	n
Unified bureaucracy	86%	14%	0%	21
Bureaucratic coalition	50%	50%	0%	2
Fragmented party	14%	86%	0%	7
Political balance	6%	38%	56%	16

opportunity for a simple majority of the population to remove the incumbent. In republics that began with either a bureaucratic coalition or fragmented Communist Party, it remained uncertain whether a popular majority could hold incumbents accountable.

Conclusion

This analysis began from the realist premise that constitutions emerge from bargaining among self-interested politicians who prefer institutions that maximize their own chances of occupying key policymaking posts and actually shaping policy once in those posts. The constitutional outcome of strategic interaction among such politicians is strongly influenced by preexisting institutions that assign leverage to these politicians over each other. In a world dominated by such politicians, democracy results not so much from the plans of the far-sighted and principled but from the failure of the self-interested and ambitious. The hope for democratization in such a world lies in balancing among self-interested politicians who are forced to reach practical compromises over the rules of the game that will permit each to continue pursuing his or her objectives. Among such politicians, the hope for democratization has less to do with the cultural or economic underpinnings of politics and more do with the structure of politics itself.

Notes

An earlier version of this essay was presented at the 28th National Convention of the American Association for the Advancement of Slavic Studies, Boston, November 14–17, 1996.

1. The labels "political economy" and "political sociology" are also commonly used to describe issue areas or subject matter. In the present context, these refer to distinctive analytic paradigms that are rooted in different assumptions about human motivations and the bases of solidarity and conflict (see Hechter 1987).

2. I develop this theme in a book manuscript entitled *Ethnicity in the State: Negotiating Post-Soviet Constitutions.*

3. I draw on those rational-choice, micro-foundational models of bargaining (see Binmore, Osborne, and Rubinstein 1992) that have become a standard tool in the repertoire of political science.

4. This figure (32.6 percent) is calculated from the report of Latvian officials that as of May 26, 1993, the eligible electorate stood at 1,245,530, while the adult population at that time was estimated to have been 1,848,514 (Bungs 1993, 48–49).

5. The justification for this surrogate measure is as follows: To be an office-holder within the republics before the 1990 elections, one normally had to be a member of the Communist Party. In the 1990 parliaments, the proportion of non-Communists is correlated with the proportion of nonofficeholders (probably the lowest estimate of that proportion in each body). To illustrate: In the Latvian legislature elected in 1990, Communist Party membership among *apparatchiks* was 100 percent, among central state officials and senior military personnel, 90 percent, among directors of parastatals, 88 percent, and among regional state leaders, 67 percent; but among nonofficeholders elected to the legislature, Communist Party membership stood at only 39 percent (calculated from the list of 166 deputies elected on March 18, 1990, published in *Sovetskaia Latviia*, March 23, 1990, 1–2 [FBIS April 18, 1990: 100–106]).

6. *Method of coding*: Single-candidate elections were coded as $p \to 0$, as were elections in which the only alternative candidates were offered by parties controlled by the regime. Uncertainty in accountability ($p \to .5$) was introduced into competitive elections when at least a third of the adult population was denied the vote; when international observers reported significant unfairness, coercion and intimidation, fraud, or other voting irregularities; or when incumbents threatened that they would not relinquish power even if they lost the vote. *Bias in coding*: Any systematic bias in coding is likely to *overestimate* the probability of popular accountability for elections under bureaucratic coalitions (coding these as 0.5 rather than 0) and to *underestimate* the probability of popular accountability under balanced polities. If there is such a systematic bias, it is not correlated positively with the relationship tested in table 8.8; indeed, it would be negatively correlated. In short, any systematic bias is likely to understate the relationship posited by the realist hypothesis. *Sources of data*: Election observer reports published by the Commission on Security and Cooperation in Europe (1993a, 1993b, 1994a, 1994b, 1994c, 1994d, 1995a, 1995b, 1995c, 1996a, 1996b, 1996c) and all annual editions of *Freedom in the World* beginning with Freedom House (1991).

9

Transitions from Communism: Putting Society in Its Place

William M. Reisinger

A little over ten years ago, Soviet leader Mikhail Gorbachev inaugurated substantive political reforms. Communist rule ended in Eastern Europe eight years ago and in the Soviet Union six years ago. Those numbers seem strikingly small given the vast changes that have occurred in the societies and polities of central Europe and Eurasia. These changes permitted (indeed, required) new forms of research on the part of those studying these countries. Much valuable information has resulted. To the extent that such information can be sifted and integrated, our collective knowledge of the formerly communist countries is much deeper now than a decade ago.

In this chapter, I categorize many different works, in a way that clearly is too simple to be taken very far. So, I apologize to anyone whom I miscategorize. I also criticize some aspects of the work. Except for an important recent book by Roeder (1993), I have tried to criticize vaguely and praise by name. Because my criticisms tend not to name names, I do want to make clear that when I discuss recent survey research, I self-consciously engage not solely in *kritika* but also in *samokritika*. I do not defend analyses or approaches that employ exclusively society-centered concepts and indicators. I call instead for more effort to ensure that every empirical analysis of political-social-economic changes in postcommunist societies rests on a theory or theoretical framework that explicitly combines societal and state-based elements, and that allows for the importance of both behaviors and institutions.[1]

Four Approaches à la Roeder

As Fleron discusses in chapter 2, Roeder (1993, 13) uses two distinctions that are central to the social sciences in positioning himself among students of Soviet politics and its collapse: (1) subjectivist versus objectivist approaches—the former stressing values and cognitions, the latter material and institutional constraints—and (2) state-centered versus society-centered approaches—the former stressing the autonomy of politics from society, the latter the dependence of the political realm on society. Roeder's first distinction is, I believe, the same as the distinction that Apter (1965) and others have made between behavioral and structural approaches. Because the terms *behavioral* and *structural* are more familiar, I will use them. Both distinctions capture commonly noticed differences in emphases and goals among those who study social phenomena, especially social change processes. These two distinctions can be combined to produce a matrix with four cells, as depicted in Figure 9.1 (cf. Fleron's Figure 2.2 in this volume).

The four resulting cells are state centered and behavioral; society centered and behavioral; state centered and structural; and society centered and structural. In each cell I have listed just a few examples of scholarship that fit within and help illustrate that cell. The top-left cell includes the tradition of elite studies prominent in comparative politics generally, including recent "transitology" approaches to democratization, and in the study of communist and now postcommunist politics. Lane (1996b), for example, sets out to defend the importance of elite interests as an analytic factor distinguishable from societal and institutional factors.

The bottom-left cell includes two distinct, though not unrelated, approaches currently prominent. In one, the expectation that there might be better and worse ways to "build" the formal institutions of democracy has led to this being dubbed "constitutional engineering" (as in the title of the recent book by Sartori [1994]). Starting from this premise, a number of scholars have set out in search of empirical regularities between key institutional features (e.g., presidential vs. parliamentary systems) and political outcomes (e.g., democratic stability or policy adaptation). The findings can even be used as a basis for recommending particular configurations of institutions for newly democratizing countries.

A different research tradition that is also state centered and structural is generally labeled neoinstitutionalism. Analyses in this tradition focus on how the formal rules of one or more institutions (such as congressional committees) shape the behavior of those operating within the institution. Much of this work in political science has involved the development of formal models based on rational-choice assumptions. Roeder (1993) places himself in this school, though he does not formalize his model.

Research that is both society centered and behavioral (in the top-

FIGURE 9.1 Four Approaches to the Study of Politics (Based on Roeder 1993)

	STATE-CENTERED	SOCIETY-CENTERED
BEHAVIORAL (VALUES AND COGNITIONS) **WHAT ROEDER TERMS "SUBJECTIVIST"**	**ELITE POLITICAL CULTURE, IDEOLOGY, OR INTERESTS** *General* Michels (1949); Mosca (1958); Rustow (1970); Putnam (1973); Przeworski (1986); O'Donnell and Schmitter (1986); Hagopian (1990); Di Palma (1990); Burton et al. (1992) *Re Communist/Postcommunist Countries* Beck et al. (1973); Welsh (1976); Willerton (1992); Higley et al. (1996); Kullberg (1996); Lane (1996)	**MASS POLITICAL CULTURE** *General* de Tocqueville (1835); Weber (1930); Almond and Verba (1963) *Re Communist/Postcommunist Countries* White (1979); Barghoorn (1965); Brown and Gray (1979); Tucker (1973); Wegren (1996)
STRUCTURAL (MATERIAL AND INSTITUTIONAL CONSTRAINTS) **WHAT ROEDER TERMS "OBJECTIVIST"**	**CONSTITUTIONAL ENGINEERING** *General* Aristotle (1995); Rae (1967); Lijphart (1984); Taagapera and Shugart (1989); Lijphart (1990); Shugart and Carey (1992); Sartori (1994) *Re Communist/Postcommunist Countries* Elster (1992); Linz and Stepan (1992); Clark (1996) **NEO-INSTITUTIONALISM** *General* March and Olsen (1989); Moe (1984); North (1990) *Re Communist/Postcommunist Countries* Roeder (1993)	**MODERNIZATION THEORY** *General* Lerner (1958); Lipset (1959); Apter (1965); Pye (1990) *Re Communist/Postcommunist Countries* Lewin (1991); Hosking (1991)

right cell of Figure 9.1) would include the many studies of political culture as an influence on a polity. Even before the opportunity to conduct surveys of public opinion within communist societies, scholars were investigating the role of political culture in explaining communist politics. More recent research opportunities, to do both surveys and other forms of fieldwork, have opened the door for more direct investigation of arguments formulated earlier.

The final, bottom-right cell in Figure 9.1 involves analyses that are both society centered and yet structural, in the sense of placing greater emphasis on the constraints that rules and norms place on individuals than they do on how values and cognitions guide behavior. One approach that flourished in the 1950s and 1960s fits this cell: studies of political development or modernization. In these approaches, the emphasis is placed on the ways in which changes in economic institutions via industrialization, urbanization, agrarian reform, the development of more complete networks of transportation and communication, and the corresponding rise in education tend to reshape societies in certain common ways. In the general comparative politics literature, this perspective coexisted relatively peacefully with analyses of political culture. Gabriel Almond and Lucien Pye, for example, helped inaugurate both foci in the 1950s and continued to defend them both in the late 1980s (see Almond 1987; Pye 1990). Among students of communist and postcommunist politics, however, the different emphases have led to a clear polarization along lines that are, to a certain extent, an extension of Russia's Slavophile versus Westernizer debate. Certainly, the antagonism between their basic tenets predates our century:

> "But what do you think are the special characteristics of the Russian laborer?" said Metrov. "His, as it were, biological qualities or the conditions in which he is placed?"
> This question already revealed an idea with which Levin could not agree. However, he went on expounding his theory that the Russian laborer's view of the land was quite different from that of other nations. And, to prove his theory he hastened to add that, in his opinion, this view of the Russian peasant was due to the consciousness of his vocation to populate vast, unoccupied tracts in the east.
> "One can be easily led astray when drawing conclusions about the general vocation of a people," said Metrov, interrupting Levin. "The condition of the laborer will always depend on his relation to land and capital." (Tolstoy, *Anna Karenina*, part 7, ch. 3)

Defending Society-Centered Approaches

Having implicitly defined four research approaches, Roeder then argues for the analytic advantages from employing one in particular—

the structural/state-centered cell in Figure 9.1. "In explaining the stagnation and collapse of the Soviet Union, I argue for the central causal effect of political institutions" (1993, 6). He further argues (17), "By treating the state as a dependent variable, cash register, or referee, society-centered analyses run the risk of diverting our attention from the power of the Soviet polity to shape society and, in particular, to select winners and losers within society and each generation."

Roeder is careful to stress that important knowledge has been produced by those working in other approaches. Indeed, he calls merely for "privileging" political institutions at the level of the state. Before exploring in more detail this issue of privileging, I want to stress at this point the limits of privileging state structures. Society is never entirely absent from political processes, especially when one seeks to understand nontrivial processes of social change. Any number of political thinkers have stressed this point. For example:

> To these three kinds of laws [constitutional, civil, and criminal] is added a fourth, the most important of all, which is engraved in neither marble nor bronze, but in the hearts of the citizens; which forms the true constitution of the state; which acquires new vigor every day, which, when other laws grow old or die out, gives them new life or takes their places, preserves a people in the spirit of its origins, and imperceptibly substitutes the force of habit for that of authority. I am speaking of moral habits, customs, and, above all, of opinion, part of our laws unknown to our political theorists, but upon which, nonetheless, the success of all the other laws depends. (Rousseau 1988, 118)

Moreover, the evidence is compelling that when a public dislikes the dominant institutions, its members can find a way to resist those institutions even under quite repressive circumstances (Scott 1985; Fitzpatrick 1994; Viola 1996). Verdery (1996, 20, italics in original) has argued:

> Communist Party states were not all-powerful: they were comparatively weak. Because socialism's leaders managed only partially and fitfully to win a positive and supporting attitude from their citizens—that is, to be seen as legitimate—the regimes were constantly undermined by internal resistance and hidden forms of sabotage *at all system levels*. This contributed much to their final collapse.

While the first sentence in this quote, especially the "comparatively," deserves further analysis, the pertinence of Verdery's observation about hidden resistance is difficult to dispute. The one-liner about workers' orientation toward communist regimes—"They pretend to pay us; we pretend to work"—is a vital part of the story of the end of communism, since declining economic productivity restricted leaders' options. As Fleron and Ahl put it in chapter 11, "While it would be inaccurate to state that the public forced perestroika and glasnost on an unwilling Soviet leadership, it appears to have been the case that growing public dissatisfaction with the status quo was a political weapon available to Gorbachev as he contemplated ways to overcome elite resistance to his initial, modest reform efforts."

In addition, once the regimes' willingness to prevent spontaneous public activity ended, members of communist societies produced a wide and surprising variety of activity quite quickly. "Informals" grew vastly in number in the late 1980s and became politically demanding. When competitive elections were called, popular front organizations were established to provide opposition to regime candidates, and they succeeded dramatically. In some Soviet republics, the popular fronts emphasized national sovereignty and gained support from all layers of society. In others, the popular fronts rallied support around the slogan of democracy and gained large numbers of mostly urban adherents. (Recall that anticommunist groups could put hundreds of thousands of people on the streets of Moscow in support of Boris Yeltsin in 1990 and 1991. This ability proved crucial at several points in bringing Gorbachev back from his periodic alliances with hard-liners.) Overall, most of the key turning points in the end of communism, in both Eastern Europe and the Soviet Union, were marked either by large-scale demonstrations or by elections or referenda. Although the public did not force glasnost and perestroika on an unwilling Soviet leadership in 1986 and 1987, members of the public certainly were critical in the downfall of the communist regimes throughout the region against the wishes of their leaderships.

In sum, both a large body of social science research and the history of political upheaval in the former Soviet bloc from 1989 through 1991 cast grave doubts on any approach to the study of political change that would exclude society (in contrast to state institutions or to state elites). It is therefore proper and unsurprising that late-communist and post-communist societies have received much scholarly attention in the 1990s. A review of this research will set the stage for a discussion of future directions.

Although communist regimes never entirely eliminated societal resistance, they did prevent the study of their societies by Western social scientists. So, with the Soviet political liberalization of the late 1980s and the end of the East European communist regimes in 1989, it suddenly became possible for Western social scientists to study formerly unreachable societies. This led to a still growing body of survey research (e.g., Hahn 1993b, 1995; Slider, Magun, and Gimpel'son 1991; Dobson and Grant 1992; Finifter and Mickiewicz 1992; Gibson, Duch, and Tedin 1992; Bahry 1993; Duch 1993, 1995; Gibson 1993a, 1996a; Gibson and Duch 1993b, 1994; Bahry and Way 1994; Miller, Hesli, and Reisinger 1994; Reisinger, Miller, Hesli, and Maher 1994; Whitefield and Evans 1994; Zimmerman 1994, 1995; Evans and Whitefield 1995; Mason 1995; Miller, Reisinger, and Hesli 1995, 1996; Rose and Carnaghan 1995; Wyman, White, Miller, and Heywood 1995; Brym 1996b; Finifter 1996; Pammett and DeBardeleben 1996; Reisinger, Melville, Miller, and Hesli 1996; White, Rose, and McAllister 1997; Wyman 1997). Much more is now known about late-Soviet and post-Soviet mass attitudes and behaviors than could have been possible without sophisticated surveys of these societies through collaboration between Western and native scholars (reviews of the findings from this literature include Willerton and Sigelman 1991; Wyman 1994; Fleron 1996b).

Of course, those studying post-Soviet transitions from a society-centered perspective have not been united in their preferred methodology. Important recent society-centered research has rested not only on survey data, for example, but on other types of quantitative data, such as electoral results and demographic trends. Often, these data are available at the local level (e.g., for republics, *oblasti* and *krais* within Russia), which permits the development of a postcommunist political geography.

Qualitative research includes historical macrosocial case studies (discussed as a research strategy in Skocpol and Somers 1980), analyses of open-ended interviews (including focus groups) and direct observation and interaction in what Fenno (1978, xiv, 249) called "soaking and poking." One of the most frequently cited recent studies of Russian politics (Fish 1995b) rests on detailed familiarity with party platforms, contact with party activists and other qualitative information. A number of recent Ph.D. theses stem from similar fieldwork in the qualitative research tradition. There is now a growing literature that attempts to strengthen qualitative work by employing bias reduction techniques developed for quantitative data analysis (e.g., King, Keohane, and Verba 1994; Lustick 1996). Such efforts may help bridge the quantitative-qualitative gap in society-centered (and other) approaches.

Beyond these methodological differences, "society-centered" approaches have differed because they can fall into either of two cells in Figure 9.1. Some of those investigating postcommunist, especially post-Soviet, societies have stressed a political cultural approach, while others have argued for the influence of societal complexification during and after communist rule. In other words, the theoretical perspectives possible from a society-centered approach can differ between those who take a more behavioral approach and those who take a more structural approach. The former have tended to, though need not exclusively, make political culture a fundamental concept. As noted earlier, the latter include those who argue that key segments of Soviet society were likely to have been influenced by the industrialization, urbanization, and other socioeconomic transformations of the Soviet period in a direction of greater complexity of thought, self-efficacy, and political demandingness. Although much is behavioral in such work, its implicit stress on how changing economic institutions shape public outlooks and values places it in the bottom-right cell of Figure 9.1 rather than the top right cell.

Thus, significant differences exist among society-centered approaches. They have produced meritorious studies with differing methodologies, concepts, and theories. Certainly, enough useful knowledge has been produced that any denigration of society's role should be questioned. Roeder's (1993) provocative defense of a neoinstitutionalist perspective does, however, usefully raise the question of which theoretical frameworks, and hence which research agendas, are most likely to advance our knowledge of transitions from communism.

Privileges, Exclusions, and Vantage Points

Although the existence of different research approaches is healthy for any area of inquiry, the debates among proponents of different approaches have produced less cross-germination than would be desirable. Scholars of postcommunist transitions need a different way of framing the question. It is now time to "privilege" not one cell in Figure 9.1 over another but theories that draw elements from more than one cell. At a minimum, this approach means using aspects of the other cells as exogenous variables. Even better is to specify them fully in the model—for behavioralists, for instance, to incorporate structure as a variable influencing popular attitudes or behaviors. Such work exists, of course, but many resist the effort to theorize across cells. One reason for such resistance is the fear of losing theoretical parsimony, and hence power and elegance. I certainly do not advocate the use of theoretical frameworks so complicated that parsimony is lost or that practical testing becomes unwieldy (structural-functionalism [e.g., Parsons 1960] and systems theories [e.g., Easton 1965] have had this problem). Nevertheless, a good deal of otherwise valuable research into postcommunist politics remains so much within a single cell in Figure 9.1 that the danger of excessive complication is distant and the rewards for better theory are near. I will now review approaches from all cells of

Figure 9.1 with these issues in mind. In each case, the possibility exists for research that combines elements from more than one cell, and I discuss these possibilities also.

Roeder's *Red Sunset*

In defending his neoinstitutional perspective, Roeder (1993) places society in the role of "object" not subject. That is, members of the mass public are acted upon by state elites, whose actions are structured by institutional rules, but the public has no theoretically important part to play in shaping elites' choices or perhaps even in shaping the institutional rules. About Soviet society, Roeder (1993, 247) states that its role in Soviet politics was not that of an actor but of an "elemental constraint like nature." Figure 9.2 presents my depiction of Roeder's perspective.

In at least one passage, Roeder's defense of a neoinstitutional approach is too sharp, when it uses the word simply (twice) to create a straw man of societal approaches:

> [T]he new institutionalist approach to authoritarian institutions stresses the importance of distinguishing state and society and in particular recognizing that the dynamics of the state are not simply derivative of the developments in society. In particular, it underscores the importance of distinguishing political development from social modernization. The former is not simply derivative of the latter. (Roeder 1993, 252)

Roeder's model is simple and elegant, and he uses it to explain the decline and fall of the Soviet Union in a thought-provoking manner. It is, moreover, applicable not just to Soviet politics but also to post-Soviet politics. Since he focuses on the centrality of state institutions in an authoritarian regime, the approach he develops in *Red Sunset* remains relevant, in part, because he considers Russia and the other post-Soviet regimes to be authoritarian at present, not democratic (see Roeder 1994). It is possible that he would acknowledge a greater role for subjective mass values and cognitions when the mass public is part of the selectorate in a democracy. His language suggests, however, that he prefers to downplay these things even when one is studying a partially or fully democratic system.

It would seem, however, that despite what Roeder says about his neoinstitutional approach, he analyses Soviet-era politics (and the ending of the USSR) in a manner that does not stay within only one cell of Figure 9.1. The story he tells (1993, 3) depends critically on a societal component: "The one-party regime ultimately fell owing to its inabil-

FIGURE 9.2 Roeder's (1993, chap. 2) Neoinstitutional Approach

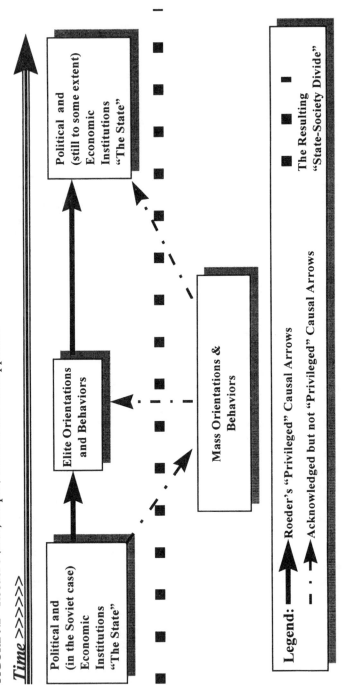

Time >>>>>>

Political and
(in the Soviet case)
Economic
Institutions
"The State"

Elite Orientations
and Behaviors

Mass Orientations &
Behaviors

Political and
(still to some extent)
Economic
Institutions
"The State"

The Resulting
"State-Society Divide"

Legend: ——▶ Roeder's "Privileged" Causal Arrows

– · –▶ Acknowledged but not "Privileged" Causal Arrows

ity to respond to immense social changes that had taken place in Soviet society—ironically, social changes that the Party itself had set in motion." His case studies bring to bear his deep knowledge of Soviet society. His own analyses, therefore, undercut the utility of drawing a thick line between state and society.

Roeder should not have argued that he would "privilege" institutions at the expense of society but instead should have focused on the way in which state institutions proffer a potentially useful *vantage point* from which to examine political change in both its elite and societal dimensions. If institutional incentives comprise the hilltop from which Roeder wishes to gain the best lines of sight, he should use that vantage point to look down at the societal valleys, not merely at the tops of nearby hills. Indeed, by the end of *Red Sunset*, he has softened the position he took at the beginning: "Yet, this case makes us aware of the need to investigate the natural history of political development alongside social modernization" (252). I would go even further and replace "alongside" with "in conjunction with."

Survey Research and Postcommunist Political Change

Having examined Roeder's neoinstitutional arguments, it is only fair to note that those conducting other types of analysis into postcommunist political and social transition frequently fail to incorporate concepts or variables from outside a single cell. Perhaps the most voluminous type of research over the past seven years has involved the analysis of data from surveys of mass publics in one or more formerly communist societies. For understandable reasons, the importance of presenting and analyzing such data to other scholars is clear. This has meant that the authors of survey-based research need not always delve deeply into the theoretical underpinnings of their interpretations of the data. It is common, for example, to deal with the question of how mass opinion relates to political change by mentioning in the introduction to an article some variant of "We all know that mass political values *have to* matter for the speed and/or success of democratization."[2]

Although the statement is correct (after all, Dahl (1989, 30) said it!), using it as a launching point serves survey researchers poorly. By itself, the assertion implies that one should gather data, set aside institutions and elites as *ceteris paribus* elements of a black box, and presume that the level of "democratic values" (of whatever kind happen to be under study) will have a monotonically positive relationship to eventual democratic consolidation.[3] Just as Roeder's neoinstitutional model could not (and, in the event, did not) tell a story of political change without bringing in society, so survey research will contribute relatively little to debates about political change unless it can incorporate institutions and elites in some defensible way.

This is not to say that researchers ought never to employ survey data gathered from the societies of Eastern Europe and the former Soviet Union to test political psychological models that omit non-individual-level variables. Given their micro objectives, political psychologists can, at times, opt to leave societal and institutional context in abeyance. Yet if an article based on survey data does propose to address political psychological theories, the authors must resist the temptation to refer vaguely to a link between the research and the democratic prospects of any country. Such boilerplate has the effect of turning the research into a study of political change without the study actually being designed as such. The resulting analyses create the impression that the author holds simplistic or naive views about processes of political change. This is to the detriment not only of the author's reputation but of survey data as a source of information.

When analyses of survey data create this misleading impression, they allow those who discount the merits of survey methodology or who worry about the continued impact of an antidemocratic political culture in the formerly communist societies to raise what I call the "Red, White, and Blue Dawn" scenario. (In a 1980s movie entitled *Red Dawn*, so I understood from the commercials, the Soviet Union invades the United States, and America is only saved because a brave band of high school students takes to the hills to resist.) The "Red, White, and Blue Dawn" scenario asks something like "If the Russian people are so democratic, how many of them would take to the streets to oppose authoritarianism if, say, General Lebed launched a coup tomorrow?" A survey researcher who tries to answer this question is a sucker. There is no good answer because not enough information has been provided. It depends on stipulating many things about which survey research alone does not and cannot provide information.

For instance, the onset of mass action in any society depends on a great deal more than the values of the (potential) participants. There must be ways to overcome the collective action problem. That is, some "space" must exist (most likely stemming from something *institutional* in nature) that makes mass protest seem relatively safe and potentially worthwhile. Also, the mass action will require leadership. Moreover, for the numbers involved to grow into significance, methods of "signaling" to other potential participants must exist. There must be, in other words, both opportunity and willingness (Russett and Starr 1989). Or, to switch metaphors, mass protest is like electricity in that it cannot flow until a connection is established.

Serious thinking about such scenarios must therefore rest on infor-

mation about how much the media would be controlled by the putsch-
ists, about which political, economic, intellectual, and/or cultural
leaders would be speaking out or keeping silent, about how quickly
military units would be deployed if at all and about much else as well.
Of course, to raise such scenarios is just to play "Rotisserie League
Russian Politics." It does clarify, though, that to theorize about mass
political action requires one to incorporate elements from several if not
all of the cells in Figure 9.1. Moreover, those analyzing survey data
from the postcommunist countries have a pressing need for explicit,
detailed theory and for theory that incorporates elites and structures,
because most of them do, in fact, view themselves as contributing important knowledge toward an understanding of transitions from communism.

The "Transitions" Approach

Many of the most celebrated recent analyses of democratization
(e.g., O'Donnell and Schmitter 1986; Przeworski 1986; Higley and Burton 1989; Di Palma 1990) have given pride of place to the role that
elites play in democratization. Not primarily because of institutional
incentives but based largely on individual calculations of potential
benefit and harm, key elites in a ruling authoritarian regime can support a breakdown of that regime—sometimes through an explicit negotiating process, or pact, between rival forces—followed by the
installation of democratic institutions. Recent instances in southern Europe and Latin America, as well as Poland and perhaps other communist countries (Bova 1991), are used as examples. This literature is often
referred to as the transitions literature, and its proponents have been
given (or coined?) the label "transitologists" (Schmitter 1995).

This literature has played an important role in breaking scholarship
out of the search for pre-conditions of democracy and refocusing attention on regime change as a political process. To the extent, however,
that transitologists neglect the mass public and downplay the organized links between elites and masses, their analyses can provide only
a limited insight into social change. This point is developed by others
(Levine 1988; Bunce 1995a, 1995b), so I will not belabor it. Nothing in
the transitions perspective prohibits creative theorizing about elites'
behaviors within institutional and societal settings that the researcher
specifies rather than assumes away.

Constitutional Engineering

An important component of the recent literature on democratization
studies how formal institutions (generally constitutional institutions

such as electoral rules and executive-legislative relations) correlate with type of political regime, political stability, the length of democratic governance, or some other attribute (a few examples are listed in the bottom left cell of Figure 9.1, but numerous other studies exist). Some research within this tradition falls prey to the willingness to allow most or all factors other than formal institutional rules to be placed in the error term, that is, to be treated as if they were equal in all the countries being studied. Correlational analyses then follow, producing results that are difficult to interpret within a theory of political change. The best of this work incorporates societal factors (e.g., the degree of cultural heterogeneity within a society) into the analyses. Thus, rather than making the bivariate claim that a certain institutional configuration is correlated in a statistically significant fashion with democratic stability, it is possible to theorize about (and test hypotheses concerning) the interplay of institutional design and social features.

Theories Stressing the Impact on Society of Economic Complexification

I placed what became known in the 1950s and 1960s as modernization theory in the bottom right cell of Figure 9.1 because some of those who tested it with quantitative data focused on the impact of changing institutions (specifically, economic development) on the mass public's beliefs and behaviors. Yet many of those who were part of this school provided more complex theories in which important concepts were examined rather than assumed away. Also, the teleological odor of some modernization analyses ("We're all going toward the same endpoint; some of us are just farther along") is not a necessary component.

The empirical regularity that certain economic changes result in important changes in mass publics has survived the flurry of challenges to "modernization" theory that arose from the 1960s on.[4]

> Far better then to recognize the formidable body of evidence that, whatever the particular cultural traits of a given society, the process of socioeconomic modernization tends to lessen the specific weight and the saliency of traditional culture. (Dallin 1988, 185)

> Capitalist development is associated with the rise of democracy primarily because of two structural effects: it strengthens the working class as well as other subordinate classes; and it weakens large landowners. The first of these must be further specified: capitalist development enlarges the urban working class at the expense of agricultural laborers and small farmers; it thus shifts members of the subordinate classes from an environment extremely unfavorable for collective action to one much more

favorable, from geographical isolation and immobility to high concentrations of people with similar class interests and far-flung communications. (Rueschemeyer, Stephens, and Stephens 1992, 58)

The factors that many authors increasingly link to Soviet citizens' receptivity to a more democratic political culture are those that result from modernization and the use of modern technology (much of it imported from advanced capitalist countries). . . . What was it that rendered those citizens receptive to those ideas in the first place? Following modernization theory, one would argue that it was the social consequences of the modernization process itself: increased functional specialization and structural differentiation created more and specialized interests in society, those interests wanted greater access in the political system; the interest intermediation structures and processes of the Soviet political system did not give them adequate access to decisionmaking; hence, they were receptive to alternative forms of interest intermediation, etc. If this is the case, then one would expect to find genuine receptivity to democracy (i.e., at the levels of both ideal and real cultural patterns) primarily among those citizens occupying positions in society that were created by the modernization process. Conversely, one would not expect to find much receptivity to democracy among segments of Soviet society relatively unaffected by modernization. Among the latter, one would find greater affinity to traditional values of Russian political culture as described in the traditional literature of Sovietology. (Fleron 1996b, 243)

Figure 9.3 provides a depiction of how a theoretical framework might stress some of the same factors that the modernization theorists did and be more explicit about processes of change over time.

Some of the recent survey research could benefit from a theoretical framework that begins with the development-social change link but that also conceptualizes and incorporates into the model the institutional features of the country under study, the ideology or interests of elites and key cultural features. By "conceptualize," I mean principally to explicate different values that these concepts can take on, so that one can generate hypotheses about what should exist empirically under different conditions. Whether the analysis is focusing on cross-national comparisons or over-time change in one country, the need for variation in the values of key concepts is critical.

Class-driven comparative historical studies, such as those of Moore (1966a), Skocpol (1979), or Rueschemeyer et al. (1992), are examples of research into social change that does not rely on concepts from only one of the cells in figure 9.1. They seek to relate how structures and societal actors (such as socioeconomic classes and the organizations that represent them) interact, producing skirmishes that drive social change. Although their methodological choices, their assumptions

FIGURE 9.3 Elements of the Argument for Economic Institutions Reshaping Society and Thereby State Institutions

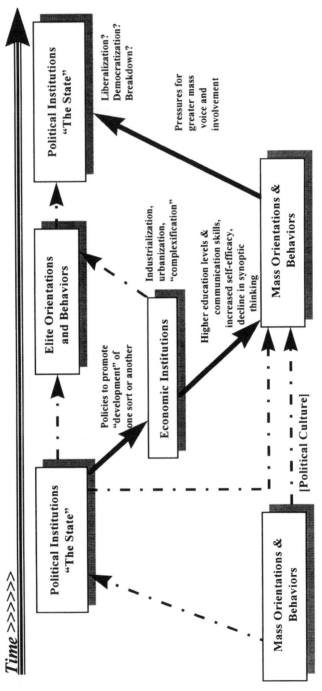

Time >>>>>

Note: Solid arrows indicate the primary lines of causation. The broken-line arrows indicate downplayed lines of causation.

about how change occurs, and the concepts they use are quite different from (often, explicitly opposed to) the choices, assumptions, and concepts of those in the "modernization" school, they also accept that economic structures are an impetus of social change, in large part because they alter the balance of power among social classes. The historical case studies are generally more theoretically complex than studies using quantitative data to examine the economics-social change link, yet there is no inherent reason for that. The quantitative researchers could lay out theoretical frameworks with four to five major concepts, which is how many the case studies tend to employ (e.g., state, civil society, class structure, and international environment), derive testable hypotheses from this framework, and employ their quantitative data to test the hypotheses.

Conclusion

The proper place for society in studies of postcommunist change is right in the thick of things. One obvious reason is that only with knowledge of society can the utility of institutional theories be assessed. When Roeder talks about how the downfall of the Soviet regime is caused by the inability of the institutions to adapt to a changing societal environment, his theory can only be properly tested by incorporating an analysis of society in some fashion. Relatedly, only by studying society can one see how institutions take practical shape and come to operate not entirely in the manner in which the institutional designers intended.

If the proper place of society is in the thick of any analysis of social change (especially of transitions away from communism), this is not to say that analyses of social change should be entirely "society centered." Different scholars will advance theories that rest on different analytic vantage points: some will place, for instance, more emphasis on state institutions, others on the mass public. Ignoring or black-boxing variables from other traditions, however, can only weaken theory development. Parsimony is crucial, but those studying postcommunist transitions have room to enrich their theoretical frameworks without abandoning parsimony.

Notes

An earlier version of this essay was presented at the 28th National Convention of the American Association for the Advancement of Slavic Studies, Boston, November 14–17, 1996.

1. I am therefore unpersuaded by Terry's (1993, 333) call to "concentrate on empirical inquiry and not to tie ourselves in conceptual knots with an excess of model-building and theory adaptation." The drawbacks to doing so are elaborated by Fleron (1996a, 264–5). See also the debate that Terry's article inaugurated: Schmitter and Karl 1994; Bunce 1995b.

2. One almost suspects that major word processing programs now come equipped with a "wizard" (a feature that simplifies the creation of a particular type of document such as a fax or memo) entitled "survey-based articles on the former communist countries." This wizard asks for author information, the conference for which the paper is being written, etc., then composes a cover sheet and introduction with this sentence in it.

3. A recent example will illustrate how assumptions of this type are attributed to survey researchers who do not attend to fleshing out their theory of social change. White, Rose, and McAllister (1997, 272) charge some survey researchers with basing their research on what they call a *destination model*, in which the researcher implicitly assumes that Russians want to become like Western citizens. I believe that they are mistaken in attributing this implicit assumption to the authors of that research. If one accepts that it is appropriate to use survey data to explore mass support for democracy in Russia, then it is appropriate to investigate those outlooks found to be correlated with support for democracy in a variety of other societies. Nothing is assumed a priori about Russian attitudes, rather, attitudes are investigated empirically. Moreover, the fact that Russians will say they would prefer to follow Russian traditions rather than a foreign model—which White, Rose, and McAllister put forth as a definitive reason for rejecting the destination model—seems quite beside the point. The pertinent questions include whether Russians want to elect their leaders, respect the rights of others, and otherwise act democratically. White, Rose, and McAllister propose an *origins model*—focusing on the continued impact on Russian outlooks of life under Soviet rule—as a superior alternative to a destination model. By counterposing the two in this way, they seem to be arguing (ironically, given the authors' breadth of experience in comparative research) against cross-national comparison in favor of cross-temporal comparison. In practice, of course, good research will build on what is known about the Soviet era as well as on cross-national findings. It seems unlikely that White, Rose, and McAllister would have read the teleological assumption into some survey-based research if those conducting it had attended more to explicating the theoretical basis of their analyses.

4. An argument against the view that communist societies were in any way engaged in modernization à la the West is made by Jowitt (1992). Yet we should remember that the match between Soviet transformations and earlier ones in the West is relative: "To [Latin American] peasants who lived seven to a room in mud huts, eating only potatoes, barefoot, unvaccinated, unschooled, and lacking electricity, sewers, and drinkable water, life in Bulgaria would seem pleasant indeed" (Rosenberg 1995, 405).

IV

POLITICAL INCLUSION

10

Lessons for the "Third Wave" from the First: An Essay on Democratization

Harry Eckstein

The "first wave" of democratization occurred in the late nineteenth century. The word *democratization* would then have denoted the creation of new citizenries: the inclusion in the political process of groups previously excluded from it. In the late twentieth century, the period of the "third wave," democratization denotes the process of transition from authoritarian rule and the full-scale fashioning of democratic institutions. But this, like the first wave, includes the creation of large new citizenries, so that it should be possible to derive lessons for contemporary democratizers from the earlier experience.

As always in making historical comparisons, there are differences between the periods and processes that enjoin caution in projecting one period onto the other. Perhaps the most notable difference is that in some cases of political inclusion, notably in the Anglo-American countries, mature institutions of representative government had largely developed before large-scale political inclusion. However, in most countries during the earlier period (e.g. France and Germany) new citizenries and new constitutional orders developed simultaneously, as they do now. In all, large new citizenries required large institutional adaptations, such as the modern systems of mass parties. Above all, the late nineteenth century, like the present period but unlike any other, was an era of unprecedented, broad-scale, and discontinuous change toward democracy. The two "waves" thus are not so dissimilar as to make it implausible to look for guidance for the later process in the earlier.[1] If these reinforce established theories about the conditions of viable democracy, the theories themselves acquire added credibility, and it seems even more prudent to base present actions on the historic lessons.

The Process of Political Inclusion

By political inclusion, I mean the extension of citizen rights to those who have not previously possessed them: legal rights to participate in the selection of incumbents of political offices and to achieve governmental office oneself. Political inclusion in the nineteenth century ended patrician privilege in politics and gave electoral preponderance to ordinary people.

In a few cases, the process can be traced back to the 1820s and 1830s. Mostly, however, it occurred, as if by contagion, in a period from roughly 1865 to 1905, with the two decades from 1865 to 1885 a particularly significant divide.[2] In each country the process took special forms, but all can be placed on a dimension that runs from more gradual and incremental change to more abrupt and broad-scale change.

As usual, Great Britain is the prototypical gradualist case, although the principal inclusionary reform, that of 1867, was radical by British standards. The more celebrated Reform Act of 1832 did not create new citizens. Rather, it is significant for the fact that it changed the electoral system from one of corporate representation to individual representation. The institution of individual representation, however, was necessary to prepare the ground for the inclusionary reforms that came later. Since the Middle Ages, representation in Parliament had been of corporate entities—boroughs, counties, universities—with the number of individuals in them disregarded, so that, among other effects, some individuals possessed plural votes as members of different corporations. This had led to glaring anomalies, especially the "rotten boroughs": constituencies without any or with little population. To remedy the anomalies, the Reform Act of 1832, for the first time in British history, related representation to size of individual population. The act was a dramatic instance of a much more general change from corporalistic to individualistic thinking, but it was not radically individualistic; even in 1865, the largest British constituency still had thirty-five times the population of the smallest.

The Reform Act of 1867, which falls into the critical period of inclusion elsewhere, was the crucial legislation. Despite using some property qualifications, it not only greatly increased the electorate but, more important, gave a preponderance of votes to members of the working class. Still, even that huge change was accomplished in a gradualist manner: only by broadening the citizenry that lived in towns. The countryside remained a stronghold of aristocratic and squirearchic privilege, until, seventeen years later, the same qualification was extended to the rural constituencies. By 1885, inclusion had become the norm. Sixty percent of adult males were enfranchised, compared with about 3 percent before the first Reform Act.

Other reforms slowly followed, intended gradually to realize fully the ideas contained in these essential reforms: the secret ballot (1872); stiffened penalties against electoral bribery and limiting the election expenses candidates could incur (1883); redistribution that abolished seats for tiny boroughs and limited to a single member all but huge ones (1885)—although it was not until 1918 that one could speak of tolerably equal constituencies; then female suffrage after World War I; the Boundary Commission, which keeps constituency size under constant review (1944); and the abolition of plural voting in 1948. The whole process was spaced out over more than a century, and it unfolded in what seems now to have been a logical sequence of first things first and next things next.

It is more difficult to generalize about the United States, because formal political inclusion was a matter for the states. The general outline, however, is clear. The United States got an early start on political inclusion during the great wave of popular politics that swept the country between 1820 and 1840, when the suffrage was granted to virtually all adult men. Slaves (and women) of course were the glaring exception. The great wave of inclusion in Europe later in the century, however, had an American counterpart in two occurrences. One was the inclusion of ex-slaves, and implicitly of all minorities, through the Fifteenth Amendment (1870). The second was the arrival of waves of new immigrants who were considerably different ethnically and in class composition from most earlier immigrants. Through immigration, the United States had to deal with a large new citizenry that was perhaps even more predominantly lower class than the new European citizenries.

The continental pattern was more abrupt. In Spain universal suffrage was instituted suddenly in 1890. In France political privilege ended all at once with the Basic Law of 1875 that instituted the Third Republic; this abruptly granted full manhood suffrage. In the newly unified Germany, less radically, the ancient method of weighting "estates" was abolished and the franchise, for the first time, was widely granted—to about 20 percent of the population, compared with 2 to 5 percent before 1871.

The Scandinavian patterns were mixed. Norway had an extensive franchise already upon its creation in 1814, at least by the standards of the time. Moreover, most of the enfranchised were ordinary people—

specifically, ordinary farmers, since a property qualification that favored landed property was used. However, there was a critical year of inclusion, 1884, when a lenient minimum income qualification replaced the property qualification, with consequences comparable to the British Reform Act of 1867. In 1900, universal manhood suffrage was introduced. Political inclusion also came early to Denmark, which instituted nearly universal male suffrage already in 1849. Finland and Sweden, however, did not have a broad suffrage until the first decade of the twentieth century, when it was instituted abruptly, in the continental manner.

The wave of political inclusion that occurred in the late nineteenth century had sources in other social changes, such as industrialization, urbanization, and working-class mobilization. The effects of these changes on politics have been widely discussed. Less known is the fact that, as in the present period of democratization, the earlier wave resulted as much from the bankruptcy of the old order as from the aspirations of the new.

The privileges of the old exclusive "political classes" had been justified in large part by the argument that good breeding and well-being made for the largess and selflessness of outlook required for true civility and statesmanship. But, in the nineteenth century, this had become transparent embellishment on a contrary reality. Economic development, even preindustrial development, presented many opportunities to use privilege for gain and thus made political positions more attractive to opportunists. Oligarchic politics became increasingly a bazaar for obtaining grants and contracts, places and sinecures. This coincided with the loss by the old order of its traditional legitimacy through ideological shifts that accompanied socioeconomic change. The forces underlying current democratization are a similar combination of socioeconomic changes and the corruption and decay of an established order.[3]

Human Nature and Democracy

After the last fifty years of political science, the first lesson that should be learned from nineteenth-century political inclusion might seem obvious and not necessary to point out. Nevertheless I will discuss it at some length here because it is fundamental—and also because, judging by contemporary writings and actions, it has in fact been hard to learn. The lesson is that *human beings do not have some natural affinity for democratic political orders; inclusive democracy, even if properly instituted, cannot be expected to develop of itself.* Effective democratization requires far more than a process of formal inclusion and the design on paper of a democratic constitution. It is an intricate and difficult task.

Expectations from Inclusion

Expectations from political inclusion in the nineteenth century, as now, were great, and the obstacles that might impede their realization were considered to be minimal. The prevailing view seemed to be that people are somehow democratic by instinct. All that was needed to achieve inclusive representative government was the opportunity to participate, a well-designed constitution, and some rudimentary popular education.

The ideas of the British utilitarians typify this. Their views are best represented by James Mill's article on representative government in the *Encyclopedia Britannica* of 1825. This became the utilitarians' holy scripture on political inclusion. Mill wrote that the "security of unselfish interest" would, and would only, be attained through an "identity of interests" between the public and the polity through full political inclusion. It was impossible for a community to act against its own interests, and it knew its interests "by instinct." Citizens needed some education, but no more than was necessary to read. Bentham similarly thought that ending parliamentary corruption and achieving liberal democracy only required universal suffrage with a literacy requirement, the secret ballot, and annual parliaments.

Even more striking is that the advocates of political inclusion thought little about obstacles to the realization of their vision. They did not think about whether or not political inclusion would make necessary structural adaptations in governmental and political organizations. They gave no thought to the possibility of public apathy. They seemed unaware of the need by the newly enfranchised for organization and leadership or of the opportunities for exploitation that might arise from this. Least of all did it occur to them that the laboring classes might not be strongly attached to liberal-democratic values themselves.

A particular psychology was associated with the liberal advocacy of political inclusion. Graham Wallas (1908) called it the psychology of "enlightened self-interest." Its model was de Tocqueville's depiction of public associations. In the participatory polity people would enlarge one another's minds and feelings through reciprocal influence; through public discussion people would become conscious of being particles of "a great community," of the interests of that community, and of the fact that personal interests and the communal interests were identical. De Tocqueville had associated this psychology with small, self-governing bodies such as the New England town meetings, but advocates of inclusion took it to hold also in mass electorates.

Liberal psychology was associated with great faith in the ability of constitutions to institutionalize viable liberal-democratic polities. Faith in constitutional contrivance had deep roots in an important element of Enlightenment thought: belief in the mechanical nature of societies. The conception of the polity as a "machinery of government" has an obvious affinity for constitutional "engineering." Mechanisms, unlike organisms, are artifacts; they function as they do principally because of their construction, and they function about the same under most conditions. The viability and working of organisms, to the contrary, depends much more on their interplay with their environments. Political inclusion and the belief that appropriate constitutional design was the only thing needed to guarantee its success thus went hand in hand.

Disillusion

Dissenting voices were few, even among conservatives. However, about a generation after the principal period of inclusion—over a period that runs roughly from 1890 to 1920—thoughts about democratization underwent a massive change. Great expectations now gave way to great disillusion. This, initially, was greatest on the part of good liberals and champions of ordinary people themselves. Graham Wallas, a gentle and moderate Fabian socialist, is a paradigmatic case in point. In *Human Nature in Politics* (1908), Wallas wonders whether representative government might not "prove to be a mistake after all"; and, he adds, "it is the growing, not the decaying, forces of society which create the most disquieting problems." Wallas, like others at the time, sought a more adequate psychology to make sense of the political behavior of the new citizenries. In fact, much of the drive that led to modern psychology and social psychology derived from mystification about the behavior that followed political inclusion. S. E. Finer (in Pareto 1966) even attributed the growing repudiation of all rational thought by men like Poincaré, Bergson, and Sorel to deep disillusion with the intellectualist trappings of liberalism.

Four perceptions were involved in this disillusion. They pervade both the scholarly and popular literatures of the time.[4] The first of these is that *political inclusion does not equalize anything, but only reratifies political life.* During the period 1895–1920, the discovery was made that "ruling elites" were being spawned in democratized societies, not least in the very political organizations of the newly included. Earlier there had been openly privileged patriciates; now, their place was taken by clandestine "elites sprung from the people." The new elites simply put effective political exclusion on an implicit and murky basis, where earlier it had been frank and transparent. Political inclusion thus was considered a fraud. Indeed, it was argued that patrician rule had better inhibited the more cynical and brutal aspects of domination, because it was explicit and based on traditional norms that also restrained elites rather than on brute success in power struggles.

Second, effective exclusion by new elites was made worse by the perception that *much of the general public, through apathy, excludes itself from full citizenship.* We have become so accustomed now to apathy in politics that it is hard for us to imagine the sense of shock, indignation, and derision that went with its initial discovery. Wallas estimated from his own experience as a politician that not more than 10 percent of ordinary people were politically aware enough to attend an occasional political meeting, and those who did were derided by their neighbors as busybodies.[5] Wallas was outraged when no one in a neighborhood could tell him where a political meeting he was to address was being held. J. E. C. Bodley (1899), the principal historian of the Third Republic at the time, wrote that the new French voters tend to avoid elections because they prefer "unalloyed recreation" to political participation; ask the great majority about elections, he went on to say, and they will reply, "Je ne m'occupe pas de politique" (a peasant may use a more vigorous verb). Just as well, says Bodley, given their fixation on picturesque personages and their lack of genuine interest in political issues.

Political apathy was the main reason that new elites could spring up in the very midst of organizations set up to mobilize and champion the newly included. Wallas had already noted the strange indifference of workingmen toward their own political organizations, but it is of course Michels (1949; originally 1910) who holds the patent here.

A third general perception of the effects of political inclusion was that *the ordinary public is not a "public" at all but a "crowd."* We are generally aware now of the elitist reaction to inclusion and of the disillusion caused by political apathy; these have continued as major themes in political science. What was involved in the belief that the public is only a "crowd" is less familiar, but this was an even more strident theme of critical writing about inclusive democracy.

The liberal idea of a "public" derived from de Tocqueville, particularly from his account of the operation and effects of small bodies of citizens, such as the New England town meetings. To account for experience with inclusion, a very different social psychology clearly was wanted. In individual psychology, perhaps not coincidentally, ideas appeared that played down ratiocination and stressed impulse and instinct, imitation, suggestibility, and conditioning, and this provided the basis for a new social psychology as well. Impulses and instincts, wrote Wallas (1908), play a large role in individual behavior, but "they increase in their importance with an increase in the number of those influenced by them." A model was now sought for what a mass public driven by impulse would be like, and the model seized upon was that of French revolutionary crowds. For a time, in fact, social psychology and the psychology of crowds were close to synonymous.

The most influential work on the subject, Le Bon's *The Crowd* (1960; originally 1893), was explicitly about behavior "attendant on the entry of the popular classes into politics." Le Bon's was a fanatical book. He was a racist, and his book has a racist contempt for ordinary people. They suffer from "socially induced stupidity"; they have "mediocre wits," a high tolerance for pious fraud, and a disposition to violence. They are childishly subject to caprice and impulse. Acting in "crowds" further reduces their wits. The public mind worships heroes, especially criminal heroes. Its morality is debased. Through the entry of the popular classes into politics we are launched on a new "tide of barbarism." And so on.

Astonishingly, this bilious and prejudiced book became, according to Allport, "perhaps the most influential book ever written in social psychology." *The Crowd* became a popular vogue book. It also influenced scholars as diverse as Sigmund Freud, Robert Park, William McDougall, and Michels. Even Max Weber, who characterized the supporters of popular leaders as "soulless followings" who had been "intellectually proletarianized," was susceptible.

Fourth, as for the new political organizations that were both to educate and channel public opinion, it was thought increasingly that *the leadership of mass political organizations operate like gangs that prey on the masses*. The advocates of civic inclusion had thought that the relationship between the new citizens and their leaders and organizers would initially be one of temporary tutelage. The better educated and more large-minded workers would guide the inexperienced citizenry through the early stages of mass citizenship.

By the end of the century, that idea was thoroughly discredited. It was particularly discredited by the discovery of the American political machine in large cities where crowds of new immigrants settled. "Crowds" and political "machines" were closely associated, having the same source. The machines themselves were internally authoritarian: they were "bossed," hierarchical, monocratic, and strictly disciplined, almost as if they were paramilitary forces. In this they resembled urban gangs, and, as Whyte (1943) has shown, they were in fact closely connected to the gangs; one graduated out of the gang into the machine, applying lessons learned in the earlier experience. At bottom, the machine's purpose was not even political, except for the use of politics for despoliation. Weber thought that machine bosses were like tax farmers and Bryce (1921) compared them to stockbrokers and called them "street vultures."

The machines did render important services to the new citizens through patron-client relations: as intermediaries to unfamiliar and threatening powers. But the people they served were also their victims, as ballot-fodder and for doing the machines' dirty work. The most cruel fraud of all was that the leaders of the urban masses tended to be social climbers who used the new politics to rise into or near the old patriciate. The new lower-class political organizations were, to a great extent, vehicles for co-optation into the old patriciate.

The political scientists who fashioned democratic theory after World War II were mainly influenced by the collapse of some democracies and the serious malfunctioning of others during the interwar period. However, long before this, a great change of mood concerning democracy had already occurred in political science. The later reconstruction of democratic theory, beginning with Schumpeter, was an extension of this. The changed mood grew from puzzlement in regard to political behavior attendant on inclusion. Its fruit has been more systematic and empirical political studies—political science as we know it. Long before World War II this had started to develop in studies of political behavior, the pioneers being men such as Wallas and Lippman, who began to wed political science to psychology, and Lasswell, through the study of elites. Later, the new political science was extended to the study of how political systems really work. The initial impetus for both of these changes came from experiences with political inclusion, so that political science may be regarded as above all a science that tries to illuminate the puzzles originating in political inclusion.

The New Optimism

I have dwelt on this subject because now, when a new wave of democratization is under way, the lessons learned earlier seem to have faded. It is a little as if there had been no political science in the meantime. A new democratic optimism that is much like the old is again developing. Giuseppe Di Palma's (1990) book, *To Craft Democracies*, is a case in point, and a good representative of the contemporary transitions-to-democracy literature.[6]

Di Palma pretty much dismisses revisionist democratic theory on the astonishing ground that the people who produced it were misled by earlier experiences with democracy. He makes some concessions to the revisionists, and we are counseled to keep expectations from the new democracies moderate. However, Di Palma also holds, as his central position, that building democracies is mainly a matter of managing properly the transitions to it. Earlier theory held that the conditions of viable democracy lie deep in social structure and culture. Not so, says Di Palma. Democratization is mainly a matter of being crafty during the transition from authoritarianism—a matter only of nursing democracy through infancy.

No doubt the management of transitions to democracy is important, and transition theorists say much that is persuasive about it. No major change can be accomplished without a transition to it, and obviously mistakes, even fatal mistakes, can be made during the process of transition. However, laying the groundwork for effective democracy after a limited period of transition to it also is a crucial problem. After all, the old failed democracies (e.g., Weimar) failed after a rather extended and apparently successful period of transition to democracy. No one thought around 1930, eleven years after its founding, that the Weimar Republic was seriously endangered. So how does one try to ensure that democratization will be more than a short-lived transition? The answer now seems again to be that we may entrust its success to human nature and well-designed constitutions. The perception of human nature is not quite the same, but the argument about democracy is similar.

How then does one "craft" democracy by transition management? First, it is presupposed that the situation in which democracy crafting can occur must be "ripe" for it. This, however, does not refer to social-economic-cultural conditions of democracy as the older democratic theorists envisioned them. It means only that there must be a prior regime crisis in the authoritarian order, a perception of its bankruptcy. In crisis, "normal" determinants of stable democracy supposedly are off; crisis makes the system available for creative artifice. It helps if the crisis situation is perceived to be a stalemate between the major interests in society—the officials, the military, owners, and labor—so that no special group can envisage a win without concessions to the others. At the deeper socioeconomic level, only a certain amount of economic development (not very high) is presupposed.[7]

The perception that an old order is bankrupt and a new one is needed as a way out no doubt is a sounder basis for building democracy than the bare belief that democracy need only exist to succeed. However, a myriad of crises have occurred in authoritarian regimes without the outcome of viable democracy. In many of these crises before our own time, mutual reconciliation in a more open polity must have been the sensible outcome. A politics of reconciliation and openness has in fact been a common outcome of regime crises in the past. The trouble is that almost always the appetite for authoritarian dominance sooner or later overcomes the former sense of deadlock, and thus the will to reconcile competing forces in open democratic competition.

The mechanism that seems to operate here is something like charisma in Weber's political sociology. Charismatic authority occurs in crises and operates outside of normal routines. However, it is itself doomed to be routinized. It may leave major traces in the routines of society (Weber thought that only charisma could overcome ingrained social rigidities), but it does not permanently suspend "normal" laws of social life, and it is not necessary that it should have any lasting effects on the reconstituted institutional life of society. Charismatic phases are as likely as not to be merely transitory periods of excitation.

Why then should the present wave of change due to crisis turn out differently from the earlier period of democratization? Because, says Di Palma, now a recipe is available for getting viable democracy out of the raw material of regime crisis. It is a simple recipe that has three ingredients. First, one should avoid "Jacobin radicalism," or the desire to reconstitute the whole social order. Second, a policy of *garantismo* should be adopted, as in Spain—the model case for the new optimism. *Garantismo* is a policy that guarantees to all major groups in society—the political left, center, and right and structural interests in society such as the church, labor, business, bureaucrats, and military officers—that they will survive democratization pretty much intact and that they will be able to realize their fundamental interests in the new regime. How is this to be done without again risking the old stalemates and the old subversions? Through formal "pacts" among the interests. What then will guarantee that the pacts will be observed more than temporarily? Here enters the third ingredient: constitutions that institute democratic rules of the new political game and guarantee the arrangements. These should be adopted quickly, says Di Palma, at the very outset of transition. They should be planted early to develop early roots. What details go into constitutions is less important than the fact that they exist, provided only that they institute the requisite amount of *garantismo*. People will get used to playing the constitutional game by playing it—presumably, rather quickly and by getting from it some tangible benefit, like civil peace.

This position differs from nineteenth-century optimism, in part, in that it supposes some modicum of social learning, rather than just relying on raw, unacculturated human nature. It makes a small concession to cultural theories of democracy. More notably, it relies more on special sectional interests than on "natural" civic spirit. Still, human nature remains the root of viable democracy. It is no longer the human nature of "enlightened self-interest," but a less pretty human nature: narrow interest, illuminated by regime failure and by formal guarantees to special and powerful interests, plus a presumed tendency of people to become quickly habituated to any institutions under which they live. But this difference, I submit, is pretty much the mixture as before: much the same in form, though somewhat different in content.

Along with this, as we saw, faith in constitutional engineering, and thus much interest in it, has reappeared. The formal legalism of the old political science, once thoroughly discredited, has been reborn, and it has been instituted in a great many new projects dealing with constitutional design. No doubt this reflects an unavoidable need for devising new institutional orders. However, one is struck by the faith again put in constitutional projects to yield viable democracies. Certainly no comparable effort is being devoted to thought about how to bring about deeper social and cultural conditions in which new constitutions might take root and flourish. The matter is not wholly ignored, as in the first wave of inclusion, but it is anything but center stage. What is different about the new faith in constitutions is only that they are now regarded as repositories of rules that interests observe in playing the "game" of politics.

Democratization and Economic Liberalization

The second lesson that should be learned from earlier experience with inclusion is that *economic liberalization is far from a sufficient condition for democracy, or even a very favorable one.* To this we may add that *the process of "marketization" of an established "command-economy" in fact occurs in tension with that of democratization.*[8] There are several reasons for this.

One reason is the simple fact that countries that earlier experienced democratization, both successfully and unsuccessfully, had market economies. More often than not, in fact, the outcome was failure. Seventeen countries, Huntington (1991, 17–21) has pointed out, adopted democratic institutions during the wave of democratization between 1915 and 1931, but only four maintained themselves throughout the 1920s and 1930s. These four cases all had market economies, but so did all the others. And market economies then were a great deal more like literally "free" markets than now—less regulated and constrained by public laws and rules, more ruggedly individualistic, less subjected to public legislation, less "commanded," and thus better equipped with the qualities that are supposed to be the link between economic and political liberalization. The new market economies that recently have sprung from the ruins of command economies are likely to be just such unrestrained and unmitigated "free" economies, in the manner of the interwar Western economies. Minimally, this suggests that market economies generally are neutral in regard to democracy and less than neutral in their ideal-typical form. Their political counterparts, on evidence, are as likely to be authoritarian as democratic.[9]

"Marketization" might conceivably play an indirect role in democratizing by promoting general economic development. One of the best-established hypotheses we have about the conditions of viable democracy is the Lipset hypothesis, linking it to level of economic development (Lipset 1960, 1994; Lipset, Seong, and Torres 1993). This hypothesis could certainly help account for earlier experiences with democratization, since it enables one to hold that most societies had not yet developed sufficiently to be ripe for successful democratization, regardless of the prevailing type of economy. However, the economic development hypothesis has become increasingly ambiguous as it has been applied and tested. It now seems clear that the hypothesis leaves a large area of indeterminacy, whether conceived, in Huntington's (1984) manner, as a zone of transition to democracy or, in Dahl's (1971), as just an area of indeterminacy. It also seems clear now that more powerful determinants of viable democracy exist that mediate the effects of economic development and that might therefore be capable of explaining stable democracy independently.[10]

An even stronger argument for the position I have taken here is that the *logical* connection between free markets and free polities is far from obvious. That we sometimes use the same word, liberalization, for processes that institute both democracy and markets does not make the processes similar or even related. "Economic man" seems in fact to be a species strikingly different from "democratic man." The ideal market actor is egocentrically absorbed in personal optimizing, in competition with and often at the expense of others. For him, the pursuit of collective benefits, as Olson (1965) and many others since Olson have shown, is highly problematic. Self-interest as identical with communal interests does not exist for him. On the contrary, the ideal democratic actor, as even the utilitarians who invented economic man knew well, is concerned with and aware of the general interest and subordinates to it personal or factional advantage. He trusts other people and works harmoniously with them to attain common goods. He is certainly an individual, but an individual who, as Aristotle said, is human only in a *polis.*

Why then is there a seemingly strong association between market economies and democracies? For two reasons, I suggest. First, we make the association because we tend to consider the totalitarian model the prototype of the command economy. The Soviet or Nazi economies, however, did not result from an earlier developed command economy that somehow contained their seeds, nor did they ultimately safeguard and preserve the authoritarian political system. Rather than being *conditions* of a political system they developed as *reflections* of the political orders they served. There is no reason then why, if they continue for a time without radical alteration, they should rule out viable democracy.

Second, I suggest that an important reason for the association is that, over a long period of adaptation, pure market relations in the utilitarian sense have been attenuated by democratic legislation and adjudication, and by the gradual evolution of what one might call market cultures. These have reduced considerably the contradictions with democracy. Democracies and markets have gradually, over a long period, adapted to one another. Such adaptations of contrary behavioral patterns—adaptations that produce viable symbioses—always take much time. A couple of generations ago, the association of capitalist markets with democracy would not have seemed at all evident, even in the United States and Britain. The countries of the ex-Soviet Union provide glaring illustrations of the principle that the liberation of greed far from suffices for instituting a smooth market economy, let alone democracy. But we should already know this sufficiently from our own history. We should also know it from Weber's (1958) analysis of the "spirit" of modern capitalism, because Weber stresses the role played in modern capitalism by values and norms that *limit* the *aura sacra fames*. One may even suspect that the development of an appropriate market culture—a complex of norms and laws that allows the potential for good of market economies to be realized while also being a safeguard against their potential for social evil—is as difficult to accomplish as a political culture appropriate to democracy.

A third argument against the hypothesis that economic liberalization is favorable to democratization is based on well-established theories that pertain to all general forms of social change. These have to do with the pace and scope of social changes intended to accomplish successful transformation.

One of these theories might be called the *discontinuity hypothesis*. This says that highly discontinuous social change (rapid change, broad in scale) generally has pathological consequences. Lipset (1960), for instance, has argued that, although level of economic development is directly related to viable democracy, the pace of development is inversely related to it. This equally important part of his argument now seems largely overlooked. Olson (1963) has argued similarly that rapid economic change has broadly dysfunctional social consequences. Kornhauser (1959) made a still stronger and more general case for linking discontinuous social change to social and political dysfunctions in *The Politics of Mass Society*. "Mass society" à la Kornhauser is a society in which typical political behavior ("mass behavior") resembles "crowd" behavior and which, according to Kornhauser and other theorists of mass society, has a particular affinity for dictatorship, even totalitarianism. Kornhauser summarizes work done on mass society by a long succession of important social thinkers, including Heberle, Arendt, and Ortega y Gassett, all of whom link mass behavior to the rise of totalitarian movements. By all odds the most important source of mass behavior, Kornhauser argues, with much evidence and reason, is discontinuous, disruptive social change.[11] In fact, he regards such change as their indispensable condition. Such change has also long been linked to the occurrence of anomie in society, and that in turn to all sorts of mild and intense social pathologies, alongside individual pathologies of the sort Durkheim studied.[12]

Contemporary changes from command economies to market economies certainly come under the discontinuity hypothesis. Marketization hardly is something that may develop smoothly and gradually, by a kind of self-generation, alongside gradually receding remnants of a command economy. In its very nature and however cushioned, the changes that marketization entails will be abrupt and large, as has in fact been the case in recent experience. If anomic pathologies in behavior follow, no one nowadays should be surprised.

The second hypothesis can be called the *sequence hypothesis*. This hypothesis has to do with the spacing in history of major, or "critical," changes. It pertains specifically to the effects of combining major changes in the social or political order. The hypothesis says that such changes are the harder to digest, and the more likely to lead to severe disorders, the more they overlap in time or occur simultaneously.

More specifically, the hypothesis argues this: (1) Certain highly consequential political issues generate especially intense conflicts. They include issues of national identity, the relations of church and state, regime structure and popular participation, and redistributive social policies. These involve deep and broad questions of the boundaries, nature, and purpose of the polity and of legitimacy. Consequently, the problems that the issues pose contain great potential for becoming "crises," in which the viability of the political order is at stake. (2) If these issues are settled sequentially—that is, one by one and in some logical order of "fundamentality" (the very deep national identity problem first, then the regime issue, then redistributive policies, or something of this kind)—then viable democracy is likely. Britain and the United States are cases in point. (3) To the extent that the issues are tackled simultaneously, as they were in Germany, for instance, the effects will be pathological, because of the much greater burden of disruptive change and the deep and complex political cleavages that are likely to result.

The gist of this hypothesis also was already intimated by Lipset, but it is now associated more with Binder et al. (1971). The hypothesis was specifically intended to explain the difference between countries in which inclusive democracy was not associated with conspicuous system failures and those in which it was. It fills this bill well.

There are, of course, newly democratizing countries in which the burden of democratization is not much added to by other transformations. The most conspicuous cases, however, are models of what to avoid in light of the sequence hypothesis. The most fundamental and cleavage-charged issues concerning the political regime and economic organization are raised simultaneously in these cases. Furthermore, any dysfunction in one area is likely to spill over into the other, and with a vengeance. Marketization would be difficult even if a stable political order were in place to oversee the process. Democratization would be difficult even if there were a reliable economy to supply basic material needs. The difficulties increase exponentially in each area if government and economy both are tenuously established.

Gradual, Incremental, and Syncretic Change

A third lesson that should be drawn from the early experience with political inclusion is that *democratization should proceed gradually, incrementally, and by the use of syncretic devices.*

The argument in the previous section implies that social transformation is only likely to be accomplished, and to be accomplished without highly destructive disorders, if it is spaced out over a good deal of time, if it is approached incrementally (i.e., sequentially), and if it builds syncretically upon an existing order rather than trying to eradicate it. This is the sense in Di Palma's counsel to avoid "Jacobin radicalism" in democratization.

There is clear evidence for this hypothesis in the history of political inclusion. The more successful cases all were countries in which inclusion was a prolonged process that had at least some features of logical sequencing. In Great Britain, as we saw, the process of inclusion was spread over generations, each step being digested before the next, and it was also carried out as if logically planned. Without the abolition of corporate representation, extending the franchise to individuals would have made no sense. Without individual representation, the idea of including the kinds of individuals who constituted a majority in society would not have been compelling. Only after highly inclusive individual representation was it really necessary to face the issue of equal districts. And so on.

Also, throughout the process, change was always tempered by continuity of aspects of the old order. Most of the old represented corporations had been territorial entities, boroughs, and counties, and most of these were retained through the use of "constituencies"—a corporate concept that is not to be confused with the individualistic concept of a voting district. Proportional representation would have been the logical expression of the idea of individualistic representation, but it would also have been a more substantial break with the past than the plurality system. The initial broad extension of the franchise occurred only in towns and cities, where the spirit of reform was most advanced. It also still involved income or property qualifications that restricted it to those more prosperous members of the working class who were most like the old patricians. And so on again.

If a hypothesis fits evidence, one should also be able to specify the reason or logic in it. This is not difficult. The great advantage of gradual and incremental processes is that they allow time to accomplish the further adaptive changes in behavior and institutions that important reforms always entail. For example, political inclusion and democratization make necessary something like a modern political party system. Parties in turn require leadership schooled in the arts of political organization; they require activists who do party work; they require party premises, party records, party bureaucracies, party treasuries, party publications, party conferences to select nominees and to define party policy. The fully developed party system has formed stable party identities in the electorate and the identification of parties with symbols; this certainly is not possible in little time. Above all, parties require skills in the arts of interest aggregation, without which party systems will be greatly fragmented and divisive.

In Britain, modern political parties in fact emerged gradually, step by step, from what had been parliamentary cliques and factions. In the early nineteenth century, being a Tory or a Liberal meant mainly being identified, usually by inheritance, with certain political notables. In the subsequent development of modern parties there were important episodes, but at no single point in, or small range of, time can one point to the beginning of modern British political parties. A date here would be as arbitrary and meaningless as saying that the Industrial Revolution occurred in 1760.[13]

In contrast to Britain (and also the United States, where parties were already highly developed when the new immigrant citizenries arrived), fully inclusive democracy came to Germany when the party system was still unripe for it. Granted, political parties antedate the Weimar Republic. In certain respects, they were even highly developed in Imperial Germany, much more so than in pre-1900 Britain. Party competition, however, had little to do with competition for power and policy, and thus with interest aggregation. The Reichstag was essentially a debating society. Under these circumstances, parties developed highly abstract and typically extreme ideologies, sometimes around mere nuances of policy. Not having any reason to compromise and coalesce, they became ideologically pure—that is, intransigent. Though well organized and well equipped with treasuries, bureaucracies, party newspapers, and the like, the parties were anything but training grounds for responsible legislative and executive leadership. Nor were they arenas for aggregating diverse interests or even, like most developed parties, electoral machines. The Weimar Republic paid a heavy price for that.

There are numerous other areas in which democratizing change imposes further imperatives to adapt. For example, early democratizing change entailed the progressive extension of public schooling, as a prerequisite for the attitudes and skills that citizenship and eligibility for office require. The extension of education in Britain in fact parallels political inclusion, always lagging some years behind; needs arising from inclusion gave impetus to educational reforms. Such reforms also cannot be achieved overnight. Schooling requires buildings and equipment, teachers, teacher training, curricula, syllabi, textbooks, and examinations; above all, it requires appropriate attitudes toward occupations and the future of one's children; and all of this takes much time even just to put in place.

In Germany, in contrast, the educational system, although, like parties, highly advanced, had not developed in symbiosis with political inclusion, or as an adaptation to it, as in Britain and the United States. If any civic training was provided, it was training in being a good subject in an authoritarian and highly bureaucratic state. Schools were in place, but what they inculcated was far from socialization for democracy. The German schools required numerous adaptations to democracy, and these are probably harder to accomplish when a system has already developed and hardened than when it is embryonic. In most currently democratizing countries, making such adaptations of established systems of education is precisely what is required.

The point is that any limited social change has repercussions in many segments of society, and these in still other social areas, so that time and experience are needed to "digest" change fully and to metabolize it into the social order.

Gradual and incremental change also allow some incorporation of the old elite into the new order—co-optation in reverse. This may spare the new order the enmity of old elites and thus the enmity of people who command resources that make for a high capacity to resist and to do mischief. Among those resources is a set for which any new order has particularly great need: "human capital," which includes education, technical skills, administrative experience, and the like. One of the great ironies of social life is that new social structures that lack well-established routines have especially great need for people who already possess such capital, which tends to be accumulated mainly by old privileged segments and which cannot be appropriated and redistributed. The result often is a paradox. This is exemplified by Kelley and Klein's (1978) important study of the Bolivian Revolution of 1951: an egalitarian revolution that initially did much to equalize but, over time, accomplished no equalization at all, precisely because the new order required human resources concentrated in the old elite. Human capital can never be created overnight, and so the cooperation of old elites becomes essential in any social transformation.

What is more generally involved here is the desirability of "syncretic" change, if real change is to be achieved effectively. Syncretic change is change that grafts onto what exists, rather than destroying it. It adapts the old to the new and vice versa. Its model is the extraordinarily successful missionary spread of early Christianity; the idea of syncretism was in fact first developed to describe religious practices and doctrines. Christianity, it has been argued, could expand from being a mere Judaic reform movement, like other such movements before Jesus, by being adapted to the universalism of Greek philosophy early on. Subsequently, missionary Christianity displayed a remarkable ability to incorporate paganism into itself. Christianity especially incorporated pagan rituals and symbolism, from gargoyle decorations on churches to Christmas trees. The Venerable Bede, writing about the successful mission to the Anglo-Saxons in the sixth century, already saw this as a major source of the spread of Christianity.

Political inclusion in Britain certainly entailed the extensive use of political syncretism. On the symbolic level of politics it hardly changed anything. A politician of the early nineteenth century would probably not feel at sea even nowadays in the House of Commons. He undoubtedly would gasp at the presence of women in the chamber, and he would be dumbfounded by the fact that the Speaker is a woman. The Speaker's wig and garb, however, would be familiar, as well as all the rest of the House's extensive ceremonialism. Today's Speaker of the House of Commons, in fact, is ideal-typical syncretism incarnate. Political syncretism during the period of inclusion is especially evident in the fact that it was the Tories, under Disraeli, who enacted the crucial Reform Act of 1867; Disraeli, it was said, "caught the Whigs bathing and stole their clothes." Disraeli's doctrine in fact was intentionally syncretic. He envisioned what he called "a union of the cottage and the throne," an alliance between the traditional oligarchy and both the old and new lower classes, to preserve tradition against a common enemy: bourgeois liberalism. What we think of as welfare state socialism, Disraeli thought of as a continuation of the best in the feudal tradition: the hegemony of uncommon people with large stakes in society, in exchange for their assuming responsibility for the welfare of ordinary people.

In the United States and Norway, syncretic adaptations could readily be accomplished because representative governmental institutions and comprehensive civil rights and liberties had developed similarly before mass inclusion, along with political parties in something like modern form. Political inclusion thus could be absorbed by a preexisting and suitable institutional apparatus. In the United States, too, political inclusion was handled incrementally early on, over quite a long period (about two decades) because of federal devolution. It did not become universal all at once; nor was there much of an "old order" to overcome. The main fact, however, is that the more problematic new citizenry, the new immigrants who started to arrive in the late nineteenth century, could be incorporated into a fully fashioned democratic order—although even so, as we saw, the process of incorporation was bumpy, giving rise to anomalies such as the urban political machine.

Democratic Culture

A fourth lesson that may be drawn from the "first wave" of inclusion is that *viable democracy requires an appropriate political and general culture, and this, in turn, a social structure appropriate for such a culture.*

A few democracies, as we saw, developed early, when economic development was still low, so that subsequent democratization could build on a substantial base. These have also been the democracies that best accommodated large-scale political inclusion. What accounts for this? It must surely be the fact that these societies already contained seeds of democracy at their inception and, to extend the metaphor, an appropriate soil in which the seeds could sprout and grow spontaneously, or in which even mature transplants could flourish. In other words, these were societies that could self-generate democracy. That surely is how democracy must have begun. The favorable conditions are more likely to be found in aspects of culture rather than in social structure or economic development, since the prototypical democracies differed little from other societies in regard to these. If so, cultural factors must surely continue to be important for the flourishing of democracy.

Consider first de Tocqueville's classic explanation of the American case.[14] De Tocqueville argued that America could be a liberal democracy even as early as 1830 because it had a culture conducive to democracy and also a social structure conducive to democratic culture. The culture came, in part, from the egalitarian and liberal attitudes associated with Puritan Protestantism, which from the outset was the thematic American culture—the culture into which young Americans were socialized and which was gradually diffused also to new arrivals. That, however, was only one face of a cultural syndrome conducive to democracy. A second crucial ingredient is less apparent but equally important, namely religion, through the moral restraints that it generates. Democracy, said de Tocqueville, is a system that particularly requires self-restraint. This is so because it liberates choice and action, and therefore also mischief, and indeed a considerable potential for tyranny. Religion disciplines democratic liberty. Thus, the liberal and restraining forces in American democracy had a common source in the culture of the settlers.

Nowadays we would recognize this argument as an early statement of what may be called the mixed-culture hypothesis (à la Almond and Verba and others). This is the hypothesis that viable democracy must have two faces, one liberal, the other not, however contradictory that may seem.

Norms and values, however, are nothing much without the ability to act upon them skillfully. Here enters the structural condition of democracy: Americans, argued de Tocqueville, could learn the proper exercise of liberal democratic citizenship and leadership in the myriad "small republics" of local government, such as the New England town meetings that practiced a highly collective democracy. They could also get a democratic civic education in the myriad more small republics of voluntary associations that existed in early America. Note that de Tocqueville never thought of education for democratic citizenship as schooling; rather, democracy was learned by practice. There are good reasons to think that this position still holds in the age of mass schooling—indeed, that there is something of a paradox in the use of the inherently authoritarian relationships of schools to instill democratic values and know-how. Structural conditions in America thus provided a framework in which behavior conducive to democracy—collective decision making, the aggregation of narrow interests, the art of compromise, and so on—could be learned. Nowadays we can recognize this thesis as the equivalent of what may be called Putnam's social-capital hypothesis.

Perhaps most important was that America was a thoroughly egalitarian society—at any rate, in the North where the dominant culture resided. De Tocqueville still believed in something like an underlying "spirit of the laws" that pervaded all aspects of a society. In America this was equality. In fact, de Tocqueville virtually equated democracy and equality. Democracy as government equalized citizenship, but this was part and parcel of a much more general egalitarian spirit that pervaded all of American social life, making for a fundamental congruence among all its segments.

Since Norway also developed liberal democratic institutions early, we should, if de Tocqueville is right, find equivalents of the American conditions there. Anyone familiar with my book on Norway (Eckstein, 1966), will know that indeed we do, and strikingly so. Egalitarianism, a long tradition of democratic local governance, the pervasive development of associations large and small, on a scale scarcely imaginable even in America—these are primary themes in Norwegian society and have been virtually from the start. One special trait of Norwegian politics, however, is especially noteworthy here; it provides perhaps the most telling corroboration of de Tocqueville's position. An extraordinarily large proportion of politicians on the national level serve long apprenticeships as legislators and officers (e.g., mayors) in local government. Local government thus is the fundamental school for national leadership. It can serve the training function well because the national government's structure and processes are simply a macroscopic version of those of local government. (I will come to this point again in the next section.)

Britain does not quite fit this mold. Local government has never played a similarly central role in Britain, although an intense and extensive associational life also developed early there. More important, Britain has been a stratified and deferential society and was emphatically so in the era of political inclusion. What, then, made the British recipe successful?

In part, I would suggest, the British mix succeeded because there existed in the earlier British oligarchy a substantial liberal culture, along with representative institutions. This could be adapted smoothly to liberal democracy. Liberalism was almost as traditional in parts of the British oligarchy as Toryism was in others. In part, I suggest further, the recipe worked because the oligarchic political class deliberately adapted to, in fact promoted, inclusive democracy. It also succeeded, as I have suggested, because the mutual adaptations of old to new and new to old were extraordinarily spaced out over time and sequentially carried out, so that mutual adaptations had a chance to be worked out. The result, say Almond and Verba, was a "civic culture" like the American but a "deferential civic culture," unlike the "participant" variety found in America.

From this argument we can extract another lesson: *the speed with which democratization can be carried out successfully varies directly with the extent to which preexisting culture and social structure are conducive to it.* To apply this hypothesis we must, of course, know what these conducive conditions are.

Through the work of contemporary political scientists, conceptions of the cultural conditions of viable democracy, and of the structural conditions conducive to democratic culture, have become less intuitive and more based on evidence and reasoning. The subject is large, but suffice it to say that de Tocqueville's position on the subject has been much elaborated and improved but never essentially altered. The overall picture that emerges is this:

1. The democratic culture is a *mixed culture,* in which disparate, perhaps even contrary, elements are balanced. Liberal and participant elements always play a vital role in it, but they require balancing by other norms and practices.
2. Democratic political culture coexists, and probably is based on, a more general culture, in which major themes are (a) high *social trust* and (b) what might be called *"civicness"*: the tendency to act "horizontally" (i.e., cooperatively) with others rather than "vertically" through hierarchical relations, such as patron-client relationships.
3. Democratic political culture is based on a highly developed *associational life in society,* the hallmark of what is now generally called "civil society."
4. Democratic culture and structure are constituted by substantially *congruent* segments, in which the norms and practices of smaller entities substantially resemble those of national governance, especially those smaller entities that play important roles in political socialization and the recruitment of politicians and leaders. Society in this way can be a school for learning democratic citizenship and governance. From this it follows that political democratization should be accompanied by a good deal of *social democratization*—the democratization of social life in a more general sense.[15]

One more point should be added. There are substantial reasons for holding that people of low socioeconomic status (poorer people, unskilled workers, etc.) are generally the least well fitted of all segments of society for incorporation into a liberal-democratic order. The phenomenon of "working-class authoritarianism" in politics was already given prominence by Lipset in the 1950s, and massive evidence to support the position that such authoritarianism is common could already then be marshaled. In my own work, I have developed the broader hypothesis that authority relations among poorer people (in families, e.g., or in predominantly lower-class schools) typically are highly authoritarian: the lower one goes on the economic scale, the more pronounced becomes authoritarian behavior, so that socialization to democracy is weakened or prevented. I have also tried to show that the adaptation of behavior to great scarcity, namely to poverty per se, is the source of this. One would expect lower-class authoritarian attitudes and practices, being highly adaptive to a given, to be especially hard to change, short of changing them at their source (Eckstein, 1984a). This point matters because the principal beneficiaries of political inclusion have been people who are far from affluent.

The Practice of Democratization

The arguments developed here may be used as a basis for prudent actions in the process of democratization. I want now to summarize some maxims of prudence that seem to follow from them.

The most fundamental of these is to recognize what problems must be solved, or alleviated, for democratization to succeed. On my analysis, there are two crucial practical tasks that face democratizers. One is short-run: to manage the transition to democracy. Contemporary transition theorists deal with that problem, often wisely. However, they say little about the most difficult question for strategy that democratic transitions pose: how to democratize at a proper pace, on a proper scale, and in a sensible sequence. The long-run problem is how to foster the emergence of democratic culture, without which transitions to democracy can bear no permanent fruit.

The Pace and Scope of Democratization

A critical problem for all ambitious social engineering is how to proceed with what the American Supreme Court has called "deliberate speed": not too rapidly and also not too slowly. We may add to this the concomitant problem of how to limit changes to a proper scope that is neither too broad nor too narrow. There will be strong pressures in the democratization process to go in both of these directions, and also strong reasons for doing so. Since this is just not possible, tricky choices must be made.

That there is no single ideal pace or scope for democratization is implicit in the hypothesis stated earlier: how rapidly and broadly one can proceed depends on the materials with which one starts. If a country already has in large degree the cultural and social traits associated with viable democracy, one can no doubt even have something like instant inclusive democracy—although in that case, inclusive democracy probably already exists, and it has existed for some time. If some of the traits are in place prior to democratization, one can proceed faster, with a higher probability of success at any pace.

Spain would furnish a good test of this assertion. After a long history of unstable democracy and stable dictatorship, Spain seems to be well on the way to becoming a stable democracy. The returns are not yet all in, but all the signs point in that direction. One should expect to find, therefore, that at least some of the traits of viable democracy were already well in place before recent democratization, but not when broad political inclusion first occurred in the late nineteenth century. I assume here, of course, that the present political order in Spain endures and functions well. One may also expect that this was not the case to nearly the same extent in Portugal. Studies of these countries, especially comparisons of them, can pay large dividends for democratic theory.

In most contemporary cases it will no doubt be necessary to proceed deliberately and on a narrow scale rather than speedily and broadly. In other words, in most cases one has to face what is probably the single most important and intractable problem in engineering social transformations: how to put brakes and limits on the process so that changes can be "digested," in the sense I spelled out earlier. There are several reasons for this difficulty.

One reason is that when an old order has substantially disintegrated, a new order cannot be long postponed without the risk of chaos. Total disintegration, to be sure, is unlikely in the first place. Even in the late Roman Empire and in the so-called Dark Ages, society went on with some degree of order. Nowadays bureaucracy will function as a powerful negentropic force even while more conspicuous institutions are in ruins or embryonic; democracy, as Weber forcefully argued, does not alter the power and permanence of bureaucracy. But even limited social entropy must be countered, or it will increase. A highly predictable new institutional order must grow from the ruins of the old.

Second, on the plain historical record, when the spirit of transformation has been unchained, there will be enormous pressures to bring change about quickly and broadly. The new order will be awaited impatiently, by both leaders and the general public, and it will be expected to transform more than a limited functional aspect of society. The more is expected from change, on the record, the greater is historical impatience. Most revolutions thus go through a phase of intense overheating—a fever, in Crane Brinton's (1965) apt analogy—to accelerate the pace of change. All too commonly, when change falls short of expectations, this involves scapegoats and bloodletting of people perceived as subversive obstacles in the path of progress. Hence, Di Palma's counsel against "Jacobin radicalism." The problem has always been *how* to avoid it.

I have already mentioned another basic reason for not proceeding radically—namely, that any partial change in a desired direction will not have the full effects intended unless accompanied by many concomitant adaptations. Being unable to move with high success on any narrow front, there will always develop a Jacobin temptation to move on all fronts simultaneously.

In addition, and quite apart from Jacobin temptations, if the pace of transformation is slow and the scope narrow, one risks the consequences of "relative deprivation" in society. One such consequence, as Gurr has shown, is political violence. Already de Tocqueville, in his other masterpiece, *The Old Regime and the French Revolution,* pointed out that the potential for upheaval is greatest when social and political conditions are being ameliorated, not when they are getting worse. The mechanism involved, relative deprivation, results from rising expectations and thus growing gaps between expectations and reality. Put this together with Jacobin temptations on the part of rulers, and you have a recipe for catastrophe.

Democratizers, therefore, must typically perform an extraordinary balancing act. The problem of how to perform it is in fact not a "problem" in the technical sense, for problems in that sense have possible solutions (Weldon 1953). Rather, it is a "dilemma," because no real solution of it is possible. Not all difficulties have solutions. Some are like the difficulty that arises when you want to have your cake and eat it, too. The logical structure of the problem of proceeding toward democratization both speedily and slowly, broadly and narrowly, is exactly like that. Nevertheless, like it or not, there is no more pressing problem for thought about prudent action in attempts to bring democracy about. Problems like what to put into new constitutions— whether, for instance, one should use a presidential or parliamentary system, one or another of the numerous varieties of electoral laws, a unicameral or bicameral legislature, and so on—pale in comparison. Not that these issues are negligible. They simply do not seem to be at the crux. Yet they have tended currently to monopolize effort and research support in studies of democratization.

Dilemmas cannot be "solved." However, they may be reduced, or at least coped with, through some *via media* between their extremes; it is always possible to eat part of a cake and to have the rest. In democratization "eating part of the cake" means proceeding in a manner that may suffice to buy time early on without overloading the process and then continuing sequentially, in some reasoned manner, over a good deal of time, so that changes can be "digested" and so that they can prepare the way for further changes. Amount and sequence of change are the core of the problem of proceeding deliberately in democratization. Current theories of democratic transition tell us much of merit in regard to disarming enmities that might destroy a nascent democracy in short order and that can thus buy time for its development. They do not, however, say much about how such development might proceed in regard to its overall pace, scope, and sequence. That, of course, is the critical problem in choosing strategies and tactics of democratization.

Here, then, are some reasoned suggestions for such strategy and tactics. Bear in mind as these are proposed that pressures toward the radical extreme of accomplishing change may be so great that no policy can overcome them.

How can one be both radical and moderate without contradictory actions? A possibility is to appear radical while in fact acting moderately—moderately enough to give change a chance and radical enough to appease pressures toward greater and faster change. A useful, and much used, way to do this involves the short-run/long-run distinction. If short-run policies explicitly aim at the achievement of the equivalent of radical transformation and if sufficient reason exists not to regard the short-run processes as dishonest dodges, then the contradiction between radicalism and gradualism might conceivably be resolved. No one can guarantee that it will be, but I know of no other way that it even has a chance.

Accordingly, I propose that one should work out a comprehensive, explicit, detailed, and scheduled agenda for proceeding from partial to full democratization, and—this is crucial—proceed with it faithfully, step by step, strictly in accordance with its schedule, so that the process of trying to accomplish large-scale change may be perceived as dependable from the start and later. The agenda must be large and comprehensive because what is sought as an outcome is big change. It must be explicit, because the whole must constantly be affirmed at least as a detailed plan while progress in pieces is pursued. It must be carried out in a reliable manner, without significant departures from plan, so that its deliberateness will not appear as evasion or betrayal. The checkered history of the implementation of *Brown v. Board of Education,* in which the "deliberate speed" principle was enunciated, is a good example of the problems that arise when one states an ultimate principle without a definite plan for approaching it. Plans can and should, of course, allow for a fair amount of flexible adaptation as experience is acquired. But in attempted social transformation it seems advisable to risk rigidity to promote perceptions of honest intent. Most people probably are far too used by now to would-be democratizers who promise but do not honestly deliver.

This raises a problem often encountered in political inquiry but far from solved: the problem of appropriate time spans. Over how long a period should one proceed in democratization? I know of only one study that can shed logical light on this: Gurr's study of the duration of regimes, which, among other things, contains measures of their overall "life expectancy" at different points of their duration. It seems that after approximately fifteen years, just about anything is still almost equally likely to occur, from quick demise to something approaching permanence. After that, however, persistence becomes more likely as time from the start increases (Gurr 1974). This is not just a quantitative finding; it also contains a certain logic. If time to "digest" major change is needed, then some span of time will always be required; and if digestion involves cultural changes—changes in orientations through learning—periods of time must be measured in generational terms. This does not necessarily mean several generations. One may suffice, at least to achieve some self-sustaining momentum. Note, for instance, that by about 1970 the present German political system appeared to have stabilized sufficiently to make persistence more likely than demise. Likewise, the Fifth French Republic by the late 1970s seemed definitively to have outlived its charismatic founder.

Thus a plan to democratize fully should probably cover some twenty-five years—more or less, depending on local conditions. That is something near the normal half-life of regimes and sufficient for at least a good deal of generational replacement. Nor is such a period beyond most people's conception of what is "reasonable" if, as it elapses, progress toward an explicit goal really is in fact made as scheduled, to signify honest intent. It will also seem honest if the earlier changes are the more essential for legitimating democracy—those that are salient in public perceptions.[16] Less essential changes can be left for more gradual introduction. In any case, one generation is about the most that historical patience will bear among latecomers to any advanced development, while less time involves a good deal of disruption.

If this principle makes sense for strategy, the first important problem for tactics is where to start. In regard to this, there is no way to avoid devising some sort of constitution early on, so that governance can proceed on a reliable legal basis, without constant arbitrary improvisation. That part of Di Palma's recipe for crafting democracy has merit. But there is still a problem with this: how to avoid hasty design and too-early rigidity of the constitutional order, without experience of how well it is adapted to prevalent conditions. If we had a lot of well-tested theories covering the effects that different constitutional formats will have under varieties of initial conditions, that problem would not arise, but we have none that come even close. In that case, having the best of both worlds might be achieved by beginning with a brief and explicitly *provisional basic law* that concentrates on the core contents of constitutions, in something like the manner of the French Third Republic at its founding. Thereafter, over time, some constitutional committee or small body should work out a more definitive constitution, profiting from experience along the way. The best outcome would be that of the French proverb, "Only the provisional endures." The provisional Basic Law of the Third Republic in fact endured longer than any other French constitution.

There is every reason to have broad public debate over particular proposals, on the lines of the Federalist Papers, over a good deal of time. This would allow constitutional provisions to become implanted in popular attention and public sense to be reflected in the provisions. There is also a potential for excitement in the open airing of basic issues, particularly in an era of mass communications. Nor is there any reason that a provisional basic law should not be amended piecemeal as experience with it grows. We have no adequate theories for adapting constitutional orders to the social conditions under which they must operate, but learning from experience with results and adjusting innovations to results as these become obtrusive is a useful alternative. The French call this *bricolage*, which is not engineering but a substitute for it and sometimes the superior process. Constitutions, in any case, must be culturally "internalized" to have reliable foundations and effects.

The part of the constitutional order that should be fixed earliest is guarantees of civil rights and liberties, together with a judicial system that can deal with violations. Openness without retribution is an absolute sine qua non in democracy and thus for its legitimacy. In the model cases of successful democratization, rights and liberties in fact were substantially established before the machinery of inclusive democratic governance was developed: the systems were "open" before being democratic. There also is evidence—for instance, from surveys in the former Soviet Union—that liberal democratic values tend to be widely agreed on at an early stage, long before adequate practical training in the subtle intricacies of democratic governance is done, or the development of structural requisites for democratic politics are developed, above all a party system. Most aspirations will usually be concentrated on rights and liberties, anyway, and especially on their reliability. Reliable political openness also is a prerequisite for the sort of deliberate discussions on which a well-adapted constitutional order must be based.

We know by now that the most salient figure in government, and often the only salient figure, is the head of state. The ideal seems to be a pompous ceremonial figure such as a monarch. The only conceivable democratic equivalent of such a figure is a plebiscitary president. There are dangers of Caesarism in such a presidency, which Max Weber wrote about presciently before the installation of the Weimar Republic. But risks must always be run, especially if we are pretty sure that the risks entailed by alternatives are greater. Democratization, after all, is a system of government, a system for directing societies. Thus, it requires some clear focus of authority, so that governance can go on, so that violent dissidence can be dealt with, and so that the progressive realization of democracy can itself occur. Clear authority at the center is especially required when democracy is young and fragile. The subject of whether in general presidential or parliamentary systems are preferable is complex, and there is a large and growing literature about it. The debate, however, largely ignores the special requisites for short-run consolidation.

As for detailed governance, it seems to me most essential to give a great deal of scope and autonomy to local governments, including quite small-scale local governments, and to do so early. In that way the load on central authority is reduced and, just as important, experimentation with various formats of governance can proceed. (A greatly decentralized system of local government also has another, even more important, advantage that I will come to in the next section.) Highly decentralized autonomy will, of course, be messy, and there will be temptations to make centralized order out of it, but remember that the one thing worse than a fragmentary mess is a uniform mess.

Three other matters also need to be done early, in the logic of democratization. One is the adoption of an electoral law, because democracy equals elections. The two others are matters about which also we are still highly ignorant: fashioning a workable system of political parties and incorporating the inherited bureaucracy into the democratic order. I will come to these a little later, for reasons that will be apparent then. Most other matters are secondary to these and thus are appropriate subjects for *bricolage*.

There is a catch in all this. However well planned one may want to proceed, one will have only partial control over the spacing and sequencing of democratizing changes. Events and conditions tend to run away from planners and authorities, with their own momentum, almost from the start. Read the epilogue to Tolstoy's *War and Peace* to see how this is so in battles and all of history. The farther away from first and early steps actions are, the more likely detailed plans for them at the start are to be moot. Initial overall sequencing therefore should be general and vague—as, according to Napoleon, should be all constitutions as blueprints of governments. The counsel to proceed syncretically with as much of the old order as can be brought into symbiosis with the new should also be observed. How to do this depends, of course, on the specific materials with which one has to work, so that it is difficult to discuss this subject in general terms.

Economic liberalization, if it must also occur, should also be gradual. The reasons for this are the same as for democratization, but even more imperative, because the satisfaction of basic material needs and wants is at stake. The principal practical issue concerning marketization is its sequencing relative to democratization—assuming that one has a choice. In light of what I argued earlier, steps toward economic liberalization clearly should follow steps toward democratization, not vice versa, though overlap will often be unavoidable. Tackling both tasks simultaneously with equal priority, as we saw, is the worst option, and the hypothesis that economic liberalization provides conditions for democracy, as we also saw, is dubious.

Fostering Democratic Culture

Democratization can proceed on three levels. One is the surface level, so to speak, of designing democratic institutions. I call this the surface level because the institutions might be or become mere facade. Another level lies deep beneath the surface; it involves trying to create social conditions and individual personalities that can provide deep roots for democracy. The third level is intermediate; it involves fostering a specifically democratic political culture, together with those particular aspects of social structure that are most closely related to such culture. The intermediate level is the critical level if democratic institutions are to be more than scenery. Without specific democratic orientations, moreover, general democratic personalities are unlikely to be formed. The deeper level of overall social structure and personality also is hard to access, except through some intermediate level. Thus, a crucial task in building democracy, perhaps the one essential task, is to provide a framework for fostering democratic culture.

The nature of culture is such that it is impossible to create it, as one may create formal institutions.[17] One can, however, try to create conditions in which an appropriate culture may have a reasonable chance to develop.

The most important condition required for fostering democratic culture, and also the only one accessible to engineered change, should be apparent in light of the analysis made earlier. It is the creation of strong, small-scale local governments ("elementary republics," in Jefferson's words), together with a large network of associations, particularly occupational associations. To some extent, associations and "small republics" can substitute for one another, since they have similar effects, but it is better to have both because they reinforce one another and because they might engage different people for different purposes.

The functionality for democracy of a vigorous associational life (or, more broadly, what is now called "civil society") is a recurrent theme in democratic theory, from de Tocqueville to the present. De Tocqueville, as we saw, argued the case for strong local government a century and a half ago, and the logic of his case, which turns on the socialization and training functions small republics can perform, does not depend on time. Most recently, Putnam (1993) has argued, convincingly, that only acting in cooperative groups fashions the sort of "social capital" on which a "working" democracy depends. The theme probably is recurrent simply because it is correct.

Associations can be mandated just as much as local governments, at any rate, provided that a preestablished structural basis for them exists, similar to locality for local governments. Occupations and professions provide such a basis in modern societies. Already Durkheim argued that occupational and professional associations would be the fundamental building blocks of societies that have an advanced, complex division of labor, as they had already been in medieval cities and even in the cities of the Roman Empire. They would be, so to speak, the "neighborhoods" of complex societies, in which interaction is close and frequent and in which incentives to mutual help and considerateness—to pursuing "collective goods"—are great. It is strange that in contemporary constitutions and writings on constitutional design associations are generally overlooked, except for the standard provision of the right to form them. A proactive approach to the forming of associations surely is conceivable. No doubt forming associations voluntarily requires preexisting social capital, but once associations are in place they themselves create such capital.

If local governments and associations are to serve a democratizing function, it is also important that they themselves have internal liberal and democratic structure. Norwegian local government, as I have described it (1966), might well serve as a model in this regard. It particularly emphasizes action in common, that is, collective decision making on all levels and thus agreement seeking. It also interweaves, in somewhat complex ways, local governmental committees with local associations and with lay participation. If local government is wanted as a school for democracy, the Norwegian model certainly provides a good start. The New England town meetings that de Tocqueville so admired also could serve as a model, though much less so in the age of bureaucracy and managerialism than when de Tocqueville wrote.

This point involves something generally overlooked in the deliberate engineering of political order: that pieces of social and political systems must fit with other pieces and that an overall aim must be the fashioning of a certain congruence and consonance among the pieces. Only thus can they mutually impinge on one another in a reinforcing manner. If the internal organization of associations is legally mandated to parallel those of local governments, and if the two are interwoven on collective local bodies as they are in Norway, fit and congruence obviously are promoted. It is particularly important to mandate and enforce democratic associational structures because, upon much evidence, the tendency toward nondemocratic organization is strong if associations are left entirely free to define their own internal structures. This tendency seems to be particularly strong in occupational associations such as trade unions. It will be especially strong if cooperation, reciprocity, and trust are not solidly rooted in the historic cultures of societies.

The recipe, then, is devolution in all phases of politics and governance, the deliberate engineering of structures that might foster democratic skills and behavior patterns and an overall interlocking and congruent fit of structures, as in coherent systems. The results of this recipe, above all initially, will be messy, but democracy values always exist in some tension with efficiency values. A certain messiness always is a built-in cost of democracy, but it also has an advantage: it is a good hedge against something highly but badly ordered.

To begin to bring about a general social structure systemically articulated with democratic governance and political culture, two considerations seem especially important.

One is socioeconomic stratification. Liberal and participatory values and behavior, as stated, do not have fertile soil in which to grow in material scarcity. That there will be a great deal of fundamental want is, on the evidence, a great risk in forming market economies from command economies. Economic liberalization should therefore be cushioned considerably by comprehensive welfare services. These mitigate some of the more cruel consequences of free markets in general, but, more important here, they guard against a condition always inimical to the formation of democratic orientations and personality.

The second factor is participatory structure in "everyday life," particularly workplace participation—social democracy to underpin political democracy. Pateman's (1970) argument that this is critical for the general formation of participatory attitudes seems to me convincing. In any case, nothing else might form a similarly general basis for democratic civic experience and training. In most advanced democracies, workplace democracy has in fact developed a great deal and often, and without harm, on a compulsory legislative basis. A considerable literature on workplace democracy already exists. Most of it is sobering in one respect: it is one thing to provide participatory frameworks and quite another to get people to use them. That point, however, is no argument against providing such frameworks.

A Case for "Indirect" Representation

A great deal of constitutional designing is done nowadays as part and parcel of democratization processes, as it must be. Even if constitutions matter less for the viability of democracy than was once thought, and now seems to be thought again, designing a formal constitutional order, provisional or permanent, is necessary and so might as well be done thoughtfully, with an eye on the future of new democracies. We have a large contemporary literature on this by now. Some of it is thoughtfully based on contemporary theory (e.g., the literature on consociational devices), but not much of it is innovative. We find almost no creative ideas, tailored to contemporary conditions and designed to help create the sociocultural bases on which the fate of democratization must ultimately rest. The old chestnuts are again discussed: federal versus unitary structures, parliamentary versus presidential systems, plurality elections versus proportional representation (PR). Choices among these surely matter. However, a great opportunity now exists to innovate in devising democratic institutions, comparable to the opportunity provided by the first wave of democratization. Innovation is required now as then, to adapt democratic structures to conditions of late democratization.

In conclusion, therefore, I want to make a proposal for a novel procedure that is based on the logic of the preceding arguments. Being novel it may seem odd, especially since the only precedent for it goes back centuries.

The logic of the arguments made here adds up to a general maxim: *In democratization, small democracy (local and associational democracy) should be as direct as possible and large democracy (national democracy) as indirect as possible.* How might this be accomplished?

A simple way to make national governance indirect is to staff national legislatures with members who represent local governments and perhaps also associations and who are elected or designated by the smaller units. As we saw, local units earlier were adapted to plurality elections as "constituencies." Nothing prevents their now being adapted as *corporate* bodies that select national representatives and leaders in the manner of electoral colleges. Corporate representation in the oldest representative government antedates 1832, but it is not necessarily bad because it is premodern, if now adapted to modern conditions.[18] Nothing like a full system of indirect national government has ever been devised, but surely, upon the logic of the analysis I have presented, the idea should be entertained. The proposal also makes sense if local government is to be the vital core of democratization.

A particularly important advantage of an indirect national representative system is that it would ensure that national political careers are based on local experience and the civic training it provides. If this experience is highly democratic, then democratic behavior on the higher level will also be encouraged. And fostering appropriate civic education is particularly important when political orders have not yet been fully developed.

Using associations similarly would realize an old idea that has undeservedly faded from attention. This is the idea of "functional representation," as canvassed by some political theorists, particularly the British "pluralists" (Figgis, Cole, Laski, and others) early in this century. The general idea behind functional representation was that the geographic division of constituencies was by then outdated, and that it would become more so. Geography once was the "natural" basis for grouping people politically; however, it was argued, with social development local differences and identities had declined and would decline much more over time. Hence, the "natural" basis of differentiation increasingly would be functional—that is, based on the division of labor in society. For the first hypothesis, the decline of local differences, there is overwhelming evidence, and the second follows from the first.

The case for functional representation of some sort in late democracies thus is strong. It has in fact been strong for a long time, as the significance of geography has declined and that of functional differentiation has increased. Using it would be a step into the remote past but also an adaptation of processes of representation to advanced modernity, the hallmark of which, it has been argued since Durkheim a century ago, is the growing complexity of functional differentiation.

Notes

An earlier version of this essay was presented at the Annual Meeting of the American Political Science Association, New York, September 1–4, 1994.

1. Throughout this essay I will use the expression "viable democracy" to mean something like a democracy in good health: able to persist, to adapt smoothly to changed circumstances, to command legitimacy, to avoid civil strife, and to do work efficaciously.

2. As always in historical periodization, these dates are somewhat arbitrary.

3. A comparative history and analysis of nineteenth-century political inclusion has not yet been written and is overdue. The subject would be ideal for a doctoral dissertation or, indeed, a larger research project.

4. I have discussed these perceptions in much more detail than here in Eckstein (1984a).

5. Wallas made a very good guess or else showed very good judgment. The systematic quantitative analysis of participation has arrived at just about the same figure now. That an estimate and a carefully measured figure, more than a half-century apart and in two quite different countries, should so closely coincide should suggest some interesting hypotheses.

6. For representative studies of transitions to democracy, see Stepan (1989) and O'Donnell, Schmitter, and Whitehead (1986).

7. Di Palma subscribes to Huntington's (1984, 1991) argument that there is a "zone of transition" between very low and very high development, in which the possibility of managing democratic transitions successfully exists. Earlier, for instance, in Dahl (1971), the argument that economic development has a strong relationship to viable democracy only at its lowest and highest levels had been used more to impugn the general economic development hypothesis than to argue as Di Palma does.

8. Note that the argument here involves the process of economic liberalization, not the political consequences of well-established market economies.

9. That, of course, might give democracy better odds than it has when a command economy exists. I use the term *quasi-totalitarian* because totalitarian in the abstract denotes a regime in which all boundaries between what is private and what is public have disappeared. Thus, a totalitarian liberal economy is a contradiction in terms.

10. There is no space here to support these arguments properly. Fortunately, that has been done already, in a masterly article by Diamond (1992). An important recent contribution to the evaluation of the hypothesis can be found in Putnam (1993).

11. "Mass society" also is the result of a structural condition: the lack or underdevelopment of what is now called "civil society"—social entities' intermediary between isolated individuals and central political power. Much more about this will be said later.

12. Still the best study of the political consequences of anomie is De Grazia (1948), a work that should have a prominent place in postwar revisionist democratic theory.

13. See McKenzie's (1963) classic study of British political parties for details.

14. I will be very brief here, because most readers will already know de Tocqueville's theses.

15. Sources for this summary include Kornhauser (1959), Lipset (1960), Almond and Verba (1963); Eckstein (1992a); and Putnam (1993).

16. I discuss later what these essential changes probably would be. This depends, of course, on actual perceptions. These will vary, but we now have adequate instruments for finding out what these are. For instance, facilities for survey research now exist almost universally.

17. The reasons for this are discussed in Eckstein (1996).

18. The advisability of various electoral systems is at present much discussed in the literature on democratization. This discussion deals almost exclusively with the merits of systems of plurality and proportional elections, in their several varieties. The fact that plurality elections originated in a third general type of electoral system—corporate representation—is overlooked, although some modernized version of it might be the most appropriate of all.

11

Does the Public Matter for Democratization in Russia? What We Have Learned from "Third Wave" Transitions and Public Opinion Surveys

Frederic J. Fleron Jr. and Richard Ahl

At the beginning of his stimulating book *The Russian Tradition*, Tibor Szamuely (1974, 3–6) juxtaposes the impressions of two earlier travelers to Russia: the Marquis de Custine and Andre Gide. The Marquis de Custine visited Russia in 1839 during the reign of Nicholas I "to seek arguments against representative government." He was an admirer of the tsarist system, a "devoted Royalist, whose father and grandfather had both died on the guillotine." Nearly one hundred years later in 1936, Andre Gide traveled to Russia during the reign of Joseph Stalin. According to the author, Gide not only approved of the new Soviet political system—"for many years he had been [its] foremost Western literary champion." Both the conservative Custine and the liberal Gide had gone to Russia to seek vindication of their ideological positions; yet both had their visions shattered by the experience. Wrote Custine, "If ever your sons should be discontented with France, try my receipt; tell them to go to Russia. It is a useful journey for every foreigner: whoever has well examined that country will be content to live anywhere else." Wrote Gide, "As it always happens that we recognize the value of certain advantages only after we have lost them, there is nothing like a stay in the USSR . . . to help us appreciate the inappreciable liberty of thought we still enjoy in France." And so, observed

Szamuely, here we have "[t]wo Frenchmen, a century and a revolution apart—two practically indistinguishable descriptions. They might almost have been travelling companions." What their descriptions have in common is testimony to "the astonishing durability of certain key social and political institutions, traditions, habits, and attitudes; their staying-power, their essential stability amidst the turbulent currents of violent change, chaotic upheaval, and sudden innovation."

The purpose of recounting these events is to remind ourselves of the durability of cultural norms and practices, especially in Russia. From the perspective of the late 1990s, it is clear that the political institutions of post-Soviet Russia have changed; what confounds analysts the world around is whether the traditions, habits, attitudes, and behavior of Russians have changed as well and in what ways they matter. And that is the subject of the following remarks as we examine the question, Does the public matter for democratization in Russia? Our answer will be based on an analysis of the transition literature and Western-sponsored survey research into Russian public values and behavior.

It is our position that the public certainly has played some role in Russian democratization, particularly at the beginning of the consolidation phase. But because of the way in which research has been oriented and the debate framed, it is at present difficult to assess the extent of that role. While it would be inaccurate to state that the public forced perestroika and glasnost on an unwilling Soviet leadership, it appears to have been the case that growing public dissatisfaction with the status quo was a political weapon available to Gorbachev as he contemplated ways to overcome elite resistance to his initial, modest reform efforts. The public did not force reform on Gorbachev, but a familiarity with public sentiment may have encouraged him to move in that direction nonetheless. As the consolidation phase (which may have begun in 1993) unfolds, the influence of the public on the evolution of political discourse, institutions, and events will probably increase, although on some key issues (e.g., the civil war in Chechnya) the public is still ignored. The nature of political cleavages in Russian society may well have an important effect on political discourse and electoral dynamics. Furthermore, it is likely that public sentiment will play a key role in shaping the calculations of any disaffected elites contemplating an extralegal seizure of power. To use the vernacular of rational choice, if elites are rational actors, they must certainly take the likely reaction of the public into account.

The following analysis is organized into four parts. First, we present several theoretical and conceptual distinctions based on the transitions literature. Second, we analyze what we have learned from in-country, Western-sponsored survey research into public values and behavior in post-Soviet Russia. Third, we discuss lessons learned about the public's role in Russian democratization. Finally, we raise some questions and challenges for those studying the role of mass publics in democratization.

Conceptual and Theoretical Distinctions

Does the public matter for global democratization? The Russian case suggests that it depends on a great number of things, for no unequivocal answer can be given to a question posed in such broad terms. Before turning to what the Russian case can tell us, we need to consider several conceptual and theoretical issues: the stages of democratization, the societal context, and the nature of the public.

Stages of Democratization

When discussing the relevance of publics in democratization, it is important to distinguish between different phases of that process. According to Mainwaring, O'Donnell, and Valenzuela (1992), democratization actually involves two transitions: (1) the transition from a previous authoritarian regime to the installation of a democratic government and (2) the transition from the installation of the first democratic government to the functioning of a democratic regime. These phases are usually referred to as transition and consolidation, respectively, and the weight of the public's role varies across these stages of democratization.

Transition and Mass Publics

O'Donnell and Schmitter (1986) identify liberalization as the first step in the transition phase. They define liberalization as the process of redefining and extending rights within an authoritarian regime to protect individuals and groups from arbitrary state action. The transition phase is "considered to have ended when a new democracy has promulgated a new constitution and held free elections for political leaders with little barrier to mass participation" (Shin 1994, 144). Similarly, Mainwaring et al. (1992, 2) state that the first transition is concluded by the holding of democratic elections. However, it is noteworthy that although there is general agreement on the beginning and end points of the transition phase there is little consensus on what happens in between. Mainwaring et al. (1992, 2) state that from case to case the sequences of events have differed but eventually led to a common outcome—democratic elections.

Although there does not seem to be an agreed-on model outlining the sequence of events in the transition phase, by definition it must at some point include the "drafting of methods or rules for resolving political conflicts peacefully" (Shin 1994, 144). There is agreement on the relative importance of political elites and mass publics in the transition phase. O'Donnell and Schmitter (1986) argue that elites are the primary determinant of whether liberalization will be pursued, thus inaugurating the first transition. Also, it seems reasonable to assert that the drafting of new rules for democratic political conflict would be an elite dominated process. In his summary of the literature, Shin (1994, 153) writes:

> As in the previous waves [of democratization], strategic elites have been a key factor in bringing about a majority of democratic transitions in the current wave. Especially in the transitions since the early 1980s elites have played a far more significant role than the mass public. For this reason, the literature does not consider the commitment of the mass public to democracy an absolute requirement for democratic transition. Indeed, it suggests that democracy can be created even when a majority of the citizenry does not demand it.

In sum, the literature emphasizes the predominance of political elites in originating the transition phase and in shaping new political rules. Later in the discussion we will consider to what extent the Russian/Soviet case confirms this emphasis.

Consolidation and Mass Publics

Once the transition phase is completed by the holding of free and fair elections, the new political regime is poised to begin the process of democratic consolidation. O'Donnell (1992, 21) argues that progress in the consolidation phase demands (1) neutralization of "unconditionally authoritarian" political actors, either through isolation or fragmentation, and (2) the imposition of democratic norms, or at least practices, on the part of those neutralized political actors. According to Mainwaring (1992, 3), the point of closure in the consolidation process is not always clear. Mainwaring (1992) views consolidation as complete once all major political actors accept the democratic selection of political leadership. For reasons discussed later, however, this may be too narrow a definition of consolidation. In an oft-quoted passage written in 1990, Juan Linz has described a consolidated democracy as one in which none of the major political actors, parties, organized interests, forces or institutions consider that there is any alternative to democratic processes to gain power, and that no political institution or group has a claim to veto the action of democratically elected decision makers. This does not mean that there are no minorities ready to challenge and question the legitimacy of the democratic process by nondemocratic means. It means, however, that the major actors do not turn to them and that they remain politically isolated. To put it simply, democracy must be seen as the "only game in town." (Linz 1990b, 158)

The scholars cited earlier clearly view the processes and outcome of consolidation primarily in terms of political elites and their commitment to democracy. Despite this, however, a consensus prevails in the literature that mass publics matter more in the consolidation phase than during the transition. One author writes:

> It is only in the consolidation of new democracies that the mass public plays a key role. As in the past waves, it appears that democracy can still be created without the demand of the masses, yet cannot be consolidated without their commitment. (Shin 1994, 154)

At first, the general emphasis on elite commitment to democracy as the key to democratic consolidation, on the one hand, and the assertion that the masses matter most during the consolidation phase, on the other, seems to be a contradiction. However, in combination these assertions suggest one potentially important role for the mass public as a potential deterrent to would-be antidemocratic plotters. In other words, when faced with the possibility of mass revolt, antidemocratic elites may be less likely to attempt a seizure of power than with a more passive public. From this perspective, then, it is possible that the masses could be "guardians" of the consolidating democracy. While this is indeed a logical possibility, it seems only fair to acknowledge that a determined antidemocratic clique, especially with collusion of the military, could overcome public opposition to a coup d'état. Perhaps the most judicious statement about the public's importance in democratic consolidation is that it has the potential to dissuade weak challenges to democratic rule.

For the public to deter antidemocratic plotters, it must satisfy at least two criteria: first, there must be considerable sentiment in favor of democracy; second, there must be considerable willingness to participate in public life and form associations, at least among those holding democratic preferences. Later, we will consider whether the Russian public meets these requirements.

Although it is not argued that the public plays no role in consolidation, the transition literature generally makes a fairly weak case for its significance. However, the public can perhaps affect the process of democratic consolidation in other ways. Consideration of this, however, requires that we distinguish between different varieties of democracy and the relationship of those types of democracy to the structure of a given society. It is to these issues that we now turn.

Societal Context and the Nature of Democracy

It is important to identify the nature of the society in which these stages of democratization are occurring. The argument has been made that societal characteristics are an important determinant of the type of democracy that emerges. Kornhauser (1959, 130–5) makes the distinction between liberal and populist variants of democracy, the former characterized by constraints on the state stemming from the pluralist organization of society and the latter characterized by the absence of such constraints on the power of government. Hence, each of these variants of democracy rests upon a distinct social foundation. Populist democracy rests on "mass society." Masses, according to Kornhauser (1959, 14) are large numbers of people who are not integrated into broad social groupings, including classes. Mass society is characterized by a relative paucity of well-defined political cleavages and low organizational density. Liberal democracy, on the other hand, rests upon a pluralist society characterized by the competition of well-defined, organized groups for influence on government action. Kornhauser (1959, 131) offers the following summary of the distinction between mass society and pluralist society and their impact on democracy:

> Pluralist society is liberal in that its social constitution limits power to certain circumscribed areas, and provides opportunities to challenge (through due process of law, freedom of expression and the like) the manner in which power is exercised. Mass society is not liberal in that its social constitution does not so limit the use of power; even where there are formal restraints on power, their effectiveness is abrogated by the lack of independent groups.

Logically, it seems reasonable to speculate that institutions will be less meaningful and more malleable in the absence of social pluralism. The relative absence of well-defined groups with competing agendas makes democratic institutions and processes less likely to be scrutinized by the public. In pluralist societies, on the other hand, democratic institutions are likely to be scrutinized by interested parties to ensure equity or compliance with the established rules of the game.

The existence of multiple, competing groups in society appears to ensure that democratic institutions would be viewed as an end in and of themselves to keep conflict between groups manageable and constrained. In the absence of pluralism, it is more likely that democratic institutions will be viewed as a means to some particular end, and, therefore, circumvention or modification of those institutions for the sake of the commonly accepted goals may be more acceptable.

Yet threats to stability of both pluralist and populist democracy do exist. Dahl (1982, 1) summarizes the dilemma of pluralist democracy as follows:

> Independent organizations are highly desirable in a democracy, at least in a large scale democracy. . . . Yet as with individuals, so with organizations; independence or autonomy creates an opportunity to do harm. Organizations may use the opportunity to increase or perpetuate injustice rather than reduce it, to foster the narrow egoism of their members at the expense of concerns for a broader public good, and even to weaken or destroy democracy itself. Like individuals, then, organizations ought to possess some autonomy, and at the same time they should also be controlled. Crudely stated, this is the fundamental problem of pluralist democracy.

In other words, the stability of pluralist democracy is threatened when the cleavages between the pluralist elements of its underlying society become so sharp as to encourage one or more groups to "defect" from democratic processes in an effort to force their will upon other elements in society (Przeworski 1991). As Dahl (1989, 254–5) put it, when a large part of any given population believes that its highest values and way of life are severely menaced by another element of the population, it is unlikely that polyarchy will endure or emerge. When the cleavages between the subpopulations of a given society become too sharp, democracy is likely to be undermined by attempts to settle the issue by force and/or circumvention of democratic processes and institutions.

Just as pluralist democracy is threatened by cleavages that become too intense for successful management through democratic institutions, populist democracy is threatened by cleavages that become so weak that the powers of the state are barely constrained. In such a case, there are no competing agendas with which the state has to contend. Under such conditions, authority is legitimated through the emphasis on widely shared goals, the rights of any distinct minority groups are unlikely to be respected, and the operation of democratic institutions is likely to atrophy.

Ironically, Lijphart (1984, 1) asserts that the "ideal" democracy is the democracy in which the actions of government are in perfect correspondence with the preferences of all citizens. This ideal democracy would have its greatest chance to triumph in a society characterized by widespread consensus on immediate goals. Paradoxically, however, too much consensus on goals may well be likely to engender political institutions and leaders too accustomed to acting without taking competing perspectives into account. It is highly unlikely that the democratic character of political institutions in such a society would endure for very long; the rationale for reliance on legal-rational authority is simply too weak. Ideal democracy as defined by Lijphart might be of such a nature that it could last only for a fleeting moment before the lack of constraints corrupted the democratic nature of political institutions.

In sum, democracy is most likely to flourish in societies with moderate levels of pluralism. A society with intense cleavages is likely to foster a pluralist democracy that degenerates into open conflict between the constituent elements of society. A society with too few cleavages, however, is likely to foster populist democracy that degenerates into authoritarianism in the name of the majority as the rationale for the operation of democratic institutions atrophies. The paucity of intermediary associations suggests that to the extent Russian democracy exists it is of the populist variant and that any further movement in that direction will have deleterious consequences for democratic consolidation.

This is another important set of theoretical issues that needs to be taken into account in assessing the role of the Russian public in democratization. More specifically, the nature of democratic development in Russia may well be shaped by the extent to which Russian society is characterized by pluralist or mass tendencies. Assessing the nature of Russian society on this dimension, and its relationship to the type of emerging polity, is an important task facing future research efforts.

The Nature of the Public: Which Publics Matter?

The nature of the public depends, in large part, on the nature of the society in which that particular public resides. Both the structure and traditions of society are important. Pluralist societies contain numerous intermediary associations through which "traditions of independent civic engagement" (Putnam 1995, 65) are established, and these associations are said to "instill in their members habits of cooperation, solidarity, and public-spiritedness" (Putnam 1993, 89–90). Mass societies lack such traditions and structures, with the result that publics will be less differentiated and less accustomed to articulating demands into the political system; in Putnam's terms, they lack "social capital" and "networks of civic engagement" and are thus unable to overcome the "dilemmas of collective action" (Putnam 1993, 167, 173–6). In addition, for countries undergoing democratization, the legacies of the *ancien régime* will play a large part in defining the nature of publics. Accustomed as they were to "passive reliance on the state" (Putnam 1995, 65), the publics in former communist countries must learn the norms of reciprocity, public trust, and civic engagement. Publics in those societies will no doubt have different characteristics than publics in societies with traditions associated with a civic culture.

But "the public" is not an undifferentiated mass. There are different publics defined by various criteria. First, and most obvious, is the fact that all publics—regardless of the type of society in which they are located—can be differentiated on the basis of certain *social categories*: age, gender, socioeconomic status (SES), education, rural-urban residence, religion, and ethnicity. Social science research has a long tradition of seeking explanations in correlations between these categories and both belief systems and overt behavior. Status systems such as social class have received considerable attention as sources of political cleavage and, therefore, as explanations of both beliefs and behavior (Lipset 1970).

Second, following Almond and Verba in *The Civic Culture* (1963), we could distinguish among parochial, subject, and participant publics on the basis of *knowledge about the political system and perceptions of self in that system*. For *parochials* in undifferentiated traditional societies, "the specialized agencies of central government might hardly touch the consciousness of townsmen, villagers, and tribesmen. Their orientations would tend to be unspecialized political-economic-religious ones, congruently related to the similarly unspecialized structures and operations of their tribal, religious, occupational, and local communities" (18). In more differentiated societies, however, parochials are more likely to be "affective and normative rather than cognitive" (19). For *subjects* "there is a high frequency of orientations toward a differentiated political system and toward the output aspects of the system, but orientation toward specifically input objects, and toward the self as an active participant, approach zero" (19). Finally, *participants* "tend to be explicitly oriented to the system as a whole and to both the political and administrative structures and processes; in other words, to both the input and output aspects of the political system" (19). Participants also "tend to be oriented toward an 'activist' role of the self in the polity, though their feelings and evaluations of such a role may vary from acceptance to rejection" (19). It is important to note, however, that parochials in a differentiated, pluralist society are quite different from citizens in an undifferentiated, mass society. Almond and Verba contrast the parochial who is "cut off from political influence" to the "isolated and powerless individual, manipulated and mobilized by the mass institutions of politics and government" (300). Neither parochials nor subjects participate in the political process; but the participation of mass publics is manipulated by elites to serve their own ends.

Similarly, distinctions among publics can be made in terms of *level of political sophistication, participation or activism* (Putnam 1993, Verba, Lehman, and Brady 1995). Neumann (1986, 170–2) differentiates among three publics based on level of political sophistication. At one end of the sophistication spectrum are the *apoliticals*, who "do not share the common norms which stress the importance of keeping informed about politics or of voting, and their behavior dramatically reflects this posture." At the other end of the sophistication spectrum are the *activists*, who "exhibit uniquely high levels of political involvement." In between these two extremes is the *mass public*, whose members are "marginally attentive to politics and mildly cynical about the behavior of politicians, but they accept the duty to vote, and they do so with fair regularity." Neumann's analysis of the American electorate found 20 percent apolitical, 75 percent mass public, and 5 percent activist. While the percentages may vary from one country to another, it is quite likely that similar inflection points can be found in the levels of political sophistication in all publics. In a similar vein, Rosenau (1961, 33–34, 50–52) differentiates members of various publics in terms of their influence in the opinion-making process: the *mass public*, "who have neither the opportunity nor the inclination to participate in the opinion-making process"; the *attentive public*, "who are inclined to participate but lack the access or opportunity to do so"; and the *opinion-making public*, who do in fact influence the opinion-making process.

Third, the public can be differentiated on the basis of what Converse (1964) terms various *issue publics*. In this view, "different controversies excite different people to the point of real opinion formation" (246). It is most often the case that the "common citizenry" is divided into "relatively narrow and fragmented issue publics." In such circumstances, a pluralism of issue publics exists. Under certain circumstances, however, it is possible for the majority of the population to become excited by the same issue, or set of issues, even though other issues may be of interest to them. Material well-being appears to be an issue on which Russians are united to the point of becoming a single, overarching "issue public." We will explore the evidence and implications of this situation later.

In light of these distinctions, it does not seem particularly fruitful to discuss the role of "the public" in democratization. A more productive approach would distinguish a variety of publics based on the three sets of criteria enumerated earlier. It is probably the case that not all of these publics matter all the time in the process of democratization. By distinguishing a variety of publics according to these three sets of criteria, we can then ask, Do some publics matter more than others? And, if so, under what conditions? Gender is significant when men count more than women. Age is significant when youth are more politically active than the aged. SES is important when wealth provides better access to the political system. Demographic factors are significant when urban publics matter more than rural publics or when publics from one region matter more than those from another region. Political participants matter more than subjects or parochials. Given different levels of participation in a population, the opinion-making public matters more than the attentive public, and the mass public would appear to matter least. A particular issue public matters more when its issue is on the public agenda and/or becomes salient to a larger portion of the population.

A realistic assessment of whether the public matters in the Russian democratization process would have to address the role of all of these publics. Which ones matter and when—that is, at which stage of the democratization process? A comprehensive analysis of this type is well beyond the scope of this essay. Given the primary focus of empirical studies to date, the following analysis will be limited to an examination of Russian publics differentiated in terms of social categories.

What We Have Learned from the In-Country, Western-Sponsored Survey Research into Public Values and Behavior in Post-Soviet Russia

Addressing the entire scope of what we have learned so far would be a monumental task due to the large volume of information generated since 1991 or so. To retain focus, we will concentrate on four major areas of investigation covered in the survey-based research published to date. First, we will give a brief summary of findings on aggregate levels of commitment to economic reform. This topic is worthy of discussion because of its emphasis in the literature and, more important, what it tells us about mass support for political change in Russia when viewed in conjunction with the survey data on aggregate levels of commitment to democratic norms and how Russians define democracy—our second and third topics. Finally, we will examine findings on the distribution of political opinion across various segments of the Russian population. This will prepare us for a discussion of what steps must next be taken to understand the institutional consequences of political cleavages in Russian society, a matter that will be discussed in our concluding section.

Here is a brief overview of the major findings to date. First, there does seem to be an emerging, if imperfect, consensus on aggregate levels of support for democratic norms and economic reform. With respect to aggregate levels of commitment to democratic norms, we see strong support for most norms in early studies and declining support in more recent studies. Some democratic norms (competitive elections, free press, multiparty system) seem to garner considerable support, while others (political tolerance and the valuation of liberty and free speech over order) receive much weaker support. Since 1992 support for democratic norms has declined, and it is still unclear whether this is the result of disenchantment with democracy as it has developed in Russia or the fact that it is increasingly acceptable to express antidemocratic views (Fleron 1996b, 247; Fleron, Hahn, and Reisinger 1997). With respect to support for economic reform, there is also an emerging consensus: that support is limited and also declining as the post-Soviet era unfolds. We will now examine these findings in more detail.

Aggregate Levels of Support for Economic Change

As already stated, an emerging consensus is apparent on aggregate levels of support for democratic principles and economic reforms. The evidence is most clear with respect to economic reform: in the early 1990s there was still considerable support for key features of the Soviet economic order, and, as the post-Soviet era unfolds, the Russian populace is evaluating key features of the Soviet economy in an increasingly positive manner.

Evidence of widespread apprehension over economic reforms can be seen in data gathered as early as 1990. Based on University of Iowa data gathered in Russia, Lithuania, and Ukraine in 1990, Reisinger and Nikitin (1993, 188) report widespread hostility to the private cooperatives legalized by Gorbachev (see also Wyman 1997, 186–7). Based on data collected in 1991, Mason (1995, 388) concludes that Russians were generally opposed to reforms aimed at creating a Western-style market economy. Millar and Wolchik (1994, 5–7) cite U.S. Information Agency (USIA) data gathered in 1991 as evidence of opposition to economic reform. Whitefield and Evans (1994, 41), Brym (1996a, 415), and Kullberg and Zimmerman (1995, 13) are generally skeptical about mass support for economic reform in Russia. But Wyman (1997, 176–8) argues that during this period there was considerable support for gradual creation of a market economy. As Gibson (1996b, 965–6) puts it in his analysis of public opinion in Russia and Ukraine, "many want the advantages of a market economy (availability of goods, incentives for harder work, etc.), while also preferring the advantages of a command economy (government social guarantees, limited inequality, restrictions on market abuses, etc.). . . . In short, many seem to want 'socialism that works.' "

Locus of Responsibility for Personal Welfare

To put the data into sharper focus, it is useful to examine support for specific issues related to economic reform. Two of the most widely considered issues are the locus of responsibility for personal welfare and tolerance of growing disparities in individual income and living standards. Finifter and Mickiewicz (1992, 858) asserted that, given Soviet history, it is necessary to examine "support for greater responsibility for individuals in social welfare as opposed to the continuation of the state's playing the major role in this area." Following their lead, additional studies have measured support for personal and state responsibility for personal welfare over the last few years.

Generally speaking, the early evidence painted a mixed picture with respect to opinions on locus of responsibility for personal welfare. In their 1989 sample, Finifter and Mickiewicz (1992, 859) found a roughly even division of respondents on this issue, as did Miller, Hesli, and Reisinger (1994, 401) in a 1992 survey. However, in a 1991 USIA sample and a 1990 sample of the European portion of the USSR, Millar and Wolchik (1994, 5–8) and Duch (1993, 598) report overwhelming support for state guarantees. Grey, Miller, White, and Heywood (1995, 195–96) report that in a 1994 sample of Russian adults, there was overwhelming support for state responsibility for the provision of employment, health care, and housing. Later surveys have been less ambiguous on this issue. In a 1993 sample, Whitefield and Evans (1994, 47–49) found overwhelming support for state guarantees. Wyman (1997, 200–2, 208) reports that in 1993, although only a modest plurality of respondents found unemployment unacceptable in principle, an overwhelming majority of Russians felt that the state should guarantee employment for those who want it. Based on 1995 surveys, Brym (1996a, 415) and Miller, Reisinger, and Hesli (1996, 158) also reported strong support for state guarantees of personal welfare, as does the 1996 *New Russia Barometer V* (Rose 1996, 44–45). Again, the weight of the evidence on this issue supports the argument that the Soviet social safety net has retained significant mass support.

Tolerance of Growing Disparities

Acceptability of growing differences in individual income and living standards is another dimension of economic reform on which numerous surveys have sought the opinions of Soviet and Russian respondents. A familiar pattern emerges from the analyses published to date: there is some willingness to accept growing disparities in the period 1989–1991 and subsequently a rejection of growing disparities.

In their 1989 sample, Finifter and Mickiewicz (1992, 859) found that only 13 percent of respondents were opposed to the growth of income differentials. Similarly, Mason (1995) reports that only one in three Russian respondents to a 1991 survey agreed that an upper level should be set on individual earnings.

Again, Duch (1993, 597–8) provides the contrary evidence for the early years of survey research; he reports very little acceptance of growth in income inequalities in the University of Houston's 1990 survey of the European portion of the USSR. Later surveys seem to support Duch's early conclusion. Based on a 1993 survey, Kullberg and Zimmerman (1995, 17) assert that mass respondents in Russia were "generally quite fearful of the economic disparities associated with marketization and privatization." Similarly, Wyman (1997, 205–6) reports that in a January 1993 survey of ten Russian cities, only 15 percent of respondents expressed positive feelings toward the "new rich" in Russian society. Comparing 1992 and 1995 University of Iowa data, Miller et al. (1996, 161) report a growth in the percentage of respondents fearing increased economic inequality from 35.9 percent to 64.0 percent.

Support for Economic Reform Summarized

In sum, with respect to economic reform the weight of the evidence seems to point to the conclusion that there is only limited support for a Western-style economy in Russia. Dobson (1994b) traces this erosion using data from June 1992, January 1993, and September 1993 surveys. He reports (30) that across these samples support for rapid privatization eroded, whereas support for gradual or no privatization increased accordingly. It is probably safe to conclude from the data that early indicators of support for economic reform represented short-term optimism about the prosperity assumed to accompany market economics and democratization. Looking at 1990 data, Miller (1993, 119–20) cautions us not to overlook the considerable support that remained for the Soviet regime. In retrospect, to the extent that opinion on economic issues is the primary concern of Russian publics, his caution was warranted.

Aggregate Levels of Commitment to Democratic Norms and Principles

At the outset, survey researchers were impressed by the generally high levels of support expressed by Soviet and Russian respondents for most democratic norms. Concluding his analysis of survey data collected in the Yaroslavl oblast in 1990, Hahn (1993b, 322) writes:

> Russian respondents . . . showed substantial support for democratic values. A clear majority favored competitive elections and a multi-party system and were highly interested in political life around them. On the whole, the picture of Russian political culture that emerges from this study is not strikingly different from what is found in Western industrial democracies.

Hahn (1993b), along with Gibson, Duch, and Tedin (1992) and Finifter and Mickiewicz (1992), represented an optimistic "first wave" of survey research into political values and norms in Russia.

These pioneering studies examined support for a variety of norms thought to be associated with a political culture supportive of democratic institutions: political efficacy, political trust, political interest, support for a multiparty system, political knowledge, political tolerance, valuation of liberty, support for the norms of democracy, rights consciousness, support for dissent and opposition, support for an independent media, acceptability of nonconventional forms of political expression, and priority of free speech over public order. A variety of subsequent works have examined these issues, as well as political participation (Bahry and Way 1994; Gibson 1993b; Kaplan 1993; Melville 1993; Hahn 1995; Hough 1994b; McAllister and White 1994; Wyman 1994; Gibson 1995; Mason 1995; Duch 1995; Reisinger, Miller, and Hesli 1995; Dobson 1996).

After the optimistic first wave of survey research, however, evidence began to mount that levels of commitment to democratic norms were in many cases more modest than originally thought, and probably declining (Grcy et al. 1995; Fleron 1996b; Brym 1996b). The evidence on commitment to democracy is characterized by both conflicting results across surveys and varying levels of commitment expressed for particular democratic norms. As Wyman (1997, 146) puts it, the evidence on commitment to democratic norms in Russia is "deeply mixed." *Political interest*, for example, is one element of a democratic political culture for which Russian respondents have exhibited consistently high levels of support. Hahn (1993b, 319; 1995, 122), Kaplan (1993, 157), and Wyman (1994, 30, 40) all provide supporting evidence for this claim. However, Wyman (1997, 124–25) reports that by late 1993 levels of political interest were beginning to decline relative to their peak levels in the 1990–91 period.

Support for *competitive elections*, on the other hand, is an example of declining commitment to a key democratic norm. Based on 1990 data, Hahn (1993b) asserts the existence of significant levels of support for competitive elections. Gibson, Duch, and Tedin (1992), Finifter and Mickiewicz (1992), Gibson and Duch (1993a), Wyman (1994, 35; 1997, 130) also report relatively high levels of support for competitive elections based on data gathered in the period 1989–91. More recent data, however, paints a different picture. Hahn (1995, 119) reports that commitment to competitive elections in Yaroslavl declined from 1990 to 1993 and, based on a 1993 survey, McIntosh and colleagues (1993, 6) report that only one in three Russians believe that it is essential for a democracy to have at least two parties competing in elections. Similarly, based on data gathered in 1992, Gibson (1995, 79) states "there is little evidence of a very deep reservoir of goodwill toward the institution of competitive elections." Political trust is another dimension of a democratic political culture for which Russians exhibited moderate levels of support (Hahn 1993a, 312–4, McIntosh et al. 1993, 8), which may now be declining, at least with respect to national governmental institutions (Hahn 1995, 119).

With respect to *political efficacy*, the empirical evidence has again been mixed. Hahn (1993a, 310–1) reports levels of political efficacy similar to those in the United States with respect to national political institutions and remarkably little efficacy with respect to local institutions in his 1990 Yaroslavl survey. Comparing this 1990 data with 1993 data from the same oblast, however, Hahn (1995, 118–9) observes declining levels of political efficacy. Wyman (1997, 129–30) reports that Russians exhibit greater skepticism than their British or American counterparts regarding the responsiveness of their political leaders to public sentiment as well as skepticism regarding the extent to which elections serve as a meaningful source of public control over policy. Similarly, in another 1993 survey, the data indicated that only 38 percent of respondents felt that their vote mattered—arguably another indication of low levels of political efficacy.

Generally speaking, the issue on which the Russian and Soviet respondents consistently exhibit the least democratic stance is *political tolerance*. Based on their 1990 survey of the Moscow oblast, Gibson, Duch, and Tedin (1992, 340–1) were the first scholars to document the apparently intolerant nature of Russian political culture. Subsequent surveys of political opinion in the European portion of the USSR supported this conclusion (Gibson and Duch 1993a, 73; Gibson and Duch 1993b, 299–301; Gibson 1995, 83; Gibson 1996b, 964–5). Wyman (1994;

1997, 134–7) reports low levels of political tolerance in a 1989 sample, and Whitefield and Evans (1994, 53) report low levels of support for *minority group rights*. Gibson (1996c, 9–10) reports that in a survey conducted in 1995/1996, it was clear that intolerance of groups on the far right of the Russian political spectrum has persisted, while intolerance of Communists has diminished considerably. He takes this to mean that although general levels of tolerance in the Russian public are still low, the situation may be improving.

A reasonable summary of the evidence on commitment to democratic norms would have to highlight the ambiguous nature of the evidence and the apparent decline of support for some democratic norms. The optimism of the first wave may well have been the product of two factors: first, the a priori expectation, based on decades of Sovietology, that Russian respondents would exhibit virtually no support for democratic norms; and, second, initial public enthusiasm for democracy as a means to an economic end.

How Do the Russians Define Democracy?

By itself this information is interesting, and its significance is revealed when viewed from the perspective of information on how Russians define democracy and prioritize issues. The published analyses that have dealt with this question suggest that Russians associate democracy primarily with personal economic outcomes. Perhaps the clearest picture of this priority of economic over political issues is offered by Dobson (1994b) using samples from June 1992, January 1993, and September 1993. His data show that across all three samples the view that economic dimensions of democracy are essential remained high and constant. By contrast, belief that protection of minority rights, freedom to criticize the government, and multiparty competition are essential features of democracy started at a lower level in the first survey and declined in the subsequent surveys. In a later analysis, Dobson (1996, 2, 33, 37) demonstrates that the priority of economic issues was also evident in data collected in 1995. Using separate 1993 samples of political opinion, Whitefield and Evans (1994, 46, 51) and McIntosh and colleagues (1993, 3–4, table 1) provide supporting evidence. Furthermore, in their analysis of elite-mass congruence, Miller, Reisinger, and Hesli (1995, 12–14) report that the Russian masses are more concerned than Russian political elites with economic reforms and are more conservative on economic questions.

A comparative study by McIntosh and colleagues (1993) found that publics' notions of democracy differ in East and West.

> While west Europeans tend to emphasize political rights, east Europeans equate democracy more with economic prosperity and social rights than with political rights. Majorities in eastern Europe select economic prosperity, security, or equality as more important in a democracy than the political rights of political pluralism, freedom to criticize the government, and a system of justice that treats everyone equally. (McIntosh et al. 1993, 4)

This difference in definitions of democracy between East and West is significant for a number of reasons, not least of which is that "the public's definition of democracy may serve as a fundamental indicator of the expectations people have of their new society—whether it is a society based on 'economic and social rights' or one that emphasizes 'political rights' " (4).

This empirical evidence is consistent with the theoretical argument about the relationship between living conditions and political values advanced by Inglehart (1990) in *Culture Shift in Advanced Industrial Society*. Inglehart (1990, 4–5, 11) argues that there is a strong relationship between the economic prosperity of a given society and the nature of the concerns emphasized by its citizens. According to Inglehart, the unprecedented high levels of material prosperity enjoyed by the citizens of most Western democracies between the end of World War II and the early 1970s have been translated into an increasing emphasis on "postmaterialist" issues including "belonging, self expression and the quality of life" (Inglehart 1990, 11). He also argues that "elite challenging" political behavior is a component of a postmaterialist orientation (1990, 4). Put simply, this perspective asserts that once physical and economic security have been achieved, the members of a given society are more likely to turn their attention to self-expression, including political expression (Gibson and Duch 1994, 6).

Gibson and Duch (1994, 16) found that only 11 percent of respondents in their 1990 survey of the European portion of the USSR qualified as "pure post-materialists." Furthermore, they found that in their sample these postmaterialists were indeed "more likely to support core democratic values" (Gibson and Duch 1994, 19). It is worth noting that Gibson and Duch (1994) found 11 percent of their respondents to be post-materialists in 1990, a time of relative economic security compared with the period of economic turmoil that events in 1991 unleashed. It is not unreasonable to speculate that the precipitous decline in the quality of life after 1990 further muted the emphasis on postmaterialist concerns.

One significant result of this situation is that acceptance or rejection of particular democratic institutions by Russians may depend on public perceptions of whether or not those institutions will be instrumental in realizing economic objectives. Based on their analysis of Russian survey data collected in late 1992, McAllister and White (1995, 57) conclude that "popular support for the emergence of a national party system based on free, competitive national elections is narrow, variable across time and space and highly conditional upon the achievement of economic and other objectives to which a rather greater priority is attached across the mass electorate."

This evidence on definitions of democracy and the priority assigned to various issues by the Russian public is central to acquiring useful information from the body of evidence on aggregate levels of support for political and economic change. Among other things, it suggests that we would be mistaken to think that only views on political issues will be politically significant. The priority of economic issues suggests that mass support for reform will be limited, regardless of any normative commitment to democratic principles that may exist. Indeed, this is borne out by the populist, state-oriented nature of Yeltsin's recent re-election campaign: he was responding rationally to the priority of and conservative bias on economic issues that the survey data portray. More important, this evidence suggests that many Russians have only an instrumental commitment to democracy. The link between support for democratic norms and economic performance underscores the fragility of democratic commitments. Under such circumstances, future support of democracy may well hinge on the ability of economic reforms to satisfy the personal material well-being of significant publics. In the absence of such economic improvement, the consolidation of democracy will be undermined unless Russian citizens adopt a more principled commitment to democratic norms (Diamond 1996, 33).

Distribution of Opinions in the Russian Population

Considerable effort has been devoted to identifying the demographic correlates of pro- and antireform sentiments in the Russian population. Generally speaking, the demographic characteristics most commonly associated with proreform sentiment are higher education levels, youth, and residence in urban areas. Many authors have taken this as evidence supporting the thesis that economic modernization has produced increasingly more westernized, democratically oriented, market-oriented generations of Russian citizens. In this view, political cleavage tends to be seen in terms of modern versus traditional sectors of Russian society and intergenerational differences in political and economic preferences. Therefore, our purpose here will be to summarize what we have learned about political cleavages in Russia from this perspective. In our subsequent discussions, we will refer back to this body of knowledge and identify key questions about its significance.

The evidence suggesting that the young and better educated are more likely to harbor reformist sentiment is indeed impressive. Miller et al. (1994, 1996), Kullberg and Zimmerman (1995, 14), Denisovsky, Kozyreva, and Matskovsky (1993, 230–1), Mason (1995, 393–4), and Wyman (1997, 178–180) all report positive correlations between education and support for economic reform. Finifter (1996, 146–7) further explores this relationship and finds that there is an urban-rural cleavage among well-educated respondents, with highly educated rural residents opposing economic reform and urban residents with higher education providing the strongest support for economic reform. With respect to the relationship between education and support for various elements of political reform, Hahn (1993b, 319–22), Finifter and Mickiewicz (1992, 869), Gibson, Duch, and Tedin (1992, 359), Kullberg and Zimmerman (1995, 14), Melville (1993, 67), Gibson and Duch (1993a, 85), Reisinger and colleagues (1994, 215), Hahn (1995, 128–9), Wyman et al. (1995), and Wyman (1997, 220–1) all report statistically significant positive relationships. However, it should be noted that this relationship is not uniform across all possible dimensions of support for democratic norms. Gibson and Duch, (1993b, 307–8), for example, found no relationship between education and political tolerance in their 1990 samples of Moscow and the European portion of the USSR. Again, Finifter (1996, 146–7) argues that there is an urban-rural cleavage among highly educated Russians. Generally speaking, there is a great deal of evidence to support claims that education is a politically significant factor.

Similarly, there is consensus on the negative relationship between age and support for reform. Bahry (1993, 544), Hahn (1993a), Gibson, Duch, and Tedin (1992), Dobson (1994a), Melville (1993, 67), Gibson and Duch (1993a, 85), Miller (1993), Denisovsky, Kozyreva, and Matskovsky (1993, 230–1), Dobson (1996, 24), and Wyman (1997, 218) all report evidence that younger Russian/Soviet respondents are more likely to support political and/or economic reform. Wyman et al. (1995, 600) note that this relationship was also evident in voting behavior in the December 1993 parliamentary elections as a large proportion of older respondents to a 1994 survey reported voting for the CPRF in those elections.

Overall, a fairly impressive consensus emerges about the demographic bases for political cleavage in post-Soviet Russia: political conflict is primarily the product of intergenerational incongruities in political and economic preferences. These differences are the product of both differing experiences (Bahry 1993) and the effect of increasing levels of education in younger generations. Generally speaking, modernization theory would seem to find an impressive body of empirical support in the Russian/Soviet case.

Summary

The foregoing discussion has identified several of the important conclusions that emerge from the survey analyses published to date. First, there is widespread lack of support for economic reform. The political significance of this is highlighted by the tendency of Russian respondents to place a high priority on economic issues and to define democracy primarily in terms of personal economic outcomes. The evidence on political values is more mixed and in hindsight probably warrants less optimism than originally generated by the early surveys. Finally, there is considerable consensus on the demographic correlates of opinion on political and economic reform. This point seems to form the foundation of our interpretation of political cleavage in Russia and to a large extent vindicates proponents of modernization theory. Although the literature is not marked by perfect harmony, a great deal of consensus exists on some key issues.

Lessons about the Public's Role in Democratization: The Russian Experience

When authoritarian regimes are in crisis or near-crisis situations, history demonstrates that publics can play an important role in terms of the extent to which they are mobilized for actions against the existing regime. Demonstrations, riots, and general strikes have all played a part in toppling authoritarian regimes. We are all familiar with the significance of the storming of the Bastille in 1789. Our aim here is to discuss just what we have learned about the role of the Russian public in the transition and consolidation phases of democratization.

The first order of business, however, must be establishing the dividing line between the transition and consolidation phases of Soviet/Russian democratization. The theoretical literature tends to see the end point in the transition phase as the promulgation of a new constitution and the holding of democratic elections for political leadership. The repeated creation of new political institutions and the holding of increasingly free elections in the period 1989–91 creates some potential for dispute over just where the Soviet transition phase ended. However, the most judicious dividing line is probably December 1993, when a new constitution was ratified and a parliament was elected in relatively free elections. At that point, Russia had a new constitution—or set of political rules—and a freely elected executive and legislature. This was the first time that post-Soviet Russia met those criteria; hence, December 1993 is taken as the dividing line between the First and Second Russian Republics. Yet if this was the beginning of the consolidation phase, it is important to point out that it was a very tentative and shaky beginning. It must be remembered that Yeltsin essentially crammed the new constitution down the throats of the public with precious little public discussion (White, Rose, and McAllister 1997, 97) just two months after he bombarded the Russian parliament and at the same time parliamentary elections returned considerable support for Zhirinovsky's Liberal Democratic Party of Russia.

Transition and the Russian Public

While the Russian public did not storm any fortresses in the quest for liberty, they did take to the streets as the Soviet Union collapsed. The most significant example was the public reaction to the August 1991 putsch, when we saw approximately a hundred thousand Muscovites take to the streets to demonstrate in support of Yeltsin and, more important, barricade themselves around the Russian "White House" to prevent the KGB from apprehending the leadership opposing the putsch.

Of course, other instances arose in which public demands manifested themselves in demonstrations and strikes. The Soviet miners' strike of 1989 was significant for its impetus to worker activism from below and a new, independent, trade union movement.[1] A national miners' strike in March 1991 went so far as to call for the resignation of President Gorbachev and Prime Minister Valentin Pavlov. Sakwa (1993, 9) argues that this strike was a "warning to Gorbachev that his alliance with the conservatives was eroding his position."

> At the opening of the Third Russian (Emergency) Congress of People's Deputies [in March 1991], called by the conservatives in an attempt to oust Yeltsin [the popularly elected president of the Russian Republic], Gorbachev ordered 50,000 Interior Ministry troops into Moscow to try to prevent a demonstration in support of Yeltsin, yet perhaps a quarter of a million people defied his ban.

Clearly, Russian and Soviet publics were willing to take to the streets as the USSR crumbled. Furthermore, the public barricades around the Russian White House very likely prevented the success of the coup plotters in August 1991, thus sustaining the transition phase. How, then, does this fit in with the emphasis in the theoretical literature on the role of the elites in the transition phase?

The short answer is that the Russian masses probably would not have taken to the streets if an elite decision had not been made to liberalize Soviet political life. As mentioned earlier, O'Donnell and Schmitter (1986) maintain that elite actions are generally the determinant of whether liberalization will be pursued, and some scholars have portrayed Gorbachev's reform efforts as an attempt to relegitimize the USSR in the eyes of its population. This line of argument follows the logic of what Huntington (1991) terms a "performance dilemma." Huntington, however, points out that in the USSR "the performance dilemma did not become a dilemma until the political sphere allowed it to." Put simply, those holding that glasnost and perestroika were manifestations of a need to relegitimate the Soviet regime overlook the fundamental role of coercion in sustaining the Soviet regime (Fish 1995b).

No widespread social unrest forced Gorbachev to liberalize Soviet political life through the introduction of glasnost in 1987. Arguably, liberalization was the product of a desire by some Soviet leaders to enhance the strategic position of their nation. This is an important point to bear in mind for it belies the simple argument that the Soviet masses destroyed authoritarianism as a result of dissatisfaction with the status quo. It does not mean, however, that Gorbachev (1987, 65–74) was unaware of public dissatisfaction with a stagnating economy. It is instructive, however, that his initial attempts at reform— "authoritarian perestroika"—made no effort to involve the public or accede to public demands (Battle 1988).

In theoretical terms, the Soviet collapse suggests several conclusions about the role of the mass public in the democratic transition. First, the emphasis in the transition literature on elites as the determinant of whether liberalization will be pursued seems warranted (Lane 1996a, 1996b); the causal chain in the demise of the USSR must start with Gorbachev's introduction of glasnost—an event hardly precipitated by public pressure, although the role of public sentiment in convincing Gorbachev that glasnost was a viable political strategy should not be trivialized. Second, once the transition has been originated by elites, the public can play a crucial role in sustaining it. This is a point not often recognized in the theoretical literature. The Russian public did not have the ability to begin the transition phase. Once Gorbachev initiated transition, however, the public did play a crucial role both in sustaining liberalization and expanding the limits of glasnost (Cohen and vanden Heuvel 1989) as well as in opposing the 1991 coup attempt. This point suggests that it may be desirable to make liberalization and transition analytically distinct phases of the democratization process and devote additional study to the role of the public in each of these phases to further develop our theoretical perspectives.

Given our belief that the decision to pursue liberalization was an elite action, we do not feel that mass-centered research has the potential to yield much insight into that process. We do feel, however, that mass-centered research does help us understand the public's role in sustaining the Russian transition. The first relevant item of information provided by mass-centered research is the finding that prodemocratic sentiment in Russia peaked in the period 1990–91.[2] Gibson, Duch, and Tedin (1992), Finifter and Mickiewicz (1992), and Hahn (1993b) all presented evidence that commitment to democratic norms and principles in Russia was higher than expected. The only democratic norm for which the public consistently expressed little support was political tolerance (Gibson, Duch, and Tedin 1992; Gibson and Duch 1993a; Wyman 1994). Subsequent studies have demonstrated declining levels of support for democratic norms in the Russian population. Hahn (1995), for example, reports declining levels of support for competitive elections and political efficacy. Miller et al. (1996) also report declining levels of support for democratic norms. Hence, public resistance to the 1991 putsch occurred when Russian enthusiasm for democratic norms had reached its highest pitch.

However, consider the extent of resistance to the putsch. According to Gibson (1993b, 12), about 1.8 percent of his respondents in a spring 1992 survey reported taking to the streets to demonstrate either in favor of or against the putsch attempt. Among the demonstrators, Gibson (1993b, 13) reports that those opposed to the coup were more numerous and that activism was more common in Moscow and Leningrad than in the rest of the USSR. What the mass-centered research tells us is that at the height of Russian enthusiasm for democratic norms only a relatively small portion of the population actively opposed the coup, and this occurred predominantly in the two largest cities of the USSR. How certain can we be that the public would have taken to the streets to defend Yeltsin in Smolensk or Tula, let alone the countryside? What mass-centered research tells us is just how fragile the process of Russian democratization was in the transition phase.

Consolidation and the Russian Public

As stated earlier, the major role usually accorded to public sentiment in the consolidation phase is that of deterrent to would-be antidemocratic coup leaders. This stems directly from the view that consolidation involves the process of winning the commitment of elites to democratic processes and discouraging those elites who cannot be won over from resorting to antidemocratic means. Those studying institutional design have generated many important insights into the effect of political rules on elite conflict. Given this emphasis in their research, however, they have not addressed the deterrent potential of the public in detail, which is where mass-centered research makes an important contribution to our understanding of political dynamics in a democratizing country.

What does the mass-centered research tell us about the potential of the Russian public to deter challenges to democratic rule? For several reasons, we feel that the potential of the Russian public to deter antidemocratic coup attempts has declined in recent years. First, as already mentioned, survey research suggests that aggregate levels of commitment to democratic norms in the Russian population are declining. Early support for democratic norms may well have been the product of widespread popular association of democracy with economic prosperity rather than deep-seated commitment to democracy as a set of procedures.[3]

Mass-centered research also demonstrates the priority of economic issues in the Russian populace and the extent to which Russians tend to define democracy in terms of economic outcomes. Given the fact that antidemocratic elites perceive declining public enthusiasm for democratic norms coupled with the primacy of economic issues, they may come to view a coup attempt as a viable means of political conflict. In addition, McAllister and White (1994, 614) conclude from surveys conducted in early 1992 that there exists "a substantial minority of citizens who consider political protest likely, and who would participate in mass political action under certain circumstances." Most important, they found that the "basis for this protest potential is economic dissatisfaction rather than political discontent." Therefore, we cannot rule out the possibility that economic issues may stimulate both elites and masses to engage in forms of anomic political behavior that would threaten democratic consolidation.

Second, survey research tells us that political participation and activity in Russia, particularly with respect to group membership, has not been particularly vibrant (Reisinger et al. 1995, 966; Kaplan 1993, 161–2) and that aggregate levels of participation seem to be declining (Hahn 1995, 124; Wyman 1994, 31–32). Furthermore, to the extent that voter turnout is a useful indicator of political participation, it seems that conservatives are becoming more active, while those harboring reform sentiment are becoming less active (Clem and Craumer 1995, 609).

In substantive terms, this suggests that the deterrent force of the Russian public has declined in recent years. Taken together with our discussion of the Russian public and liberalization, a broader theoretical conclusion is possible. Liberalization and coup attempts are both generally discussed in terms of the importance of political leadership. However, elite decisions to pursue these paths are likely to be shaped—at least in part—by anticipated public reaction. Gorbachev probably would not have embarked on liberalization had he not expected popular approval. Antidemocratic elites are probably much less likely to stage a coup if they expect popular resistance. While the public may not directly precipitate these events through conscious action, it could be a more important consideration in elite calculations than is generally recognized.

Summary: Transition, Consolidation, and the Russian Public

The foregoing remarks suggest several conclusions about what we have learned so far about the role of the Russian public in the process of political change. First, the decision to pursue liberalization was an elite decision made in the absence of compelling public pressure. However, Gorbachev's anticipation of the public's role as his ally in political reform may well have encouraged him to proceed with liberalization. Put another way, Gorbachev was not operating in a social vacuum; while the public may not have been a "stick," it may well have been the "carrot" that drew Gorbachev down the path of fundamental reform. In keeping with this logic, we need to consider how public sentiment may encourage or deter elites in the consolidation period. The evidence collected to date suggests that the likelihood of public sentiment deterring a challenge to democratic rule has declined in the last several years and the future of democracy in Russia may well rest on the shoulders of elites now more than ever.

Questions and Challenges for Those Studying the Role of Publics in Democratization

In the previous section, we asserted that political elites do not operate in a social vacuum; even if they have considerable freedom to make decisions, they are unlikely to ignore the potential reaction of the public. In our discussion of the questions and challenges that need to be addressed by those studying the public's role in post-Soviet politics, we intend to further develop this theme in several ways. First, we discuss the relationship between societal context and the likely direction in which Russian political institutions and discourse will evolve. Second, we address the question of just which segments of the public are likely to be most relevant in shaping elite calculations.

Societal Context and Russian Politics

Democracies are not necessarily alike; indeed, they are quite different in terms of their historical genesis, institutional forms, and societal contexts (Fischer 1996, 1–2). Using Kornhauser's (1959) distinction between pluralist and populist democracies has the potential to enhance our understanding of the type of political system that is developing in Russia and its relationship to Russian society and the public. Kornhauser argues that pluralist democracy is characterized by constraints on state power stemming from the pluralist constitution of society, whereas populist democracy is characterized by a lack of constraints on state power resulting from the low organizational density in mass societies.

In keeping with the points made earlier ("Societal Context and the Nature of Democracy"), we believe that the extent to which Russian society is characterized by mass or pluralist tendencies may well help us understand how political institutions, competition, and discourse will evolve in post-Soviet Russia. At the very least, evaluating the nature of Russian society on this dimension requires us to determine the extent to which meaningful cleavages divide the Russian populace into distinct groups.

Despite some minor variations, essentially three major perspectives on political cleavages in Russia have been presented in the published works on contemporary Russian politics. The first perspective combines the assumptions of modernization theory and economic rationality. This "group interests" perspective argues that economic modernization in the postwar era has created the elements of a pluralist society in Russia and that different Russian demographic groups are pursuing their perceived interests. These demographic groups are seen as the primary source of emerging political cleavages. One of the earliest statements of this group interests perspective was offered by Hough (1988), who argued that perestroika was a middle-class revolution supported most strongly by bureaucrats and professionals who expected to benefit from the introduction of more individualism into the Soviet economy. He believed that Soviet blue collar workers had the most to lose from reform and would therefore be its most vigorous opponents.

Some survey researchers, such as Finifter and Mickiewicz (1992) and Miller et al. (1994), have also voiced the expectation that better-educated Russians were better positioned than other groups in society to benefit from economic reform and that this was, in part, responsible for the greater tolerance of reform exhibited by these groups. More recently, Fish (1995a, 367) has argued that socially based political cleavages are emerging in Russia. He bases this view on the claim that "whether or not the market has 'succeeded,' it has begun to completely re-shape the interest bases of politics." Furthermore, he states that the main political issues in Russia are ideologically loaded and not characterized by broad consensus.

A second perspective emphasizes cleavages built around differences in opinion on normative political issues such as respect for minority rights, respect for free speech, and support for competitive elections. This approach also owes a heavy intellectual debt to modernization theory. In this case, however, the emphasis is on cultural changes precipitated by economic development and the associated spread of education. This "cultural change" perspective holds that the spread of education in Russia over the last few decades has created a populace that is much less tolerant of authoritarian practices. Since younger generations tend to be better educated, intergenerational cleavages are emphasized. It should be noted that these first two perspectives are, in many cases, complementary, as some authors have argued that better-educated Russians are both normatively committed to democracy and better positioned to benefit from economic reform.

Hahn's (1993b) article "Continuity and Change in Russian Political Culture" is one of the best known statements of this position. Based on a 1990 survey conducted in Yaroslavl, Hahn (1993b, 322–3) concludes that

> the weight of the evidence . . . favors the argument that support for democratic institutions in the Russian political culture is more likely to be found among the young who are also better educated. . . . The generational differences in political culture found in our sample are clearly related to higher educational attainment, an important consequence of economic development.

In sum, Hahn argues that increased education resulting from modernization has undermined the social basis for a return to Soviet-style politics. A variety of other studies—including Gibson, Duch, and Tedin (1992), Gibson and Duch (1993a), Reisinger and colleagues (1994), Hahn (1995), and Kullberg and Zimmerman (1995)—have reached similar conclusions about the positive relationship between education and support for democratic norms in Russia.

Miller et al. (1996, 153) also acknowledge the role of modernization theory in shaping interpretations of survey data collected in the former Soviet Union. In summarizing the relationship between modernization and political change in the former Soviet Union, they state, "[A]s the years passed and Soviets became better educated and more aware of other cultures, they began to demand more rights, more individual opportunities, and greater self-determination for both the individual and the various ethnic populations of the USSR." In that same article, they assert that the data collected for the Soviet Interview Project "appear to support the modernization argument." Similarly, Melville (1993, 56, 57) argues that modernization produces a civic culture favorable to the development of democracy and that modernization has fostered the emergence of civic culture values among the young and highly educated citizens of the former USSR.

This is but a small sampling of the scholars who have embraced to at least some extent the argument that modernization has produced the building blocks of structured political cleavage in Russia. Whether their expectations are based on economic rationality or the cultural impact of economic modernization, all of the authors cited see a relationship between membership in various demographic groups and the likelihood of benefiting from, and/or supporting, reform in Russia. Both perspectives are consistent with a pluralist characterization of Russian society.

The third perspective focuses on the nature of Soviet social structure and social policies, and their impact on post-Soviet Russia. In the view of Fish (1995b, 98–101), the Soviet social structure, with its emphasis on egalitarian wages, did not allow for the sort of stratification that forms the basis of political cleavages in many Western polities. There are several reasons for this phenomenon:

> The Brezhnev-era policy of *uvravenie* (equalization) of wages, combined with the long-standing ban on private property and entrepreneurship and near-total state control over employment, production, distribution, and services, limited severely the social-structural effects of economic change. Furthermore, neither the black market nor the corruption and privileges of the apparat induced genuine class formation and differentiation. Black markets do not create middle classes; and, as one scholar [Remington] has remarked, "The embourgeoisement of the political elite is not the same as the rise of a Soviet bourgeoisie." (Fish 1995b, 99)

> The weak and peculiar stratification of Russian social structure therefore established very different "conditioning parameters" [Kirchheimer] around political life than those evident in many other—particularly non-socialist—cases. (Fish 1995b, 99)

> In its efforts to develop a true "citizen's consciousness" in Russia, the Democratic Union "held that totalitarianism had erased any notion of citizenship and even independent personality." (Fish 1995b, 108)

Put simply, the Soviet economic experience homogenized Russian society to the extent that programmatic politics were not viable. In the absence of an economic rationale, electoral competition in the early 1990s revolved around the personal qualities of contending candidates and leaders. Fish (1995b, 101–3) terms this "socioeconomic realism." Connor (1994, 331) provides a similar argument, pointing out that as of 1993 the Russian state was still by far the largest employer. This situation tended to create a pattern of shared interests across broad segments of the Russian population from the top levels of management down to unskilled labor; all had something to lose from the withdrawal of state subsidies.

This third perspective suggests that the bases for pluralism in Russian society may have been muted by the Soviet experience and that Russian society may bear a strong resemblance to the mass society described by Kornhauser. Fish (1995b) does, however, leave open the possibility that economic reform will eventually create meaningful political cleavages between demographic groups in Russian society, and in more recent writings, Fish (1995a, 1996) has shifted to the group interests perspective on Russian politics owing to his belief (1995a, 367) that "massive privatization and the formation of markets of every kind are now established facts in Russia."

Nevertheless, it is Fish's (1994, 33) position that one of the legacies of Communist rule in Russia was a society in which "the intermediary realm between state and society was driven out of existence. In sociopolitical terms, Soviet Russia consisted on the one hand of a state that monopolized all associational life, and on the other of an ultraprivate realm of networks of individuals bound together by ties of kinship, ethnicity, personal friendship, or informal economic exchange." In other words, Soviet society was a dual society that paralleled the dual persona at the individual level.[4] The types of relationships in this "ultraprivate realm" are usually described as primary relationships that "serve profoundly particularistic needs" (Fish 1994, 34), in contrast to the secondary relationships that serve more universalistic, public needs (Diamond 1994, 6).[5]

Pluralist and civil societies are characterized by a multiplicity of these secondary relationships. Mass societies are characterized by the predominance of primary relationships. In the post-Soviet era, however, proliferating intermediary associations based on secondary relationships become a threat to the existing social fabric based on primary relationships. Likewise, the development of a legal market based on principles of formal contract and secondary relationships are a threat to existing networks of primary relationships for informal economic exchange. As a result, the continuing "unofficial Russia" based on primary relationships coexists with a new "official Russia" based on secondary relationships.

We have little reason to suspect that mass publics in Russia will easily give up existing patterns of primary social relationships and quickly embrace new and proliferating secondary relationships of a more pluralist, civil society. Indeed, as Fish (1994, 33) points out:

> With the state fractured and disintegrating and the ban on autonomous associations only a memory, the enormous breach between the state and the individual has become a powerful vacuum. Rushing in to fill that vacuum are the remnants of the old Soviet order—fragments of the old party-state, as well as outgrowths of private interpersonal networks.

Hence, mass society as the basis for populist politics is likely to exist for some time to the detriment of the development of a pluralist, civil society that can serve as the basis of a more liberal democratic politics. Among other things, a "feeble civil society . . . creates ample opportunities for the emergence and empowerment of populist elites" (Fish 1994, 40). Fish (1994, 35) goes so far as to conclude, "Lacking a richer and more differentiated civil society, democratic consolidation has little hope in Russia."

These issues suggest several important questions that need to be answered if we are to further our understanding of the relationship between Russian publics and the process of democratization. First, we need to assess which of the aforementioned perspectives on Russian political cleavages is more accurate. The group interests perspective is clearly the dominant interpretation of Russian political culture, but its accuracy is not beyond question.[6] In many cases the regression coefficients for the relationship between demographic characteristics and opinions on economic and political reform are statistically significant but modest. As McIntosh et al. (1993, 11) put it in an analysis of political opinions in postcommunist Europe: "none of the demographic variables account for much of the variance in support for liberal democratic values." One of the most significant dangers that we must navigate, then, is the possibility of confounding substantive and statistical significance (Brym 1996b, 755). Hence, an important task facing mass-centered researchers is the reevaluation of where meaningful political cleavages lie in Russian society and the degree to which the findings that young, better educated Russians are more reformist are *substantively* (as opposed to statistically) significant.

Once we have established which characterization of Russian political cleavages is more accurate, we can better assess the likely effect of societal context upon the course of political events and institutions. This might best be accomplished by assessing what a rational, power-seeking politician would do when confronted with a mass or pluralist society. This could be a useful avenue of research both across nations and across the regions of Russia.

Consequences of Democratic Institutions for Economic Performance

As Keech (1995, 214) has reminded us, democratic institutions do have consequences for economic performance in the form of certain costs. One such cost relates to "the backward-looking accountability issue." Because government officials are accountable to the public through the ballot box, "government agents will try to make their performance look misleadingly good at the time that contracts are renewed (i.e., at election time)." A second cost relates to the "forward-looking choice issue" that involves "the inevitable uncertainty about the consequences of choices that electorates make." This produces yet another cost in "the failure of the public to appreciate the consequences of the actions it supports." While in established democracies these costs are "modest and bearable," they may be neither modest nor bearable in societies that are simultaneously undergoing democratization and marketization. Especially noteworthy in the case of Russia has been the failure to follow through with marketizing economic reforms for fear of retaliation by voters at election time. Witness Yeltsin's manipulation of the public just before the 1996 presidential election by (at least temporarily) increasing pensions, paying wages that were many months in arrears (with the help of a $10 billion loan from the International Monetary Fund), granting a $5 billion subsidy to farmers, reducing commercial electricity rates by half, and pledging $2 million for construction of a new barracks at a military college.[7]

Fish (1994, 34–35) rebuts the view that "the absence of a vigorous civil society might even be seen as an advantage." In his opinion, "Both political institutionalization and the progress of liberal economic reform have been the most impressive in those countries where civil society is the most robust." As Linz and Stepan (1996b, 29) suggest, however, "when people's assessments about politics are positive, they can provide a valuable cushion for painful economic restructuring." They present evidence (1996b, 30) from *The New Democracies Barometer III* (Rose and Härpfer 1994) to support the "loosely coupled" hypothesis of a weak relationship between attitudes on political and economic reform: Eastern European "respondents judged that, in important areas directly affected by the democratic political system, their life experience and chances had overwhelmingly improved, even though they also asserted that their own personal household economic situations had worsened." In other words, "the deterioration of the economy does not necessarily translate into rapid erosion of support for the political system" (Linz and Stepan 1996b, 30). This point confirms findings of Finifter and Mickiewicz (1992) and Finifter (1996) that attitudes toward political and economic reform are not unidimensional, but it contradicts those of Miller et al. (1996) that support for economic and political reform are positively and strongly correlated. These contradictory findings suggest that we shift our focus away from a preoccupation with the negative effects of marketization on democratization and look more closely at the possible positive effects of democratization on marketization.

Institutions and Masses: What Causes What?

The importance of institutions can be illustrated by Jack Knight's (1992, xi) suggestion that "the rationality of social institutions" could best be explained "in terms of their distributional effects." This view relates to the "locus of responsibility" issue that, in turn, has an impact on support for democracy. For many Russians, there appears to be a strong connection between economic well-being and affect toward democracy. When their economic situation is threatened or worsens, they blame it on democracy.

Not only can people learn to be democrats within the context of democratic institutions, but through their distributional effects those institutions can have a strong impact on citizen affect toward democracy. The problem for Russia is that this impact can be either positive or negative, depending upon economic performance. This is illustrated in the finding by Kullberg and Zimmerman (1995, 22) of "a connection between economic conditions and the level of individual attachment to philosophical and political liberalism."

In terms of what causes what, Kullberg and Zimmerman (1995, 5) directly challenge a main assumption of the transitions literature that institutions matter more than values and attitudes (Kitschelt 1992b; Di Palma 1990). Whereas some students of post-Soviet politics (Roeder 1993; Bova in chap. 7) maintain that institutions matter, Kullberg and Zimmerman (1995, 3) argue that "masses matter." Clearly this is an issue of great practical and theoretical significance that requires further exploration.

Will Mass Publics Accept Uncertain Outcomes?

Przeworski (1986, 58) argues, "The process of establishing a democracy is a process of institutionalizing uncertainty, of subjecting all interests to uncertainty." This conception of democratization appears to be flatly contradicted by rational choice institutionalists. As described by Stoner-Weiss (1995, 54):

> The classic dilemma of collective action is the lack of enforceable commitments. Rational choice institutionalists argue that institutions provide these commitments by rendering the behavior of other actors more predictable. Institutions accomplish this task by providing information that makes commitments between actors both enforceable and credible. As a result, actors who would otherwise not cooperate opt to do so because they recognize that they will gain from this behavior. In sum, by providing information about the behavior of other actors, institutions not only reduce uncertainty, but the transaction costs of cooperative exchange are similarly reduced.

This joins an important question about the role of institutions in the democratization process. Do they reduce uncertainty or institutionalize uncertainty? They may do both. And this relates to Przeworski's (1986, 59) principal thesis that "[d]emocratic compromise cannot be a substantive compromise; it can be only a contingent institutional compromise." If institutions reduce uncertainty (as the rational choice institutionalists maintain), then they must do so only with regard to the "rules of the game," but not with regard to substantive outcomes. This appears to be the gist of Przeworski's point about the importance of "institutional agreements" that are "compromises about the institutions that shape prior probabilities of the realization of group-specific interests" (60). And that is why the struggle over constitutional principles looms so large in contemporary Russia.

According to this criterion, argues Shevtsova (1996, 32), "the Russian polity after August 1991 can be classified as the institutionalization of uncertainty" and therefore a democracy. But, she says, this was "due more to the existence of a weak, unconsolidated regime and the absence of rules of the game approved by all actors than to a victory of traditional democracy." In other words, Schumpeter's definition of democracy does not apply to Russia, but Przeworski's does. For Shevtsova (1996, 32), the Russian polity does not permit "the choice between elites by voting in regular and competitive elections." "New elites have not really yet emerged; the replacement of the old nomenklatura is far from complete. As a result, there is no opportunity for the development of elite competition on the basis of agreed-upon rules." But, she argues, institutionalized uncertainty does exist. There appears to be a contradiction here, for institutionalized uncertainty can exist only where there is agreement on the rules of the game.

By way of contrast, Hahn (1996b, 245) argues, "In the end, democratic consolidation did not proceed in Russia because relevant elites in both legislative and executive institutions were unwilling to accept uncertain outcomes." This is a clear violation of Przeworski's (1991, 14) dictum that "The decisive step toward democracy is the devolution of power from a group of people to a set of rules."

How can we reconcile these two opposing views? Public attitudes toward uncertain outcomes may provide important clues. Based on surveys by the Russian Center for Research on Public Opinion in May and June 1996 during the height of the presidential election, Brym and Kosova (1996) report that nearly two-thirds of the respondents regarded postponement of either the presidential election or the upcoming parliamentary election as "impermissible." They concluded that "for most Russians, democratic process matters more than electoral outcomes." In contrast to the contradictory evidence on Russian elites, this is evidence that Russian publics are willing to accept uncertain outcomes, at least with regard to elections, and therefore represents a positive step toward democratic consolidation (Fischer 1996, 3).

Unfortunately, these findings and optimistic conclusion are contradicted by another recent study. Based on surveys conducted by the Russian Institute of Complex Social Studies about the time of the December 1993 Russian parliamentary election, Pammett and DeBardeleben (1996) found considerable cynicism and skepticism concerning the electoral process. The bulk of their evidence supports the view that "electoral institutions still lack a sustained basis of public support" (373) in Russia. Most important, they found that "evaluation of the electoral institutions is closely linked to satisfaction with political/economic outcomes and outputs" (378). This observation suggests that Russian publics are not willing to accept uncertain outcomes.

These contradictory findings are one very important example of a problem in survey research into post-Soviet Russian values and behavior that appears to be widespread: the findings may well be the result of the timing of surveys, the types of questions asked, and the nature of the sample populations. Only additional and more sophisticated research will be able to resolve these methodological questions and the resulting contradictory findings reported throughout this analysis.

Synoptic Thinking and the Malleability of Political Culture

Much of Sovietology has provided us with a pessimistic scenario for the prospects of democracy in Russia based on the antidemocratic traditions and ideology-based legitimacy of both pre-Soviet and Soviet era political culture. Regarding the role of ideology, Huntington (1991, 106) has argued that one of the "[f]actors contributing to the breakdown or weakening of authoritarian regimes in the 1970s and 1980s" was the general absence of ideology-based legitimacy for authoritarian regimes other than one-party systems." And this, in turn, was the result of "the prevalence of democratic norms globally and in many individual countries."

In this regard, it is important to note that Yeltsin has been anything but ideological to the point that he has been criticized by some in his own camp for failure to give Russia some new sense of national identity. Giorgi Saratov, a leading political adviser to Yeltsin, stated during the presidential campaign:

> When totalitarianism was being destroyed, the idea of ideology was being destroyed, too. The idea was formed that a national idea is a bad thing. But the baby was thrown out with the bath water. Our Kremlin polls show that people miss this. In 1989, 1990, and 1991 there was a real sense of mission to destroy communism. After that seemed to be resolved, there was a vacuum that followed. Partly this is why the Communists are doing so well. (Remnick 1996, 46; see also Hanson 1997)

It is Remnick's view (1996, 46) that

> the Yeltsin government decided it was unnecessary to try to put forward an ideology, a national idea, to replace the old one. The largely unspoken understanding in the first years of the Yeltsin era was that the new Russia would be more or less democratic, more or less market-oriented—in other words, more or less like the United States, Western Europe, or Japan. Russia, in other words, had abandoned not only the Marxism-Leninism of the twentieth century, but also the Slavophile notion of the eighteenth and nineteenth centuries that declared Russia a "special role" in the world, a degree of particularity and messianism that set it off from all other nations.

Some recent evidence suggests that the Yeltsin government's assessment may be well founded.

Both the Slavophile and Marxist-Leninist traditions in Russia produced a political culture characterized by what Zimmerman (1995, 631) calls synoptic thinking: the view that there is "only one correct philosophy." Based on the results of 1992–1993 surveys, Zimmerman (1995, 636) found that 60 percent of the general public, 81 percent of university attendees, and 93 percent of elites who answered the question "Is there only one right philosophy" rejected synoptic thinking. In contrast to other recent assessments (Fleron 1996b), this led him to the conclusion that "the connection between orientation to market and, to a lesser extent, to the political system, and the disposition to reject the idea that there is only one right philosophy reinforces the view that those who support notions congruent with liberal democracy are not simply giving lip service to such a conception" (640).

The implications of this line of reasoning have considerable theoretical import, for they suggest that "attitudes core to a political culture are knowledge driven and not constant" (Zimmerman 1995, 640). As a result, "culture is relatively malleable," and concerns about the weight of the Russian and Soviet pasts on the postcommunist present are not well founded. This bodes well for the consolidation of democracy in Russia for it suggests, contrary to the received wisdom of much of Sovietology, that Russians can learn to become democrats. Indeed, survey research suggests that they are becoming democrats. Yet additional research is required in order to tell us whether other aspects of traditional culture are equally malleable.

Conclusion: What Will It Take to Consolidate Democracy in Russia?

Linz and Stepan (1996b, 16) argue that democratic consolidation must involve behavioral, attitudinal, and constitutional dimensions:

> *Behaviorally*, a democratic regime in a territory is consolidated when no significant national, social, economic, political, or institutional actors spend significant resources attempting to achieve their objectives by creating a nondemocratic regime or seceding from the state.

> *Attitudinally*, a democratic regime is consolidated when a strong majority of public opinion, even in the midst of major economic problems and deep dissatisfaction with incumbents, holds the belief that democratic procedures and institutions are the most appropriate way to govern collective life, and when support for antisystem alternatives is quite small or more-or-less isolated from prodemocratic forces.

> *Constitutionally*, a democratic regime is consolidated when governmental and nongovernmental forces alike become subject to, and habituated to, the resolution of conflict within the bounds of the specific laws, procedures, and institutions sanctioned by the new democratic process.

What continues to confound analysts is that there appears to be a contradiction between the attitudinal and behavioral indicators of democratic consolidation. On one hand, survey research has demonstrated that the Russian public holds many values strongly supportive of democratic norms. On the other hand, those same publics gave considerable support to potentially antidemocratic elements in the 1993 and 1995 parliamentary elections and the recent presidential election. At the same time, there are important political actors (and groups of actors) spending "significant resources attempting to achieve their objectives by creating a nondemocratic regime [Zhirinovsky, Zyuganov] or by seceding from the state" (Chechnya), or even attempting to restore the USSR (Tatar Communists and proindependence nationalists).[8] How are we to account for this apparent contradiction?

One answer is that it is one thing to express one's affection for abstract democratic norms in a public opinion survey, but what really matter are material conditions and self-interest, democratic practices embodied in actual social practices, and particularistic social ties (Fleron 1996b). And this takes us back to Szamuely's description of the Russian tradition discussed at the outset. What had impressed Szamuely (1974, 6) about the experiences of the Marquis de Custine and Andre Gide in Russia was "the astonishing durability of certain key social and political institutions, traditions, habits, and attitudes; their staying-power, their essential stability amidst the turbulent currents of violent change, chaotic upheaval, and sudden innovation."

Clearly certain key political institutions have changed. A constitution has been promulgated, legislative bodies have been established, and relatively fair parliamentary and presidential elections have been held. Mass-based survey research suggests that many traditional Russian political attitudes have changed and Russian political culture seems more malleable than heretofore conceived. Contrary to the received wisdom of Sovietology, it now appears that the outlooks of Russian publics do not rule out the eventual consolidation of democracy. This is an important finding supported by a wide range of empirical studies conducted by highly competent scholars, and it has great theoretical and practical significance. But there is nothing inevitable about democratic consolidation in Russia, and the jury is still out concerning other social institutions, traditions, and habits (Tucker 1992; Sergeyev and Biryukov 1993; Ragsdale 1996). Indeed, there are indications that basic values have not changed in any fundamental way (Brym 1996b). Although both common sense and theory suggest that publics do matter, no research to date, survey based or otherwise, has demonstrated that the public *really* matters for the process of democratization. This presents us with an important challenge.

Going beyond the Linz-Stepan conceptualization of consolidation, Diamond (1996) has argued in a seminal article that genuine democratic consolidation requires *liberal* democracy, not merely formal *electoral* democracy. Minimalist conceptions of democracy stress the importance of "regular, free, and fair electoral competition and universal suffrage" and " 'vertical' accountability of rulers to the ruled" (23). According to these criteria, says Diamond, Russia can be considered a democracy. But a more expansive notion of *liberal* democracy also includes the following criteria:

1. "the absence of 'reserved domains' of power for the military or other social and political forces that are not either directly or indirectly accountable to the electorate"
2. " 'horizontal' accountability of officeholders to one another; this constrains executive power and so helps protect constitutionalism, the rule of law, and the deliberative process"
3. "extensive provisions for political and civic pluralism, as well as for individual and group freedoms"

According to these criteria, Diamond maintains that Russia has not yet achieved democratic consolidation.

Regarding the public's role in democratization, it is clear from our analysis that Russia has not yet acquired "extensive provisions for political and civic pluralism." In addition, although individual political rights appear to be reasonably secure, due process rights continue to lag behind Western standards of liberal democracy (Sharlet 1994; Korkeakivi 1994; Juviler 1995).[9] Even according to the minimalist criteria of democracy cited by Diamond, however, we have good reasons to believe that Russia has not yet fully achieved the status of an electoral democracy. Democracy implies both restraints on rulers and responsiveness to the public. Yet there are indications that voting is being used more for elite legitimation than for registering public preferences by "fair electoral competition" (see Treisman 1996).

It is important to distinguish between democratic elections and democratic campaigns. Democratic *elections* are based on universal suffrage and the absence of violence and intimidation. According to these criteria, recent Russian elections score well. But a democratic election also requires that incumbents leave office if they lose, and there are indications that Yeltsin would not have relinquished the presidency if he had lost the recent election. In addition, Yeltsin appeared prepared to cancel the election altogether if his campaign advisors concluded that he would not win. This suggests a more cautious appraisal of Russian elections.

Democratic *campaigns* require relatively free and open access to important resources, especially the media. Yet there was obvious bias in Russian television coverage of the presidential campaign that can be traced to the fact that two of the eight channels available to Russian viewers were government controlled and the advertising revenues of the remaining six were controlled by two companies whose executives were Yeltsin supporters. Furthermore, Yeltsin's position as both candidate and incumbent enabled him to adopt a "full pockets" approach to the "targeted allocation of 'pork' " (Treisman 1996, 66–72). In buying voters on credit, Yeltsin exhibited a crassness that exploited the baser instincts of the Russian public for personal self-aggrandizement. One recent analysis described the 1996 presidential campaign as a "rough-and-ready campaign rather than competition within the rules of an established democracy" (White, Rose, and McAllister 1997, chap. 12). This is not the stuff of democratic campaigns, and it represents a cynical attitude toward the role of the public in democratic consolidation.

Both the comparativist and the area specialist have important reasons to ask whether the public matters for democratization in post-Soviet Russia. For the comparativist, the former communist countries provide an exciting opportunity to test in a new setting the assertions, hypotheses, and propositions of the literature on democratic transition and consolidation. For the area specialist, a reexamination of the role of the public in democratization in the former Soviet Union is long overdue. Considerable effort has been directed toward designing and financing mass surveys and, based on the results, drawing conclusions about the future of Russian democracy. What we still do not know, however, is how these survey results are related to political behavior. Further examination of the role of the public in democratization is needed to focus our interpretations of survey results on the likely consequences of public sentiment and cleavages for political events. To return to the question posed at the beginning of this chapter, we have important logical reasons to suspect that the public does matter for democratization. To this point, however, mass-based research has made only a limited contribution to understanding that role. It is in the direction of the public's impact on specific processes and institutions that we must expand our efforts.

Notes

An earlier version of this paper was presented at the Distinguished Lecture Series, Center for International and Comparative Studies, University of Iowa, September 30, 1996. The authors wish to thank Erik P. Hoffmann for helpful comments on earlier drafts of this chapter and for several substantive examples.

1. For details, see Rutland (1990), Bergsten and Bova (1990), and Sakwa (1993, 268–70). For a discussion of trade unions, strikes, and labor unrest in the post-Soviet period, see Connor (1996).

2. This is not an assertion that there was overwhelming commitment to democracy in the Russian population at that time; rather, levels of commitment to democracy were relatively higher than they are today.

3. For a detailed critique and analysis of the early literature on post-Soviet political culture and democratic norms, see Fleron (1996b).

4. For the classic statement of Russia as a dual society, see Tucker (1960). For an analysis of the impact of the dual persona on the results of survey research on Russian political culture, see Fleron (1996b).

5. For more on particularism, see O'Donnell (1996, especially 40–41).

6. Ahl (1997) found that demographic groups were not a meaningful source of cleavage with respect to evaluations of economic experience and opinion on economic issues. Given the priority of economic issues indicated in the survey research published to date, this suggests that demographic groups may still not be an important basis for political cleavage. As a result, Fish may have abandoned his 1995 argument prematurely.

7. *Time,* May 27, 1996, 52.

8. *OMRI Daily Digest I,* 138 (July 18, 1996).

9. The 1995–96 Freedom House (1996) survey rates Russia 3 on political rights and 4 on civil liberties on a scale of 7. This gives Russia the same ranking as nine other Partly Free countries: Albania, Bangladesh, Central African Republic, Guinea-Bissau, Mozambique, Nepal, Thailand, Ukraine, and Zambia.

V
CONCLUSION

12

State–Society Relations in the Soviet Union and Post-Soviet Russia

Erik P. Hoffmann

This book has explored the nexus between state and society in the Soviet Union and post-Soviet Russia. Our contributors have presented state-centric and society-centric approaches and have employed various social science paradigms. We have focused on elite-mass linkages, a key component of the state–society nexus. Following Harry Eckstein, we have emphasized the importance of "congruent authority patterns" in the polities and societies of authoritarian and democratic countries, as well as "balanced disparities" in developing and consolidated democracies. But state–society relations are often disjointed and disruptive, especially in posttotalitarian and postauthoritarian regimes. And global and regional power configurations are often unbalanced and contentious, especially in the multipolar international system emerging after the disintegration of the Soviet bloc and the Soviet Union. Hence, academic, governmental, and other professional analysts of post-Soviet Russia are confronted with formidable challenges in the post-cold war era.

To understand the performance and potential of the emerging Russian polity, one must understand the unstable bonds between Russia's state and society. These bonds are being shaped by a large number of variables: tsarist and Soviet legacies, formal and informal institutions, leadership priorities and personalities, policy outputs and outcomes, socioeconomic and demographic trends, psychological and cultural adaptation, technological and environmental conditions, international and transnational relations, and others. The interaction between state and society became increasingly volatile in the final half decade of the Soviet Union, when socioeconomic and international pressures for

331

change intensified, prompting Mikhail Gorbachev, Boris Yeltsin, Andrei Sakharov, Eduard Shevardnadze, Aleksandr N. Yakovlev, and others to launch reforms that quickly weakened or severed the ties among core elements of the state-centric political system. And post-Soviet Russia's fitful and still derailable transition from totalitarianism to democracy depends, above all, on the building of stable and responsive relationships between a much weaker and decentralized state and a much more self-reliant and organized society.

The Soviet Union

State-society relations in Soviet ideology contrasted sharply with democratic theories. The official Soviet conception of politics was much broader than Western conceptions, and the activities of the Soviet party-state were much more extensive than the combined activities of Western executive, legislative, and judicial institutions. No governmental body in the West assumes responsibility for making key foreign and domestic political and economic decisions at the national, regional, and local levels; for "guiding" the organizations that must implement these decisions; for recruiting and deploying personnel in all leadership and administrative positions in all major bureaucracies in the country; and for designing and conducting political and atheistic education programs for the entire citizenry (adults and children) in an ethnically and religiously diverse society. However, these were precisely the responsibilities that the post-Stalin Communist Party of the Soviet Union (CPSU) assumed, in accordance with the ideology of Marxism-Leninism. And the CPSU's national and regional apparatuses carried out these responsibilities to the extent that they possessed the power and knowledge to do so, increasingly relying on Leninism rather than Marxism to legitimize rather than to motivate their actions. Soviet theory and practice were never congruent, and the gap between them always intensified political and social tensions.

Karl Marx and Friedrich Engels distinguished sharply between a nation's political "superstructure," including governmental institutions and policies as well as public attitudes toward authority and law, and its economic "base," including both the "social relations of production" and "productive forces." These production relations included the power of capitalists to extract surplus value from the labor of exploited workers, purportedly enlarging an increasingly poor and radicalized proletarian class; and productive forces included the power of technology and know-how to enhance economic growth and labor efficiency. Marx emphasized the upward impact of productive forces on the social relations of production and, in turn, on the superstructure. But he also acknowledged the downward influence of the superstructure on the social relations of production and, in turn, on the productive forces, as well as the superstructure's direct influence on productive forces.

In other words, Marx was keenly sensitive to the reciprocal relationships between state and society, and he stressed the increasing capability of the latter to mold the former, thereby producing a "bourgeois revolution," then a "socialist revolution," and eventually a classless and harmonious "communist" political order. Socioeconomic forces were deemed so powerful that they could weaken and dismantle the inherently coercive "feudal" and "capitalist" governments. Under full communism the state and law would "wither away," and all citizens would enjoy economic security and social justice in a myriad of highly decentralized communes.

Vladimir Lenin, in sharp contrast to Marx, stressed the predominance of the political-administrative superstructure over the socioeconomic base, especially in underdeveloped capitalist and quasi-feudalist countries such as Russia. The complex ideological, practical, psychological, and ethical relationships between Leninism and Marxism have been succinctly summarized by Daniels:

> [Lenin believed] that history is made in the last analysis not by classes or the forces of production, but by willful individual leaders and by ideas. This was an outlook he shared with practically all pre-Marxist Russian social thinkers. . . .
>
> For Lenin the revolution was not inevitable at all; it had to be brought about by the deliberate action of conscious revolutionaries, *against* the natural flow of history. If the spontaneous forces of history were not interfered with, Lenin implied, the moral imperative of revolution would never become a reality. Hence, it was on willful revolutionaries, sustained by a sense of moral duty, that Lenin had to rest his hopes. How to guarantee, however, that the revolutionaries would keep striving in the right direction against the frustrating spontaneity of the passive herd? Lenin's answer was the same on which any religious movement relies to assure individual rectitude: the proper doctrine, the true faith [Marxism as read by Lenin]. (Daniels 1993, xxi-xxii, italics in original)

Relying on the Jacobin tradition of the Russian revolutionary movement, Lenin created the Bolshevik party, which espoused his organizational principle of "democratic centralism," carried out a successful coup d'etat in November 1917, and emerged victorious from the bloody civil war immediately thereafter. Then, drawing on both the coercive and pedagogical branches of Russian populism as well as selected short- and long-term goals of traditional Marxism, Lenin's nascent single-party system began to "construct socialism" in Soviet Russia. This was a major step toward uniting "workers of all countries in one World-Wide Socialist Soviet Republic," according to the 1924 constitution.

But Lenin and Joseph Stalin concentrated much less on expanding the Communist International (Comintern) than on state building, especially the formation of the Red Army and Cheka (security police), the creation of disciplined regional and local party organizations, and the recruitment of "bourgeois specialists" into industrial ministries and large factories. The New Economic Policy (NEP) delayed the socialist "cultural revolution" and economic reforms Lenin had promised, with the notable exceptions of successful literacy campaigns and nationalization of key industries. The expansion and staffing of political and administrative institutions, according first to Lenin's and then Stalin's preferences, were the top priorities under the NEP. Forced collectivization of agriculture, complete nationalization of industry and commerce, destruction of all independent institutions and groups, and blood purges of every social stratum culminated in the emergence of one-man rule by the late 1930s. Stalin ruled "over" rather than "through" the party (in Leonard Schapiro's [1959] classic formulation), and the unspeakably repressive Stalinist state ruled "over" rather than "through" the profoundly alienated and atomized society it had created. In a word, the terrorist and intrusive totalitarian state tried hard to obliterate the very distinction between state and society. Citizens were viewed as "cogs" in the machinery of government, and constitutionally granted liberties could be exercised only in the pursuit of socialist goals as defined by the top party-state leadership.

Courageous individuals and nascent groups privately retained their unofficial beliefs and identities even at the height of Stalin's "cult of personality," and publicly expressed their dissent on several occasions under Nikita Khrushchev's liberalizing one-party rule and on many occasions under Leonid Brezhnev's stagnating oligarchy. Valentyn Moroz (1971, 134, 138–40, italics in original), a Ukrainian dissident, lucidly analyzed the predicament of the masses in totalitarian societies and poignantly voiced the aspirations of independent-minded citizens oppressed by their own state.

> The ruling power claims to be the only fount of "the mind, honor, and conscience" of the whole society—and then solemnly proclaims the "politico-moral unity of society." In so far as the Cog [a programmed person] is concerned, the eternal question, "Where to go?," is made into a formula which requires no exertion of the intellect: "Wherever they lead me." . . .

Nothing will replace the free, unregimented thought of an individual whose creative ability is the only motive force of progress. We owe progress to those who have kept their ability to think and have preserved their individuality despite all attempts to erase it. A person without an individuality becomes an automaton who will *execute* everything but will not *create* anything. He is spiritually impotent—the manure of progress, but not its motor.

Top Soviet leaders, from Lenin to Gorbachev, distinguished between state and society, and they deemed it necessary for a powerful national government to transform its domestic and international environments. Stalin was by far the most ambitious and ruthless reshaper of society. He focused on "socialism in one country," spurred heavy industrialization and urbanization through the institutionalization of terror, and diminished the role of the CPSU vis-à-vis the state's military command, secret police, economic ministries, and pseudo-representative bodies (the national and subnational soviets). Moreover, Stalin's foreign policy was tailored to domestic goals, especially the preservation of his "third revolution" and personal dictatorship. For example, Stalin transformed the Comintern into a weapon in his power struggle with political enemies during the mid-1920s; Soviet foreign trade organizations exchanged confiscated agricultural goods for Western machinery throughout the 1930s; and the new East European empire was plundered to help rebuild the shattered Soviet economy after World War II.

Gorbachev recognized the decline of domestic economic capabilities and the need for improved East–West relations to foster scientific-technological progress, and he adjusted Soviet policies and political-administrative institutions accordingly. Gorbachev gradually reduced the role of the CPSU vis-à-vis other institutions, especially the increasingly assertive regional and local party organizations and soviets, as well as the emboldened mass organizations and mushrooming associational interest groups. Also, he abandoned the Ministry of Foreign Trade's monopoly on international commerce, thereby trying to induce factories and farms to modernize technology and improve the quality of their products for export, as well as to spawn privately owned cooperatives and joint ventures to increase economic growth and productivity. And, most important, Gorbachev reversed the strategic and conventional weapons buildup launched two decades earlier by Brezhnev. Like Khrushchev in the late 1950s, Gorbachev began to reduce the size of the bloated military-industrial complex and to transfer scarce resources from military to civilian industries and agriculture.

The essence of Stalinism was the binding of society to the state in an autarkic international environment, and the essence of Gorbachev's perestroika was the unbinding of society by the state in an increasingly interdependent world. Stalin deliberately unleashed the USSR's super-structure on its socioeconomic base, and Gorbachev unintentionally helped the base take "revenge" on its superstructure. Initiatives "from above" began to dismantle the Soviet party-state, discredit the bureau-cratic authorities, and transform the elite and mass political cultures; responses "from below" and "from abroad" accelerated these proc-esses. But many official and unofficial political orientations persisted, many formal and informal social networks survived, and many na-tional and subnational nomenklatura cadres thrived in the increasingly privatized economy. Bonds between the weakening communist state and emerging civil society were never established, and attitudinal and institutional disconnections between the fragmented state and multi-national society are important legacies of the Soviet and tsarist eras.

Sovietology

The state–society nexus has been the focus of some of the best Western scholarship on Soviet and tsarist Russia. Two of the earliest post-World War II studies of the Soviet Union stressed the reciprocal influences of the Soviet polity and its socioeconomic environment: namely, Barring-ton Moore Jr.'s (1965) *Soviet Politics—The Dilemma of Power* (also Moore 1966b) and Merle Fainsod's (1965) *How Russia Is Ruled* (also Fainsod 1958).

Moore's work had a significant central theme: the impact of political ideas on social change, and vice versa. Moore carefully examined the ways in which the aims and accomplishments of Soviet leaders influ-enced one another in different time periods. He also judiciously ana-lyzed the situational constraints on Soviet policy makers, the responsiveness of party officials to rapidly changing conditions and unexpected events, and the evolving functions performed by the val-ues, attitudes, and beliefs of political elites. Moore forcefully argued that the Bolshevik "ideology of means," exemplified in Lenin's words and actions and in the Russian revolutionary tradition, had a tremen-dous influence on the formation and development of the Soviet polity, economy, and society. This instrumental ideology had a substantially greater effect on the behavior of generations of CPSU officials than did the much less authoritarian goals and ideals of classical and Russian Marxism. Lenin's and Stalin's cardinal operational principle—"the end justifies the means"—underscored the importance of goal-*seeking* feed-back, not goal-*changing* feedback. And, until Gorbachev's policy of glasnost, party cadres studied public opinion only to speed the implementation of decisions already made by top party leaders.

Fainsod, too, presented a distinctive and prodigiously documented theoretical interpretation of the Soviet system. His emphasis on the concept of "totalitarianism" helped to bridge the gap between macro- and microtheories and contributed to middle-range theories of modernization, communication, and organization. Fainsod is not usually thought of as a "conflict" theorist, because he stressed the dictatorial nature of Soviet policy making. But he was acutely aware of the importance of inter- and intraorganizational conflict in the implementation of national policies and of the top leaders' continuous efforts to prevent "the pluralization of authority." Also, Fainsod fully understood that Stalin relied on terror to spur socioeconomic and political transformation and that he adroitly altered career incentives and the legal system to stabilize many new socioeconomic and political relationships. Furthermore, Fainsod's research in the extraordinary Smolensk Archives, which included classified CPSU and secret police directives as well as letters from ordinary citizens to party and state officials, documented the quest for goal-seeking feedback by the Soviet bureaucratic elites and the outpouring of goal-changing feedback by the general population.

Granted, much of Western Sovietology focused on national politics or "the view from the top," especially in the heyday of Kremlinology and the Cold War. But there were increasing opportunities to study "the view from the bottom." Westerners began conducting limited archival and field research in the late 1950s, and bibliographical and travel restrictions selectively diminished thereafter. Moreover, Soviet policies and policy-making procedures were liberalizing under the energetic and impatient reformer, Khrushchev, and Politburo control over the regional and local party organizations was loosening under the aging and stolid bureaucrat, Brezhnev. In a word, the core elements of the Soviet polity were adjusting to new conditions, and Sovietologists were chronicling these changes through on-site observations as well as careful reading of the increasingly divergent print media.

One scholar who focused on the state-society nexus throughout the entire Soviet era was Robert C. Tucker (1960, 1971, 1973a, 1973b, 1981, 1987, 1990). He analyzed political leadership and mass culture and their interrelationships. His concept of "dual Russia" encapsulated and highlighted the wide gulf between the Russian elites and masses. Moreover, Tucker's historical studies of tsarist and communist Russia, as well as his in-depth psychological studies of Stalin and other Soviet leaders, helped to explain the causes and consequences of "dual Russia." Tucker used a wide variety of written sources and personal experiences to delineate and link key variables, such as the "we/they" mentality throughout Russia, but his evidence did not include survey research. Today, with the help of public opinion polls, scholars such as Judith Kullberg and William Zimmerman (1995; 1996) have further documented the enduring and adaptive nature of dual Russia. If these cleavages between elites and masses persist, they will continue to be major obstacles to democratization in the post-Soviet political order.

Allen Lynch affirms that Gorbachev clung to his view of the Communist Party as "an agent of reform," even though the party itself was unreformable, and to his view of "the state as the dominant allocator of economic resources, even in an economy with significant market components." Lynch (1996, 320) concludes:

> What Gorbachev did, in effect, was to conduct a grandiose test of the hypothesis that the roots of Soviet and Russian socialism ran deeper than the Stalinist legacy. In successfully uprooting Stalinism in all of its political and institutional manifestations—an historically and moral accomplishment of the first magnitude—Gorbachev thereby destabilized the system he was trying to save. Factors such as the incentives provided by the centrally owned economy and the constitutional legitimacy of nationally defined republics, compounded by the Gorbachev-Yeltsin rivalry that saw Russia pitted against the Soviet Union, then served to propel the decomposing system into a rapid fragmentation along formerly national lines.

The disintegration of the Soviet Union was hastened by its dramatically increased interaction with other countries. The Chernobyl nuclear disaster forced Gorbachev to think seriously about global issues and to participate actively in international organizations. Also, as noted earlier, Gorbachev encouraged foreign trade by republic and local governments and by established production enterprises and new business cooperatives. Most important, Gorbachev accelerated and accepted the breakup of the Soviet external empire in Eastern Europe, thereby heightening the desire for autonomy by leaders and citizens of the Soviet internal empire, especially in the Baltic republics. The combination of these three factors had a profoundly destabilizing impact on Soviet institutions and policies. Environmental degradation, world markets, and ethnonational ambitions quickly upset the "congruent authority patterns" in the USSR's multinational state and society and virtually eliminated the possibility of "balanced disparities" throughout the disintegrating polity.

In short, powerful politicians and influential political theorists, as well as comparativists and area specialists, have long and insightfully analyzed the state-society nexus, especially elite-mass relationships, in communist polities. If the rapidity of the Soviet Union's demise has taught us only one thing, it is that the Soviet polity was a *system*, the Soviet bloc was an even larger *system*, the Cold War bipolar international order was a still larger *system*, and the *symbiotic* linkages among these three systems were irreparably damaged by Gorbachev's attempts to reform state–society relations in the USSR. And if the remarkably peaceful disintegration of the Soviet internal and external empires has left us with just one insight, it is that several core elements of the Soviet state and society have survived and are adapting themselves to new conditions throughout the Commonwealth of Independent States and, to a much lesser extent, in the Baltic and East European countries.

Post-Soviet Russia

Some students of "third wave" democratization have highlighted state-society relations, and their research increasingly encompasses postcommunist Russia and Eastern Europe. Linz and Stepan (1996a) identify five "arenas" of a modern democracy—two of which are the "state apparatus" (based on "rational-legal bureaucratic norms") and "civil society" (based on "freedom of association and communication"). The other three arenas are connecting links between the state apparatus and civil society—"political society" (based on "free and inclusive electoral contestation"), "rule of law" (based on "constitutionalism"), and "economic society" (based on an "institutionalized market").

Significantly, Linz and Stepan identify each arena's "necessary support from other arenas" and each arena's "primary mediation upon other arenas." For instance, civil society needs the state apparatus to protect civil liberties and "generates ideas and helps monitor the state apparatus and economic society." And the state apparatus needs political society to authorize and collect taxes and enforces upon civil, political, and economic societies "democratically sanctioned law and procedures established by political society." Moreover, political society "needs legitimacy in the eyes of civil society" and "produces [an] overall regulatory framework for economic society." Rule of law must be supported by a "legal culture with strong roots in civil society and respected by political society and the state apparatus" and establishes "a hierarchy of norms that make actions by, and upon, other arenas legitimate and predictable." And economic society must be grounded on a "legal and regulatory framework produced by political society, respected by civil society, and enforced by the state apparatus," and "produces the indispensable surplus to allow the state to carry out its

collective good functions and provides a material base for the pluralism and autonomy of civil and political societies" (Linz and Stepan
1996a, 7–15 ff.).

Neither state nor society is "privileged," and their interconnections
and interdependence are underscored, in Linz and Stepan's theoretical
framework but not in all their case studies. Analyzing the USSR and
post-Soviet Russia, for example, the authors do not develop the theme
of "complementarity" between civil society and political society, especially their changing relationships in different phases and spheres of
posttotalitarianism and democratic transition. Instead, Linz and
Stepan emphasize the "crafting" of democratic institutions by national
political elites, rather than subnational governments' initiatives and
grassroots democratization—a top-down rather than an interactive
top-down/bottom-up approach (Linz and Stepan 1996a, see, e.g., 8–9,
366–400). Whether Linz and Stepan have chosen their approach because of unusual conditions observed in Russia or because they consider it appropriate to the early phases of democratization in all
postcommunist countries is unclear. In the Russian context, however,
an overly heavy focus on the establishment of national governmental
institutions can minimize the weakness of state structures and capabilities. A state-centric focus can exaggerate the authority of regime-
founding leaders, their consensus on policies and metapolicies, and
their influence on bureaucratic, ethnic, and socioeconomic networks
surviving from the previous communist system. It is especially important not to presume the Russian state's control over or unrespon-
siveness to the powerful new "adjacent" organizations such as freely
elected regional governments and fabulously wealthy business/media
conglomerates. But the national government's stifling of or impervi-
ousness to associational interest groups and neocommunist, ultrana-
tionalist, and centrist political parties can be underscored, at least for
the immediate future.

In the USSR's democratic, protodemocratic, and nondemocratic successor states, the progress toward a full democracy and the mix of
Linz and Stepan's five arenas of democracy vary considerably. But to
exclude one or more of these arenas a priori, or because previous research in a particular arena was flawed, reduces one's understanding
of the systemic nature of stable democracies and of the multifaceted
challenges of democratic transitions in postcommunist polities, economies, and societies. Consider Fish's (1995b, 27, 200, italics in original)
"statist, institutional approach to *political-societal* change," especially the
emergence of political protoparties and social "movement organizations" under Gorbachev and their decline under Yeltsin:

Just as ideology and belief systems will be deemphasized in treatment of the state, notions of popular political culture and psychology will play no part in explanations of the organization and behavior of societal actors. . . . [I]ndividual behavior will be explained in terms of political opportunity structures and political entrepreneurship, not political psychology or culture. Precisely the latter approaches, rather than use of meaningful comparative concepts such as "totalitarianism," checked the theoretical advancement of sovietology over the decades. . . . (See also chap. 3, e.g., 77 ff., and chap. 4, e.g., 93 ff.)

But elite belief systems and policy priorities *did* shape or reinforce the institutions and activities of the party-state in the Gorbachev and Yeltsin years. The international "new political thinking" and domestic "ideology of renewal" were not merely post facto justifications, especially considering Gorbachev's innovative foreign policy and the over three hundred amendments to the USSR constitution. Also, the preservation of power and the acquisition of property were predominant elements of the bureaucratic elites' operational ideology, especially during the rapid and extensive "nomenklatura privatization" under Yeltsin. Old patron-client networks of the national and subnational nomenklatura were not indifferent to rising counterelite and public expectations and were not impervious to intensifying domestic and international pressures. We should credit many former CPSU elites with pragmatic adaptation to an increasingly decentralized polity and multipolar world; to more assertive economic institutions, mass media, interest groups, and social movements; and to other liberating manifestations of glasnost, perestroika, demokratizatsiia, and "postcommunism" before and after the watershed events of late 1993.

Also, the following questions are pertinent: Were not the short- or long-term "political opportunity structures" and the goals or methods of "political entrepreneurship" influenced by government leaders' personal idiosyncrasies, pecuniary drives, ethnic bonds, geographical loyalties, and perceptions of scientific-technological modernization and socioeconomic development at home and abroad? Did not "the beliefs, ideas, and political orientations" of national, subnational, and civic leaders help to remold and sometimes rigidify "the structure and character of state power," especially as parliamentary and governmental factions spawned new democratic and nondemocratic protoparties, and as regional and local governments and ethnic and economic interest groups asserted themselves? Why would, and how could, the members of nascent democratic parties and social movements try to free themselves from their ideologically and culturally grounded cognitive orientations in the "subjective . . . process of identity formation"? And were the aspirations of the Baltic peoples, Ukrainians, Tatars, Chechens, and other national minorities unimportant "notions of popular culture and psychology" (cf. Fish 1995b, 27, 93, 200)?

The increasing fragmentation and weakness of the Russian state, which Fish rightly underscores, make it even more important to understand the cognitive processes of the national and subnational elites and of organized and unorganized groups among the masses. The Soviet "center" disintegrated in a struggle over power *and* policy, and a democratic post-Soviet "center" has failed to emerge because of a similar struggle. National elites have not been able to agree on fundamental policies on how to make policy. This inability to institutionalize and legitimize metapolicies has fueled explosive political and bureaucratic disputes about the powers of individual governmental structures, and it has greatly weakened the power of the national government as a whole. Bitter conflicts within the president's apparatus, within the prime minister's government, between the national executive and legislative branches, and between national and subnational governmental bodies show few signs of subsiding—the firing of national security adviser Aleksandr Lebed, the comeback of Anatolii Chubais, and the nearly three dozen bilateral treaties between the president and regional leaders notwithstanding. Indeed, conflicts among elites have been exacerbated by Yeltsin's serious health problems, the national government's inability to collect taxes, the regional governments' resistance to federal authority, the weakness of the judiciary at all levels, the vast property redistribution, the disintegration of Russia's armed forces, and the manipulation of election campaigns and financing and of television ownership and programming.

Political dissatisfaction has overflowed from interelite to elite-mass arenas. Because national governmental and business oligarchs and their "clans" have been remarkably unresponsive to the material and nonmaterial needs of average citizens, we have witnessed the mounting distress and resourcefulness of countless individuals as well as the largely ineffectual protestations and demands of key workers' organizations (e.g., miners' unions), interest groups (e.g., environmentalists), bureaucracies (e.g., the armed forces), and professions (e.g., medicine, education, and science). Only in agriculture, where Soviet collective farms remained largely intact, have hopelessness, inertia, and resistance to innovations stifled virtually all political and professional initiatives.

Much stronger bonds between Russia's elites and masses are the sine qua non of a future democracy. The process of democratization is more than national institution building and rule setting; it includes the remolding of elite and mass political cultures and the building of myriad institutions and behaviors linking the governors and the governed, especially widespread respect for the law, fiscal federalism, effective interest groups, legislator-constituent responsiveness, independent mass media, and fair elections and campaigns. Also, the products and processes of democratization interact with one another. Policy-making procedures shape policy outputs and outcomes, which can have powerful effects at home and abroad. In turn, these policy consequences influence the stability and legitimacy of the new metapolicies and the capabilities and effectiveness of the political system as a whole. And the state apparatuses of stable and would-be democracies, as well as their entire socioeconomic foundations, are now much more permeable to international and transnational influences than ever before.

To be sure, interelite pacts and constitution drafting may be especially important in the final phases of authoritarian withdrawal and the initial phases of democratic transition. But relations among elites do not take place in a political, economic, and social vacuum. The state–society nexus is likely to have portentous short- or long-term ramifications, even if the masses are ignored by elites who presume they are, for the time being or forever, impervious to their domestic and international environments.

For an important example, constitutionalism and rational-legal bureaucratic norms must be legitimized by the general population. This may be especially important in the early phases of democratization, when regime-founding elites often find it very difficult to agree on new decision-making rules, and fragile metapolicies are easily reversible. Also, large segments of the public will not immediately benefit from socioeconomic and ethnonational reforms, and counterelites will try to mobilize this discontent to enhance their power, support their policies, and revise basic metapolicies. Furthermore, popular support for democratic constitutions and institutions is likely to be strongest during the socioeconomic tumult and revolutionary exuberance immediately after the collapse of authoritarian rule and immediately before all or most elites can be blamed for ineffective or unjust social and economic policies. And average citizens are less likely to blame democracy and democrats for policy failures and personal hardships if a broad spectrum of society is represented in the policy-making process.

The legitimacy and effectiveness of a national constitution are considerably influenced by the processes of its framing and promulgation. Some kind of a constitutional convention or assembly, with considerable elite and mass inputs, will almost always produce a more democratic constitution than one imposed from above. A democratically crafted constitution is much more likely to enjoy the support, or at least the acquiescence, of the groups that were able to voice their preferences during its formulation. After all, the functions performed by a constitution are much more important than its contents, and these functions and contents will have begun to shape one another well before its formal ratification. The broader political context, especially changing authority patterns in state institutions and societal units, will have a major impact in determining whether a new constitution will lead to constitutional democracy or constitutional authoritarianism (rule of law or rule by law).

A case in point is the 1993 Russian constitution, which is rightly termed "Yeltsin's constitution" and was crafted on a battlefield rather than a negotiating table. Having just ordered the bombing of parliament, the president enjoyed limited success in persuading the electorate to view the constitution as much more than a self-serving cudgel. In the constitutional plebiscite, only 31 percent of the eligible Russian voters reportedly supported the document, whose significantly revised final version they had about one month to read and digest, with virtually no critiques or impartial analysis permitted on state-run television. And the claimed 31 percent support was almost surely inflated to circumvent a key provision of the constitutional referendum statute. As Sharlet (1996, 496) observes, "It is generally accepted in Russian political circles that the Constitution was not ratified according to procedure which required participation of a minimum of 50 percent of the registered voters in the referendum. The Central Election Commission headed by Nikolai Riabov has not to date released the 1993 data on participation." Needless to say, this constitution was not a social contract between the elites and masses, or even a pact among key national and regional elites.

For another example, postcommunist studies could profit from a sharper focus on political economy. Especially significant are the sequencing of progress toward a civil society, civil economy, and civic culture, as well as the reciprocal influences between stages of political socialization and institutionalization and of marketization and privatization. Haggard and Kaufman (1995b) contend that the deeper the economic crisis accompanying a democratic transition, the greater the need for quick and decisive action by political and economic elites. They do not laud or condemn executives who try "to overcome legislative and interest-group stalements through presidential decrees and plebiscitarian appeals" or "stabilization packages and broader reform initiatives [that come] from small, closed circles of technocrats rather than [emerge] from a broader process of legislative or interest-group consultation or pact-making." They conclude that "such exercises of executive power are as much a reflection of the weaknesses of democratic institutions as their cause." And the authors express the hope that these weaknesses can be overcome through enhanced economic growth and productivity, as well as responsiveness to the economic deprivations and dislocations caused by "shock therapy" (Haggard and Kaufman 1995b, 227).

Thus, a focus on metapolicies is fine, but inattention to substantive policies is problematic, because the outcomes of the latter affect the performance of the former. An essentialist rather than a mechanistic (goal-seeking) or cybernetic (goal-changing) view of metapolicies is problematic, too. Arguably, Stalin's one-man dictatorship differed considerably from the one-party dictatorship that preceded it and the one-party oligarchies that followed. But even if one accepts the contention that the "Leninist constitution" survived for over seventy years, it is important to analyze how these clusters of metapolicies adapted to changing socioeconomic, scientific-technological, and international contexts (cf. Roeder 1993, especially chap. 2). The national political leadership's consensus on metapolicies was shattered by Gorbachev's mostly liberalizing but oscillating reforms, which encompassed domestic and international policies and policy-making procedures. Simultaneously, these reforms fueled mounting public criticisms of socioeconomic conditions and their historical antecedents, together with a revolution of rising expectations about more inclusive policy making and less intrusive policies. Subnational elites increasingly encouraged these criticisms and heightened these expectations in order to enhance their own power and their regions' autonomy. The Soviet political system disintegrated but did not dissolve as a result of these momentous pressures and choices. And Soviet institutional, attitudinal, and ecological legacies continue to have an impact on high politics, socioeconomic conditions, and everyday life in post-Soviet Russia.

Post-Sovietology

The challenges facing post-Sovietologists are formidable. Elite and mass beliefs, perceptions, motivations, policy preferences, property grabs, and conflict resolution mechanisms, as well as national elite ties with like-minded subnational elites and segments of the masses with widely differing expectations and skills, need to be identified and their interrelationships analyzed. Likewise, the evolving political psychologies and cultures of all strata of the elites and the masses, especially the seemingly persistent gap or ideological dualism between state and society, cannot be dismissed or "held constant." And public opinion is becoming increasingly important to politicians and scholars because of more competitive elections and controversial decrees as well as greater interest articulation and unfulfilled expectations. True, many Russians have soured on the very concept of "democracy" because of their elected president's authoritarian proclivities and substantive policies. But the Russian population's attitudes toward civil liberties and political inclusion are diverse. And the mix and malleability of Russian public opinion do not preclude an eventual democratic consolidation or balancing of disparities, as the survey research reported by Frederic J. Fleron Jr. and William Reisinger in this volume documents.

Obviously, all variables are not of equal significance in explaining political change and continuity, and one cannot study everything simultaneously and intensively. One can hypothesize about the relative importance of state or society, structure or process, and macro- or microbehavior. But one should be keenly sensitive to the many presuppositions underlying one's preferred approach. For an important example, the structure/process and macrobehavior/microbehavior dichotomies call into question the state/society dichotomy. Structural and macrolevel analysis focuses on the institutions of state power as well as the components of socioeconomic modernization, with emphasis on the "objective" constraints imposed by the latter on the former (shades of Marx?). Procedural and microlevel analysis focuses on the coalitions and rivalries among governmental and nongovernmental elites, with emphasis on the malleability of "subjective" orientations and political environments (shades of Lenin?). Moreover, Kitschelt (1992b, 1028, italics in original) succinctly notes:

> What is at stake between structure- and process-oriented political regime change is a more fundamental division concerning the *concept of choice in political action itself.* For structuralists, choices represent calculations in light of given preferences and institutional constraints. For process-oriented scholars, choices are caught up in a continuous redefinition of actors' perceptions of preferences and constraints.

Most political scientists favor one or another theoretical approach and do not use combinations of approaches. And the result is usually acontextual or one-sided analysis, which obscures the complexities of revolutionary or reformative transitions and contributes little to comparative or social theory.

Ideally, interdisciplinary teams of social scientists would scrutinize the interrelationships between state and society, structure and process, and macro- and microbehavior. One's "vantage point" should be used to explore a wide terrain, as William Reisinger rightly observes. And one's focus on state, society, or the state-society nexus can employ a variety of analytical paradigms, including political economy, political sociology, or political realism, as Philip Roeder forcefully argues. His primary focus is the state, and his primary paradigm is political realism. But other scholars have fruitfully employed different combinations of foci and paradigms, including multiple foci and paradigms.[1] If the type of political system under examination is disputed by informed researchers, or if it is a hybrid or highly unstable system—maybe not a system at all—a variety of foci and paradigms should be marshaled in the quest for insight and understanding. Inclusive, especially dynamic and holistic, approaches are preferable to exclusive, especially single-level and single-factor, approaches, when one's dependent or independent variable is multifaceted, nonrecurring, and sequential (e.g., democratization—the shift from a noncivil society, noncivil economy, and noncivic culture to a civil society, civil economy, and civic culture).

Theoretical and methodological pluralism is especially needed in the study of the post-Cold War international order and postcommunist polities, because core elements are in flux or gestation. It is useful to describe important components of the nascent Russian Federation, but it is especially fruitful to explain the continuous interaction among these components and between components and contexts. More than ever, these contexts include the international system and provincial and local subsystems, as well as ethnonational, socioeconomic, and scientific-technological conditions at home and abroad.

New political rules of the game are emerging throughout the former Soviet Union and Soviet bloc, and they vary considerably among and within countries. In post-Soviet Russia, for instance, old political and economic elites, as well as bureaucratic and clientelistic networks, are vying for power to establish formal and informal metapolicies nationwide or on their geographical or policy "turf." But there are enormous variations among the eighty-nine "constituent entities" of the Russian Federation and serious tensions among the different levels and branches of government and within the national executive branch. Even more important, the fundamental values and identity of the country, as well as its external borders and internal subdivisions, are in dispute. Perhaps never before has a colonial metropole (Russia) remained in such close geographical proximity to its former colonies (the Commonwealth of Independent States, the Baltic countries, and Eastern Europe), and the political, military, economic, social, cultural, ethnic, and environmental ramifications of this proximity are far from settled.

Briefly stated, the very nature of our subject matter and the relevance of our questions are in constant need of reassessment. The unstable mix of continuity and change in various arenas of the Russian state and society, as well as their international and transnational arenas, are not well understood or agreed upon. Even if one concludes or presupposes that interelite relations are crucial in the initial phases of post-communist transitions, one must still study elite-mass relations to make the case for their relative insignificance. Some form of eliminative analysis is essential in the verification of one's hypotheses, and such analysis necessitates empirical investigation of the factors presumed to be less important. Hence, only by analyzing state–society linkages, including weak and nonexistent linkages, can one begin to understand the disintegration and reintegration produced by Gorbachev's communist liberalization and Yeltsin's postcommunist democratization.

In summary, I am calling for more than "peaceful coexistence" or "detente" between state- and society-centered approaches to postcommunist politics. I am calling for entente. If Gorbachev could comprehend that "mutual security" was a multiple-sum game, surely post-Sovietologists can understand that the Russian state and society and their international and transnational environments are becoming much more interactive. Internal and external pressures for change could abruptly weaken these interactions in the current decade, but mounting pressures will probably broaden and deepen the state–society nexus in Russia in subsequent decades. For both intellectual and practical reasons, it is essential to discern the changing contours of this nexus and their causes and consequences. It is time to privilege linkages, synergies, and symbioses and to be inclusive, interdenominational, and ecumenical.

Notes

I wish to thank Frederic J. Fleron Jr., Nadia Kavrus-Hoffmann, and Robert Sharlet for their very helpful comments on an earlier draft of this chapter.

1. For thoughtful analyses "linking," "combining," and "bridging the gap" between various approaches in non-Russian contexts, see Coleman (1990), especially chapter 1; Rueschemeyer, Stephens, and Stephens (1992); Kitschelt (1992a); and O'Neil (1996). For methodological guidance on using both qualitative and quantitative data, see King, Keohane, and Verba (1994), and for critiques of this book, see Review Symposium (1995). Also, for its multifaceted approach and methodology, see Putnam (1993), as well as laudatory and critical reviews of this work, such as Laitin (1995) and Tarrow (1996).

13

Russia and the Conditions of Democracy

Harry Eckstein

Few problems of political inquiry have generated more hypotheses than the problem of the determinants of the success or failure of democracies. Which of these hypotheses (to use Roeder's evocative word) should one "privilege"? Which identify the decisive factor or factors? How do we choose among them when we attempt to answer the question in the title of this book: whether democracy can "take root" in the case of Russia? I will deal with these questions in the first part of this chapter; in the second I will apply the results to the case of democratization in Russia.

It will be apparent that the abundance of hypotheses about the determinants of the performance of democracies is not matched by an abundance of information about Russia pertinent to them. Some degree of doubt, of course, attaches to all of the hypotheses, as it does to all theories. However, "democratic theory" is much more developed and more firmly established than empirical information about Russia pertinent to such theory. Hence, while some tentativity is necessary in the first part of this chapter, a great deal of it is required in the second. In fact, the discussion there probably indicates mainly an agenda for future empirical researches into Russian democratization rather than the processing of abundant data, via theory, into confident prognosis. We can make a start on this, using the materials available, but the application of democratic theory to Russia must be a long-continued enterprise.

From this process, as is pointed out in several essays in this book, we can no doubt also learn much that may help in the further development of democratic theory. This is particularly so because, in many ways, as has also been pointed out earlier in this book, Russia provides a sort of laboratory setting for that purpose. Not least, Russia allows us to use hypotheses about the performance of democracy in predictive tests—always the strongest, most telling tests of theories—just because Russian democratization, as historical time goes, is still in early infancy.

Causes, Etiology, "Conditions"

So far the search for a particular "cause" of the success or failure of democracies has proved fruitless, and there is reason to think that it will always prove to be so. The reason, I would argue, is that causal thinking per se is a stultifying way to go about explaining this and similar phenomena.

By "causal thinking," I mean thought that involves the essential idea of a cause as an antecedent occurrence or condition that brings about a subsequent condition or occurrence. This is the notion that Aristotle called "efficient causation," one of four types of causation that he considered necessary for the full explanation of phenomena. Three of these—material, formal, and teleological causation—were discredited long ago and dropped out of conventional thought. Thinking in terms of efficient causation, however, is deeply embedded in our culture and governs the idea of explanation in the social sciences.

Now, clearly, efficient causation occurs, but it occurs plainly only in the triggering of unique and discontinuous (or "catastrophic") events. It makes sense to say that the cause of X's death was that Y put a large dose of strychnine in her soup, or that the cause of damage to a house was an earthquake, or that the cause of Mary Slaney's losing an Olympic race was that she was tripped and fell. Science, however, is not concerned with such contingent (accidental, fortuitous) occurrences that trigger unique events. It is concerned with discovering regularities exhibited by phenomena and the general "laws" that govern, or underlie, occurrences, including those that are unique and "catastrophic."

The whole idea of efficient causation seems to have dropped out of the advanced sciences. For instance, it plays no role whatever in Hempel's (1965) elucidation of the nature of "scientific explanation" or in the epistemologies of any of the other major philosophers of science (e.g., Popper, Watkins, Ayer, Feigl, Reichenbach, etc.), at any rate since Cohen and Nagel (1934) amplified John Stuart Mill's notion of the logic of experiments.[1] There are good reasons for this, the most essential being that causal thought produces more problems than it solves.

A familiar reaction to the deficiencies of causal thinking in the social sciences has been to attribute the deficiencies to "monocausal" thinking and to propose "multivariate" thought as a corrective. This, however, leads to the same, indeed additional, problems. For instance, from a logical point of view, there is no difference between monovariate and multivariate explanations, if by the latter we mean something like a bundle of circumstances that brings about events. The "bundle" in that case is itself a "unit" that simply is complex but to which we can give a single name, as to any part of it. If, on the other hand, we mean that numerous antecedent conditions, singular or bundles, can produce the same effects, then we simply have numerous ways to get to the same destination, each of which is "monocausal" in nature. More commonly, however, as in multiple regression, the idea of multicausality seems to involve the question of what antecedents are "more causal" than others—which have the greater share of the cause of a condition or occurrence. It seems unnecessary to show that this idea of percentage shares of causality raises profound problems of its own, if indeed it is not *prima facie* absurd.[2]

In some fields of inquiry (e.g., medical science), the idea of causation has been replaced largely by that of etiology. Etiology literally means the science of causes, but in medicine it has come to refer to the chain of events that leads from some initial occurrence to actual illnesses or disabilities—their "natural histories," so to speak. In medical science, the word *cause* is certainly used, but generally in quotation marks and simply to denote the initial events believed to start an etiological sequence (Beeson and McDermott 1975). Note also that causes in medical science are just about always regarded as more uncertain than etiology as a process. This is because they are always "distal" in the chain of effects that leads to an outcome, with each link in the chain diluting overall probability.

Etiology as process avoids some of the problems of causality, but it also entails difficulties. Like efficient causation, it can be used sensibly in analyzing the occurrence of particular events, especially an "abnormal" event (such as person X getting the flu), and it makes sense particularly when classes of such events (e.g., flu in general) are to be explained. However, for some states of affairs even just raising the question of etiology seems absurd. For instance, one would certainly not inquire into the etiology of *generally* healthy or sick organisms, or strong and weak, efficient and inefficient, short-lived and long-lived organisms. In such cases, "functional" thinking makes more sense than causal or etiological thought, but functional thought has also given rise to much discussed difficulties.

An alternative to both causal and etiological thinking is based on the idea of "suitable conditions." By this is meant an appropriate set of *internal (endogenous) traits* of an entity (which can be thought of structurally and functionally) plus traits of its context (or *exogenous environment*) that together govern whether the entity lives or dies, flourishes, or is stunted. This sort of thinking seems to me to be most fruitful for accounting for such phenomena as the endurance or collapse, efficacy or inefficacy of political orders—"such phenomena" being all ill or healthy, enduring or short-lived, efficient or inefficient entities.

An analogy might clarify this. Suppose that the problem is to explain the flourishing (or languishing) of a plant. Plainly, this depends on many conditions. To start with, you need a good seed that has the potential for growth and for endurance through satisfying its systemic needs as a plant. Then, to realize that potential, the seed must be planted in a suitable soil. It must be treated in special ways in order to germinate and to make the transition from seed to established plant. When established, the plant needs proper space (overcrowding impairs it), proper amounts of sun or shade, water and fertilizer (but not too much of either), and careful tending (weeding, hoeing, pruning, etc.). For every species of plant there is a set of such conditions that is ideal for its flourishing. To the extent that these conditions are approximated, the plant thrives; to the extent that they are not, it languishes or dies.[3]

Explanation of this sort, based on approximation to an ideal set of conditions, applies to any entity or system. It is proper when one tries to explain the "health" or lack of health, strength or weakness of a human being; it applies also to mechanisms. To thrive, every entity and system needs proper internal structure (or "constitution"), a proper environment, and appropriate exchanges between internal structure and external environment. Polities, plainly, are complex "entities," or at least "systems,"[4] so that explanation by approximation to ideal conditions is appropriate for them.

Granted that one could express all the relationships involved in such explanation in a causal language; everything can be said in many languages. We could say that the seed "causes" the flourishing plant, or the soil does, or water does, and so on. But then causal explanation is no longer what it is normally understood to be: explanation by efficient causation. Soil or water per se do not cause flourishing (try it, if doubtful); they are parts of a proper general environment for it. In any case, using causal language instead of the language of conditions in no way is a help either to understanding or to being able to base actions on sound scientific reasons. The language of etiology is less problematic, but it applies well only to a *succession* of events that is ideal for a transition from potential to actuality.

The Democracy Syndrome

In chapter 8, Roeder treats some explanations of the success or failure of democracies as "privileged" over others—more important, or having more explanatory power. Claims of privilege for certain variables are conventional in democratic theory, but different inquirers have claimed privilege for many different conditions. Reisinger (in chap. 9) has given a useful typology and list of the conditions, based on broad distinctions between endogenous and exogenous, objective and orientational (subjective) conditions.

I also will make a claim of "privilege" for an *explanans* later in this essay, but on a basis different from Roeder's and consistent with "conditional" explanation. For the present, I will just sketch the syndrome of conditions associated in current theory with the performance of democracies (in the sense of "performance" discussed in chap. 1). I assume that each item in the syndrome is required for ideal performance and that each can explain approximations to, or departures from, this ideal.

Transition

To have a history at all, an entity must be established in the first place. Democracies, of course, begin with transitions from authoritarian rule.

The authors of this book generally agree that accomplishing transition is almost exclusively a matter for "elites," especially their choices in regard to constitutional design. However, it seems doubtful that transition could be successfully accomplished without some level of support by the general public, or at least its acquiescence, and unless there is at least a modicum of success concerning maintaining public safety and well-being. Elite choices are not made, or elite goals accomplished, in a vacuum. It is in fact doubtful that there is anything special about the role of elites in transitions to democracy as against "normal" democratic politics. In both, political elites decide (which is what makes them political elites), but the general public, even if it participates little, surely is part of the "environment" of government and thus a source of consequences for it.

It seems generally agreed that the first required step in the transition to democracy is the recognition by old elites that the authoritarian order is bankrupt, so that they will acquiesce in, or even try to bring about, major change in the governmental order. After that, the general principle that most decides whether the transition to democracy succeeds on a long-term basis is that it should proceed gradually, by increments and by the use of syncretic devices—that is, by incorporating much of the old order instead of eradicating it.

The speed of transition, as I have pointed out in chapter 10, may vary according to the extent to which other conditions of democratic performance are satisfied at the start, but the general principles of gradualism and syncretism still apply. One may expect an almost instantly successful transition to democracy if something like an ideal environment for it has come into existence before the constitutional transition; however, in most cases of deliberate democratization that will be far from the case. In most cases, therefore, the transition to well-established democracy should be treated as a long continued, gradually unfolding process, as it was in democracies that developed spontaneously. This is not to say that history could not be hurried along by careful political artisanship; surely it can. But neither is it to say that political contrivance can quickly achieve successful results, regardless of particular circumstances.

This general principle is what underlies the recommendation by numerous contemporary political scientists that democratizers should follow a policy of pacts with former elites (or *garantismo*, the policy pursued—successfully, it seems—in Spain). After the collapse of the authoritarian order, old elites remain and still have the lion's share of "human capital"; as well, old ways of doing things are ingrained even when discredited. Thus, it is advisable to try to co-opt former elites into the democratic order and, similarly, to develop new, democratic ways of doing things by grafting onto the old rather than building from the ground up.

This principle, however, only covers the early stages of democratization. After infancy, democracy, to be fully realized, must still develop and cannot be expected to do so simply of its own accord—no more than a mature plant can be grown simply by putting a seed into the ground and having it germinate. Careful nurture and contrivance, over extensive time, in a step-by-step manner, are required.

A principle closely related to that of gradualism is that the success of transitions to democracy depends on the sequence in which critical problems that face all polities are resolved. "Critical problems," in gist, are fundamental issues that no polity can avoid and that tend to be both very consequential and very divisive. The most basic such issues are generally considered to be the definition of the political community (what is included in the polity), problems concerning the nature of its regime (the broad nature of the constitutional order), and basic problems of distributive justice. The argument is that these fundamental problems are best dealt with one at a time and in the sequence listed. The basic reason for this is that the resolution of each problem has potential for creating deep "cleavages"; that if they arise simultane-ously the cleavages will be especially deep and intense; and that, if simultaneously faced, they will lead to "cross-cutting cleavages," ex-pressed in splintered, as well as deeply divided, leadership groups and party systems. Thus, stable and effective democratic government will be impeded in what is most required for it in complex societies: stable cooperative coalitions that reconcile differences.

Of course, gradual and sequential changes are not always open op-tions to democratizers. It may simply not be possible to co-opt old elites—to avoid having to eliminate them. Popular expectations, pres-sures, and disillusions may preclude a slow and piecemeal process of change. And it is not necessarily possible to avoid having to deal with problems of defining the political community, regime, and basic distri-bution simultaneously. In such cases, there simply is a high probability of failure of a full transition to democracy, no matter what actions are taken.

The Constitutional Order

A critical task in the transition to democracy is to construct a consti-tutional order for it—formal-legal (explicit) rules governing elections, executive and legislative structures, powers and relations, policy-making processes, civil rights and liberties, and so on. Obviously, the formal definition of such rules is particularly necessary when con-ventional democratic ways of doing things have not yet been devel-oped. Where, as in Great Britain, liberal democracy gradually evolved over a long period, thereby itself becoming a traditional order, consti-tutional blueprints for government are not needed; otherwise, contriv-ance, or "constitutional engineering," cannot be avoided. Modern democracy, in Jacob Burckhardt's phrase, necessarily is "a work of art," although, over time, it can become a way of life.

When designing a constitution, as in designing anything, one wants of course to get things right, on the assumption that constitutional rules matter to the emergence of a new institutional order that is val-ued and practiced. But what is right in devising constitutional orders? We have many studies of the supposedly intrinsic merits and short-comings of different constitutional arrangements—different electoral laws, different executive arrangements, different ways of relating na-tional to local governments, and so on. However, none of these should be regarded as intrinsically good or bad, regardless of context. It seems advisable, as I have argued in chapter 10, always to fit constitutional blueprints to particular initial conditions, as in all engineering; and it is also likely that arrangements that might work well early in transition might not be advisable in a permanent order.

Political science, it has been suggested,[5] can best serve constitutional engineers by devising something like a handbook of options available for the central tasks of constitution making, stating their supposed advantages and disadvantages, in general or under particular conditions.

Rules could then be fit to contexts by working constitutional "engineers," politicians, but with choices informed by such political science "wisdom" as exists.

But will such choices have decisive consequences for performance? Until about the 1950s, this question would not have been raised; governmental performance was explained chiefly on the basis of constitutional provisions. Polities had long been treated in mechanistic terms—as "machineries of government"—and this was the fundamental framework from which constitutional explanations were derived. The operation of machines depends almost entirely on their construction and thus on the designs followed in constructing them. Moreover, they work similarly, by and large, in different environments; context plays a role—a spanner may be thrown into the works; a machine may soon rust in a humid climate—but context does not intrinsically determine how machines operate. Context, given the mechanistic outlook, thus could be virtually ignored.

The formal-legal approach to explanation became discredited by interwar experiences, so that, until recently, explanations emphasized chiefly "exogenous" conditions. Now, however, explanations on the basis of constitutional design are prominent again, but on a different basis: that of "utility," or self-interested ("rational") choice. Constitutional rules in this framework are regarded as the rules of a competitive game observed by politicians intent upon winning. Since the politicians, as rational games players, will adapt their behavior to the rules, these, it is thought, can be used to engineer predictable, desired patterns of behavior. This is one thing denoted by a widely current and rather ambiguous term: the "new institutionalism."[6]

Philip Roeder, in chapter 8, puts his finger on the essential problem in this new formal legalism. If the behavior of self-interested politicians requires adaptation to the rules of competition, then self-interested politicians will surely also selfishly manipulate the rules. In that case the rules may still conceivably explain high or low performance, but they will not be designed to achieve successful performance in the first place; they will be designed to promote sectional, not general, interests. However, we need not tackle the issue of what animates constitutional design here. The issue here is not how to explain the design of constitutions but whether governmental performance can be sufficiently explained and predicted on the basis of constitutional design.

On logical grounds alone, ignoring experience, the answer to this question clearly must be no. If constitutions must be fitted to contexts, then, logically, we must know the contexts to explain performance via formal rules. Another obvious argument against explanations based on constitutional rules is that nothing guarantees that rules will be followed in practice. Indeed, if the rules express utilitarian choices, they will not even be constant but will themselves express the waxing and waning of politicians' fortunes and/or societal forces, and they thus will explain only eccentric patterns of performance. This point does not imply that constitutional rules have no consequences. It means that to know their consequences much more must be known that goes deeper than formal rules.

Support

Constitutional arrangements will be binding on agents only if considered legitimate. Support for a political order thus is a "deeper" level of explanation than formal rules. The latter will have consequences of their own for performance, but not unless supported and observed. This is simple. However, complications arise from the fact that support varies not only extensively but also by the depth, or level, of supportive attitudes and thus their reliability over time.

Easton's (1965, pt. III) familiar distinction between specific and diffuse support is particularly relevant here. Specific support is based on the delivery of desired results (e.g., good economic conditions), while diffuse support endures largely regardless of results; the former, unlike diffuse commitment, is conditional and so may be quickly granted and quickly withdrawn. Similarly, supportive attitudes may just be "momentary"—current attitudes that lack roots in history and culture and thus are unreliable. The attitudes may even just express antipathy to a former regime, not commitment to the present order—rather like protest votes. Or they may merely express expectations that a regime will achieve desired results.

The lasting success of governments clearly depends on deep, diffuse, unconditional, historically and culturally rooted legitimacy. It may be that long-term legitimacy might gradually be built on the short-term satisfaction of desired outcomes. In that case, one must of course take into account not only current attitudes toward a regime but also the extent to which it achieves expected ends, and one might do so long enough to allow support to become "rooted."

Political Culture

These remarks point to a still deeper level of explanation: the general "political culture" of a society. Support for the governmental order, diffuse or specific, is an aspect of that culture, but it is coupled with numerous other aspects of culture that are also related to overall performance. Political culture, as it affects the performance of democracies, is itself a syndrome.

I use the concept of political culture here in the sense it originally was given by Almond and Verba (1963), as elaborated by many others, including Thompson et al. (1990) and myself (especially in 1988, 1996, and 1997). Political cultures consist of general "orientations" toward "political objects" (the political order, oneself as a member of it, others as members of it) prevalent in a society, the orientations being formed by processes of socialization that link generations. Such general orientations provide molds, as it were, that particular attitudes and patterns of behavior must fit, that shape them, and that give coherence to sets of attitudes and behaviors. They are, according to Thompson et al. something like general political "ways of life," not merely particular attitudes toward particular policies or indeed values.

A telling set of facts that points especially strongly to the need for an explanation deeper than support is provided by interwar experience in Europe. Failures of democratic regimes occurred widely during this period, but in no case because of lack of majority preferences for democratic government. Consider the Weimar Republic. Toward its end, in two elections in 1932, it came closer than any of the other failed European democracies to broad electoral support for antidemocratic parties. However, from the start, the democratic constitutional order devised after World War I was supported by a very large majority of the public and of political elites;[7] the so-called Weimar coalition of parties always received large majorities in elections; even in the last two the prodemocratic Weimar parties still predominated, and the antidemocratic forces *lost* support in the second election of 1932, the last before the end. Was this support for Weimar democracy merely "conditional"? Hardly, since it was granted despite disastrous economic conditions and much political turmoil in the period 1919–25, and again in 1930–32.[8]

The best inference is that Germany lacked a more general culture appropriate for democracy. Such a culture was required not just for dependable support; equally important, it was also required for the ability to operate the supported order effectively. Constitutional and unconstitutional dictators achieved power in Germany and other European democracies when, in the face of economic crisis and wide public disorder, democratic governments, using normal procedures, were paralyzed. Governments are never so unconditionally supported that they need not even govern to retain legitimacy, and of course steering and directing is their irreducible function. On much of the continent, under severe stress, governing largely was accomplished only by surrendering power to dictators exercising *plein pouvoir*. In effect, the dictators governed as much by abdication as by the seizure of power.

What, then, are the traits of political cultures appropriate for democracy? Two hypotheses about this seem well established. One is the "civic culture hypothesis" propounded by Almond and Verba (1963). This says, in gist, that a mixed political culture, consisting of elements that at first glance may seem inconsistent, is required. Participatory orientations are an important element of the culture, but so are "subject" orientations (which involve compliance) and "parochial" orientations (which denote detachment from the polity). The argument, on extensive evidence, is that these different orientations must exist both in segments of populations and in the same individuals. The underlying rationale for the hypothesis is that democratic governments are not just systems of public inclusion and participation but remain governments that must discharge the functions for which governments exist. Their effectiveness thus requires both attitudes of compliance and attitudes that limit the load of demands on government.

The fact that democratic governments must govern also accounts for the second hypothesis: the "ideologism hypothesis." This says that an "ideological" style of thinking and acting is inimical to effective democracy, while a nonideological style is conducive to it.

An ideological style may be broadly distinguished from a "pragmatic" style. The principal differences between the two styles have been elucidated best, in my view, by Putnam (1973, 31–63), in a comparative study of British and Italian legislative and bureaucratic elites. The following are basic differences between the two styles as I see them, based on these studies:[9]

> Ideologists think about politics deductively, pragmatists do not. The beliefs of ideologists derive from some central, underlying belief, or set of related beliefs, forming a unified deductive "system." The beliefs of pragmatists are less logically related, more tied to special situations, and more improvised to suit the situations. This difference between the two styles is generally regarded as the fundamental difference on which others load.
>
> The belief systems of ideologists are "comprehensive," because they are based on central beliefs that are considered applicable to all situations. Pragmatists think and act in a piecemeal fashion.
>
> Ideologists hold their political beliefs dogmatically, as based on abso-

lutely valid premises; they follow orthodoxy and see other beliefs as heterodox. Pragmatists are less concerned with the abstract validity of policies than with their usefulness.

Ideologists "moralize" issues on the basis of normative dogma. Pragmatists treat problems and issues as mainly technical in character.

Ideologists tend to base beliefs and preferences on general theories of history. Pragmatists are concerned only with the here and now.

Pragmatists tend to make political acceptability a criterion of good policy, ideologists do not.

Pragmatists put emphasis on the costs of policies as criteria of their desirability. Ideologists tend to ignore costs on the ground of higher principles.

A rather simple train of reasoning underlies the ideologism hypothesis. Effective decision making in democracies always requires bargaining and compromise; this in turn requires tolerance toward adversaries and a certain skepticism toward one's own beliefs; and tolerance and skepticism will not be associated with thinking in terms of deductive validity, orthodoxy and heterodoxy. Thus, decisional efficacy will be low where the ideological style is typical.

If policy decisions are made without regard for the particularities of situations and costs, they are likely to be ineffective in the "real" world. This is particularly so if specific situations are interpreted through some abstract theory about the nature of history. Moreover, if policies fail, ideologists are precluded from blaming their premises, since these are absolute; therefore, they are likely to blame (and persecute) scapegoats instead of learning from experience. Pragmatists, on the other hand, will try some other way that might work better.

Authority Culture

Political scientists will be familiar with the idea of political culture. They will not be as familiar with the idea of a more general "authority culture" in societies. That culture involves general orientations toward governance and direction, superordination and subordination, not just orientations toward the polity. Political culture in the narrower sense can be regarded as embedded in such a more general authority culture. This is necessarily so on culturalist premises, since most people's experiences with authority do not involve government nearly as much as family, school, workplace, or association.

The idea that societies have general authority cultures at a deeper level than their specifically political cultures is logically implied by congruence theory, as explained in chapter 1. The congruence hypothesis does not imply that the authority cultures of societies are always monotonic. As with political culture, indeed anything cultural, societies may be characterized by fragmented authority cultures that may even coexist in contradiction. The hypothesis, as we saw in chapter 1, only implies that governmental performance will be impaired to the extent that the components of authority cultures are dissimilar. Further, if "mixed" political cultures are the most appropriate for democracies, then the hypothesis also implies that mixed general authority cultures are appropriate for them, as posited in the "balanced disparities" hypothesis explained in chapter 1.

Since congruence theory, and thus the idea of authority cultures and their role as conditions of governmental performance, have been explained at length in that chapter, I will say no more about the subject now. However I will come back to the congruence condition shortly, to explain why it should be considered to have a special role among the conditions of democracy.

The Democratic Society

It should go without saying that polities are embedded in overall societies. In political science we distinguish between the political and other aspects of society "analytically," but analytical distinctions, by definition, are artificial: merely conceptual and used for convenience. Societies are "seamless webs," as has been said about history. No one can really pinpoint a time when, for example, the Middle Ages ended and the Renaissance began. In the same way, there is no real boundary where politics ends and nonpolitical society begins. In view of this, it would be truly astonishing if the general social environments of governments did not have important effects on their performance.

There has been much discussion in this volume about the relative merits of endogenous versus exogenous explanations of performance. In general, the writers agree that it would be advisable not to choose between them. If polities are not isolated islands in societies, detached from the social mainland by real and rigid boundaries, this surely is the sensible tack to take; and if democracy can have "roots," it surely must be in society, not just in the print of constitutions. The real problem, then, is not which kind of explanation to "privilege" but how to treat their conjunction.

True, much has been made recently of the "autonomy of the State." If by that is meant that governments are not mere expressions of socio-economic conditions and that they can determine such conditions instead of only being conditioned by them, then amen. But strong dissent if the expression means that governments are immune from social conditioning. Perhaps combining endogenous and exogenous explanatory conditions should be avoided because it sacrifices "parsimony," but this is not necessarily so. It depends on how they are combined; and, anyway, parsimony as a scientific value is always relative to other considerations, including explanatory power (or, as Popperians say, "empirical content").[10]

A great many social "correlates" of democracy have been posited—in fact, about all that are imaginable. Here I will mention those on which there is some convergence in democratic theory, on evidence and/or reasoning. No doubt, actual democracies will not score high in regard to all of the correlates, and some correlates can never be satisfied fully.[11] However, as stated, the better the performance of democracies, the more the societies in which they exist should resemble an imaginary society that is "ideal" for democracy, as specified in pertinent hypotheses.

One of the best-established hypotheses about the performance of democracies says that *the success of democracy is associated with a high level of economic development.*[12]

This hypothesis has been investigated very extensively,[13] probably more extensively than any other in democratic theory. For the most part, the hypothesis has been strongly supported by research, but it also has encountered difficulties. For instance, the hypothesis seems to hold categorically only at the low or high extremes of economic development. In between, it seems, almost any kind of government may turn up, although it has been argued recently that this has been due largely to a kind of "structural lag"—that is, in many cases it has taken time (until the current wave of democratization) for political structures to "catch up" with levels of economic development.[14] Another difficulty is that the hypothesis seems to hold better if, for economic development, we substitute a much more general notion, "quality of life," which contains economic development but also other conditions. These, however, are important difficulties only if we think in purely causal terms. By now, we know almost certainly (about as certainly as anything inductive is ever known) that level of economic development is an important ingredient of the democratic syndrome.

The level-of-economic-development hypothesis originally came coupled with another that says that *the success of democracy is associated with a slow rate of economic development.* This hypothesis has not been much investigated compared with the other. Probably this is due in large part to perceived measurement problems and the current fixation in political science on quantitative exactitude.[15] However, the rate hypothesis, as explained in the original (Lipset 1960), made just as much sense as the level hypothesis. It also fits well with other well-established conditions of successful democracy, particularly those that generally posit advantages for continuity and gradual development in general. In the ideal democratic society, then, level of economic development will be high as a result of slow and prolonged growth.

A hypothesis about economic structure that is now widely advanced is that *liberal democracies are associated with (perhaps require) market economies*. This statement may seem truistic, in that a monolithic command economy can hardly be conducted by democratic means. (In fact, it probably cannot be conducted by any political system significantly short of totalitarianism.) However, the hypothesis does raise an important question: whether a full market economy must always precede or develop in conjunction with a democratic polity, or whether, for the sake of limiting burdens of contriving and enduring change, its development can be delayed or slowed while political democracy is being constructed. It also raises the question of just how much market freedom democracy requires. Certainly democracy has been compatible with a good deal of central economic planning and direction and with welfare-state distributive policies. Democracy may, in fact, be most compatible with hybrid economies that deviate greatly from the model of the pure market economy.

One should also note that market economies seem to have been "neutral" in regard to governmental structure, short of totalitarian autocracy. As pointed out in chapter 10, market economies are associated not only with successful democracies but also with authoritarian regimes and failed democracies. No doubt markets are part of the democratic syndrome, but in what ways exactly and to what extent still are open questions.

A hypothesis established just about as strongly as the level-of-economic-development hypothesis says that *successful democracy is associated with the existence in society of a large number of voluntary associations and much membership and participation in them.* The first to point out this association and to explain it was de Tocqueville. Still the best (though outdated) summary treatment of the extensive evidence concerning the hypothesis is to be found in Kornhauser (1959), and the single most convincing empirical study supporting it is Putnam's (1993). The hypothesis also has turned up as an extension of, or as implied in, others—for instance, the civic-culture and the congruence hypotheses. Our knowledge of the hypothesis, as with the economic development hypothesis, approaches certainty about as closely as is possible.

In somewhat more general terms, we could say that *successful democracy is associated with strong "civil society,"* that is, the existence of any and all participatory organized life intermediate between the central state and its individual members. Civil society in this sense would include not just voluntary associations in the conventional sense but also autonomous and participatory local governments, firms that allow workers' participation in management, self-directing shop floors, homeowners' associations, and a great variety of clubs and leagues. Putnam has explained the association between the efficacy of democracy and group life through the concept of "social capital," which means having the skills and habits required for effectively participating in cooperative decision making, for forming collaborative coalitions and producing agreement out of opposition. Obviously, democracies require such habits and abilities in high degrees, and Putnam argues, surely with compelling reason, that they can only be acquired by learning from actually participating in collective life.

An even more general hypothesis comprises this civil society hypothesis but enlarges it. It says that *successful democracy occurs in societies organized on the basis of horizontal (or cooperative), not vertical (or hierarchical) social relationships.* Horizontal relationships can be regarded as the basic "atomic" components of democratic societies, as participatory groups might be regarded as their "molecular" units; and the latter are unthinkable without a basis in the former. There are societies in which the molecular building blocks are not collaborative but hierarchic dyadic relationships, typically patron-client relationships. If, in these, you want something, you use a patron to obtain it for you, in exchange for goods and services rendered to the patron. At the core of such "exchanges" are subservience and dominance, not cooperation. Patrons are regarded as "higher" people who possess powers, knowledge, and connections needed to get things (jobs, justice, etc.) that ordinary people cannot acquire for themselves—hence their subservience. In horizontally organized societies, on the other hand, you use cooperation with others to attain desired ends—symmetrical, not asymmetrical, exchanges.

We should mention another commonly held hypothesis in connection with the group, civil society, and horizontal relationship hypotheses—namely, that the democratic society is characterized by a great deal of "individualism." This hypothesis is not italicized here because, on the basis of the other hypotheses, one should strongly dissent from it. None of these hypotheses is consistent with social "atomization." Democratic societies are collaborative, and democratic citizens pursue collective benefits. In fact, overwhelming evidence indicates the effect that atomized societies consisting of isolated individuals—"mass societies"—breed political extremism, even totalitarian dictatorships.[16] This point, it should be noted, is also highly relevant to the evaluation of the democracy-markets nexus, for reasons discussed in chapter 10.

Another hypothesis is related to this point. It is widely agreed, and strongly supported by evidence and reasoning, that *democratic societies are characterized by high social trust.* They cannot be characterized by the assumption that everyone is out only for egoistic interest, so that everyone is a threat to everyone else. Rather, they should contain strong cultural norms that constrain means used for interest seeking and that especially prohibit deceptions or intimidation. Cooperative relationships and groups and the collective pursuit of collective benefits obviously suppose trust and collaboration. Democratic societies do not necessarily "presuppose" them in any strictly causal sense. It is more likely that trust and collaboration have a reciprocal relationship. The ideal democratic society thus is characterized by a virtuous cycle in which trust, cooperation, and group life constantly reinforce one another; that circle, of course, can become a vicious circle if impaired at any point. Trust and the propensity to cooperate themselves are core aspects of a general syndrome of behavioral propensities that are associated with successful democracy, such as tolerance, self-discipline (inner restraints on egotism), acceptance of ambivalence and disagreement, and competition without conflict.

A hypothesis that long played a major role in democratic theory is that *the performance of democracy is associated with the dominant religious order of society.* This hypothesis seems almost to have dropped out of democratic theory—unaccountably so, because of the large role played in such theory by traits of culture and because religion in most societies has been fundamental to the formation of culture; even where it has ceased to be the core of culture, religion has left important sediments in general culture and so, presumably, important consequences for democracy. Originally, the hypothesis referred to Catholic versus Protestant cultures and was inspired mainly by experiences with democracy in Southern Europe and France. One does not hear much about the deleterious consequences of Catholicism any longer, perhaps because of changes in its structure and doctrines. However, much the same point now is often made in country and regional studies about other religions or quasi-religious belief systems—for instance, Confucianism and Islam.

Another important and fundamental hypothesis about the traits of democratic societies is that *successful democracies are associated with high levels of equality in all aspects of social life.* This hypothesis has been most strongly and cogently argued by de Tocqueville, along with much else in democratic theory. The hypothesis can be considered even more fundamental in his scheme of explanation than the group-hypothesis because democracy, to de Tocqueville, meant social equality in all its aspects. It stood for a general animating "spirit" of society that was manifested in equality of political participation but, as necessary correlates, in other kinds of equality as well, especially equality of wealth, status, and education. Of course, democratic society as a society of equals is something that can only be more or less approximated; and clearly democracy can tolerate fairly considerable degrees of inequality. However, these seem best tolerated in what Almond and Verba (1963) called "deferential civic cultures" (such as Britain's) or other kinds of limited democracies; and, in all cases, there are strict limits on inequalities that do not undermine democracy. From this standpoint, such tendencies as increasing equality of the sexes, economic leveling, and greatly expanded higher education all indicate the continued development of democracy where it is already well established.

From the equality hypothesis it follows that, contrary to widely held belief, an emphasis on rewards purely for merit is only compatible with democracy within considerable limits. After all, aristocratic and oligarchic orders were based on supposed merit. To be sure, aristocratic merit in traditional European society was merit by ascriptive status, but this is not the only possible basis for aristocracy. Note that the original Greek idea of aristocracy was government by the *aristoi*, the "best," and this was always contrasted by the Greeks with leveled democracy in which the mass predominated. In modern democracies, high scores on admission exams are not required for the right to have a vote nor for achieving office (obviously); nor are extra votes awarded for educational achievement, as they used to be in Britain to certain university graduates. Popular democracy is, so to speak, the most extreme form of affirmative action. Reward by merit—any kind of merit—leads easily to all sorts of social inequalities, and every inequality potentially taints political equality, which is the essence of democracy.

Democracy and what has been called "meritocracy"[17] may go hand in hand in general social development, but they are hardly mutually reinforcing. Rather, they are more like two opposite faces of a single coin. The ultimate meritocracy, in fact, is not democracy but bureaucracy, with its objective qualifying exams, promotions and status by performance, impersonal criteria of all kinds, and also rigid hierarchy and blind submission to superiors.

Another long-argued hypothesis—one that may possibly be related to the equality hypothesis—says that *the success of democracy is associated with the degree of homogeneity in a society's population.* This hypothesis was the principal way in which "exogenous" society was brought into political explanation during the long dominance of formal-legal explanations. It seemed to make obvious sense, for the more people are alike, the less they are likely to have divergent interests, disagreements, and conflicts, and the easier it will be to aggregate interests into stable coalitions and accepted policies. The hypothesis is still commonly argued about certain countries that have had conspicuously successful democracies (especially the Scandinavian countries). However, since all large populations are bound to contain substantial dissimilarities, it has gradually been transformed into another, which singles out particular kinds of heterogeneities as fateful for democracy.

This hypothesis says that *successful democracies are unlikely to exist in plural societies.* "Plural societies" are societies divided along ethnic, religious, or linguistic lines, these differences being considered especially divisive and hard to reconcile—sources of bitter contention that sometimes call into question the very nature of the political community. It should be noted, however, that it is now common to argue, à la Lijphart, that plural societies can sustain democracy if their elites are committed to cooperation and if certain constitutional devices are used. On the other hand, it has also been conceded that democracy only works in plural societies if it is highly limited by structural devices, like Grand Coalitions and privileges to minorities, that offset its cleavages but also compromise its "democraticness."

Summary

The "successful democracy syndrome" can now be summarized. *Endogenously,* it comprises a constitutional order that is well adapted to the social and cultural characteristics of the larger society; it developed gradually and by grafting onto predemocratic society; it is widely supported as legitimate, and it has a civic (mixed) and nonideological political culture. *Exogenously,* the polity is embedded in a society that has a highly developed economy as a result of a slow rate of economic growth; it has a market or mixed economy; it contains numerous organized groups that have large memberships, and it has in a more general sense a strong "civil society"; its basic building blocks are horizontal social relationships; its members trust one another, are tolerant, restrict egotistic action, and accept disagreements; its culture is not based on an authoritarian religion or quasi-religion; it is a highly leveled society; and it is not a "plural society."

The Special Role of Congruence

It will be noticed that I have omitted one condition from this summary—namely, a coherent, or congruent, authority culture. I have done this because the congruence variable, in my view, is not coequal with the other conditions because it plays a special role in the democracy syndrome.

I have argued here that no particular aspect of the syndrome should be regarded as privileged over others—that is, considered to give valid explanations while others do not or even to have strong effects while others have only weak ones. No particular element of any syndrome should ever be so regarded; it is the overall syndrome that counts as if it were, logically, a single variable. For instance, in explaining the thriving of plants one would not want to single out, say, water explanations over light explanations, over fertilizer, soil, seed, or gardening-care explanations. It takes compounds of conditions to make plants thrive, or people healthy, or polities stable and effective. When a particular entity does badly, of course, the difficulty may lie in one or another aspect of the compound, but failures or weaknesses in general may result from any aspect of the syndrome.

This may seem inconsistent with my emphasis, in chapter 1, on the congruence of authority patterns as a special basis of explanation. The congruence hypothesis, however, is not treated as special because it is valid while other hypotheses are not. Rather, it is singled out because it is not just a component part of the democracy syndrome alongside others. Its special role is to tie the syndrome together so that it is more than just a random aggregate of conditions. Put otherwise, its function is to explain why and how the various aspects of the syndrome have consequences for the fate of democracies.

The congruence condition seems to me to do this in two ways, both of which were discussed in chapter 1 but which bear repeating. In the first place, congruence is a "relational" (or "field") variable that combines exogenous and endogenous variables in a unified package. It overcomes perhaps the most bothersome problem in explaining the performance of democracies—whether to emphasize their internal structure or external context, when it is obvious that they depend on both, in some systematic way. Second, congruence is treated as the consideration that governs the extent to which, and the conditions under which, other conditions in the syndrome affect the overall performance of governments—why they have a certain explanatory power and not more. It is, as stated in chapter 1, a "higher-order" theory; as such, it unifies other hypotheses but does not impugn or replace them. In the original statement of the theory, I tried to demonstrate this point in regard to four conditions: religion, level of economic development, rate of economic development, and the civil society hypothesis. The analyses there still strike me as sensible, but showing how the whole syndrome of conditions may be filtered through the congruence variable is an unfinished task. This task is considerable and may result in failure, for congruence theory still is not as solidly established as it should be. Epistemologically, it is a candidate theory like others and must be tested independently.

An important point should now be added. The hypotheses I have summarized identify "empirical regularities" that are well supported by evidence. However, if indeed the conditions to which they refer are connected with the performance of democracies via the congruence condition—if their essential role is to promote or hinder congruence in democracies—then it is conceivable that a significant degree of congruence might be found even where other conditions are not satisfied to any great extent. This may not be likely, but it is *conceivable*.

Consistent with the general argument here, it is likely to occur only in what one might call "minimal" democracies. An example of minimal democracy is what might be called "Schumpeterian" democracy, a system based on electoral competition between elites but lacking most other traits generally associated with liberal democracy. There are other forms of minimal, or at least limited, democracy, too; and one of these, as I will argue in the next section, may be particularly promising for the future of democracy in Russia.

Russia and the Democracy Syndrome

The syndrome of conditions outlined here should help in arriving at a reasoned prognosis of the likely outcome of any process of democratization, and it can also be a basis for thoughtful policy in building democracy. It represents the current "state of the art" in democratic theory, and it will therefore undergo changes as knowledge advances. Such as it is, however, it can be used to arrive systematically at a prognosis for the future of Russian democratization, using information furnished in this book. This might tell us something both about Russia and about the state of contemporary democratic theory.

Support

I will start with the question of support for democracy, since lack of it probably would make further discussion superfluous. Unfortunately, the picture in regard to it is fuzzy.

A great deal of survey research has been done since 1990 to elicit Russian attitudes toward democracy and its institutional correlates (e.g., political parties). Reisinger (in chap. 6) refers to thirty publications based on such research for the period 1991–96, and several essays in this book have referred to that literature extensively (Fleron in chap. 2; Fleron and Ahl in chap. 11; Reisinger in chaps. 6 and 9; and Hoffmann in chap. 4).[18] The researches converge on the finding—at first quite unexpected given Russia's past—that democracy there in fact has broad popular support.

The very fact that the results converge creates a presumption that they reveal a reservoir of genuine legitimacy for democracy. However, there are stronger reasons for doubts about this. Survey researches, like all empirical methods, have intrinsic shortcomings, but these are not the issue here. Rather, doubts arise from the survey findings themselves.

An especially noteworthy fact is that responses favorable to democracy have been declining since 1992. At a minimum, this suggests that positive attitudes toward democracy were not deeply rooted, nor could one reasonably have expected them to be after such a short time. More likely, the responses indicated alienation from the old order rather than solid attachment to the new; thus, the quick erosion of support as great expectations from the change of orders were, inevitably, disappointed. Relative deprivation theory would lead us to expect a progressively wider and deeper erosion of support on this basis in the future. If that expectation is confirmed, then we can probably safely ignore the initial survey findings altogether.

Certainly the support indicated by the surveys was not "diffuse." This emerges clearly in the facts that democratic processes have not been valued in themselves and that, likewise, there has been little valuation of intrinsic aspects of democracy such as political pluralism or freedom to criticize. Democracy is supported mainly as a means to other valued ends, especially economic well-being and "social rights." In fact, democracy, to Russians, seems to *mean* affluence and social rights. For this reason, the new order, to retain support, must "deliver"—live up to social and economic expectations—which hardly is possible in conditions of upheaval and the fundamental reordering of society.

There is a more subtle sense, rooted deeply in Russian history, in which the Russian conception of democracy differs from ours. The Russian conception, as Hoffmann argues in chapter 4, seems strongly based on the idea of *sobornost*, which, as I understand it, means something close to Rousseau's General Will: the collective, "correct," consensual will of the collectivity per se, not just of some competing segment or coalition, even if a majority. It means genuinely collective will, not pluralism, and that conception of democracy has made trouble for working democracy from the start (in the French Revolution).

The idea is associated particularly with the *mir*, the village commune, which has often been considered a deeply rooted cultural basis for democracy in Russia. The decision-making structure of the traditional village commune was a direct democracy of the heads of families—that is, the corporate cells of village society. Decisions were made by deliberations aimed at consensus, and, once made, were to be treated as the "real" preferences of all, as if made by themselves. In very broad terms, the village democracy of the *mir* was a direct democracy of discussion and deliberation, but not of tolerance of dissent or special interests.

The idea of *sobornost* may seem superdemocratic, and abstractly it is; but in an advanced, complex, large modern nation it is likely to have nondemocratic effects. Modern democracy, unlike traditional village democracy, in practice means nothing if not plural, competing interests and the formation of "winning coalitions" among these, often on a cynical basis, and this is almost the reverse of *sobornost*. Under modern conditions that idea might indeed furnish a basis for government, but this would be very different from democracy as we conceive it. The idea of *sobornost* can in fact readily support the rule of autocrats, indeed of totalitarian leaders who purport to speak for the people as an undifferentiated mass. Democracy as it is likely to work in complex, large modern societies will probably only alienate support based on the idea of *sobornost*.

Still another special doubt about the survey responses comes from the well-established conception of a prevalent "dual personality" among Russians.[19] This involves a disjunction between public and private personae, traceable to the tsarist past and strongly reinforced by the communist experience. The public persona expresses attachment to perceived "official" values, while the private persona does not act in accordance with these values, even scoffs at them. Among Russians, so the argument goes, exists a "double morality," a "divided consciousness," "cross-thinking." The survey responses, needless to say, will have tapped the public pose of Russian respondents, not the private reality. They are likely to express only people's conceptions of "correct" responses (Fleron 1996b).

Political Culture

This point raises a critical question. Do we have any reason to think that current support for democracy in Russia expresses something deep in the society's political culture rather than ephemeral responses to questions asked under passing conditions?

A very important argument about this has been made by Nikolai Petro (1995) in the aptly titled *The Rebirth of Russian Democracy*. Petro dissents sharply from the standard interpretation of Russia's historic political culture. This interpretation considers the culture to be captured in the formula Orthodoxy, Autocracy, and Nationality; it equates it with the lack of significant institutional restraints on leaders, generally personalistic authority, and bureaucratic servility. Petro argues, on the contrary, that *two* political cultures have existed side by side in Russia for centuries—one autocratic, the other an "alternative culture" of democracy. Support for democracy on this basis is not shallow and new but stems from the reemergence of a strain long and deeply ingrained in Russia's culture.

The alternative democratic culture manifested itself in the *zemskie sobory*—popular assemblies dating to the sixteenth century. It emerged in the elected legislative commission of Catherine the Great's reign. It emerged again in the *zemstvos* of the nineteenth century—elected bodies representing landowners, peasants, and inhabitants of cities. It provided the spirit of the Duma of 1905 and, initially, of the Communist revolution. During the communist period, as before, the culture was transmitted in the family, in other intimate arenas of private life, in underground literature, in "subversive" art, and the like—in the "Russian psyche." It simply surfaced once again, largely intact, first under Gorbachev, then, more fully, in and after 1990.

Is Petro's thesis convincing? There can be no doubt about its facticity, but his interpretation of the facts seems to me doubtful. An alternative interpretation that I consider better is that Russia has a dominant political culture, the culture of autocracy, and also a subordinate reformist culture. The latter emerges periodically, but only in relatively short-lived reactions against failures of the dominant culture. It is neither deeply rooted nor generally shared, its lack of depth being indicated by the fact that it has always been difficult to institutionalize. As Fleron and Ahl point out in chapter 11, the autocratic strain has had much greater staying power; and Hoffmann notes in chapter 4 that there have been thirteen attempts at reforming autocracy since the sixteenth century, all of them reversed or faded away.

What Petro considers to be an alternative culture thus has not been much of an alternative. It is probably better considered to be a "counterculture" of periodic protest by the disaffected rather than as a genuine alternative set of liberal orientations throughout either the elite or the public. Even if Petro is right in arguing that democracy has "reemerged" in Russia, history strongly suggests that it probably will not last long.

The outlook for stable democracy in Russia would not be rosy even if there were two coequal strains in Russian political culture. The likely course of events then would be pendulum swings between two unreconciled political orders, as in France from the Revolution to the Fifth Republic.

One might find some reassurance in the civic culture hypothesis (and the balanced disparities hypothesis discussed in chap. 1), which holds that a compound of democratic and nondemocratic attitudes is healthy for democracy. However, the civic culture hypothesis says that participant, subject, and parochial orientations should *coincide* in society and in individuals, not that the civic compound may consist of periodic swings between tuning into and tuning out of politics, knuckling under and rebelling. The hypothesis certainly does not say that subject orientations may be greatly dominant in the compound or that it may be a mix of autocratic domination, servile bureaucracy, and rebellious dissidence. There are explosive as well as stable compounds.

The hypothesis that a substantially "idealistic" political culture also is inimical to successful democracy does not offer more hope in the case of Russia. The authors of this book seem to agree than "synoptic" thinking is typical in Russia. Marxist-Leninist doctrine certainly epitomized that mode of thinking, and the mode of thinking probably persists even if the specific contents of Marxist-Leninism are discredited. More subtly, aspects of the idea of *sobornost* may also fit into synoptic thinking—for instance, the belief that there are single "correct" decisions, that these somehow become revealed, and that dissent from them is reprehensible. Nonideological thinking, as we saw, does not involve conceptions of abstract, absolute correctness or even of consistency in action but rather improvisation without constraint of doctrine as situations unfold. It does not accommodate the conception of an undifferentiated, sacred General Will.

Whether there is, in fact, a general tendency to think synoptically in Russia can be tested in the realm of economic policy. Synoptic thinking would induce the rigid pursuit of "market" policies, regardless of failures in practice, just as the collective idea once decided such policies in the face of obtrusive facts. This seems to be happening now. Western "capitalist" societies (though not their right wings in politics or certain professional economists who themselves are given to synoptic thinking) have been more circumspect about "free markets," more willing to be theoretically inconsistent in regard to them, and more willing to let "mixed" economies emerge from practical responses to specific problems. Synoptic thought about democracy is likely to hinder a similar approach to the economy in Russia, and, if so, is also likely to hinder the emergence of a benignly mixed, nondoctrinaire democratic civic culture in Russia.

The Process of Change

As there are explosive compounds, so there are "explosive" processes of change, and the change to democracy in Russia, according to the pertinent hypotheses, is a model of what social and political change should not be to succeed.

The fundamental hypothesis—that gradual and incremental change is desirable and rapid transformation is not—has already been violated dramatically in Russia. The perestroika period promised a process of gradual change toward a liberal regime, but the present process has aimed at immediate full-scale democracy. The result has been something close to chaos. Present-day Russia seems to confirm the hypothesis that highly discontinuous change leads only to a certain "formlessness" of structure (Eckstein 1988).

Something that is formless, ipso facto, is not predictable. Rather than having any kind of probable outcome, formlessness is manifested in great swings between inconsistent states and by much ambivalence and ambiguity.

The only certainty in formlessness is that *ultimately* some institutionalized order will emerge from it, but one cannot foresee its nature or how long it will take to emerge.

How do people manage to live with social formlessness? A typical response to it (as to extreme despotism) is what Merton (1957, 153–3, 188–9) has called "retreatist" behavior: withdrawal into small private networks of kin or friends, or indeed into some purely personal world detached from social life (as children, when threatened, tend to withdraw into a daydream world). In this condition, a coherent central government may seem to exist on paper (constitutional or journalistic), but practical life occurs mainly in small, parochial contexts.

The most dramatic example of formlessness in social and political life probably was the state of Europe after the disintegration of the Roman Empire and before the emergence of a settled feudal order. The so-called Dark Ages appear "dark" (to historians) because it is hard to discern any settled social form in them. Roman emperors still existed; life seemed to go on as before; but, in practical terms, it was confined more and more to small-scale units and personalistic ties between prefeudal patrons and their clients. In this world, the latter accepted subordination for the sake of security in a society of unchecked marauders, so that the building blocks of society increasingly became small groups having "contractual" obligations to petty "barons." I do not argue that this is also to be the fate of the ex-Soviet empire in Russia, but the case of Rome and the Dark Ages does provide an exaggerated model of what it might become, perhaps in some respects already has become, before a new coherent order has developed.

In this condition syncretic change—grafting a new order on the old—is possible only to a very limited extent; nor are there available, intact old elites with whom to make pacts to ensure smooth, uncontested transition. Of course, the old order and elites may reemerge from the ruins of social and political life. This, in fact, seems the most likely outcome, for three reasons: former elites still have the preponderance of human capital; old ways of doing things, through cultural inertia, remain familiar alternatives to still chaotic new ways of behaving; and regression is a typical general reaction to inordinate stress.

The sequence hypothesis—that "critical" political changes should be accomplished one at a time and in a particular order—also is violated dramatically in the Russian case. The always critical issue of national identity has to be dealt with because of secessions, rebellion (as in Chechnya), and the claims of ethnic and religious minorities (for Russia is a prototypical plural society). At the same time that critical problems of national identity are faced, so is the problem of working out a new "regime," even a new society. So also are fundamental issues of material distribution, indeed the very nature of the economic order— which also manifests formlessness, perhaps even more extreme than the political variety.

The prototypical case in point for the sequence hypothesis was always Germany after unification. Present-day Russia has, if anything, even greater critical problems to resolve simultaneously. From this, as in Germany, complex and deep political cleavages, hence splintered (themselves "formless"?) multiparty systems that include extremist parties, are likely to emerge. As a result, cooperative coalitions, without which democracy simply cannot work, will be virtually impossible to form.

The Socioeconomic Context

Democracy has always been considered part of a general syndrome of "modernity." Russia certainly is a "modern" country in most respects, despite somewhat uneven development in different sectors of society and a good deal of economic decline in recent years. It is certainly nothing like a Third World country. From this, however, it does not follow that successful democracy is practically assured—*pace* Huntington's (1991) "catching up" hypothesis, which, as will be recalled, says that if economic development is advanced, then democracy will occur, though sometimes only after a certain lag time. It is not necessary for all aspects of a syndrome to coexist, even if one may suppose that any aspect of a syndrome probably favors the existence of others. Also, of course, modernity is a very general "form" that can accommodate a great variety of "content."

Certain particulars of Russian modernity hardly are promising for democracy. One of these, much commented on in this book, is the ex-

treme weakness of civil society—the lack of associational life, of organized groups intermediary between the state and individuals. A result
of the totalitarian state, as might be expected, has been an atomized
society—a "mass society"—which differs from pluralistic society both
in structure and effects. The most noteworthy of its effects is that atomized individuals, on much evidence,[20] have an affinity for political extremism and support of despotic rule, whereas organized individuals
tend to be moderate and liberal.

Russian society does have "molecular" building blocks, as it must
have, but these, as might be expected, are mainly of a kind consistent
with individual atomization. As pointed out by Hoffmann in chapter
4 and Reisinger in chapter 5, the cells of society tend to be patron-client
relationships that link isolated individuals, not horizontal cooperative
relations between connected individuals. Patron-client relations even
seem to play a large role within the public bureaucracy (which, in that
sense, is not fully bureaucratic); they also played a large role in Communist Party life. The relations can be considered an aspect of an even
more general pattern in the organization of Russian society: the fact
that, as Fleron points out in chapter 2, social relations tend to be highly
"personalistic" rather than defined by impersonal institutional norms.
Within the bosom of modernized society, therefore, Russia seems to
contain individual relationships and social building blocks more characteristic of premodern societies and of a kind considered to be hin-
drances to successful democracy.

As will be expected from this, the general personal orientations that
relate individuals with their fellows in Russia also differ from those
characteristic of successful democracies. Russians, it has been pointed
out in these pages, lack social trust; they have low tolerance for social
differences, ambiguities, and disagreements; they tend to equate these
with "disorder," while greatly valuing strict order and predictability;
and they are deficient in the self-discipline that cooperative relations
with other people always require.

The Authority Culture, the Constitutional Order, and the Question of Congruence

One thing should be evident from this discussion: short of extremely
underdeveloped societies, it would be hard to think of a less likely case
for successful democratization than Russia. Only the ancient structure
of village decision making offers a credible historic basis for democracy, which, as we saw, has ambivalent implications. Support for the
idea of democracy is at best tenuous and instrumental, it has no strong
roots in an accustomed central political culture, the current processes

of change militate against it, and the social context is inhospitable to it in almost all respects.

Just for this reason, however, Russia might provide a very strong test of congruence theory—a "crucial test," as I have defined it elsewhere (Eckstein 1979a). Just about all pertinent hypotheses lead to the prediction that democratization will fail in Russia. Thus, if political reform fails for the fourteenth time in four centuries, the current body of democratic theory (including the congruence hypothesis) stands, but it is not strengthened. Nothing will require better theory, and nothing will indicate ways to improve it.

But what if Russian democratization should succeed? If it could be demonstrated that, *pace* all else, this success occurred in conjunction with a significant degree of congruence between governmental and social authority patterns—a governmental order well adapted to be a term in a coherent overarching authority culture—then the congruence hypothesis would be hugely strengthened. The other hypotheses would not be "disproved," for they still identify empirical regularities related both to congruence and the performance of democracies. However, the argument that the congruence condition has a special role in the democracy syndrome, as a "filter" for the effects on democracy of other conditions, would be decisively corroborated.

Russell Bova's argument in chapter 7 is especially important for this point. Through proper constitutional engineering, says Bova, a system of government might be instituted that is somehow a congruent part of a general authority culture. If so, then, of course, success would be predicted by the congruence hypothesis. This point deserves a closer look.

If a general authority culture wholly lacks "democratic elements" (in the sense discussed in chap. 1), then no governmental order that is even minimally democratic can be congruent with it. A question that arises, therefore, is whether there are any such elements in characteristic Russian authority practices. Undoubtedly, the pervasive themes in such practices are authoritarian, autocratic, and hierarchical. However, as pointed out, the decision-making structure of the village commune was a glaring exception to this. Granted, the village commune is a thing of the past. However, as also noted, cultural orientations, through their inherent inertia, may survive as cultural "sediments" long after the conditions in which they appeared have ended. They would in that case undergo changes, but not necessarily in their essentials.

This, arguably, has in fact happened with village decision making in Russia. Bova points out that the practices of village decision making were transplanted to cities by peasant migrants. He also points out that, even under communism, it was practiced in the governance of workplaces by bodies composed of management, party, and trade union officials, as "elders" of a sort. The collective decision makers, according to Bova, related to subordinates in highly authoritarian and hierarchical ways and did not tolerate dissent; however, the point remains that the process of decision making itself had traits of direct democracy, undiluted even by elected representation.

This pattern, in the abstract, somewhat resembles Leninist "democratic centralism." In practice this was hardly democratic in any sense. However, the general *idea* of democratic centralism, perhaps intentionally conveyed by the name, may be considered to contain a democratic germ. Decisions are worked out collectively, by a process of discussion and deliberation; then the decision makers take united responsibility for them—dissent among them ceases; and collective responsibility is crystallized in a single responsible head, whose powers, however, are more nominal than real.

This, as far as it goes, could well be a broad description of cabinet government in Britain. A missing ingredient of "minimal democracy" as we think of it is, of course, the popular election of "oligarchs," but that surely could be synthesized with the idea of democratic centralism without changing its essential nature. Electoral representation, after all, is a substitute for literal self-government. Moreover, in Britain the inclusive democracy of voting rights is grafted onto institutions and orientations that antedate inclusive democracy yet are entirely compatible with it—indeed, the seeds from which inclusive democracy developed.

An important aspect of democratic centralism certainly is entirely foreign to the British practice: the exaction of strict compliance on the part of subordinates and strict limitations on dissent. Some other important things also are missing from the analogy: an integrated party system to contest elections and to alternate in office; the clear definition of supporters and opponents of the government in the legislature; a lively parliament oriented to the criticism of leaders and to holding them answerable if not accountable—a body that is oppositional but not mutinous. However, the point is not that Britain has democratic centralism but that the Russian practice of democratic centralism might contain some germ, or seed, of "democraticness" on which to base a minimally democratic polity that is a congruent part of a coherent authority culture.

In this sense, the constitutional order of 1993 seems to have some potential for being well adapted to the Russian authority culture. It is based on the conduct of elections but also locates extraordinarily strong, virtually autocratic, central powers in the president. Bova calls the system "semipresidential" in that it has some traits both of presidential government and of the parliamentary variety. However, the system could also be called "superpresidential," since, instead of balancing presidential powers with others, it gives the president just those powers that *strengthen* leaders in parliamentary systems—the power to dissolve the legislature, for example, and special powers to govern by emergency decrees, in this case even when there is no real emergency. At least a central core for developing democratic centralism thus seems to have been constituted.

It remains to be seen whether the new constitutional order will in fact develop into a full-fledged institutional order, but it is certainly conceivable that some lasting embodiment of the idea of democratic centralism might emerge from the current chaos. Essentially this would be an order of highly concentrated presidential powers, with the collective decision-making traits of democratic centralism as a basis for and constraint on these powers. The present constitution, at least, does not in itself hinder the development of an elective democratic centralism.

If the idea of democratic centralism is indeed a crucial aspect of the Russian authority culture, then one might in fact expect it to emerge in time as a fully institutional order, much like the Fifth French Republic. Originally, the Fifth Republic also originated in governmental crisis and was tailored largely to a single heroic leader. It was generally predicted that it would not survive de Gaulle's death.

But it did survive it and clearly has become a rooted institutional order. In all likelihood this occurred because the constitutional order on which it was based was well adapted to the existence of two French authority cultures by synthesizing them. So, perhaps, it might be in Russia.

A democratically centralized order obviously contains large risks and perils for democracy, most obviously the strong possibility of presidential coups. All "minimal democracy" is precarious. However, that does not mean that the order *must* fail, and it may be the only democratic order that has a reasonable chance to succeed in the short run and, possibly, to become a basis for further democratic development in the longer run.

Conclusion

Recurrent references have been made throughout this book to congruence theory, which, we think, has high potential for forecasting and explaining the outcomes of attempts to democratize. So do other hypotheses about the conditions in which democracy tends to flourish;

but if the congruence hypothesis governs the effects on democracy of other conditions, the power to predict would be greatly increased. So would the possibility of informed constitutional design, and so also the likelihood that constitutional blueprints will become full-fledged "institutions."

The catch, of course, is "if it holds." The congruence hypothesis, at present, may be highly plausible, for the reasons summarized in chapter 1, but it has not yet been strongly tested. For a long time it has been a theory in search of a strong and practicable test. The future of democracy in Russia may well furnish that test.

Notes

1. Popper (1959) uses the word *causality*, but not in the conventional sense of efficient causation, and he generally puts the word *cause* in quotation marks to denote this. He writes, "To give a *causal explanation* of an event means to deduce a statement which describes it, using as premises of the deduction one or more *universal laws*, together with certain singular statements, the *initial conditions*" (59). This is identical with what Hempel (1965) simply calls "scientific explanation," without begging questions by using the language of causality.

2. Consider this: If X, a condition of society, is associated with the occurrence of revolutions at a probability of 0.5, what does this imply for X as a "cause"? That it causes half-revolutions or perhaps half of all revolutions? The basis of the difficulty is, of course, that a certainty cannot be divided into chunks of probability.

3. I ignore the decline inherent in a plant's normal life cycle.

4. David Easton has discussed the properties and needs of "political systems" in numerous works, notably in 1965.

5. By Rein Taagepera, a political scientist and colleague who played an important role in deliberations on the new constitutional order of Estonia.

6. I consider this concept unfortunate, since the word *institution*, as used in the social sciences, long denoted a repeated pattern of actual behavior, not a blueprint, or formal prescription, for behavior that might only be honored in the breach. Moreover, numerous different definitions of the concept now abound. The version in the text is my understanding (or misunderstanding) of its meaning in gist.

7. This point is supported extensively by Bermeo (1997).

8. The argument about Weimar applies still more clearly to other European countries in which democracy failed during this period (Bermeo 1997).

9. I do not follow Putnam exactly here. However, my meaning and his coincide in essentials.

10. De Tocqueville (1966), in *Democracy in America*, combines the two kinds of conditions in his very conception of democracy. He thinks of democracy as a general condition of society, not just its polity, its defining characteristic being

equality. In the manner of Montesquieu, he argues that, to be realized in its special political sense, it must be the "spirit" of a whole society—for instance, of its distribution of wealth and education.

11. This is due to the fact that they are dimensions the poles of which are purely abstract, like zero or infinity.

12. The classic statement of the hypothesis is in Lipset (1960).

13. For an excellent summary and evaluation of work on the level-of-economic development hypothesis, see Diamond (1992).

14. By Huntington (1991).

15. Level of economic development has always been measured by easily obtainable quantities, the favorite being per capita GDP. Comparable data for rates of economic development do not exist at present but could be obtained easily—for instance, by the amount of time it took for societies to pass beyond specified thresholds of development, however these are measured.

16. See especially Kornhauser (1959).

17. The originator of this expression was Burnham (1960).

18. For references, see the chapters listed.

19. See Fleron in chapter 2 and especially White (1979, 111) and Tucker (1987, 184).

20. See especially Kornhauser (1959).

Bibliography

Ackerman, Bruce. 1991. *We The People: I Foundations*. Cambridge, MA: Harvard University Press.

Ahdieh, Robert. 1997. *Russia's Constitutional Revolution: Legal Consciousness and the Transition to Democracy, 1985–1996*. College Park, PA: Pennsylvania State University Press.

Ahl, Richard. 1997. "Values, Interests, and Political Cleavages in Post-Soviet Russia." Ph.D. diss., State University of New York, Buffalo.

Almond, Gabriel A. 1987. "The Development of Political Development." In *Understanding Political Development*, ed. Myron Weiner and Samuel P. Huntington. Boston: Little, Brown.

———. 1990a. "The Return to the State." In *A Discipline Divided: Schools and Sects in Political Science*, ed. Gabriel A. Almond. Newbury Park, CA: Sage.

———. 1990b. "The Study of Political Culture." In *A Discipline Divided: Schools and Sects in Political Science*, ed. Gabriel A. Almond. Beverly Hills, CA: Sage.

Almond, Gabriel A., and Sidney Verba. 1963. *The Civic Culture: Political Attitudes and Democracy in Five Nations*. Princeton, NJ: Princeton University Press.

———. 1980. *The Civic Culture Revisited*. Boston, MA: Little, Brown.

Anderson, Richard D., Jr., Valery I. Chervyakov, and Pavel B. Parshin. 1995. "Words Matter: Linguistic Conditions for Democracy in Russia." *Slavic Review* 54: 869–95.

Apter, David E. 1965. *The Politics of Modernization*. Chicago: University of Chicago Press.

Aristotle. 1995. *Politics*. New York: Oxford University Press.

Aron, Leon. 1995. "Russia between Revolution and Democracy." *Post-Soviet Affairs* 11: 305–39.

Aslund, Anders. 1995. *How Russia Became a Market Economy*. Washington, D.C.: Brookings Institution Press.

Baaklini, Abdo, and Helen Desfosses, eds. 1997. *Designs for Democratic Stability: Studies in Viable Constitutionalism*. Armonk, NY: Sharpe.

Bagehot, Walter. 1978. *The English Constitution*. 2d ed. London: Oxford University Press.

383

Bahry, Donna. 1993. "Society Transformed? Rethinking the Social Roots of Perestroika." *Slavic Review* 52: 512–54.

Bahry, Donna, and Brian D. Silver. 1990. "Soviet Citizen Participation on the Eve of Democratization." *American Political Science Review* 84: 821–47.

Bahry, Donna, and Lucan Way. 1994. "Citizen Activism in the Russian Transition." *Post-Soviet Affairs* 10: 330–66.

Barghoorn, Frederick C. 1965. "Soviet Russia: Orthodoxy and Adaptiveness." In *Political Culture and Political Development*, ed. Lucian W. Pye and Sidney Verba. Princeton, NJ: Princeton University Press.

Bates, Robert H. 1996. "The Death of Comparative Politics?" *APSA-CP* (Newsletter of the APSA Organized Section in Comparative Politics) 7(2): 1.

Batkin, Leonid. 1995. "The Minefield of Russian Constitutionalism: Before and after October 1993." In *Remaking Russia: Voices from Within*, ed. Heyward Isham. Armonk, NY: Sharpe.

Battle, John M. 1988. "Uskorenie, Glasnost' and Perestroika: The Pattern of Reform under Gorbachev." *Soviet Studies* 40: 367–84.

Baun, Michael J. 1995. "The Federal Republic of Germany." In *Political Culture and Constitutionalism: A Comparative Approach*, ed. Daniel P. Franklin and Michael J. Baun. Armonk, NY: Sharpe.

Beck, Carl, Frederic J. Fleron Jr., Milton Lodge, William A. Welsh, and M. George Zaninovich. 1973. *Comparative Communist Political Leadership*. New York: Mackay.

Beeson, Paul B., and Walsh McDermott, eds. 1975. *Textbook of Medicine*, 14th ed. Philadelphia: Saunders.

Bergsten, Gordon S., and Russell Bova. 1990. "Worker Power Under Communism: The Interplay of Exit and Voice." *Comparative Economic Studies* 32: 47–72.

Bermeo, Nancy. 1987. "Redemocratization and Transition Elections: A Comparison of Spain and Portugal." *Comparative Politics* 19: 213–231.

———. 1997. "Getting Mad or Going Mad: Citizens, Scarcity, and the Breakdown of Democracy in Interwar Europe." Research Monograph Series No. 7, Center for the Study of Democracy, University of California, Irvine.

Berry, William D. 1993. *Understanding Regression Assumptions*. Newbury Park, CA: Sage.

Binder, Leonard, et al. 1971. *Crises and Sequences in Political Development*. Princeton, NJ: Princeton University Press.

Binmore, Ken, Martin J. Osborne, and Ariel Rubinstein. 1992. "Noncooperative Models of Bargaining." In *Handbook of Game Theory*, vol. 1, ed. Robert J. Aumann and Sergiu Hart. Amsterdam: Elsevier Science.

Bodley, J. E. C. 1899. *France*, rev. ed. London: Macmillan.

Bojcun, Marko. 1995. "The Ukrainian Parliamentary Elections in March–April 1994." *Europe–Asia Studies* 47: 229–49.

Bova, Russell. 1991. "Political Dynamics of the Post-Communist Transition: A Comparative Perspective." *World Politics* 44: 113–38.

Bratton, Michael, and Nicolas van de Walle. 1997. *Democratic Experiments in Africa: Regime Transitions in Comparative Perspective*. New York: Cambridge University Press.

Brennan, Geoffrey, and James M. Buchanan. 1985. *The Reason of Rules: Constitutional Political Economy.* Cambridge: Cambridge University Press.

Breslauer, George W. 1982. *Khrushchev and Brezhnev as Leaders: Building Authority in Soviet Politics.* London: Allen & Unwin.

———. 1990. "Soviet Economic Reforms Since Stalin: Ideology, Politics, and Learning." *Soviet Economy* 6: 252–80.

———. 1991. "Evaluating Gorbachev as Leader." In *Milestones in Glasnost and Perestroyka: Politics and People,* ed. Ed A. Hewett and Victor H. Winston. Washington, D.C.: Brookings Institution Press.

Breslauer, George W., and Catherine Dale. 1997. "Boris Yel'tsin and the Invention of a Russian Nation-State." *Post-Soviet Affairs* 13: 303–332.

Breslauer, George W., and Philip Tetlock, eds. 1991. *Learning in U.S. and Soviet Foreign Policy.* Boulder, CO: Westview.

Brinton, Crane. 1965. *The Anatomy of Revolution.* New York: Vintage Books.

Bronfenbrenner, Urie. 1970. *Two Worlds of Childhood: U.S. and U.S.S.R.* New York: Russell Sage Foundation.

Brown, Archie. 1989. "Ideology and Political Culture." In *Politics, Society, and Nationality Inside Gorbachev's Russia,* ed. Seweryn Bialer. Boulder, CO: Westview.

Brown, Archie, and Jack Gray, eds. 1979. *Political Culture and Political Change in Communist States,* 2d ed. New York: Holmes & Meier.

Brown, Bess. 1992."Whither Tajikistan?" *RFE/RL Research Report* 1 (June 12): 1–6.

———. 1993. "Central Asia: The First Year of Unexpected Statehood." *RFE/RL Research Report* 2: 25–36.

Brudny, Yitzhak. 1995. "Ruslan Khasbulatov, Aleksandr Rutskoi, and Intra-Elite Conflict in Postcommunist Russia, 1991–1994." In *Patterns in Post-Soviet Leadership,* ed. Timothy J. Colton and Robert C. Tucker. Boulder, CO: Westview.

Bryce, James. 1921. *Modern Democracies.* 2 vols. New York: MacMillan.

Brym, Robert J. 1996a. "The Ethic of Self-Reliance and the Spirit of Capitalism in Russia." *International Sociology* 11: 409–26.

———. 1996b. "Re-evaluating Mass Support for Political and Economic Change in Russia." *Europe–Asia Studies* 48: 751–66.

Brym, Robert J., and Larissa Kosova. 1996. "The 1996 Russian Presidential Election: A Post-Mortem." Typescript, University of Toronto.

Brzezinski, Zbigniew K. 1976. "Soviet Politics: From the Future to the Past." In *The Dynamics of Soviet Politics,* ed. Paul Cocks, Robert V. Daniels, and Nancy Whittier Heer. Cambridge, MA: Harvard University Press.

Bunce, Valerie. 1995a. "Comparing East and South." *Journal of Democracy* 6(3): 87–100.

———. 1995b. "Should Transitologists Be Grounded?" *Slavic Review* 54: 111–27.

Bungs, Dzintra. 1993. "Twenty-three Groups Vie for Seats in the Latvian Parliament." *RFE/RL Research Bulletin* 2 (June 4): 48–49.

Burnham, James. 1960. *The Managerial Revolution.* Bloomington: Indiana University Press.

Burton, Michael, Richard Gunther, and John Higley. 1992. "Elite Transformations and Democratic Regimes." Introduction to *Elites and Democratic Consolidation in Latin America and Southern Europe*, ed. John Higley and Richard Gunther. New York: Cambridge University Press.

Byzov, Leonty, Vladimir Petukhov, and Andrei Ryabov. 1997. "Politicians Appeal to the Masses in Vain." *Obshchaya gazeta* 41, October 16–22, 4. (Translated in *Current Digest of the Post-Soviet Press* 49[41] [November 12], 14.)

Cerny, Philip. 1990. *The Changing Architecture of Politics: Structure, Agency, and the Future of the State*. Newbury Park, CA: Sage.

———. 1997. "Globalization and the Residual State: The Challenge to Viable Constitutionalism." In *Designs for Democratic Stability: Studies in Viable Constitutionalism*, ed. Abdo Baaklini and Helen Desfosses. Armonk, NY: Sharpe.

Clark, William A. 1989. *Soviet Regional Elite Mobility after Khrushchev*. New York: Praeger.

———. 1996. "Presidential Power and Democratic Stability under the Russian Constitution: A Comparative Analysis." *Presidential Studies Quarterly* 26(3).

Clem, Ralph S., and Peter Craumer. 1995. "The Geography of the Russian 1995 Parliamentary Election: Continuity, Change, and Correlates." *Post-Soviet Geography* 36: 587–616.

Cocks, Paul. 1976. "The Policy Process and Bureaucratic Politics." In *The Dynamics of Soviet Politics*, ed. Paul Cocks, Robert V. Daniels, and Nancy Whittier Heer. Cambridge, MA: Harvard University Press.

Cohen, Morris, and Ernest Nagel. 1934. *An Introduction to Logic and Scientific Method*. New York: Harcourt, Brace.

Cohen, Stephen F. 1985. *Rethinking the Soviet Experience: Politics and History since 1917*. New York: Oxford University Press.

Cohen, Stephen F., and Katrina vanden Heuvel. 1989. *Voices of Glasnost: Interviews with Gorbachev's Reformers*. New York: Norton.

Coleman, James S. 1990. *Foundations of Social Theory*. Cambridge, MA: Harvard University Press.

Collier, David. 1993. "The Comparative Method." In *Political Science: The State of the Discipline II*, ed. Ada W. Finifter. Washington, D.C.: American Political Science Association.

Colton, Timothy J. 1988. "Gorbachev and the Politics of System Renewal." In *Gorbachev's Russia and American Foreign Policy*, ed. Seweryn Bialer and Michael Mandelbaum. Boulder, CO: Westview.

———. 1995. "Boris Yeltsin: Russia's All-Thumbs Democrat." In *Patterns in Post-Soviet Leadership*, ed. Timothy J. Colton and Robert C. Tucker. Boulder, CO: Westview.

Colton, Timothy J., and Robert C. Tucker, eds. 1995. *Patterns in Post-Soviet Leadership*. Boulder, CO: Westview.

Commission on Security and Cooperation in Europe. 1990. *Elections in the Baltic States and Soviet Republics: A Compendium of Reports on Parliamentary Elections Held in 1990*. Washington, D.C.: Commission on Security and Cooperation in Europe.

———. 1993a. *Human Rights and Democratization in Estonia*. Washington, D.C.: Commission on Security and Cooperation in Europe.

———. 1993b. Human Rights and Democratization in Latvia. Washington, D.C.: Commission on Security and Cooperation in Europe.

———. 1994a. *Report on the March 7, 1994, Parliamentary Election in Kazakhstan.* Washington, D.C.: Commission on Security and Cooperation in Europe.

———. 1994b. *Report on the Moldovan Parliamentary Elections, February 27, 1994.* Washington, D.C.: Commission on Security and Cooperation in Europe.

———. 1994c. *Russia's Parliamentary Election and Constitutional Referendum, December 12, 1994.* Washington, D.C.: Commission on Security and Cooperation in Europe.

———. 1994d. *Ukraine's Parliamentary Elections, March 27, 1994, April 10, 1994.* Washington, D.C.: Commission on Security and Cooperation in Europe.

———. 1995a. *Report on Armenia's Parliamentary Elections and Constitutional Referendum, July 5, 1995.* Washington, D.C.: Commission on Security and Cooperation in Europe.

———. 1995b. *Report on the Parliamentary Election in Kyrgyzstan, February 5, 1995.* Washington, D.C.: Commission on Security and Cooperation in Europe.

———. 1995c. *Report on the Parliamentary Election in Turkmenistan, December 11, 1994.* Washington, D.C.: Commission on Security and Cooperation in Europe.

———. 1996a. *Report on Azerbaijan's November 1995 Parliamentary Election.* Washington, D.C.: Commission on Security and Cooperation in Europe.

———. 1996b. *Report on the Russian Duma Elections of December 1995.* Washington, D.C.: Commission on Security and Cooperation in Europe.

———. 1996c. Report on the U.S. Helsinki Commission Delegation to Georgia and Azerbaijan, April 22–29, 1996. Washington, D.C.: Commission on Security and Cooperation in Europe.

Connor, Walter D. 1994. "Labor Politics in Post-Communist Russia: A Preliminary Assessment." In *The Social Legacy of Communism,* ed. James R. Millar and Sharon L. Wolchik. New York: Cambridge University Press.

———. 1996. *Tattered Banners: Labor, Conflict and Corporatism in Postcommunist Russia* Boulder, CO: Westview.

Constitution of the Russian Federation. 1993. In *Current Digest of the Post-Soviet Press* 45(45): 4–16.

Converse, Philip E. 1964. "The Nature of Beliefs in Mass Publics." In *Ideology and Discontent,* ed. David E. Apter. New York: Free Press.

Converse, Philip E., and Roy Pierce. 1986. *Political Representation in France.* Cambridge, MA: Harvard University Press.

Critchlow, James. 1992. "Democratization in Kazakhstan." *RFE/RL Research Report* 1 (July 24): 12–14.

Crowther, William. 1994. "Moldova after Independence." *Current History* 93: 342–347.

Crozier, Michel. 1964. *The Bureaucratic Phenomenon.* Chicago: University of Chicago Press.

Crummey, Robert O. 1987. "The Silence of Muscovy." *Russian Review* 46: 157–64.

————. 1988. Review of *Kinship and Politics* by Nancy Shields Kollmann. *Slavic Review* 47: 111–2.

Dahl, Robert. 1956. *A Preface to Democratic Theory*. Chicago: University of Chicago Press.

————. 1971. *Polyarchy: Participation and Opposition*. New Haven, CT: Yale University Press.

————. 1982. *Dilemmas of Pluralist Democracy*. New Haven, CT: Yale University Press.

————. 1989. *Democracy and Its Critics*. New Haven, CT: Yale University Press.

Daily Report: Central Eurasia. Washington, D.C.: Foreign Broadcast Information Service, 1991–1996 (with occasional *Supplements*).

Dallin, Alexander. 1988. "The Uses and Abuses of Russian History." In *Soviet Society and Culture: Essays in Honor of Vera S. Dunham*, ed. Terry L. Thompson and Richard Sheldon. Boulder, CO: Westview.

Daniels, Robert V. 1987. "Russian Political Culture and the Post-Revolutionary Impasse." *Russian Review* 46: 165–76.

————. 1988. *Is Russia Reformable? Change and Resistance from Stalin to Gorbachev*. Boulder, CO: Westview.

————. 1993. "Introduction: The Evolution of the Communist Mind—In Russia." In *A Documentary History of Russia: From Lenin to Gorbachev*, ed. Robert Daniels. Hanover, NH: University Press of New England.

Davidson, William L. 1915. *Political Thought in England: The Utilitarians from Bentham to J. S. Mill*. London: Butterworth.

De Grazia, Sebastian. 1948. *The Political Community: A Study of Anomie*. Chicago: University of Chicago Press.

Denisovsky, Gennady M., Polina M. Kozyreva, and Mikhail S. Matskovsky. 1993. "Twelve Percent Hope: Economic Consciousness and a Market Economy." In *Public Opinion and Regime Change: The New Politics of Post-Soviet Societies*, ed. Arthur H. Miller, William M. Reisinger, and Vicki L. Hesli. Boulder, CO: Westview.

de Tocqueville, Alexis. 1955. *The Old Regime and the French Revolution*, trans. Stuart Gilbert. New York: Doubleday.

————. 1966. *Democracy in America*. New York: Harper and Row.

Diamond, Larry. 1992. "Economic Development and Democracy Reconsidered." *American Behavioral Scientist* 35: 450–99.

————. 1994. "Toward Democratic Consolidation." *Journal of Democracy* 5(3): 4–17.

————. 1996. "Is the Third Wave Over?" *Journal of Democracy* 7(3): 20–37.

Diamond, Larry, and Marc Plattner, eds. 1995. *Economic Reform and Democracy*. Baltimore, MD: Johns Hopkins University Press.

————. 1996. *The Global Resurgence of Democracy*, 2d ed. Baltimore, MD: Johns Hopkins University Press.

Di Palma, Giuseppe. 1990. *To Craft Democracies: An Essay on Democratic Transitions*. Berkeley: University of California Press.

Dobson, Richard B. 1994a. "Communism's Legacy and Russian Youth." In *The Social Legacy of Communism*, ed. James R. Millar and Sharon L. Wolchik. Cambridge: Cambridge University Press.

————. 1994b. "Whither Russia? Trends in Russian Opinion since 1991." Paper presented at the meeting of the World Association for Public Opinion Research, Danvers, MA.

————. 1995a. "Russians Disenchanted with Leaders and Institutions." M-40–95. Washington, D.C.: U.S. Information Agency.

————. 1995b. "Russians' Disillusion Deepens." M-105–95. Washington, D.C.: U.S. Information Agency.

————. 1996. "Is Russia Turning the Corner? Changing Russian Public Opinion, 1991–1996." R-7–96. Washington, D.C.: U.S. Information Agency.

Dobson, Richard B., and Steven A. Grant. 1992. "Public Opinion and the Transformation of the Soviet Union." *International Journal of Public Opinion Research* 4: 302–20.

Dostoevsky, F. M. 1991. *The Brothers Karamazov*, trans. Richard Pevear and Larissa Volkhonsky. New York: Vintage Books.

Dragunskii, Denis. 1995. "The Sign of Our Times: Democracy, Authoritarianism, or . . ." In *Remaking Russia: Voices from Within*, ed. Heyward Isham. Armonk, NY: Sharpe.

Duch, Raymond M. 1993. "Tolerating Economic Reform: Popular Support for Transition to a Free Market in the Former Soviet Union." *American Political Science Review* 87: 590–608.

————. 1995. "Economic Chaos and the Fragility of Democratic Transition in Former Communist Regimes." *Journal of Politics* 57: 121–58.

Easton, David. 1965. *A Systems Analysis of Political Life*. New York: Wiley.

Eckstein, Harry. 1966. *Division and Cohesion in Democracy: A Study of Norway*. Princeton, NJ: Princeton University Press.

————. 1969. "Authority Relations and Governmental Performance: A Theoretical Framework." *Comparative Political Studies* 2: 269–326.

————. 1971. *The Evaluation of Political Performance: Problems and Dimensions*. Beverly Hills, CA: Sage.

————. 1979a. "Case Study and Theory in Political Science." In *Handbook of Political Science*, ed. Fred I. Greenstein and Nelson W. Polsby, vol. 7 New York: Wiley.

————. 1979b. "On the 'Science' of the State." *Daedalus* 108(4): 1–20.

————. 1980. "The Natural History of Congruence Theory." Monograph Series in World Affairs, vol. 18, no. 2, University of Denver.

————. 1984a. *Civic Inclusion: The Political Aspect*. Working Papers on Authority Relations, no. 3, University of California, Irvine.

————. 1984b. "Civic Inclusion and Its Discontents." *Daedalus* 113: 107–146.

————. 1988. "A Culturalist Theory of Political Change." *American Political Science Review* 82: 789–804.

————. 1992a. *Regarding Politics: Essays on Political Theory, Stability, and Change*. Berkeley: University of California Press.

————. 1992b. "A Theory of Stable Democracy." In *Regarding Politics: Essays on Political Theory, Stability, and Change*, ed. Harry Eckstein. Berkeley: University of California Press. Originally published as Research Monograph Number 10, Center of International Studies, Princeton University. Subsequently published as Appendix B in Eckstein, *Division and Cohesion in Democracy: A Study of Norway*. Princeton: Princeton University Press, 1966.

———. 1996. "Culture as a Foundation Concept for the Social Sciences." *Theoretical Politics* 8: 471–97.

———. 1997. "Social Science as Cultural Science; Rational Choice as Metaphysics." In *Culture Matters: Essays in Honor of Aaron Wildavsky*, ed. Richard S. Ellis and Michael Thompson. Boulder, CO: Westview.

Eckstein, Harry, and Ted Robert Gurr. 1975. *Patterns of Authority: A Structural Basis for Political Inquiry*. New York: Wiley.

Election Observation Report. 1994. Washington, D.C.: International Republican Institute.

Elster, Jon. 1988. Introduction to *Constitutionalism and Democracy*, ed. Jon Elster and Rune Sladstad. New York: Cambridge University Press.

———. 1992. "Making Sense of Constitution-Making." *East European Constitutional Review* 1:15–17.

Evans, Alfred B., Jr. 1990. "Rethinking Soviet Socialism." In *Developments in Soviet Politics*, ed. Stephen White, Alex Pravda, and Zvi Gitelman. Durham, NC: Duke University Press.

Evans, Geoffrey, and Stephen Whitefield. 1995. "The Politics and Economics of Democratic Commitment: Support for Democracy in Transition Societies." *British Journal of Political Science* 25: 485–514.

Fainsod, Merle. 1958. *Smolensk under Soviet Rule*. Cambridge, MA: Harvard University Press.

———. 1965. *How Russia Is Ruled*, 2d ed. Cambridge, MA: Harvard University Press.

Fearon, James D. 1991. "Counterfactuals and Hypothesis Testing in Political Science." *World Politics* 43: 169–95.

Fenno, Richard. 1978. *Home Style: House Members in Their Districts*. Boston, MA: Little, Brown.

Feshbach, Murray, and Alfred Friendly Jr. 1992. *Ecocide in the USSR: Health and Nature under Siege*. New York: Basic Books.

Festinger, Leon. 1957. *A Theory of Cognitive Dissonance*. Stanford, CA: Stanford University Press.

Filatov, Sergei, and Liudmila Vorontsova. 1995. "New Russia in Search of Identity." In *Remaking Russia: Voices from Within*, ed. Heyward Isham. Armonk, NY: Sharpe.

Finer, S. E. 1971. *Comparative Government*. New York: Basic Books.

Finifter, Ada W. 1996. "Attitudes Toward Individual Responsibility and Political Reform in the Former Soviet Union." *American Political Science Review* 90: 138–52.

Finifter, Ada W., and Ellen Mickiewicz. 1992. "Redefining the Political System of the USSR: Mass Support for Political Change." *American Political Science Review* 86: 857–74.

Fischer, Mary Ellen, ed. 1996. *Establishing Democracies*. Boulder, CO: Westview.

Fish, M. Steven. 1994. "Russia's Fourth Transition." *Journal of Democracy* 5(3): 31–42.

———. 1995a. "The Advent of Multipartism in Russia, 1993–95." *Post-Soviet Affairs* 11: 340–83.

———. 1995b. *Democracy from Scratch: Opposition and Regime in the New Russian Revolution*. Princeton, NJ: Princeton University Press.

———. 1996. "Russia between Elections: The Travails of Liberalism." *Journal of Democracy* 7(2): 105–7.

———. 1997. "The Predicament of Russian Liberalism: Evidence from the December 1995 Parliamentary Elections." *Europe–Asia Studies* 49: 191–220.

Fitzpatrick, Sheila. 1994. *Stalin's Peasants: Resistance and Survival in the Russian Village after Collectivization*. New York: Oxford University Press.

Fitzpatrick, Sheila, Alexander Rabinowitch, and Richard Stites, eds. 1991. *Russia in the Era of NEP: Explorations in Soviet Society and Culture*. Bloomington: Indiana University Press.

Fleron, Frederic J., Jr. 1969. "Co-optation as a Mechanism of Adaptation to Change: The Soviet Political Leadership System." *Polity* 2: 176–201.

———. 1970. "Representation of Career Types in the Soviet Political Leadership." In *Political Leadership in Eastern Europe and the Soviet Union*, ed. R. Barry Farrell. Chicago: Aldine.

———. 1993. "Comparative Politics and Lessons for the Present." *Harriman Institute Forum* 6(6–7): 3–13.

———. 1996a. "The Logic of Inquiry in Post-Soviet Studies: Art or Science?" *Communist and Post-Communist Studies* 29: 245–74.

———. 1996b. "Post-Soviet Political Culture in Russia: An Assessment of Recent Empirical Investigations." *Europe–Asia Studies* 48: 225–60.

Fleron, Frederic J., Jr., Jeffrey W. Hahn, and William M. Reisinger. 1997. "Public Opinion Surveys and Political Culture in Post-Soviet Russia." *Kennan Institute Occasional Paper* 266, 1–39.

Fleron, Frederic J., Jr., and Erik P. Hoffmann, eds. 1993. *Post-Communist Studies and Political Science: Methodology and Empirical Theory in Sovietology*. Boulder, CO: Westview.

Fleron, Frederic J., Jr., Erik P. Hoffmann, and Robbin F. Laird, eds. 1991. *Soviet Foreign Policy: Classic and Contemporary Issues*. Hawthorne, NY: Aldine de Gruyter.

Freedom House. 1991. *Freedom in the World, 1990–1991*. New York: Freedom House.

———. 1996. *Freedom in the World: The Annual Survey of Political Rights and Civil Liberties, 1995–1996*. New York: Freedom House.

Frieden, Jeffry A. 1991. *Debt, Development, and Democracy: Modern Political Economy and Latin America, 1965–1985*. Princeton, NJ: Princeton University Press.

Friedgut, Theodore, and Jeffrey Hahn, eds. 1994. *Local Power and Post-Soviet Politics*. Armonk, NY: Sharpe.

Fukuyama, Francis. 1995. "The Primacy of Culture." *Journal of Democracy* 6(1): 7–14.

Fuller, Elizabeth. 1992a. "Georgian President Flees, Opposition Seizes Power." *RFE/RL Research Report* 1 (January 17): 4–7.

———. 1992b. "The Ongoing Political Power Struggle in Azerbaijan." *RFE/RL Research Report* 1 (May 1): 11–13

————. 1992c. "Azerbaijan after the Presidential Elections." *RFE/RL Research Bulletin* 1 (June 26): 1–7.

Gibson, James L. 1993a. "Perceived Political Freedom in the Soviet Union." *Journal of Politics* 55:936–74.

————. 1993b. "Mass Opposition to the Soviet Putsch of August 1991: Collective Action, Rational Choice, and Democratic Values in the (Former) Soviet Union." Revised version (1.0) of paper presented at the annual meeting of the American Sociological Association, Miami Beach, FL.

————. 1995. "The Resilience of Mass Support for Democratic Institutions and Processes in the Nascent Russian and Ukrainian Democracies." In *Political Culture and Civil Society in Russia and the New States of Eurasia*, ed. Vladimir Tismaneanu. Armonk, NY: Sharpe.

————. 1996a. "A Mile Wide But an Inch Deep(?): The Structure of Democratic Commitments in the Former USSR." *American Journal of Political Science* 40: 396–420.

————. 1996b. "Political and Economic Markets: Changes in the Connections Between Attitudes Toward Political Democracy and a Market Economy Within the Mass Culture of Russia and Ukraine." *Journal of Politics* 58: 954–984.

————. 1996c. "Political Intolerance in the Fledgling Russian Democracy." Paper presented at the annual meeting of the Midwest Political Science Association, Chicago.

Gibson, James L., and Raymond M. Duch. 1993a. "Emerging Democratic Values in Soviet Political Culture." In *Public Opinion and Regime Change: The New Politics of Post-Soviet Societies*, ed. Arthur H. Miller, William M. Reisinger, and Vicki L. Hesli. Boulder, CO: Westview.

————. 1993b. "Political Intolerance in the USSR: The Distribution and Etiology of Mass Opinion." *Comparative Political Studies* 26: 286–329.

————. 1994. "Postmaterialism and the Emerging Soviet Democracy." *Political Research Quarterly* 47: 5–39.

Gibson, James L., Raymond M. Duch, and Kent L. Tedin. 1992. "Democratic Values and the Transformation of the Soviet Union." *Journal of Politics* 54: 329–71.

————. 1994. "Postmaterialism and the Emerging Soviet Democracy." *Political Research Quarterly* 47: 5–39.

Goldmann, Kjell. 1996. "International Relations: An Overview." In *A New Handbook of Political Science*, ed. Robert Goodwin and Hans-Dieter Klingemann. New York: Oxford University Press.

Gorbachev, Mikhail. 1987. *Perestroika: New Thinking for Our Country and the World*. New York: Harper & Row.

Gorer, Goeffrey, and John Rickman. 1962. *The People of Great Russia*. New York: Norton.

Gorshkov, Mikhail. 1997a. "Survey: Russian Citizens' Autumn Worries—Citizens Fear Ruble Revaluation and Dream of Returning to Brezhnev's Time." *Nezavisimaya gazeta*, October 17, 5. (Translated in *The Current Digest of the Post-Soviet Press* 49[41] [November 12], 1–5.)

———. 1997b. "Three-Fourths of Russian Residents Surveyed Rate 1996 as Bad for Themselves, and 90% Rate It As Bad For the Country, Too." *Nezavisimaya gazeta,* January 16, 5. (Translated in *Current Digest of the Post-Soviet Press* 49[3] [February 19, 1997]: 1–3.)

Grancelli, Bruno. 1988. *Soviet Management and Labor Relations.* Boston: Allen & Unwin.

Grey, Robert D., William L. Miller, Stephen White, and Paul Heywood. 1995. "The Structure of Russian Political Opinion." *Coexistence* 32: 183–215.

Grofman, Bernard, and Arend Lijphart, eds. 1986. *Electoral Laws and Their Political Consequences.* New York: Agathon.

Gurr, Ted Robert. 1974. "Persistence and Change in Political Systems." *American Political Science Review* 68: 1482–1504.

Gustafson, Thane. 1981. *Reform in Soviet Politics: Lessons of Recent Policies on Land and Water.* Cambridge: Cambridge University Press.

Haggard, Stephan, and Robert Kaufman. 1995a. "The Challenges of Consolidation." In *Economic Reform and Democracy,* ed. Larry Diamond and Marc Plattner. Baltimore, MD: Johns Hopkins University Press.

———. 1995b. *The Political Economy of Democratic Transitions.* Princeton, NJ: Princeton University Press.

Hagopian, Frances. 1990. "Democracy by Undemocratic Means? Elites, Political Pacts and Regime Transition in Brazil." *Comparative Political Studies* 23: 147–70.

Hahn, Jeffrey W. 1993a. "Attitudes Toward Reform Among Provincial Russian Politicians." *Post-Soviet Affairs* 9: 66–85.

———. 1993b. "Continuity and Change in Russian Political Culture." In *Post-Communist Studies and Political Science: Methodology and Empirical Theory in Sovietology,* ed. Frederic J. Fleron Jr. and Erik P. Hoffmann. Boulder, CO: Westview.

———. 1995. "Changes in Contemporary Russian Political Culture." In *Political Culture and Civil Society in Russia and the New States of Eurasia,* ed. Vladimir Tismaneanu. Armonk, NY: Sharpe.

———. 1996a. *Democratization in Russia: The Development of Legislative Institutions.* Armonk, NY: Sharpe.

———. 1996b. "The Development of Local Legislatures in Russia: The Case of Yaroslavl." In *Democratization in Russia: The Development of Legislative Institutions,* ed. Jeffrey W. Hahn. Armonk, NY: Sharpe.

Hall, Peter A., and Rosemary C. R. Taylor. 1994. "Political Science and the Four New Institutionalisms." Paper presented at the annual meeting of the American Political Science Association, New York.

Hammer, Darrell P. 1990. *The USSR: The Politics of Oligarchy.* Boulder, CO: Westview.

Hanson, Stephen. 1997. "The Role of Ideology in Russian Party Transformation." *Kennan Institute Report* 14, 8.

Harasymiw, Bohdan. 1969. "Nomenklatura: The Soviet Communist Party's Leadership Recruitment System." *Canadian Journal of Political Science* 2: 493–512.

Hechter, Michael. 1987. *Principles of Group Solidarity*. Berkeley: University of California Press.

Heckathorn, Douglas D., and Steven M. Maser. 1987. "Bargaining and Constitutional Contracts." *American Journal of Political Science* 31: 142–68.

Hellie, Richard. 1987. "Edward Keenan's Scholarly Ways." *The Russian Review* 46: 177–90.

Helmer, John. 1997. "Communist Reform: A Success Story." *The Russian Magazine*, November, 40–41.

Hempel, Carl Gustav. 1965. *Aspects of Scientific Explanation*. New York: Free Press.

Herrmann, Richard. 1985. *Perceptions and Behavior in Soviet Foreign Policy*. Pittsburgh, PA: University of Pittsburgh Press, 1985. This chapter is excerpted in Fleron, Hoffmann, and Laird 1991.

Higley, John, and Michael G. Burton. 1989. "The Elite Variable in Democratic Transitions and Breakdowns." *American Sociological Review* 54: 17–32.

Higley, John, Judith Kullberg, and Jan Pakulski. 1996. "The Persistence of Postcommunist Elites." *Journal of Democracy* 7(2): 133–47.

Hockstader, Lee. 1996. "For Russia's Reformers, a Time of Despair." *Washington Post National Weekly Edition*, January, 8–14, 23.

Hodnett, Grey. 1981. "The Pattern of Leadership Politics." In *Domestic Context of Soviet Foreign Policy*, ed. Seweryn Bialer. Boulder, CO: Westview.

Hoffman, David. 1994. "Peasant Culture and Urban Migration in the 1930s." Kennan Institute Meeting Report 11 (14).

Hoffmann, Erik P. 1992. "Ivan Karamazov: His Rebellion, Suffering, and Regeneration." Typescript, State University of New York, Albany.

———. 1993. "Nurturing Post-Sovietology." *Harriman Institute Forum* 6(6–7): 14–23.

———. 1994."Challenges to Viable Constitutionalism in Post-Soviet Russia." *Harriman Review* 7(10–12): 19–56.

———. 1997. "Can Viable Constitutionalism Take Root in Post-Soviet Russia?" In *Designs for Democratic Stability: Studies in Viable Constitutionalism*, ed. Abdo Baaklini and Helen Desfosses. Armonk, NY: Sharpe.

Hoffmann, Erik P., and Robbin F. Laird. 1982. *The Politics of Economic Modernization in the Soviet Union*. Ithaca, NY: Cornell University Press.

Hoffmann, Stanley. 1974. "The Rulers: Heroic Leadership in Modern France." In *Decline or Renewal? France since the 1930s*, ed. Stanley Hoffmann. New York: Viking.

Hosking, Geoffrey. 1990. *The Awakening of the Soviet Union*. Cambridge, MA: Harvard University Press.

Hough, Jerry F. 1969. *The Soviet Prefects: The Local Party Organs in Industrial Decision-Making*. Cambridge, MA: Harvard University Press.

———. 1972. "The Bureaucratic Model and the Nature of the Soviet System." *Journal of Comparative Administration* 5: 134–67.

———. 1988. *Russia and the West*. New York: Simon & Schuster.

———. 1994a. "Rational Choice Theory and Reform of Communist Economies: Evidence from a 1993 Russian Election Study." Paper presented at the annual meeting of the American Political Science Association, New York.

————. 1994b. "The Russian Election of 1993: Public Attitudes Toward Economic Reform and Democratization." *Post-Soviet Affairs* 10: 1–37.

————. 1997. *Democratization and Revolution in the USSR, 1985–1991*. Washington, DC: Brookings Institution Press.

Huntington, Samuel. 1984. "Will More Countries Become Democratic? *Political Science Quarterly* 99: 191–218.

————. 1991. *The Third Wave: Democratization in the Late Twentieth Century*. Norman: University of Oklahoma Press.

————. 1996. *The Clash of Civilizations and the Remaking of World Order*. New York: Simon and Schuster.

Huskey, Eugene. 1995. "The Rise of Contested Politics in Central Asia: Elections in Kyrgyzstan, 1989–90." *Europe–Asia Studies* 47: 813–33.

————. 1996a. "Democracy and Institutional Design in Russia." *Demokratizatsiya: The Journal of Post-Soviet Democratization* 4: 365–387.

————. 1996b. "The Making of Economic Policy in Russia: Changing Relations between Presidency and Government." *Review of Central and East European Law* 4: 453–73.

Inglehart, Ronald. 1988. "The Renaissance of Political Culture." *American Political Science Review* 82: 1203–30.

————. 1990. *Culture Shift in Advanced Industrial Society*. Princeton, NJ: Princeton University Press.

"Is the Kremlin Planning Electoral Reform?" 1997. *Jamestown Foundation Monitor*, May 28. Johnson's Russia Listserv (May 28, 1997).

Isham, Heyward, ed. 1995. *Remaking Russia: Voices from Within*. Armonk, NY: M. E. Sharpe.

Ishiyama, John T. 1993. "Founding Elections and the Development of Transitional Parties: The Cases of Estonia and Latvia, 1990–1992." *Communist and Post-Communist Studies* 26: 277–99.

Johnson, Juliet. 1997. "Russia's Emerging Financial-Industrial Groups." *Post-Soviet Affairs* 13: 333–365.

Jones, Stephen F. 1996. "Georgia's Return from Chaos." *Current History* 95: 340–45.

Jowitt, Ken. 1983. "Soviet Neotraditionalism: The Political Corruption of a Leninist Regime." *Soviet Studies* 35: 275–97.

————. 1992. *New World Disorder: The Leninist Extinction*. Berkeley: University of California Press.

Joyce, John M. 1984. "The Old Russian Legacy." *Foreign Policy* 55: 112–53.

Juviler, Peter. 1995. "Human Rights and Russia's Future." *Parker School Journal of East European Law* 2: 495–523.

Kangas, Roger D. 1994. "Uzbekistan: Evolving Authoritarianism." *Current History* 93: 178–82.

Kaplan, Cynthia S. 1993. "New Forms of Political Participation." In *Public Opinion and Regime Change: The New Politics of Post-Soviet Societies*, ed. Arthur H. Miller, William M. Reisinger, and Vicki L. Hesli. Boulder, CO: Westview.

Kavrus-Hoffmann, Nadezhda. 1997. "The Russian Orthodox Church Today: Restoration or Transformation?" Paper presented at the Mid-Atlantic Slavic Conference, Albany, NY.

Keech, William R. 1995. *Economic Politics: The Costs of Democracy.* Cambridge: Cambridge University Press.

Keenan, Edward L. 1986. "Muscovite Political Folkways." *Russian Review* 45: 115–84.

Kelley, Jonathan, and Herbert J. Klein. 1978. *Revolution and the Rebirth of Inequality: A Theory Applied to the Revolution in Bolivia.* Berkeley: University of California Press.

Khazanov, Anatoly M. 1995. *After the USSR: Ethnicity, Nationalism, and Politics in the Commonwealth of Independent States.* Madison: University of Wisconsin Press.

Kiewiet, Roderick, and Mathew McCubbins. 1991. *The Logic of Delegation: Congressional Parties and the Appropriations Process.* Chicago: University of Chicago Press.

Kim, Ted. 1997. "Chubais Promises Cleaner Privatization Process." *The Russian Magazine,* November, 34–35.

King, Gary, Robert O. Keohane, and Sidney Verba. 1994. *Designing Social Inquiry: Scientific Inference in Qualitative Research.* Princeton, NJ: Princeton University Press.

Kionka, Riina. 1992. "Estonian Political Struggle Centers on Voting Rights." *RFE/RL Research Report* 1 (June 12): 15–17.

Kitschelt, Herbert. 1992a. "The Formation of Party Systems in East Central Europe." *Politics and Society* 20: 7–50.

———. 1992b. "Political Regime Change: Structure and Process-Driven Explanations?" *American Political Science Review* 86: 1028–34.

Knight, Jack. 1992. *Institutions and Social Conflict.* Cambridge: Cambridge University Press.

Koenker, Diane P., William G. Rosenberg, and Ronald Grigor Suny, eds. 1989. *Party, State, and Society in the Russian Civil War: Explorations in Social History.* Bloomington: Indiana University Press.

Kollmann, Nancy Shields. 1987. *Kinship and Politics: The Making of the Muscovite Political System, 1345–1547.* Stanford, CA: Stanford University Press.

Konstitutsiia Rossiiskoi Federatsii: The Constitution of the Russian Federation. 1994. Moscow: Iuridicheskaya Literatura.

Korkeakivi, Antti. 1994. "Russia on the Rights Track: Human Rights in the New Constitution." *Parker School Journal of East European Law* 1: 233–53.

Kornhauser, William. 1959. *The Politics of Mass Society.* Glencoe, IL: Free Press.

Koshkaryova, Tatyana, and Rustam Narzikulov. 1997. "How Things Really Stand." *Nezavisimaya gazeta,* September 25, 1. (Translated in *The Current Digest of the Post-Soviet Press* 49[39] [October 29], 4–5.)

Kovalev, Sergei. 1995. "The Ruling Element and Society: Who Will Prevail?" *Moscow News,* August 11–17, 2.

Kryshtanovskaya, Olga. 1995. "To Russian Democrats: Don't Unite," *New York Times,* September 14, A27.

Kubiček, Paul. 1994. "Delegative Democracy in Russia and Ukraine." *Communist and Post-Communist Studies* 27: 423–41.

Kuhn, Thomas. 1970. *The Structure of Scientific Revolutions,* 2d ed. Chicago: University of Chicago Press.

Kullberg, Judith S. 1994. "The Ideological Roots of Elite Political Conflict in Post-Soviet Russia." *Europe–Asia Studies* 46: 929–53.

Kullberg, Judith S., and William Zimmerman. 1995. "Liberal Elites and Socialist Masses: Public Opinion and Problems of Russian Democracy." Paper presented at the annual meeting of the American Political Science Association, Chicago.

———. 1996. "Bringing the Masses Back In: Societal Forces in Postcommunist Transitions." Paper presented at the American Association for the Advancement of Slavic Studies national convention, Boston.

Kutkovets, Tatyana, and Igor Klyamkin. 1997. "Russian Ideas: Is Accord Possible in a Split Society?" Monthly supplement to *Nezavisimaya gazeta*, January 16, 2–3. (Translated in *Current Digest of the Post-Soviet Press* 49[3] [February 19, 1997]: 4–7.)

Laitin, David D. 1995. "The Civic Culture at 30." *American Political Science Review* 89: 168–73.

Lane, David. 1996a. "The Gorbachev Revolution: the Role of the Political Elite in Regime Disintegration." *Political Studies* 44: 4–23.

———. 1996b. "The Transformation of Russia: The Role of the Political Élite." *Europe–Asia Studies* 48: 535–49.

Le Bon, Gustave, 1960. *The Crowd: A Study of The Popular Mind.* Reissue. New York: Viking.

LeDonne, John P. 1991. *Absolutism and Ruling Class: The Formation of the Russian Political Order 1700–1825.* New York: Oxford University Press.

Lerner, Daniel. 1958. *The Passing of Traditional Society: Modernizing the Middle East.* Glencoe, IL: Free Press.

Levada, Yury. 1995. "A Democracy of Disorder Has Been Established in Russia." *Sevodnya*, April 15, 3. (Translated in *Current Digest of the Post-Soviet Press* 47[14] [May 3, 1995], 4–6.)

Levi, Margaret. 1988. *Of Rule and Revenue.* Berkeley: University of California Press.

Levine, Daniel H. 1988. "Paradigm Lost: Dependence to Democracy." *World Politics* 40: 377–94.

Lewin, Moshe. 1991. *The Gorbachev Phenomenon,* rev. ed. Berkeley: University of California Press.

Lewis-Beck, Michael S. 1980. *Applied Regression: An Introduction.* Beverly Hills, CA: Sage.

Lichbach, Mark, and Alan Zuckerman, eds. 1997. *Comparative Politics: Rationality, Culture, and Structure.* New York: Cambridge University Press.

Lijphart, Arend. 1971. "Comparative Politics and Comparative Method." *American Political Science Review* 65: 682–93.

———. 1975. "The Comparative Cases Strategy in Comparative Research." *Comparative Political Studies* 8: 158–77.

———. 1977. *Democracy in Plural Societies: A Comparative Exploration.* New Haven, CT: Yale University Press.

———. 1984. *Democracies: Patterns of Majoritarian and Consensus Government in Twenty-one Countries.* New Haven, CT: Yale University Press.

———. 1990. "The Political Consequences of Electoral Laws, 1945–1985." *American Political Science Review* 84: 481–96.

Likhachev, Dmitri. 1990. "The National Nature of Russian History." Harriman Lecture, Columbia University, November 13.

Lindblom, Charles. 1977. *Politics and Markets: The World's Political-Economic Systems*. New York: Basic Books.

Linz, Juan J. 1990a. "The Perils of Presidentialism." *Journal of Democracy* 1(1): 51–69.

———. 1990b. "Transitions to Democracy." *The Washington Quarterly* 13: 143–64.

Linz, Juan J., and Alfred Stepan. 1992. "Political Identities and Electoral Sequences: Spain, the Soviet Union and Yugoslavia." *Daedalus* 121: 123–39.

———. 1996a. *Problems of Democratic Transition and Consolidation: Southern Europe, South America, and Post-Communist Europe*. Baltimore, MD: Johns Hopkins University Press.

———. 1996b. "Toward Consolidated Democracies." *Journal of Democracy* 7: 14–33.

Linz, Juan J., and Arturo Valenzuela. 1994. *The Failure of Presidential Democracy*. Baltimore, MD: Johns Hopkins University Press.

Lipset, Seymour Martin. 1959. "Some Social Requisites of Democracy: Economic Development and Political Legitimacy." *American Political Science Review* 53: 69–105.

———. 1960. *Political Man: The Social Bases of Politics*. New York: Doubleday.

———. 1970. "Political Cleavages in 'Developed' and 'Emerging' Polities." In *Mass Politics: Studies in Political Sociology*, ed. Erik Allardt and Stein Rokkan. New York: The Free Press, 1970.

———. 1994. "The Social Requisites of Democracy Revisited." *American Sociological Review* 59: 1–22.

Lipset, Seymour Martin, and Stein Rokkan, eds. 1967. *Party Systems and Voter Alignments: Cross-National Perspectives*. New York: Free Press.

Lipset, Seymour Martin, Kyoung-Ryung Seong, and John Charles Torres. 1993. "A Comparative Analysis of the Social Requisites of Democracy." *International Social Science Journal* 45(2): 155–175.

Löwenhardt, John. 1981. *Decision-Making in Soviet Politics*. New York: St. Martin's.

———. 1995. *The Reincarnation of Russia: Struggling with the Legacy of Communism, 1990–1994*. Durham, NC: Duke University Press.

Lustick, Ian S. 1996. "History, Historiography and Political Science: Multiple Historical Records and the Problem of Selection Bias." *American Political Science Review* 90: 605–18.

Lynch, Allen. 1996. "Review of Jack Matlock, Jr., *Autopsy of an Empire*," *Nationalities Papers* 24:317–322.

Maddox, Graham. 1982. "A Note on the Meaning of 'Constitution,'" *American Political Science Review* 76: 805–9.

Mainwaring, Scott. 1992. "Transitions to Democracy and Democratic Consolidation: Theoretical and Comparative Issues." In *Issues in Democratic Consoli-*

dation: The New South American Democracies in Comparative Perspective, ed. Scott Mainwaring, Guillermo O'Donnell, and J. Samuel Valenzuela. Notre Dame, IN: University of Notre Dame Press.

———. 1993. "Presidentialism, Multipartism, and Democracy: The Difficult Combination." *Comparative Political Studies* 26: 198–228.

Mainwaring, Scott, Guillermo O'Donnell, and J. Samuel Valenzuela, eds. 1992. *Issues in Democratic Consolidation: The New South American Democracies in Comparative Perspective*. Notre Dame, IN: University of Notre Dame Press.

Mair, Peter. 1996. "Comparative Politics: An Overview." In *A New Handbook of Political Science*, ed. Robert Goodwin and Hans-Dieter Klingemann. New York: Oxford University Press.

March, James G., and Johan P. Olsen. 1984. "The New Institutionalism: Organizational Factors in Political Life." *American Political Science Review* 78: 734–49.

———. 1989. *Rediscovering Institutions: The Organizational Basis of Politics*. New York: Free Press.

Mason, David S. 1995. "Attitudes toward the Market and Political Participation in the Postcommunist States." *Slavic Review* 54: 385–406.

McAllister, Ian, and Stephen White. 1994. "Political Participation in Postcommunist Russia: Voting, Activism, and the Potential for Mass Protest." *Political Studies* 42: 593–615.

———. 1995. "Democracy, Political Parties and Party Formation in Postcommunist Russia." *Party Politics* 1: 49–72.

McFaul, Michael. 1996. "The Vanishing Center." *Journal of Democracy* 7(2): 90–104.

McIntosh, Mary E., Martha Abele Mac Iver, Richard B. Dobson, and Steven A. Grant. 1993. "The Meaning of Democracy in a Redefined Europe." Paper presented at the annual meeting of the American Association for Public Opinion Research, St. Charles, IL.

McLean, Iain, ed. 1996. *The Concise Oxford Dictionary of Politics*. New York: Oxford University Press.

McKenzie, Robert T. 1963. *British Political Parties: The Distribution of Power in the Conservative and Labour Parties*. New York: St. Martin's.

Mead, Margaret. 1955. *Soviet Attitudes toward Authority*. New York: Morrow.

Melville, Andrei Yu. 1993. "An Emerging Civic Culture? Ideology, Public Attitudes, and Political Culture in the Early 1990s." In *Public Opinion and Regime Change: The New Politics of Post-Soviet Societies*, ed. Arthur H. Miller, William. M. Reisinger, and Vicki L. Hesli. Boulder, CO: Westview.

Merriam, Charles. 1944. *Public and Private Government*. New Haven, CT: Yale University Press.

Merton, Robert. 1957. *Social Theory and Social Structure*, rev. ed. Glencoe, IL: Free Press.

Meyer, Alfred G. 1967. "The Soviet Political System." In *The USSR after 50 Years: Promise and Reality*, ed. Samuel Hendel and Randolph L. Braham. New York: Knopf.

Michels, Robert. 1949. *Political Parties*. Glencoe, IL: Free Press.

Migdal, Joel S. 1988. *Strong Societies and Weak States: State-Society Relations and State Capabilities in the Third World*. Princeton, NJ: Princeton University Press.

———. 1991. "A Model of State-Society Relations." In *New Directions in Comparative Politics*, ed. Howard Wiarda, 2d ed. Boulder, CO: Westview Press.

———. 1997a. "Studying the State," *APSA-CP* (Newsletter of the American Political Science Association Organized Section in Comparative Politics), 8(1), 14.

———. 1997b. "Studying the State." In *Comparative Politics: Rationality, Culture, and Structure*, ed. Lichbach and Zuckerman. New York: Cambridge University Press.

Migdal, Joel, Atul Kohli, and Vivienne Shue. 1994. *State Power and Social Forces: Domination and Transformation in The Third World*. New York: Cambridge University Press.

Migranyan, Andranik. 1997. "Realities: Autumn of the Patriarch—The President's Political Rehabilitation Has Still Not Taken Place." *Nezavisimaya gazeta*, October 14, 5. (Translated in *The Current Digest of the Post-Soviet Press*, 49[40] [November 5], 1–3.)

Mill, J. S. 1873–1875. *Dissertations and Discussions*. New York: Holt.

Millar, James. 1995. "From Utopian Socialism to Utopian Capitalism: The Failure of Revolution and Reform in Post-Soviet Russia." *Problems of Post-Communism* 42(3): 7–14.

Millar, James R., and Sharon L. Wolchik. 1994. "The Social Legacies and the Aftermath of Communism." Introduction to *The Social Legacy of Communism*, ed. James R. Millar and Sharon L. Wolchik. Cambridge: Cambridge University Press.

Miller, Arthur H. 1993. "In Search of Regime Legitimacy." In *Public Opinion and Regime Change: The New Politics of Post-Soviet Societies*, ed. Arthur H. Miller, William M. Reisinger, and Vicki L. Hesli. Boulder, CO: Westview.

Miller, Arthur H., Vicki L. Hesli, and William M. Reisinger. 1994. "Reassessing Mass Support for Political and Economic Change in the Former USSR." *American Political Science Review* 88: 399–411.

Miller, Arthur H., William M. Reisinger, and Vicki L. Hesli. 1993. *Public Opinion and Regime Change: The New Politics of Post-Soviet Societies*. Boulder, CO: Westview.

———. 1995. "Comparing Citizen and Elite Belief Systems in Post-Soviet Russia and Ukraine." *Public Opinion Quarterly* 59: 1–40.

———. 1996. "Understanding Political Change in Post-Soviet Societies: A Further Commentary On Finifter and Mickiewicz." *American Political Science Review* 90: 153–66.

Moe, Terry M. 1984. "The New Economics of Organization." *American Journal of Political Science* 28: 739–77.

Mondak, Jeffrey J. 1995. "Media Exposure and Political Discussion in U.S. Elections." *Journal of Politics* 57: 62–85.

Moore, Barrington, Jr. 1965. *Soviet Politics—The Dilemma of Power*, 2d ed. New York: Harper & Row.

———. 1966a. *Social Origins of Dictatorship and Democracy: Lord and Peasant in the Making of the Modern World*. Boston: Beacon.

———. 1966b. *Terror and Progress—USSR*, 2d ed. New York: Harper & Row.

Moroz, Valentyn. 1971. "A Report from the Beria Reservation." In *Ferment in the Ukraine*, ed. Michael Browne. New York: Praeger.

Mosca, Gaetano. 1958. *The Myth of the Ruling Class*. Ann Arbor: University of Michigan Press.

Moses, Joel C. 1981. "The Impact of Nomenklatura in Soviet Regional Elite Recruitment." *Soviet Union/Union Sovietique* 8: 62–102.

Naylor, Thomas H. 1988. *The Gorbachev Strategy: Opening the Closed Society*. Lexington, MA: Lexington Books.

Nelson, Lynn D., and Paata Amonashvili. 1992. "Voting and Political Attitudes in Soviet Georgia." *Soviet Studies* 44: 687–97.

Neumann, Sigmund, ed. 1956. *Modern Political Parties: Approaches to Comparative Politics*, Chicago: University of Chicago Press.

Neumann, W. Russell. 1986. *The Paradox of Mass Politics: Knowledge and Opinion in the American Electorate*. Cambridge, MA: Harvard University Press.

Nissman, David. 1994. "Turkmenistan (Un)transformed." *Current History* 93: 183–6.

North, Douglass C. 1979. "A Framework for Analyzing the State in Economic History." *Explorations in Economic History* 16: 249–59.

———. 1990. *Institutions, Institutional Change and Economic Performance*. New York: Cambridge University Press.

North, Douglass C., and Barry R. Weingast. 1988. "Constitutions and Commitment: The Evolution of Institutions Governing Public Choice in 17th Century England." Working Papers in Political Science, P-88–11, Hoover Institution, Stanford, CA.

Nourzhanov, Kirill, and Amin Saikal. 1994. "The New Kazakhstan: Has Something Gone Wrong?" *The World Today* 50: 225–9.

Nove, Alec. 1987. *The Soviet Economic System*. London: Allen & Unwin.

O'Donnell, Guillermo. 1992. "Transitions, Continuities, and Paradoxes." In *Issues in Democratic Consolidation: The New South American Democracies in Comparative Perspective*, ed. Scott Mainwaring, Guillermo O'Donnell, and J. Samuel Valenzuela. Notre Dame, IN: University of Notre Dame Press.

———. 1994. "Delegative Democracy." *Journal of Democracy* 5(1): 55–69.

———. 1996. "Illusions about Consolidation." *Journal of Democracy* 7(2): 34–51.

O'Donnell, Guillermo, and Philippe C. Schmitter. 1986. *Transitions from Authoritarian Rule: Tentative Conclusions about Uncertain Democracies*. Baltimore, MD: Johns Hopkins University Press.

O'Donnell, Guillermo, Phillipe C. Schmitter, and Laurence Whitehead, eds. 1986. *Transitions from Authoritarian Rule: Prospects for Democracy*. 4 vols. Baltimore, MD: Johns Hopkins University Press.

Olson, Mancur, Jr. 1963. "Rapid Growth as a Destabilizing Force." *Journal of Economic History* 23: 529–52.

———. 1965. *The Logic of Collective Action: Public Goods and the Theory of Groups*. Cambridge, MA: Harvard University Press.

O'Neil, Patrick. 1996. "Revolution from Within: Institutional Analysis, Transitions from Authoritarianism, and the Case of Hungary." *World Politics* 48: 579–603.

Ordeshook, Peter C. 1995. "Institutions and Incentives." *Journal of Democracy* 6(2): 46–60.

Ordeshook, Peter C., and Olga Shvetsova. 1997. "Federalism and Constitutional Design." *Journal of Democracy* 8(1): 27–42.

Pammett, Jon H., and Joan DeBardeleben. 1996. "The Meaning of Elections in Transitional Democracies: Evidence from Russia and Ukraine." *Electoral Studies* 15: 363–81.

Pareto, Vilfredo. 1966. *Sociological Writings.* Selected and with an introduction by S. E. Finer. New York: Praeger.

Parker, John. 1992. "A Place Reborn: A Survey of Russia." *The Economist* (December 5): 58.

Parsons, Talcott. 1960. *Structure and Process in Modern Societies.* New York: Glencoe.

Pateman, Carole. 1970. *Participation and Democratic Theory.* Cambridge: Cambridge University Press.

Petro, Nicolai N. 1995. *The Rebirth of Russian Democracy: An Interpretation of Political Culture.* Cambridge, MA: Harvard University Press.

"Poll Shows Russians Trust Lebed More Than Yeltsin." 1997. Russia Today, http://www.russiatoday.com, January 17.

"Poll Shows Standing of Presidential Candidates." 1997. Interfax. Johnson's Russia Listserv, May 28.

Popper, Sir Karl Raimund. 1959. *The Logic of Scientific Discovery.* New York: Basic Books. (Translation of *Logik der Forschung,* 1934.)

Przeworski, Adam. 1986. "Some Problems in the Study of the Transition to Democracy." In *Transitions from Authoritarian Rule: Prospects for Democracy,* ed. Guillermo O'Donnell, Phillipe C. Schmitter, and Laurence Whitehead. Baltimore, MD: Johns Hopkins University Press.

———. 1988. "Democracy as a Contingent Outcome of Conflicts." In *Constitutionalism and Democracy,* ed. Jon Elster and Rune Slagstad. New York: Cambridge University Press.

———. 1991. *Democracy and the Market: Political and Economic Reforms in Eastern Europe and Latin America.* Cambridge: Cambridge University Press.

Przeworski, Adam, Michael Alvarez, José Antonio Cheibub, and Fernando Limongi. 1996. "What Makes Democracies Endure?" *Journal of Democracy* 7(1): 39–55.

Przeworski, Adam, and Henry Teune. 1970. *The Logic of Comparative Social Inquiry.* New York: Wiley.

Pulzer, Peter G. 1967. *Political Representation and Elections: Parties and Voting in Great Britain.* New York: Praeger.

Putnam, Robert D. 1973. *The Beliefs of Politicians: Ideology, Conflict and Democracy in Britain and Italy.* New Haven, CT: Yale University Press.

———. 1993. *Making Democracy Work: Civic Traditions in Modern Italy.* Princeton, NJ: Princeton University Press.

———. 1995. "Bowling Alone: America's Declining Social Capital." *Journal of Democracy* 6(1): 65–78.

Pye, Lucian W. 1990. "Political Science and the Crisis of Authoritarianism." *American Political Science Review* 84: 3–20.

Rae, Douglas W. 1967. *The Political Consequences of Electoral Laws*. New Haven, CT: Yale University Press.

Ragsdale, Hugh. 1996. *The Russian Tragedy: The Burden of History*. Armonk, NY: Sharpe.

Raitsin, Leonid. 1997a. "The Big Easy." *The Russian Magazine*, October, 12–13.

———. 1997b. "The Selling of Svyazinvest." *The Russian Magazine*, September, 42–45.

Reisinger, William M. 1993. "Conclusions: Mass Public Opinion and the Study of Post-Soviet Politics." In *Public Opinion and Regime Change: The New Politics of Post-Soviet Societies*, ed. Arthur H. Miller, William. M. Reisinger, and Vicki L. Hesli. Boulder, CO: Westview.

———. 1995. "The Renaissance of a Rubric: Political Culture as Concept and Theory." *International Journal of Public Opinion Research* 7: 328–52.

———. 1996. "Establishing and Strengthening Democracy." In *Democratic Theory and Post-Communist Change*, ed. Robert D. Grey. New York: Prentice Hall.

———. 1997. "Establishing and Strengthening Democracy." In *Democratic Theory and Post-Communist Change*, ed. Robert Grey. Upper Saddle River, NJ: Prentice Hall.

Reisinger, William M., Andrei Yu Melville, Arthur H. Miller, and Vicki L. Hesli. 1996. "Mass and Elite Political Outlooks in Post-Soviet Russia: How Congruent?" *Political Research Quarterly* 49: 77–101.

Reisinger, William M., Arthur H. Miller, and Vicki L. Hesli. 1995. "Public Behavior and Political Change in Post-Soviet States." *Journal of Politics* 57: 941–70.

———. 1997. "Russians' Views of the Law." *Journal of Communist Studies and Transition Politics* 13(3): 24–55.

Reisinger, William M., Arthur H. Miller, Vicki L. Hesli, and Kristen Hill Maher. 1994. "Political Values in Russia, Ukraine and Lithuania: Sources and Implications for Democracy." *British Journal of Political Science* 24: 183–223.

Reisinger, William M., and Alexander I. Nikitin. 1993. "Public Opinion and the Emergence of a Multi-Party System." In *Public Opinion and Regime Change: The New Politics of Post-Soviet Societies*, ed. Arthur H. Miller, William M. Reisinger, and Vicki L. Hesli. Boulder, CO: Westview.

Remnick, David. 1993. *Lenin's Tomb: The Last Days of the Soviet Empire*. New York: Random House.

———. 1996. "Hammer, Sickle, and Book." *The New York Review of Books* 43(9): 45–51.

"Results of 1995 Russian State Duma Elections." 1997. OMRINet. http://www.omri.cz/Elections/Duma95, January 27.

Review Symposium. 1995. "The Qualitative-Quantitative Disputation: Gary King, Robert O. Keohane, and Sidney Verba's *Designing Social Inquiry: Scientific Inference in Qualitative Research*." *American Political Science Review* 89: 454–481.

Roeder, Philip G. 1989. "Modernization and Participation in the Leninist Developmental Strategy." *American Political Science Review* 83: 859–84.

———. 1993. *Red Sunset: The Failure of Soviet Politics*. Princeton, NJ: Princeton University Press.

———. 1994. "Varieties of Post-Soviet Authoritarian Regimes." *Post-Soviet Affairs* 10(1): 61–101.

Rogowski, Ronald. 1993 "Comparative Politics." In *Political Science: The State of the Discipline II*, ed. Ada Finifter. Washington, DC: American Political Science Association.

Rose, Richard. 1992. "Toward a Civil Economy," *Journal of Democracy* 3(2): 13–26.

———. 1993. "Origins and Destination Models for Civil and Uncivil Economies." Paper presented to the International Institute of Public Finance, 49th Congress, Berlin, August 23–26.

———. 1994. "Postcommunism and the Problem of Trust." *Journal of Democracy* 5(3): 18–30.

———. 1996. *New Russia Barometer V: Between Two Elections*. Glasgow: University of Strathclyde, Centre for the Study of Public Policy.

Rose, Richard, and Ellen Carnaghan. 1995. "Generational Effects on Attitudes to Communist Regimes: A Comparative Analysis." *Post-Soviet Affairs* 11(1): 28–56.

Rose, Richard, and Christian Härpfer. 1993. "Mass Response to Transformation in Post-communist Societies." *Europe–Asia Studies* 46: 3–28.

———. 1994. *New Russia Barometer III: The Results*. Glasgow: University of Strathclyde, Center for the Study of Public Policy.

Rosenau, James N. 1961. *Public Opinion and Foreign Policy*. New York: Random House.

Rosenberg, Tina. 1995. *The Haunted Land: Facing Europe's Ghosts after Communism*. New York: Vintage Books.

Rosenberg, William G., and Lewis H. Siegelbaum, eds. 1993. *Social Dimensions of Soviet Industrialization*. Bloomington: Indiana University Press.

Rousseau, Jean-Jacques. 1988. *Rousseau's Political Writings*, ed. Alan Ritter and Julia Conaway Bondanella, trans. Julia Conaway Bondanella. New York: Norton.

Rowen, Henry S. 1995. "The Tide Underneath the Third Wave." *Journal of Democracy* 6(1): 52–64.

Ruble, Blair. 1982. *Soviet Trade Unions: Their Development in the 1970s*. New York: Pergamon.

Rueschemeyer, Dietrich, Evelyn Huber Stephens, and John D. Stephens. 1992. *Capitalist Development and Democracy*. Chicago: University of Chicago Press.

Rumyantsev, Oleg. 1995. "The Present and Future of Russian Constitutional Order." *Harriman Review* 8(2): 21–35.

Russett, Bruce, and Harvey Starr. 1989. *World Politics: The Menu for Choice*, 3d ed. New York: Freeman.

"Russia's Reforms in Trouble." 1997. *The Economist*, November 22–28, 23–26.

Rustow, Dankwart A. 1970. "Transitions to Democracy: Toward a Dynamic Model." *Comparative Politics* 2: 337–63.

Rutland, Peter. 1990. "Labor Unrest and Movements in 1989 and 1990." *Soviet Economy* 6: 345–384.

———. 1994. "Democracy and Nationalism in Armenia." *Europe–Asia Studies* 46: 839–61.

Sakwa, Richard. 1989. *Soviet Politics: An Introduction*. London: Routledge.

———. 1990. *Gorbachev and His Reforms, 1985–1990*. New York: Prentice Hall.

———. 1993. *Russian Politics and Society*. New York: Routledge.

———. 1995. "Subjectivity, Politics and Order in Russian Political Evolution." *Slavic Review* 54: 943–64.

———. 1996. *Russian Politics and Society*, 2d ed. New York: Routledge.

Sartori, Giovanni. 1976. *Parties and Party Systems: A Framework for Analysis*. Vol. 1. New York: Free Press.

———. 1994. *Comparative Constitutional Engineering: An Inquiry into Structures, Incentives and Outcomes*. New York: New York University Press.

Sautman, Barry. 1995. "The Devil To Pay: The 1989 Debate and the Origins of Yeltsin's Soft Authoritarianism." *Communist and Post-Communist Studies* 28: 131–51.

Savelyev, Oleg. 1997. "Russians Polled on President, Government." *Trud*, May 24. (Translated by RIA Novosti, Johnson's Russia Listserv, May 28, 1997.)

Schapiro, Leonard. 1959. *The Communisty Party of the Soviet Union*. New York: Random House.

Schmitter, Phillipe C. 1995. "Transitology: The Science or the Art of Democratization?" In *The Consolidation of Democracy in Latin America*, ed. Joseph S. Tulchin. Boulder, CO: Riener.

Schmitter, Phillipe C., and Terry Lynn Karl. 1994. "The Conceptual Travels of Transitologists and Consolidologists: How Far to the East Should They Attempt to Go?" *Slavic Review* 53: 173–85.

Schonfeld, William R. 1976. *Obedience and Revolt: French Behavior toward Authority*. Beverly Hills, CA: Sage.

Schumpeter, Joseph. 1975. *Capitalism, Socialism, and Democracy*. New York: Harper & Row.

Scott, James C. 1985. *Weapons of the Weak: Everyday Forms of Peasant Resistance*. New Haven, CT: Yale University Press.

Sedov, Leonid. 1995. "Boris Yeltsin Falls Victim to Boris Yeltsin." *Sevodnya*, April 8, 3. (Translated in *Current Digest of the Post-Soviet Press* 47[14], 1–3.)

Sergeyev, Victor. 1998. *The Wild East: Crime and Lawlessness in Post-Communist Russia*. Armonk, NY: Sharpe.

Sergeyev, Victor, and Nikolai Biryukov. 1993. *Russia's Road to Democracy: Parliament, Communism and Traditional Culture*. Brookfield, VT: Elgar.

Sharlet, Robert. 1978. *The New Soviet Constitution of 1977: Analysis and Text*. Brunswick, OH: Kings Court.

———. 1994. "Citizen and State under Gorbachev and Yeltsin." In *Developments in Russian and Post-Soviet Politics*, ed. Stephen White, Alex Pravda, and Zvi Gitelman. Durham, NC: Duke University Press.

———. 1996. "Transitional Constitutionalism: Politics and Law in the Second Russian Republic." *Wisconsin International Law Journal* 14: 495–521.

Shevtsova, Lilia. 1995. "The Two Sides of the New Russia." *Journal of Democracy* 6(3): 56–71.

———. 1996. "Parliament and the Political Crisis in Russia, 1991–1993." In *Democratization in Russia: The Development of Legislative Institutions*, ed. Jeffrey W. Hahn. Armonk, NY: Sharpe.

———. 1997. "The Young Reformers and the Party of Power." *Izvestiia*, October 9, 4. (Translated in *The Current Digest of the Post-Soviet Press* 49[40] [November 5], 3–4.)

Shin, Doh Chull. 1994. "On the Third Wave of Democratization: A Synthesis and Evaluation of Recent Theory and Research." *World Politics* 47: 135–70.

Shlyakhov, Vladimir, and Eve Adler. 1995. *Dictionary of Russian Slang and Colloquial Expressions*. Hauppauge, NY: Barron's Educational Series.

Shugart, Matthew Soberg, and John M. Carey. 1992. *Presidents and Assemblies: Constitutional Design and Electoral Dynamics*. New York: Cambridge University Press.

Singer, J. David. 1961. "The Level-of-Analysis Problem in International Relations." In *The International System: Theoretical Essays*, ed. Klaus Knorr and Sidney Verba. Princeton, NJ: Princeton University Press.

———. 1969. "The Behavioral Science Approach to International Relations: Payoff and Prospects." In *International Politics and Foreign Policy: A Reader in Research and Theory*, ed. James N. Rosenau, rev. ed. New York: Free Press.

Sirotin, Boris. 1997. "The Big FIGS." *The Russian Magazine*, September, 30–31.

Skilling, H. Gordon, and Franklyn Griffith, eds. 1971. *Interest Groups in Soviet Politics*. Princeton, NJ: Princeton University Press.

Skocpol, Theda. 1979. *States and Social Revolutions: A Comparative Analysis of France, Russia and China*. New York: Cambridge University Press.

———. 1985. "Bringing the State Back In: Strategies of Analysis in Current Research." In *Bringing the State Back In*, ed. Peter B. Evans, Dietrich Rueschemeyer, and Theda Skocpol. Cambridge: Cambridge University Press.

———. 1994. *Social Revolutions in the Modern World*. New York: Cambridge University Press.

Skocpol, Theda, and Margaret Somers. 1980. "The Uses of Comparative History in Macrosocial Inquiry." *Comparative Studies in Society and History* 22: 174–97.

Slider, Darrell, Vladimir Magun, and Vladimir Gimpel'son. 1991. "Public Opinion on Privatization: Republic Differences." *Soviet Economy* 7: 256–75.

Smith, Raymond. 1989. *Negotiating with the Soviets*. Bloomington: Indiana University Press.

Sneider, Daniel. 1991. "Democratic Spirit Sweeps Armenia." *The Christian Science Monitor*, October 17, 3.

Sourzhansky, Andrew. 1997. "On the Future of FIGS: Interview with Oleg Soskovets," *The Russian Magazine*, September, 27–29.

Starovoitova, Galina. 1995. "Modern Russia and the Ghost of Weimar Germany." In *Remaking Russia: Voices from Within*, ed. Heyward Isham. Armonk, NY: Sharpe.

Steele, Jonathan. 1994. *Eternal Russia: Yeltsin, Gorbachev, and the Mirage of Democracy*. Cambridge, MA: Harvard University Press.

Steinmo, Sven, Kathleen Thelen, and Frank Longstreth, eds. 1992. *Structuring Politics: Historical Institutionalism in Comparative Analysis*. Cambridge: Cambridge University Press.

Stepan, Alfred. 1988. *Rethinking Military Politics: Brazil and the Southern Cone.* Princeton, NJ: Princeton University Press.

———. 1989. *Democratizing Brazil: Problems of Transition and Consolidation.* New York: Oxford University Press.

Stepan, Alfred, and Cindy Skach. 1993. "Constitutional Frameworks and Democratic Consolidation." *World Politics* 46: 1–22.

Stoner-Weiss, Kathryn. 1995. *Local Heroes: Political Exchange and Governmental Performance in Provincial Russia.* Typescript, Princeton University, Princeton, NJ.

———. 1997. *Local Heroes: The Political Economy of Russian Regional Governance.* Princeton, NJ: Princeton University Press.

Suny, Ronald Grigor. 1994. "Revision and Retreat in the Historiography of 1917: Social History and Its Critics." *The Russian Review* 53: 165–82.

Szamuely, Tibor. 1974. *The Russian Tradition.* New York: McGraw-Hill.

Taagapera, Rein, and Matthew Soberg Shugart. 1989. *Seats and Votes: The Effects and Determinants of Electoral Systems.* New Haven, CT: Yale University Press.

Tarrow, Sidney. 1996. "Making Social Science Work across Space and Time: A Critical Reflection on Robert Putnam's *Making Democracy Work.*" *American Political Science Review* 90: 389–397.

Teague, Elizabeth. 1994. "Who Voted for Zhirinovsky." *RFE/RL Research Report* 3(2): 4–5.

Terry, Sarah Meiklejohn. 1993. "Thinking about Post-Communist Transitions: How Different Are They?" *Slavic Review* 52: 333–37.

Thompson, Dennis F. 1976. *John Stuart Mill and Representative Government.* Princeton, NJ: Princeton University Press.

Thompson, Michael, Richard Ellis, and Aaron Wildavsky. 1990. *Cultural Theory.* Boulder, CO: Westview Press.

Tolz, Vera. 1994. "Problems in Building Democratic Institutions in Russia." *RFE/RL Research Report* 3(9): 1–7.

Treisman, Daniel. 1996. "Why Yeltsin Won." *Foreign Affairs* 75(5): 64–77.

Tucker, Robert C. 1960. "The Image of Dual Russia." In *The Transformation of Russian Society: Aspects of Social Change Since 1861,* ed. Cyril E. Black. Cambridge, MA: Harvard University Press.

———. 1971. *The Soviet Political Mind: Stalinism and Post-Stalin Change.* New York: Norton.

———. 1973a. "Culture, Political Culture and Communist Society." *Political Science Quarterly* 88: 173–90.

———. 1973b. *Stalin as Revolutionary, 1879–1929: A Study in History and Personality.* New York: Norton.

———. 1981. *Politics as Leadership.* Columbia: University of Missouri Press.

———. 1987. *Political Culture and Leadership in Soviet Russia.* New York: Norton.

———. 1990. *Stalin in Power: The Revolution from Above, 1928–1941.* New York: Norton.

———. 1992. "Sovietology and Russian History." *Post-Soviet Affairs* 8: 175–96.

———. 1995. "Post-Soviet Leadership and Change." In *Patterns in Post-Soviet Leadership,* ed. Timothy J. Colton and Robert C. Tucker. Boulder, CO: Westview.

Urban, Michael E. 1989. *An Algebra of Soviet Power: Elite Circulation in the Belorussian Republic 1966–1986*. Cambridge: Cambridge University Press.

Valenzuela, Arturo. 1995. "Chile: Origins and Consolidation of a Latin American Democracy." In *Politics in Developing Countries: Comparing Experiences with Democracy*, ed. Larry Diamond, Juan J. Linz, and Seymour Martin Lipset. Boulder, CO: Rienner.

Verba, Sidney, Kay Lehman, and Henry R. Brady. 1995. *Voice and Equality: Civic Voluntarism in American Politics*. Cambridge, MA: Harvard University Press.

Verba, Sidney, and Norman H. Nie. 1972. *Participation in America: Political Democracy and Social Inequality*. New York: Harper & Row.

Verdery, Katherine. 1996. *What Was Socialism and What Comes Next?* Princeton, NJ: Princeton University Press.

Viola, Lynne. 1996. *Peasant Rebels under Stalin: Collectivization and the Culture of Peasant Resistance*. New York: Oxford University Press.

Walder, Andrew G. 1986. *Communist Neo-Traditionalism: Work and Authority in Chinese Industry*. Berkeley: University of California Press.

Walker, Edward W. 1993. "Post-Sovietology, Area Studies, and the Social Sciences." *Harriman Institute Forum* 6(6–7): 24–28.

Wallas, Graham. 1908. *Human Nature in Politics*. London: Constable.

Watkins, John W. 1984. *Science and Scepticism*. London: Hutchinson.

Weber, Max. 1958. *The Protestant Ethic and the Spirit of Capitalism*, trans. Talcott Parsons. New York: Scribner.

Wegren, Stephen K. 1996. "Understanding Rural Reform in Russia: A Response to Reisinger." *Europe–Asia Studies* 48: 317–29.

Weldon, Thomas Dewar. 1953. *The Vocabulary of Politics*. Baltimore, MD: Penguin.

Welsh, William A. 1976. "Elites and Leadership in Communist Systems: Some New Perspectives." *Studies in Comparative Communism* 9: 162–186.

———. 1979. *Leaders and Elites*. New York: Holt, Rinehart & Winston.

White, Stephen. 1979. *Political Culture and Soviet Politics*. New York: St. Martin's.

———. 1983. "Political Communications in the USSR: Letters to Party, State and Press." *Political Studies* 31: 43–60.

White, Stephen, Richard Rose, and Ian McAllister. 1997. *How Russia Votes*. Chatham, NJ: Chatham House.

Whitefield, Stephen, and Geoffrey Evans. 1994. "The Russian Election of 1993: Public Opinion and the Transition Experience." *Post-Soviet Affairs* 10(1): 38–60.

Whyte, William F. 1943. *Street Corner Society*. Chicago: University of Chicago Press.

Willerton, John P. 1992. *Patronage and Politics in the USSR*. New York: Cambridge University Press.

Willerton, John P., and Lee Sigelman. 1991. "Public Opinion Research in the USSR: Opportunities and Pitfalls." *Journal of Communist Studies* 7: 217–34.

———. 1993. "Perestroika and the Public: Citizens' Views of the 'Fruits' of Economic Reform." In *Public Opinion and Regime Change: The New Politics of Post-Soviet Societies*, ed. Arthur H. Miller, William M. Reisinger, and Vicki L. Hesli. Boulder, CO: Westview.

Witte, John F. 1980. *Democracy, Authority, and Alienation in Work: Workers' Partic-ipation in an American Corporation.* Chicago: University of Chicago Press.

World Bank. 1997. *World Development Report 1997: The State in a Changing World.* 1977. New York: Oxford University Press.

Wortman, Richard. 1987. "Muscovite Political Folkways and the Problem of Russian Political Culture." *The Russian Review* 46: 191–98.

Wuthnow, Robert. 1989. *Communities of Discourse: Ideology and Social Structure in the Reformation, the Enlightenment, and European Socialism.* Cambridge, MA: Harvard University Press.

Wyman, Matthew. 1994. "Russian Political Culture: Evidence from Public Opinion Surveys." *Journal of Communist Studies and Transition Politics* 10: 25–54.

———. 1997. *Public Opinion in Postcommunist Russia.* London: Macmillan.

Wyman, Matthew, Stephen White, Bill Miller, and Paul Heywood. 1995. "Pub-lic Opinion, Parties and Voters in the December 1993 Russian Elections." *Europe–Asia Studies* 47: 591–614.

Yakovlev, Alexander M. 1995. "The Presidency in Russia: Evolution and Pros-pects." In *Remaking Russia: Voices from Within,* ed. Heyward Isham. Armonk, NY: Sharpe.

Yanov, Alexander. 1977. *Detente after Brezhnev: The Domestic Roots of Soviet For-eign Policy.* Policy Papers in International Affairs, no. 2, University of Califor-nia, Berkeley.

———. 1987. *The Russian Challenge and the Year 2000.* Oxford, England: Basil Blackwell.

Yanowitch, Murray. 1977. *Social and Economic Inequality in the Soviet Union.* White Plains, NY: Sharpe.

Yavlinsky, Grigory. 1995. Interview in *New York Times,* August 4, A1–2.

Yeltsin, Boris. 1997. "Invitation to Get Down to Work on State Business" (Ad-dress to the Federation Council). *Rossiiskiye vesti,* September 25, 1. (Trans-lated in *The Current Digest of the Post-Soviet Press* 49[39][October 29], 4–5.)

Zimmerman, William. 1994. "Markets, Democracy and Russian Foreign Pol-icy." *Post-Soviet Affairs* 10(2): 103–26.

———. 1995. "Synoptic Thinking and Political Culture in Post-Soviet Russia." *Slavic Review* 54: 630–41.

Index

411

About the Authors

Richard Ahl received his Ph.D. from the State University of New York, Buffalo, and is conducting research on the nature of political cleavages in Russia.

Russell Bova is Associate Professor of Political Science at Dickinson College. His current research focuses on issues of democratic consolidation in Russia and other postcommunist states. His publications related to Russian politics include articles in *World Politics, Journal of Democracy,* and *Soviet Studies.*

Harry Eckstein is Distinguished Research Professor at the University of California, Irvine. His most recent book is *Regarding Politics: Essays on Political Theory, Stability, and Change* (1992). His many contributions to comparative politics are honored in a special issue of *Comparative Political Studies* (1998).

Frederic J. Fleron Jr. is Professor of Political Science at the State University of New York, Buffalo. His current research concerns democratization, political culture, public opinion, and political parties in post-Soviet Russia. His most recent publications include *Post-Communist Studies and Political Science: Methodology and Empirical Theory in Sovietology* (1993; co-editor with Erik P. Hoffmann) and articles in *Europe–Asia Studies, Communist and Post-Communist Studies,* and *Journal of Communist Studies and Transition Politics.*

Erik P. Hoffmann is Professor of Political Science at the State University of New York, Albany. His current research is on the theory and practice of democratization, especially state-society relations, viable constitutionalism, and federalism in post-Soviet Russia. Author or editor of nine books and many essays on Russian domestic and international politics, his most recent publications are *Post-Communist Studies and Political Science: Methodology and Empirical Theory in Sovietology* (1993; co-editor with Frederic J. Fleron Jr.), three articles in *The Harriman Review*, and chapters in several books.

William M. Reisinger is Professor of Political Science at the University of Iowa. His current research concerns democratization in the former communist states, post-Soviet public opinion, and Russian legal orientations. He is author of *Energy and the Soviet Bloc: Alliance Politics since Stalin* (1992), author or co-author of numerous articles and chapters, and co-editor of *Public Opinion and Regime Change: The New Politics of Post-Soviet Societies* (1993) and *Constitutional Dialogues in Comparative Perspective* (1998).

Philip G. Roeder is Associate Professor of Political Science at the University of California, San Diego. He is author of *Red Sunset: The Failure of Soviet Politics* (1993) and *Soviet Political Dynamics: Development of the First Leninist Polity* (1988), as well as articles in *American Political Science Review*, *World Politics*, and other professional journals. He is currently completing a manuscript entitled *Ethnicity in the State: Renegotiating Post-Soviet Constitutions*.